Path of No Path
Contemporary Studies in Pure Land
Buddhism Honoring Roger Corless

Roger Corless
(1938–2007)

Path of No Path
Contemporary Studies in Pure Land Buddhism Honoring Roger Corless

Edited by Richard K. Payne

Institute of Buddhist Studies and
Numata Center for Buddhist Translation and Research
2009

First Printing, 2009
ISBN: 978-1-886439-41-2
Library of Congress Catalog Card Number: 2009920743

Published by
Numata Center for Buddhist Translation and Research
2620 Warring Street
Berkeley, California 94704

Printed in the United States of America

Contents

Foreword *by Arthur Holder* vii
Preface: Appreciating Roger *by Gordon Bermant* xi
Acknowledgments *by Richard K. Payne* xix

Practice

Vajrasattva Meditation: Healing through Crosscultural Perspectives *by Harvey B. Aronson* 3

A Tang Esoteric Manual for Rebirth in the Pure Land: *Rites for Contemplation of and Offerings to Amitāyus Tathāgata* *by Charles D. Orzech* 31

Shinran's Secret Transmission to Nyoshin: The *Hōri hachiman chō* *by James H. Sanford* 57

American Jōdo Shinshū Practice: A Fork in the Road *by Gordon Bermant* 77

Transmission

Yuan Hongdao and the *Xifang helun:* Pure Land Theology in the Late Ming Dynasty *by Charles B. Jones* 89

Spiritual Kinship and Lineage in Major Buddhist Traditions *by Charles S. Prebish* 127

How Not to Talk about Pure Land Buddhism: A Critique of Huston Smith's (Mis)Representations *by Richard K. Payne* 147

Interpretation

The Supremacy of Amida's Vows in Rennyo: The Case of Women *by Alfred Bloom* 175

Shinran's Pure Land Buddhism as a Way of Being Religious: Some Twenty-first–century tasks for Shin Buddhist Theology *by Ruben L. F. Habito* 189

Amida and Pure Land within a Contemporary Worldview: From Shinran's Literal Symbolism to Figurative Symbolism *by Kenneth K. Tanaka* 215

Contributors 243
Bibliography 245
Index 257

Foreword

Arthur Holder
Dean and Vice President for Academic Affairs
Graduate Theological Union, Berkeley

When I graduated from Duke University with a bachelor's degree in 1973, the school yearbook generated some controversy. Eschewing the usual pictures of club meetings and football games, the student editorial staff had turned the yearbook into a collection of black-and-white art photographs. Most of the photos depicted campus scenes and people, but they weren't labeled as such. Some were whimsical, some irreverent, and a few quite risqué. The athletes and student government types deplored the yearbook's untraditional character, but for me the photos captured the essence of those heady years of questioning, experimentation, and protest toward the end of the counterculture and the Vietnam War.

There was only one prose piece in the entire volume: a short essay by Roger Corless in which the young professor of religion likened the college experience to medieval alchemy. The purpose of a college education, said Roger, is not to prepare you to get a job or find your place in society, any more than the purpose of alchemy was to turn base metals into gold. The true purpose of a college education is actually the same as the alchemists' quest, which is the transformation of consciousness.

The aim of all education—higher or otherwise—is enlightenment, or wisdom. That was what Roger Corless believed, and it was how he taught for over thirty years. Teaching for transformation of consciousness got him in trouble with the university administration from time to time, but it also brought generations of eager students to his door.

It was my privilege to study with Roger in a graduate seminar on "Buddhist Thought and Practice." He had come to Duke only three years before, in 1970. I was an undergraduate religion major who went on to divinity school; eventually I became an ordained Episcopal priest, seminary professor, and dean of the ecumenical and interreligious Graduate Theological Union in Berkeley, California But I took Roger's seminar on Buddhism primarily for personal reasons. Like many Christians before and since, I had an inkling that Buddhism could teach me something about ultimate reality. I was interested in prayer and meditation (of course), but also in the appeal of a religious tradition that affirmed paradox and put as much emphasis on practice as on dogma. I wanted to get "out of my head"—spiritually speaking—and into the mystery.

My consciousness may or may not have been transformed in Roger's class, but I certainly learned something about the study of religion in general, and Buddhism in particular. Looking back from a vantage point more than three decades on, I can identify three things that Roger taught me, for which I am profoundly grateful.

First, language matters. Much of our time in Roger's Buddhism course was devoted to the definition and interpretation of words. Learning any new religion is in many ways like learning a new language with its own vocabulary, grammar, and syntax. But learning Buddhism from Roger was truly a multilingual experience. As he lectured and wrote rapidly on the blackboard, in those days before PowerPoint presentations, we students dutifully copied down the (transliterated) key terms—first in Sanskrit, then in Pāli, Tibetan, Chinese, and Japanese. I remember being thankful more than once for Roger's professorial stammer because it gave us time to catch up with his precise dictation of those polysyllabic words. He would break each term (in each language) down into its component parts, discuss the etymologies, and patiently explain the shifts of nuance as the word passed from culture to culture and period to period.

Very few of the words have stayed with me over the years, but I have never forgotten the methodological principle that the scholar of religion has to learn the language of the tradition's primary texts. For my work in the history of medieval Christian spirituality, it has been Greek and Latin rather than Pāli and Japanese, but the principle is the same: first, learn the language; then read and interpret the texts.

Second, religions should be studied from the inside out, not the outside in. The course I took with Roger was in his early years of teaching, when he was still using textbooks written by Western scholars with a history of religions approach. But he was already beginning to experiment with the "reinvention" (as he called it) of teaching Buddhism to a Western audience "Buddhistically"—which is to say that he replaced the historical chronology of the standard textbooks with a presentation based on the twelve acts of the Buddha. The eventual fruit of that pedagogical reinvention was his now-classic textbook *The Vision of Buddhism: The Space Under the Tree.*[1]

It seems so obvious now that I wonder why it had to be explained to me, but it was Roger who first told me that I couldn't expect to understand

Buddhism as long as I persisted in applying categories derived from my own Christian tradition. If I am going to see something new, I first have to learn to look at things in a different way. It is not Buddhism's job to solve my Christian problems.

This was (and is) a hard saying, but it was easier for me to hear coming from Roger because he was both a Catholic Christian (a Benedictine oblate, even) and a Buddhist practitioner. He was the first person of my acquaintance to claim what we now call "multiple religious belonging." Throughout the many years of his involvement in Buddhist-Christian relations, Roger was able to carry on the dialogue while talking to himself! He always insisted to me that his Buddhism made him a better Christian, and I expect he told his Buddhist friends the same thing in reverse. Not every scholar of religion can go as far as Roger did in coming to know another religion from the inside, but we can at least strive to emulate the integrity of his commitment to appreciative scholarship.

Third, the study of religion, like religion itself, is a form of play. It is perhaps an indication of Roger's longstanding engagement with Jōdo Shinshū that his textbook *The Vision of Buddhism* concludes with a section on Pure Land Buddhism. There he acknowledges that Christian scholars have sometimes compared Shinran's practice of the nenbutsu to Martin Luther's conviction that he could be saved only by faith, not by works. But repeating the insight he first made in an article on "The Playfulness of *Tariki*," Roger suggested that it would be better to say that Shinran "had discovered how to play his practice rather than to work it."[2] This was true of Roger as well.

Anyone who knew Roger would soon experience his wry sense of absurdist humor. Despite years of living in North Carolina, he never completely mastered the art of transforming his native British accent into a Southern drawl. However, that never stopped him from mischievously mocking the pretensions of his adopted culture, even after he settled into a happy retirement in the more politically and culturally congenial San Francisco Bay Area. Roger relished a good story, especially if it included a comeuppance for some figure of authority.

But his playfulness was very much a part of Roger's teaching as well. I remember his amusement at some of us Christian students in the Buddhism seminar who professed to be scandalized when we discovered that some Buddhist monks circumvented strictures against handling money by wearing gloves and using begging bowls. "Did you think your own religion had a monopoly on hypocrisy?" he asked us. Of course he then went on to explain this practice not as hypocrisy but as an adaptation of monastic rules to changing times, and to caution us against applying our own puritanical morality out of context. Still, it was the gentle chiding with a smile that effectively deflated our self-righteous attitude.

Roger Corless was certainly a scholar of both Buddhism and Christianity, and a teacher of renown. But he never thought that he needed to hide his personal practice of these religions in order to study them or teach them to others. He delighted in singing Handel's *Messiah* with the Duke Chapel Choir at Christmastime, and I will always remember the radiance of his face as he stood on the chapel steps singing the "Hallelujah Chorus" with all his might (and no trace of a stammer). The Hebrew word *hallelujah* means "praise the Lord," and in Handel's famous piece the continual repetition of this phrase catches singers and audience up into what Roger liked to call "the alchemy of praise." I think he would want us to see the connection with another practice to which he was equally devoted:

> The Nembutsu is not a mantra that beings recite to the Buddha, it is the Buddha's invitation to beings to accept the liberation that he has already obtained for them. . . . When this realization is experienced, it comes as a moment of ecstatic, bodily, dancing joy. Nothing needs to be done! Everything is right as it is! *"Namu Amida Butsu!"* we shout in gratitude.[3]

For every student of Pure Land Buddhism, and for all of us who mourn the loss of our friend and colleague Roger Corless, this collection of essays is a further cause for gratitude. I am so appreciative of what I have learned from him, both in thought and in practice, in life and in death. *Deo gratias!* Thanks be to God!

Notes

1 Roger Corless, *The Vision of Buddhism: The Space Under the Tree* (New York: Paragon House, 1989).

2 Ibid., p. 279.

3 Ibid., p. 278.

Preface
Appreciating Roger

Gordon Bermant
Lecturer, Department of Psychology
University of Pennsylvania

As I get older, my friends die more often. Perhaps something so obvious should not be an occasion for sad reflection, but it is. And reflection goes where it will. For example, when your friend dies, I feel sorry for you. When my friend dies, I feel sorry for myself, which is worse. My self-sorrow is more pointed, painful, and meaningful to me than my sorrow for you. Nothing is more objective than the death of a body, but its significance is created by subjectivity: my consciousness. This is old news for Buddhists, but the updates are arriving more often.

Roger Corless died on January 12, 2007. The contributors to this book had hoped to present a completed manuscript to Roger in appreciation for his life and work. His time ran out before we could get it done.

Roger had known of his serious illness for more than a year. True to his fashion, he faced the details of his deteriorating biology with the zeal of a medical student and the detachment of a person without illusions. His incisive humor did not fail him. Few people can find humor in the travails of wearing a colostomy bag—Roger was one who could. He shared the details of his condition in e-mail messages to a circle of friends, displaying a remarkable grasp of medical vocabulary, physicians' strengths and foibles, and his dwindling chances of a full recovery. Ironically, but not out of character, Roger's detailed communications kept us focused on completing this volume in his honor; they were dispatches from a front where he was both combatant and correspondent. It was clear that time was of the essence. Though Roger died before we could present him with a manuscript, he knew we were working on it. Had he known of our worry about "making it on time," perhaps he would have counseled us that the book would be the book, regardless of his condition at the time of its publication. The rest of our concern, he might have said, comprises our wishes for things to be different than they are.

What follows is not an assessment of Roger as a scholar. It is an appreciation of him as a dharma teacher by a Shin Buddhist layman who became one of his many friends.

Roger moved gracefully and tirelessly in numerous communities: academic, Buddhist, Christian, gay/lesbian/bisexual/transgender, recovering alcoholic, and various combinations of these. In my experience, he was open to anyone who was open to him. But he could express elegant disrespect for those he found to be hypocritical or closed-minded. He had slight regard for pomp and privilege, frequently playing the sly needle that popped overblown balloons. He delighted in finding humor in the midst of what others treated with (too) high seriousness. He seemed like a gifted student whose stance in the world was at an acute angle to that of his more traditional classmates. Pressed to find a single word to characterize his perspective, the best word I can find is *outside.* I mean that Roger was welcomed in many communities and drew comfort from them, but that his participation in them was always, in part, observational.

Roger symbolized the breadth of his religious devotion with three altars he fashioned in one room of his home in Benicia, California, where he moved after he had retired from Duke University and had spent some time in Hawai'i. The altars were, in the order he showed them to me, Buddhist, Christian, and a syncretic form of his own devising. I wish I could explain the insights he shared with me then, but my memory and understanding are insufficient. I hope other friends will share accounts of Roger's devotional space.

Roger's Shin Buddhist writing will survive as a special gift to those whose eagerness for devotion is tempered by ingrained skepticism and concern for being led down (yet another) rosy religious path to a dead end. His several publications in *The Pure Land,* the journal of the International Association of Shin Buddhist Studies, are artful combinations of religious insight and scholarly reference. It was through these writings that I discovered Roger and because of them that Reverend Kenryu Tsuji and I originally invited him to Ekoji Buddhist Temple to conduct weekend seminars early in the 1990s. Roger was a recurrent guest at Ekoji and in my home, a double treat for me and my family.

This collection of essays is the first volume of a three-volume series commemorating Roger's work. The third volume will be a collection of his essays, and I recommend in particular two articles, "The Pathless Path for North America" and "Self-Power Practice with Other-Power Attitude,"[1] as representative of Roger's unique contributions published in *The Pure Land.* It was only later, in conversation with Roger about the scope of the book, that he mentioned an earlier article, "The Playfulness of *Tariki*,"[2] as a favorite of his. He added with satisfaction that Ruth Tabrah had told him that the article was his best writing about Jōdo Shinshū. I hastened to read it. Tabrah's accolade was well deserved. The article is a small jewel that reflects the light from Roger's broad learning and religious insight. Below I emphasize some features of these articles that display Roger's contributions to the comprehension of Jōdo Shinshū by someone like me who is, as Roger once characterized himself, "a dumb *gaijin* and an inveterate hairy barbarian."[3] Fortunately, the articles will also be present, in the third volume of this series, to speak for themselves.

"The Playfulness of *Tariki*"

Roger prepared this paper as a contribution to a conference pursuing a theme of "Shin Buddhism as a Member in the Global Communities of Faith." Perhaps for that reason, or perhaps just because it was how his mind worked, Roger developed his theme by placing Shin concepts in the light of religious and secular themes drawn from diverse languages, disciplines, and historical periods. Appropriate to its theme, the text moves quickly and deftly through diverse allusions in support of his theme that Amida Buddha permits, invites, and encourages us, in a popular phrase, to lighten up.

The article begins by amending the distinction between "salvation by works" and "salvation by faith," which some scholars have imported from its Christian context in order to illuminate Shinran's rejection of any human act as contributing to one's own salvation.[4] Roger changed the significance of the distinction by transmuting "works," connoting good deeds, into "work," connoting earnest effort.

What a difference an "s" makes! With this amendment Roger unlocked a treasure chest of cultural references ranging over centuries and across cultures.[5] From the Western canon he introduced St. Francis of Assisi, Dante, and the Faust legend as told by Marlowe and Goethe. To these classical sources he added two more from the twentieth century: Johan Huizinga's mid-century masterpiece on the deep nature of play and Mihály Csikszentmihály's introduction of "flow" as a term to capture the peak experience and presence of being when a person is at one with his or her actions.[6] From the Asian canon Roger introduced Chinese and Tibetan sources as well as references to Hōnen and Shinran, and modern commentators on all of them.

In the space of nineteen pages Roger deployed these resources as coherent beams of light illuminating a profoundly simple idea: Play is the disappearance of the self that measures the progress or outcome of its activities. Play is natural as effort can never be. The heartfelt nenbutsu of gratitude is thus play. It is tempting, but wrong, to say that we should take such play seriously. We do better to cultivate a lightheartedness that goes "all the way down," like the very tall stack of turtles that supports the universe.[7]

"Self-Power Practice with Other-Power Attitude: An Interpretation of Mind in Shin Buddhism"

This article returned to the themes of the 1987 article while wearing academic robes for most of its forty pages. Roger set himself the task of working through the distinctions among self-power (*jiriki*), other-power (*tariki*), and absolute other-power (*zettai tariki*) that sit at the core of Shinran's teaching and also are early stumbling blocks for many "dumb *gaijin*" who discover Jōdo Shinshū as adults. His purpose, as it emerges in the article, was to save Shinran's teaching from a futile interpretation of these distinctions that, Roger believed, had become a harmful, unnecessary orthodoxy. His method was to show that the distinction between power of the self and power beyond the self pervades all of Buddhism, no Buddhist teaching is grounded in self-power only; and that, in any case, the categories of self and other are porous to each other, or empty, in a Buddhist sense.

Along the way to his conclusion, Roger introduced the reader to abhidharma, Mādhyamika, and Yogācāra as alternative Buddhist frameworks corresponding approximately to the worldviews of modern physics, literary criticism, and cognitive science. His reason for noting the correspondences seems to have been to give modern Western and ancient Asian themes mutual support in their insistence on the weakness of hard boundaries between apparently separate entities, including especially self and other. His conclusion, to be fair to its breadth, could benefit from more justification than Roger provided for it here. Perhaps others will pick up the gauntlet or have done so already.

In a similar fashion Roger announced that traditional English translations of Śākyamuni Buddha's last words are significantly mistaken. The mistake, he claimed, arises from reading the Pāli as if the Buddha was addressing members of the sangha as individuals rather than as a collective. The distinction is important because, assuming that Roger's interpretation is correct, the "refuge" or "lamp" on which each member should rely is not the member's individual insights but the sangha's collective wisdom, which is the repository of the dharma. The self is part of the (collective) other, and the other works for the benefit of the self's enlightenment. Separation between self and other on the path to enlightenment is illusory.

The article continues to move through the tricky apparent dualities of Buddhist doctrine to show how Mahayana teaching guides practitioners (at least those with a taste for this sort of thing) to an appreciation of an existential status that is "not two" without being "one." The conditions of nirvana and samsara, and of pure mind and defiled mind, are of this sort: the members of each pair pervade each other without becoming each other. Major Mahayana texts show how pervasion becomes deepened into static and dynamic forms.

Roger's development of these themes leads him to Tanluan, the subject of his 1973 doctoral dissertation and, perhaps, his true teacher. Roger concludes that Tanluan's doctrine of "double *dharmakāya*" (essential and operational) is the insight that allows Tanluan to develop his advocacy for the Pure Land and the power of Amida Buddha's vows. I hear resonances between the themes Roger is developing here and one of the stanzas in Shinran's *Shōshinge,* in the section devoted to Tanluan:

> In his commentary on the treatise of Bodhisattva Vasubandhu, [Tanluan] shows that the cause and attainment of birth in the fulfilled land lie in the Vow. Our going and returning, directed to us by Amida, come about through Other Power; the truly decisive cause is *shinjin.*[8]

For Roger, Shinran's teaching is the final development of the dynamic pervasiveness of pure and impure consciousness, so "that the question 'who is being enlightened by whom?' is a non-question."[9] But that does not mean that Shinran's teaching is discontinuous from other Mahayana teaching or from Buddhism generally.

Having established Shinran at an apogee of Mahayana teaching, Roger criticizes what he believed were unnecessary and harmful interpretations of Shinran's meaning, particularly for Western Buddhists. In the article's final major section, "Implications for Practice," he suggests that the organized church and some of its scholars have established doctrinal positions that obscure the fluid relationship between self and other by a misplaced emphasis on the absolute other-power of Amida Buddha and insistence that faith, as it were, entails complete individual docility in all religious (and social/political) matters. His arguments take several forms, of which a historical one is particularly trenchant. He invites us to note that

> although many accomplished teachers (Dōgen, Bankei, Milarepa, and Shinran are his examples) speak in terms of spontaneity, letting be, or other-power, they do so only at the conclusion of a painful path of apparent self-power. . . . All of them came to the limits of their endurance, and practically gave up in despair. But at that very instant, the breakthrough occurred.[10]

What Roger does not do, however, is claim that these strenuous efforts and sufferings were the proximate causes of the breakthroughs. His personal experience of Dharmākara's eighteenth, nineteenth, and twentieth vows brings him to the position that

> one always practices with total reliance and both self-power and other-power. Because of relying on self-power, one practices assiduously; because of relying on other-power, one practices playfully, not expecting any results.[11]

Thus at the end of his exposition, Roger returned to the theme of his 1987 article, with its advocacy for lightheartedness and play.

"The Pathless Path for North America"

This 1997 article is substantially more practical or "applied" than the two earlier articles. In one sense it picks up where the previous articles end, because it situates Jōdo Shinshū in today's United States. Roger makes a pessimistic assessment of Shinshū's future unless changes are made in how Shinran's message is made available, in particular to newcomers. Roger was hardly alone in raising these concerns, but he brought his unique wit and style to bear in his critique.

The article emphasizes history and the significance of embedding religious practice in cultures. Ethnic animosity directed toward Japanese immigrants on the mainland and in Hawai'i led to certain accommodations which, in Roger's view, now hinder the healthy future development of Jōdo Shinshū in the United States. The years of internment did nothing to encourage the hierarchies or memberships in Japan and the United States to find new ways to make the doctrine available to those outside the community.

Roger's recommendations are reasonably specific but, in my view now, a bit misleading. First, he says, "Shin must be presented as Buddhism."[12] But the Buddhism he is talking about is not one for which he has much respect. He shows little regard for what has happened to much of Zen and Insight practices, which, he claims, combine "formless sitting" with inattention to the dharma to create a thin broth of "sitting and psychobabble."[13] He cites *Tricycle* magazine as the flagship communicator of Buddhism for newcomers, and characterizes it as "a kind of *People* magazine for upwardly mobile Caucasian Buddhists."[14] Despite these disparagements (and perhaps they were just Roger being playful), he recommended that Shin must engage such "formless Dharmalessness on its own ground."[15] As a consequence he seems to be recommending that Shin Buddhism find what sells in the Buddhist market and sell it in order to gain a larger market share.

I believe, however, that Roger meant something else, though his wit and disaffection with some current trends led him to offer barbed *bon mots* that were more clever than useful. But he also provided a positive critique. For example, he urged the temples of the Buddhist Churches of America to offer regular meditation practice opportunities. Roger emphasized that this recommendation has a sound doctrinal justification. And indeed there is a movement among BCA temples in this direction; Roger's was one voice among several who have spoken out for the wholesomeness of this change in temple practices.

Roger used the phrase "pathless path" in the 1992 article to describe a going and returning with a sense that change occurs in the midst of stasis. By the time of the 1997 article, he used "pathless path" to characterize practice as play. And so here, as in the previous articles, the advocacy of play as the model of practice is a major theme of Roger's dharma message.

Appreciating Roger

People occasionally pass the time by talking about what they would be if they were beings of a different sort: birds, four-legged animals, and flowers are often chosen in this little game. Thinking about Roger, I imagine that, as a bird, he would choose to be a hummingbird; as a four-legged animal, he would choose to be a fox rather than a hedgehog;[16] and as a flower, he would choose to be a tulip, brightening the ground early in the season, and gone before it gets too hot.

Notes

1 Roger Corless, "The Pathless Path for North America," *The Pure Land*, n.s., 13–14 (December 1997): pp. 6–18; "Self-Power Practice with Other-Power Attitude: An Interpretation of Mind in Shin Buddhism," *The Pure Land*, n.s., 8–9 (December 1992): pp. 166–205.

2 Roger Corless, "The Playfulness of *Tariki*," *The Pure Land*, n.s., 4 (December 1987): pp. 34–52.

3 Corless, "The Pathless Path for North America," p. 8.

4 See, for example, Alfred Bloom, *Shinran and the Gospel of Pure Grace* (Tucson, AZ: University of Arizona Press, 1965), p. 45.

5 Roger Corless's source citations will be included in the articles that will comprise the third volume of this three-volume series.

6 William Butler Yeats famously captured the nonduality of being and action in the final lines of his poem "Among School Children" (*The Collected Poems of W. B Yeats* [New York: Macmillan, 1959], p. 212):

> O chestnut-tree, great-rooted blossomer,
> Are you the leaf, the blossom, or the bole?
> O body swayed to music, O brightening glance,
> How can we know the dancer from the dance?

7 The story of the "little old lady" who challenges a famous scientist by claiming that the universe is supported on the back of a turtle, which is at the top of a stack of "turtles all the way down," appears in Stephen W. Hawking, *A Brief History of Time* (New York: Bantam Books, 1988), p. 1. Hawking says that the story may have originated with Bertrand Russell.

8 Shinran Shōnin, *The Collected Works of Shinran,* 2 vols. (Kyoto: Jodo Shinshu Hongwanji Ha, 1997), I.72, stanza 2.

9 Corless, "Self-Power Practice with Other-Power Attitude," p. 192.

10 Ibid., pp. 194–195.

11 Ibid., p. 200.

12 Corless, "The Pathless Path for North America," p. 12.

13 Ibid., p. 13.

14 Ibid., p. 14.

15 Ibid.

16 Perhaps some will disagree. See Isaiah Berlin, "The Hedgehog and the Fox: An Essay on Tolstoy's View of History," in *The Proper Study of Mankind: An Anthology of Essay,* ed. Henry Hardy and Roger Hausheer (New York: Farrar, Straus and Giroux, 1997), p. 436.

Acknowledgments

Richard K. Payne

Dean, Institute of Buddhist Studies, Berkeley

It had been our hope to be able to present this collection of essays honoring the contribution of Roger Corless to the interpretation of Pure Land Buddhism while he was alive. That would have meant that it could be referred to as a *festschrift,* writings celebrating the work of a fellow scholar. Unfortunately, Roger died before the work was finished, and so it must stand as a memorial volume, helping us to recall the man and his thought by acknowledging his influence on each of the contributors.

I would like to thank those contributors myself, since it is they who made the work possible: Kenneth K. Tanaka, Alfred Bloom, Charles B. Jones, Charles S. Prebish, Charles D. Orzech, Ruben L. F. Habito, Gordon Bermant, Harvey B. Aronson, James H. Sanford, and Arthur Holder. The title, "Path of No Path," reflects the name of one of Roger's essays, "The Pathless Path for North America." Beyond that, however, it points to the idea of "just come as you are" (Jpn. *sono mama*) that Gordon Bermant, in his essay included in this collection, identifies as the appealing character of Shin for contemporary Americans such as himself. Looking through the lens of Buddhist studies, the phrase points even further afield, however, to the ideas of *tathāgatagarbha* and inherent awakening found frequently throughout Mahayana Buddhism. This idea of the "path of no path," of "just come as you are," provides an underlying commonality that sectarian exceptionalism and triumphalism of all kinds have tended to obscure.

This is the first of what is planned to be a series of three works, a "Corless trilogy." Roger always wanted to revise his doctoral dissertation on Tanluan's *Commentary,* producing his own subcommentary. Although unfinished at the time of his death, his work will be edited for publication as part of the trilogy. Third, a collection of Roger's own essays on Pure Land Buddhism will be published to complement his subcommentary on Tanluan's *Commentary.*

Roger sincerely believed in the personal significance and beneficial potential of Pure Land Buddhism for individual human life. This conviction on his part was based on his own personal life story, and, I believe fair to say, his struggles within that life. At the same time, he was not an exclusivist. At one academic conference in which we were both participating, I remember him mentioning that he planned not only to go to an Alcoholics Anonymous meeting on Saturday night, but also to attend Catholic mass on Sunday morning. He also became involved with Soka Gakkai International, and its San Francisco branch organized memorial services for him at the time of his death. Far from being a dilettante who dabbled superficially in one thing after another, it seemed to me that Roger was actively, purposely constructing his life. Without intending to be, he was, therefore, a postmodern person.

My special thanks to Gordon Bermant for the photograph of Roger on the frontispiece, taken at the opening of the Jōdo Shinshū Center in Berkeley, California, a few months before his death. Despite his illness, evident in the baldness that resulted from chemotherapy, the joy and excitement with which he greeted change is evident in his smile.

Thanks also to Natalie Quli for copyediting, Marianne Dresser for editorial and production work and indexing, Mushim Ikeda-Nash for proofreading, and Arlene Kato for cover design.

Practice

Vajrasattva Meditation: Healing through Crosscultural Perspectives

Harvey B. Aronson
Dawn Mountain Tibetan Temple, Community Center, and Research Institute, Houston

Prologue: A Jōdo Shinshū Contribution

This article began as a set of reflections on the healing Vajrasattva meditation as practiced in the Nyingma tradition of Tibetan Buddhism, and in large measure it remains so. However, since its inception, Richard Payne, Dean of the Institute of Buddhist Studies at the Graduate Theological Union, Berkeley, California, requested a contribution for a *festschrift* on Jōdo Shinshū honoring Professor Roger Corless and mentioned that my piece might fit well in this project because of some writing Roger himself had done on the relationship of Jōdo Shinshū and tantric practice. In the late 1960s Roger and I were graduate students under Richard Robinson and Min Kiyota at the University of Wisconsin and it warms my heart to have the opportunity to honor our relationship in this way.

Through a variety of contacts with Richard Payne over the last five years, I have been reading some elementary material on Jōdo Shinshū and had come to theorize its approach as one end of a spectrum that spanned Theravāda "self-power" and Jōdo Shinshū reliance on "other-power" in its gratitude-filled recitation of nenbutsu. As a practitioner of Tibetan Buddhism, I became somewhat sensitive to occasions when texts or teachers talked of either "self-" or "other-"power.

Then in October 2004 I was asked to participate in a conference on Buddhism and psychotherapy organized by Naoki Nabeshima (Ryūkoku University), Richard Payne, Mark Unno (University of Oregon), and David Eckel (Boston University). During the course of this conference Dake Mitsuya (Ryūkoku University) attempted to disabuse me of my comfortably encrusted characterizations and informed me that his teacher explained the practice of nenbutsu in a way more subtle than "self-" or "other-power" but rather in a nondual fashion. Dake was kind enough to send me a copy of *A Life of Awakening: The Heart of the Shin Buddhist Path*[1] by Takamaro Shigaraki, and it is based on this fascinating text that I would like to make some observations.

While there may be material in the Tibetan tradition that mirrors some of Shigaraki's observations, I am not aware of any. What he says comes from within the Jōdo Shinshū tradition, and its context is that tradition's understanding of Amida's vow, and from within some particular lineages of scholarly and practical reflections that are part of the tradition. At the outset of this paper, however, I would like to suggest that with respect to recitation and visualization, Shigaraki's observations have much to offer practitioners of Tibetan tantric practice. And even if his perspective is not explicitly articulated in the Tibetan traditions as such, I feel that for practitioners of Tibetan tantra to be able to allow the overtones of his observations to gently infiltrate their practice would be of great value to them. Furthermore, it is my sense that Shigaraki's interpretations, while not unique, have not been the main presentation of Shinran's ideas in the West, and I feel moved to make the richness and depth of his spiritual insight available to practitioners from a broad range of spiritual traditions.

First, regarding mantra. While there may be much written about mantra in certain scholarly parts of the Tibetan canon, when it comes to practice, teachers may provide only the minimum of theory. Instructing their students in the way to recite a mantra, the mantra is explained as being the sound of the deity—the essence of a specific buddha. Emphasis is placed on receiving consecrated mantra from those who have fully accomplished (Skt. *siddha;* Tib. *sgrub*) the practices associated with a particular deity and his or her mantra. The mantra is sacred and it is an avenue to realization of oneness with the deity. In the practice of Vajrasattva, to be discussed more fully below, there is first the purificatory mantra of Vajrasattva, and then the essential mantra of Vajrasattva, which allows the practitioner to imaginatively experience him- or herself as Vajrasattva. How helpful it is to have Shigaraki's observation framing recitation in the following relational manner:

> When we continue to call out the Name of the Buddha . . . our selves become emptied and we experience deeply the truth of something long forgotten—that our saying of the Name, in which we call out to the Buddha, is itself the Buddha's calling out to us.[2]

Second, regarding faith and visualization of a deity. Faith is a huge topic, and so Shigaraki distinguishes between secular faith, religious faith in general, and faith as understood in the Shin tradition. He sees secular faith as something resting on reason and proof; religious faith as often oriented to a transcendent object and requiring a leap beyond reason; and faith (Jpn. *shin*) in Shin Buddhism as a particular state in which one's heart and mind are pure and joyous. "This form of *shin* is completely nondualistic and subjective in nature. It does not imply that we must do something vis-à-vis some object."[3]

Briefly put, Shigaraki sees the practice of the recitation of the name as allowing practitioners to realize something long forgotten (Jpn. *omoiataru*).[4] The deepest faith occurs as *shinjin*, a "transcendent, religious experience of awakening,"[5] "equivalent to the state of *samādhi* in which one visualizes the Buddha."[6] While it is of course the case that for some there is a unidirectional recitation, what is of significance is to come to the state of

> a real religious experience—a profound experiencing of the truth of something long forgotten—in which what has been recited is heard coming from the opposite direction.[7]

From Shigaraki's viewpoint, for followers of Shinran, *shin* is not a dualistic trust in Amida as an object but rather the practitioner becomes Amida, just as Amida becomes the practitioner.[8]

Indeed in Nyingma, there is the definite presentation that practice is to restore ourselves to our already existent, but covered over, realized state of buddhahood. The goal of practice is also articulated as nondual realization of one's inner nature as enlightened being; in the practice of Vajrasattva, this would mean one's nature as this deity. (That one's inner nature is comprised of various buddha manifestations is simply a given to Tibetan Buddhist practice.) In coming to realize one's inner nature, the mantra ineluctably must transform from something that "we" are doing into the very sound of the deity. Once when practicing, I noticed that I was moving toward a more nondual state in my recitation, and asked my teacher Khetsun Sangpo if that was positive. He said, "Nondual is better." For us in the West, steeped in our individualized culture, I offer Shigaraki's observations drawn from the Jōdo Shinshū tradition as avenues for easing our movement home, to something we have long forgotten.

Introduction to Vajrasattva Meditation

The practice of meditation on Vajrasattva was recently identified as the most important healing meditation in that tradition by the respected

Buddhist scholar Tulku Thondup, author of two major popular works on this topic.[9] It thus seems like an ideal candidate for crosscultural reflection on healing. The word "heal" is related to three major English words: *hale, whole,* and *hallow.*[10] Health, wholeness, and the sacred are all ingredients to our sense of healing. Coming from a different time and place, the vision of healing presented in the Vajrasattva meditation will be one particular way of visioning the relationship of health, wholeness, and the sacred. The large frame for this paper is then the worldview that contains and is expressed through this particular practice of healing. Through a dialogical process I hope our crosscultural reflections on this practice will deepen our understanding of it and ultimately of ourselves.

There is a secondary frame for my reflections as well. In 1996, while on a trip to Nepal to translate teachings by the Venerable Khetsun Sangpo Rinpoche, one of the few remaining senior teachers of the Nyingma tradition who had trained in Tibet prior to the Chinese invasions of the 1950s, I had the opportunity to relay a question from one of Rinpoche's American students regarding the healing and purifying practice of Vajrasattva. In brief, the question was, "How do I—within the frame of this practice—in good conscience make the strong commitment to abstain from nonvirtuous acts in the future, when I know that there are some forms of nonvirtuous actions that I will no doubt repeat in the future?" Khetsun Rinpoche's response was that it was necessary to put such thoughts out of mind and indeed important to make such a commitment.[11] As a translator, I realized during the course of this conversation that I was having one of those moments when I was somehow not doing justice to either the questioner or the respondent. I intuitively knew that there was a way in which I was not creating contact between the two on the question at hand, but I could not see a way to repair this breech. This paper is my attempt to understand the issues at play in that rather brief interchange, which left me with a long-lingering sense of incompleteness.

I have since that time become aware of Richard Shweder's work on crosscultural psychology, and would like to use this particular incident and Shweder's frame as an opportunity for some extended crosscultural reflection on the healing practice of Vajrasattva meditation.

The Crosscultural Framework

In brief, Richard Shweder suggests that there are four movements in our process of reflection on another culture, or "thinking through it."[12] First, we *think by means of the other,* which allows us to use the frame of another's vision to broaden and deepen our understanding of our own experience.

Next, it is important to *get them straight*, which means understanding the internal logic of the other. Ultimately this leads us to the third movement, when we *deconstruct and go beyond the other*, in the sense that we see what another has dogmatically hidden. Fourth, during the course of doing all this we *witness in the context of the other*, namely, we are participant to an *open-ended, self-reflexive dialogic experience* entailed in this whole process.[13]

Using such an approach, we can, as Jeffrey Kripal so eloquently states, have

> a kind of postmodern religious experience in which transformation and transcendence are discovered not within a particular tradition or culture but between at least two. . . .[14]

It is my fervent hope that during the course of the following explorations there may be opportunities for a variety of awakenings to take place that open heart and mind in the space in between ourselves and the subjects of our reflection. Also, I would like to suggest that here we will consider healing through a crosscultural perspective and arrive at some modicum of a healing experience ourselves through the medium of our reflections.[15]

The Meditation on Vajrasattva: A Sacred Dance of Healing and Wholeness

Our first two movements are to *think through the other* and *get them straight*. Here, this involves understanding the worldview within which the Vajrasattva practice occurs and the nature of the practice itself.

Situated in the ethical universe of karma, the Buddhist practitioner knows that he or she has accumulated a variety of ethical and non-ethical behavior in the past that affects the quality of his or her present experience.[16] Being ensnared in the cycle of rebirth and its attendant suffering is in part maintained by karmic obstructions and the continued operation of emotional afflictions and subtle obscurations.[17] The only way out is understanding. However, the practitioner is in some type of catch-22. Due to the very workings of the obscurations and obstructions that have been obtained from time immemorial, vision is clouded and there is no way for new insight to occur. If deeply obstructed by soot-covered glasses, all new visual information we take in will be obstructed by soot, unless we do something about the soot. How can we see clearly enough to eradicate the source of the soot? We need an intervention that is outside of the limited visual world of glass, soot, and obstructed vision. In that instance some mechanical process of removing the soot will work. Similarly, to allow for new types of spiritual information to be experienced, it is necessary to have a procedure for eradicating the obstructions to clear vision. This, then, is where the meditation on Vajrasattva is useful.

One is instructed to sit in the lotus posture and visualize a lotus on one's head. Upon this lotus is a moon disc, and in this moon disc is the letter *hūṃ,* which turns into Vajrasattva. This is one's own teacher in the form of Vajrasattva.[18] He has all the adornments of a complete enjoyment body and is in union with his consort. His body has the consistency of a rainbow; it is made of light. Having a sense of shame for misdeeds previously performed, the practitioner determines to reveal all of those misdeeds to Vajrasattva, and reflects in the following way:[19]

> I will purify the ten non-virtues that I have done since time without beginning. I will cleanse the five heinous acts that I have accumulated. In the past I have broken the vows of individual liberation, those of Bodhisattvas, and the tantric ones. Please cleanse all of these. I have lied and broken many oaths; please purify them.[20]

The ten nonvirtuous actions are: killing, stealing, sexual misconduct, lying, divisive speech, harsh words, senseless talk, covetousness, harmful thoughts, and wrong view.[21] The five heinous acts are killing one's mother or father, killing an arhat, malevolently drawing the blood of a buddha, or creating a split in the spiritual community.[22] The vows of individual liberation allude to the various commitments and rules of training that practitioners undertake when seeking their individual liberation as an arhat. The bodhisattva vows are the rules of training for those seeking to become enlightened into buddhahood for the sake of all others. The tantric pledges refer to training guidelines for those seeking buddhahood rapidly using the very special techniques taught in tantric Buddhism.

This then comprises the first two parts of a fully qualified act of confession.[23] The first part requires that we have a pure base to whom we confess, in this case Vajrasattva. The purification is conceived interpersonally as part of the liturgy within which one imagines Vajrasattva and states, "I ask you for refuge and to cleanse my sins. . . ." The second part of a fully qualified act of confession is the strong sense of remorse associated with the liturgical confession of misdeeds done in the past—the act of contrition.[24]

Within this liturgical recitation the practitioner asks for refuge, requests the purification of his or her misdeeds, and finally vows to abstain from such misdeeds in the future, "though it cost my life."[25] This, then, is the third part in the act of confession, "a strong intention to avoid repeating the deeds in the future."[26] The liturgy continues by describing the visualization of a moon disc on Vajrasattva's heart upon which the letters of his hundred-syllable mantra are rotating. At the same time, the practitioner is reciting the hundred-syllable mantra. This is the fourth part in the act of confession, the application of antidote behavior.[27] As the hundred-syllable mantra is recited, the practitioner imagines a cloud of white nectar coming forth from the mantra that descends into his or her head and body. As skill in this visualization practice develops, the practitioner is to imagine other beings performing this visualization at the same time.

As the white nectar fills the body, it washes away the three poisons (anger, desire, and ignorance), the three classes of disease (wind, bile, and phlegm), and the three demonic influences (Poden Gyalpo, the manifestation of anger; Modon Dremo, the manifestation of desire; and Ludon Sadak, the manifestation of ignorance).[28] The three poisons flush out as ink, smoke, coal dust, or dirt.[29] The three diseases wash out as rotten blood and pus. And the three demonic influences wash out in the form of poisonous insects, scorpions, snakes, fish, tadpoles, lice, spiders, and frogs.[30]

Through the orifices at the bottom of one's body and the soles of one's feet these impurities flow out.[31] The practitioner imagines the earth opening up and, at a depth of nine stories, are gathered the messengers and workers of the Lord of Death, and all beings with whom one has some obligation. These are individuals who can harm and shorten life. All of one's impurities descend and are then transformed into what it is that these beings desire. They become satisfied and content, and the earth then closes up again.

The practitioner then imagines his or her body as being filled with nectar, and feels filled with joy.[32] Here one continues with the liturgy, again confessing to having broken one's pledges in the past and requesting to be guarded in the future against such behavior by Lama Vajrasattva. One again takes refuge in the "leader holding a *vajra,* whose nature is great compassion," and beseeches Vajrasattva, saying, "Please cleanse and purify all my masses of defilement."[33] Vajrasattva smiles and laughs, and answers that all obstructions and sins are purified.[34]

At this point Vajrasattva and his consort melt into light and dissolve into the practitioner, who now imagines he or she is Vajrasattva together with his consort, having a body of light.[35] At the practitioner's heart is a small disc the size of a mustard seed with the five seed syllables of Vajrasattva on it sending out five colors of light. At the end of the rays offering goddesses offer objects pleasing to the five senses to buddhas and bodhisattvas throughout space. With these offerings the accumulation of merit is completed, and the last obstructions are purified. The pleased buddhas and bodhisattvas emit light returning to the practitioner, endowing him or her with all spiritual accomplishments, in particular full buddhahood. Then light pours forth from the letters and goes into all of the six realms of rebirth where beings (all of whom have been related to us as our mother in the past[36]) are freed from every form of suffering and are in turn transformed into Vajrasattva, and their environs are transformed into the pure lands of Vajrasattva. One recites the seed syllables of Vajrasattva, and the visualization is dissolved into light, which is absorbed into one's heart. One's heart also then dissolves, and one remains in a space-like equipoise. As one reemerges, one considers oneself to be in a pure land, that all beings are Vajrasattva, and that all appearances are the illusions of a magician.

The Narrative Frame: Context of Healing in Crosscultural Perspective

Along with providing an overall frame for considering practice from another culture, Richard Shweder also provides the useful template of *narrative* from which to consider various cultural practices. Shweder discerns three major forms of narrative that people over time have used to try to make sense of experiences that otherwise seem inexplicable: the karmic, bewitchment, and the bio-psychological.[37]

Today, in the modern West, when it comes to healing, our primary narratives are biological and psychological. In contrast, those who come from traditional perspectives might discuss healing in a language that invokes karma, other ethical laws, or a narrative that involves spirits of various kinds. When we are able to see the constraints our narratives impose, most often in an unconscious manner, then the power of these narratives will hopefully be made palpable.

In its biological sense, healing is the purview of modern medicine, where goals of improving the functioning or the duration of life of an individual who is ill are of major concern. Of course, one of the ongoing major ethical concerns is whether it is duration or function that has priority, but these two are the major concerns that set the parameters of modern medicine. In its most limited forms, modern medicine restricts itself to considering etiology related to pathogens, environmental pollutants, genetic predisposition, and mechanical irregularities. At its more enlightened, some sensitivity to sociological and psychological factors as contributors to disease is included. The task of modern medicine ends at death.

Psychological healing has to do with the alleviation of emotional and psychosomatic symptoms, and improving functioning in relationships. Often summed up in the rubric that mental health is the capacity to work and love, the purview of this form of healing is the individual in his or her immediate social environment. Some of the less pragmatic forms of therapy, such as the existential, the humanistic, and the transpersonal, do concern themselves with larger issues of meaning and life. However, the mainstream of the psychotherapeutic profession limits its concerns to the more circumspect spheres of vocation and immediate relationships. There is some division today within the world of psychology as to the significance of nature and nurture. While there is a pharmaceutical revolution underway in the treatment of disturbances like depression, at the same time talk therapy proceeds with tools that look at earlier history as well as current relationships, and the way individuals relate to themselves during the course of their lives. The task of modern psychology ends at death.

Hale through Purification

The meditation we are considering here has a very different frame. In terms of time, the practice is oriented toward eliminating all of the obstacles accumulated within beginningless rebirth. In terms of the future, successful practice means that one becomes a buddha and continues to work for the enlightenment of limitless beings over the course of future lifetimes. The practice has no range of beginning in its applicability, and no finite range of conclusion in its effect.

In a curious presaging of Shweder's identification of explanatory narratives, the liturgy mentions operations in three narrative frames—purification of demonic forces (bewitchment), purification of illness (biological), and purification of misdeeds (karmic). Nevertheless, the goal of the practice transcends the realms of each of these as it ultimately concerns itself with becoming free of any narrative that is related to conditioned reality. One practices not merely to become free from possession, to become healthier, or to improve one's rebirth—though these may be intermediate epiphenomena. Rather, one practices to cleanse oneself in order to become a vessel capable of understanding the nature of reality.

Thereby, one becomes a buddha, capable of orienting and leading all other beings. It is this feature of promoting purification for the sake of buddhahood that moved Tulku Thondup to identify this as the foremost form of healing.[38]

In the practice of Vajrasattva, to be *hale* in the most profound sense is to be free of karmic obstructions, free of interfering illness, and free of demonic forces so that one can become a buddha and thereby help others. While ensconced in what is arguably a practice primarily oriented toward karma, this practice ultimately leads beyond karma, bewitchment, and ordinary biology and psychology, presaging a different kind of narrative—the narrative of liberation.

Whole and Hallowed

The practice is undertaken in a vision of all others practicing with oneself. One is in a hierarchical relationship with all of one's teachers, and one is going through steps that include rectifying relationships with others, and imaginatively enlightening all others as a prelude to actually doing so. The practice is a veritable operatic performance with multiple chorale—all beings surrounding us initially, practicing together; teachers above us in the form of Vajrasattva; our creditors below us; and, in the conclusion, all beings in the ten directions ultimately becoming enbuddha-ed with all environments becoming pure heavenly realms. The meditation includes several layers of interdependence and interrelatedness. It is a given that all beings are considered to have been in a close, supportive relationship in the past.[39] There are, in addition, the relationships between student and teacher, and creditor and debtor. Within this vast web, the meditation is enlivening a *holistic* vision of relation and concern. One is rehearsing in meditation what one hopes to ultimately do in reality. One is enacting the sacralization of all others and is envisioning each being's sacred potential—*all* are *hallowed* and in a process of healing.

Cultural Expectations

As mentioned above, I have been actively involved in the transmission of meditative practices such as the Vajrasattva visualization described here across the cultural boundaries that define traditional Tibetan religious culture and our own modern Western society. During that time, I have seen that when we in the West approach a practice such as Vajrasattva, there are many ways that we bring our cultural lenses into operation in our understanding of the practice.

It may ultimately behoove us to slow down and really consider carefully the cultural nexus within which the Vajrasattva practice arose and the features of religious practice in that context, so that we can more sensitively appreciate it.

Pragmatic applications. Because of the cleansing, purifying, and healing aspects of this practice, there is an inclination to want to apply this form of practice to the medical and psychological domains. Occasionally, I've heard of therapists teaching their clients elements of this practice, and I myself have sometimes used some elements of its structure in offering guided imagery to patients with cancer, suggesting they imagine light purifying and healing their condition.

There is no denying that clients may feel immediate benefits from doing elements of this practice. At the same time, it seems appropriate to note ways that in doing so there may be a gradual movement of elements of the tradition away from their original context of meaning. In bold terms, when Asian spiritual traditions oriented toward liberation from the cycle of rebirth are brought to the West, they are often subsumed to the much narrower and more circumscribed pragmatic agendas of modern psychology or medicine.

Of course, this has already happened in a larger scale with meditation as a whole. Nowadays, meditation has been adopted in the field of mental health as an intervention for virtually every form of diagnosis in the *Diagnostic and Statistical Manual of Mental Disorders.*[40] For example, one interesting application of meditation is in the alleviation of obsessive-compulsive disorder.[41] In traditional Buddhist practice, however, meditation had its place in the karmic-liberative narrative.

A metaphor that might be useful here is that of a ballerina who, through her practice of leg lifts, developed the capacity to lift forty pounds with her right foot extended horizontally. This is a real pragmatic result and perhaps of much interest to a weight trainer or physical fitness enthusiast. Within the ballerina's context, her primary concern, and ours as well as that of her audience, is that she is able to perform with beauty and grace as a swan in *Swan Lake.* Her muscular talent is an epiphenomenon that may not even receive any note from her. If, however, we talked with a weight trainer who had just met the principal of the Houston Ballet and all he discussed was her pragmatic capacity to lift forty pounds with her foot extended horizontally, we would feel that this individual had really missed the big picture.

This type of thing happens when the ballet of Buddhist spirituality is translated into the bio-psychological narrative of our culture. There is often no mention of morality, karma, or liberation—the *Swan Lake* of the spiritual life. Meditations are isolated from their soteriological context and transplanted into circumstances that support the stereotypical American values of pragmatism in the fields of psychology and medicine. Due to cultural forces larger than any individual, there seems to be a gradual slide away from meditation as an opportunity to liberate us from ensnarement in this life toward assimilating this practice not only to our pragmatism but also to our social values of peak performance and hedonism—witness, for example, psychoanalyst Jeffrey Rubin's praise of meditation for "appreciating art, listening to others, participating in athletics, and experiencing love."[42]

I am reminded of an incident that serves as a striking metaphor for what is happening here. In 1971 I was staying in a very primitive hostel in Sarnath, India, the location of Buddha's first sermon. We only had one water faucet for a hostel of fifty people; the water only ran twice a day and there was no bathroom. We shared our hostel with pilgrims from Ladakh. One day a wizened old lady came and asked me for two stick-on bandages, which I was happy to give her, no questions asked. But imagine my amazement when I saw her later that evening with the bandages neatly plastered to her temples, in order to alleviate her headache! She had correctly surmised that we apply these plastic strips to areas of pain and had figured out a way of dealing with her own. She was happy, and so are we when we meditate ten minutes a day to lower our blood pressure. But we may then have no more idea of what meditation was originally trying to ultimately accomplish than this woman had about the germ theory of disease. In both instances the means employed may provide the desired effects. Yet in both instances, fuller appreciation of the context of intervention provides a much richer opportunity for understanding the rationale for intervention, exploring other opportunities for intervention, and appreciation for the chosen intervention in a broader theoretical and practical framework. Without this, we are consigned to the oversimplified pragmatic formula "If it works, it is good."

It is thus interesting to reflect on the Vajrasattva meditation coming to the West from within the context of karma and liberation, since the way this practice is seen, understood, and applied often has as much to tell us about ourselves as it does about the practice itself. First I should say that Tibetan Buddhism does not lack for specific meditations linked to longevity or physical well-being. Meditation on the goddess Tara or long-life initiations and practices related to Amitāyus (Infinite Life) Buddha can be done with an orientation toward longevity. Furthermore, there are meditations related to the Medicine Buddha (Bhaiṣajyaguru) for working with physical illness.[43] These are, however, distinct from the goals associated with the Vajrasattva visualization practice.

Specific spiritual goals of Vajrasattva practice. Curing medical illness or lengthening our lives are not the ultimate goals of the Vajrasattva meditation, although purification from all illness and pacifying forces that might shorten our lives are aspects of the visualization. The overall practice is related to a liberative narrative. Seeing life as subject to karma, Buddhists came up with a whole trajectory of ways to move out of karma, though in the initial stages of practice one uses karma to create the appropriate context for practice.

When considering health and healing in the Asian Buddhist context, it is important to identify and highlight the liberative frame, for in a sense it is from this frame that the priorities of life are clearly set. This frame differs so greatly from our own. Through familiarity with this distinctly different frame, some of our own native priorities become much clearer.

The Vajrasattva practice is a purification, assisting the practitioner to arrive at the understanding that is present from the beginning, understanding that will ultimately flourish into the liberation of buddhahood.[44] As such one is no longer chained by karma and is free to help others in infinite ways.

It is to clarify one's understanding of any stain or obstruction that one does the practice. Here, the three poisons, the three diseases, and the three demonic influences are all ways in which our understanding can be clouded. Impediments that shorten life shorten our capacity to practice. The healing is oriented toward the liberated state of buddhahood.

Vajrasattva and curing illness. I have heard rumor of instances of individuals who recovered from some disease by doing the Vajrasattva practice. On a recent visit, I talked with Tulku Thondup about the use of this meditation for health purposes. Thondup had some sense of perhaps hearing of this in Tibet but could not be sure. He was sure that there was the tale of a famous teacher who early in his career could not remember things whatsoever, yet who went on to become a great and learned abbot due to the practice of Vajrasattva.[45] Here the practice is seen in its capacity to purify karma, leading to improved cognitive capacity in the service of the larger religious purpose.

One would think, from hearing the description of the meditation, that it might be used as a medical intervention. However, this is not how I have seen it contextualized. In all the instances when I have been ill around lamas—and I have had my share of amoebic dysentery and giardiasis—they have never suggested that I do this practice as a way to overcome the physical illness. Nor have I heard that they, when themselves ill, were doing this practice. Here the notion of narrative helps.

While couched in terms that seem to refer to illness and its elimination and appeasing forces that might shorten our lives, the practice has its larger purpose in a narrative of liberation. It is not set forth in pragmatic bio-psychological terms. It is interesting to consider this in terms of Shweder's third movement, "deconstructing the other." From our bio-psychological perspective this absence of any emphasis on pragmatic results may be seen as an incompleteness.

We can detect some very subtle shifts as practices migrate from Asia to the United States. Because of the rapidity of cultural transfer now, and because of the availability of information from both source and target cultures, the process of cultural assimilation is visible to us in an *in vivo* environment. As we have seen, the Vajrasattva meditation mentions abandoning all physical illness, though physical healing is not its larger purpose, and from what I have been exposed to, this was not its traditional use in general. However, we in the West are for the most part immersed in a bio-psychological narrative. So it becomes understandable that when meditation was arriving at our shores in the 1950s through the 1980s, the rubrics for understanding it would be those of mental and behavioral health, though those are not the rubrics used in traditional culture.

Furthermore, whether intended or not, when a practice arrives it will be tested against our narratives. I'm reminded of the famous essay on the origin of roasted pork, where the pig accidentally fell in the fire, the person extends his hand to remove it, burns his hand, sucks on it to cool it off, and realizes it's tasty. We know that we've seen Zen married to every noun in the English language, as though Zen had fallen into every imaginable fire—from swordsmanship to motorcycle repair—and been tasted and found satisfying. Thus, when the Vajrasattva meditation comes into our context, it is almost predictable that it will be applied to either the psychological or biological sphere.

In fact, Tulku Thondup tells the inspiring story of Harry Winters, a long-term Buddhist practitioner. Winters was given six months to live with lung cancer but he successfully underwent two surgeries, and rejected a third surgery five years later at the onset of relapse. All the while Winters had been successfully employing the traditional Vajrasattva meditation as an adjunct to his medical treatment.[46] Winters went on to live at least another six years after the third surgery had been suggested and rejected. This is inspiring.

I am also aware of the pressures upon me, as a Western teacher of and author about Buddhism, to transform traditional Buddhist practice so that it fits into the modern Western narrative.[47] I am aware that audiences in the West and book publishers would love to hear about techniques that are oriented to lengthen life or reduce illness, but the push is to excise these from traditional teachings about suffering, cyclical rebirth, and the significance of liberation. *Viva* drive-through self-improvement! So I see myself as part of a larger process of cultural assimilation, wherein there is pressure to take the traditional Buddhism I know, with its deep profound view, and truncate it in order to serve the immediate cultural mandates of the moment. In the West, when the ideas of rebirth and liberation are lost during the importation of Buddhist practice, the tradition is deracinated—stripped of the cognitive context that provides its rationalizing justification. The danger in succumbing to such pressures is that practices meant to facilitate a one-way exit to the fresh air of freedom can, through the gradual assimilation to our cultural preferences, become a revolving door that merely return us to the smoke-filled world of samsaric values. In contemplating this already-in-place cultural trend, I become aware of our own limitations and incompleteness.

"Henceforth I Will Refrain from Them at the Cost of My Life":[48] The Milieu of Practice

I wish to return now to the question that started me thinking anew about this practice. The Western student asked, "How do I commit to not doing nonvirtue in the future when there are some nonvirtues that I know I will do again?" Here the Buddhist teacher's response was, "Indeed, you must make the strong commitment to never do such a thing again." We are now in a position to engage Shweder's fourth movement, "open-ended self-reflexive dialogic experience," with respect to this question and answer.

My first reaction was to see the Buddhist teacher's counsel as a call to some intense effort of moral intention. I now think, however, that this interpretation misses several critical differences in the milieu of practice.

Tibetan culture is a traditional sociocentric culture with a preference to considering matters with respect to the concrete occasion and set of relations that are entailed.[49] Much like the Oriyas of Bhubaneswar, India, studied by Richard Shweder, the Tibetans would much rather discuss a question about a specific person, in a specific situation, with a specific condition, than engage in an abstract discussion of, let us say, euthanasia. The latter is what we in the United States prefer, that is to say, an abstract style of conversation—identifying, for example, a person's traits, "friendly," "angry," "trustworthy," rather than considering the specific contexts of their discrete behaviors.[50]

When Khetsun Sangpo Rinpoche sits and reflects on never committing nonvirtue, he is emphasizing his act of commitment at the moment. He is not reflecting on human nature (an abstraction), or even his own personal inclinations (another abstraction). Rather, he is making a concrete commitment, at a concrete time, with all good intention and sincerity. We as Westerners may find this a very different universe than our own. We run across this universe of values over and over, when we try to plan things in the far-extended future with Tibetan teachers. They would much prefer to respond to circumstances within maybe a three-month frame, while we are ready to talk of two to five years into the future. The picture is enriched when we consider how respective cultural values affect each practitioner as they contemplate making a commitment with respect to the future.

Willingness or Willfulness

Part of the difficulty with the Westerner's question to the lama has to do with issues related to will, vulnerability, and perfection or completeness. My reading of modern Western spiritual values is that there is some concern about the appropriateness of willfulness as an approach to the spiritual life.

Gerald G. May, in *Will and Spirit*, writes:

> The idea of being able to accomplish one's own salvation is held as anathema by every major spiritual tradition in the world, not only because of its fundamental implausibility but also because of the destructive narcissism it cultivates. . . .[51]
>
> [T]he desire to be the master of one's soul is nothing but willfulness.[52]

This spiritual perspective then seems almost at odds with the more general cultural norm for the West as articulated, for example, by Clifford Geertz:

> The Western conception of the person as a bounded, unique, more or less integrated motivational and cognitive universe, a dynamic center of awareness, emotion, judgment, and action organized into a distinctive whole *and set contrastively both against other such wholes and against a social and natural background* is, however incorrigible it may seem to us, a rather peculiar idea within the context of the world's cultures.[53]

So in the West there is some tension between the cultural norm that sees the individual willfully opposed to others and the environment, and a spiritual norm that such willfulness can never serve ultimately in the path to God.

The Buddhist vision on this is complex and nuanced somewhat differently. Seemingly, it goes from an extreme of self-power in Theravāda, where on his deathbed the Buddha informs the assembled to "Try to accomplish your aim with diligence," offering no recourse to divine support.[54] This particular form of willfulness apparently escaped Gerald May's notice. On the other end of the geographical and historical map is the belief in the salvific grace of Amida Buddha—the other-power teaching described by some authors of Jōdo Shinshū.[55]

Tibet, geographically in the middle, takes a path that shares features of both self- and other-power. Here in the practice of Vajrasattva we see the practitioner vowing to hold his or her vows even at the risk of his or her own life. When I asked Tulku Thondup about this particular passage, he stated that his teachers had said that even though we know that we will fall from our vows, we repeat this type of strong commitment in order to strengthen our ability to hold the vows.[56] He also pointed out that during some periods of political oppression some lamas did in fact object to destroying religious statues for the Chinese and were imprisoned as a result. Some died in prison. The significance of individual intentionality, willfulness if you like, toward ideal spiritual behavior cannot be minimized in our attempts to understand indigenous Tibetan Buddhist practice. We had evidence of this during a recent visit of some Tibetan practitioners. When I asked one—who was clearly nodding off due to extreme exhaustion—if he was tired, he said no and immediately closed his eyes and went to sleep. Holding the intention of not being tired was important even in the face of massive override by physical reality.

At the same time practice is contextualized in such a way that practitioners understand that their undertaking cannot be done alone. The meditator prays to all his or her teachers, in the form of Vajrasattva, for refuge, for purification of past transgressions, and for protection against future transgressions. The instrument of purification is the blessings of the teachers in the form of nectar. The ability of the four powers of confession to work include the delicate mix of one's own confession, and one's own intention (willfulness) to not transgress in the future, with the reliance on the pure sacred object, in this case Vajrasattva (willingness), and engagement in pure, prescribed activity to effect purification (both willful and willing).

Tulku Thondup made a wonderful crosscultural observation when he visited Houston in February 2001. He stated that when Westerners do visualization, they are very concerned with both the visualization and the recitation, but also with the nature of their experience and feelings as they engage in the process. In contrast, Tibetans traditionally emphasized the first two, together with an attitude of deep faith toward the buddha, bodhisattva, or teacher whom they were visualizing. Traditional practitioners would mix fervent intentionality (willfulness) and deep open-hearted receptivity (willingness). As the practice moves West there may be some decided trend toward emphasizing the action of recitation and visualization over moral intentionality. There may also be a self-oriented attentiveness toward experience associated with practice and a correlative atrophy in open-hearted reliance. Because of our orientation toward self-reliance and independent strength, as a matter of course we may be assimilating this practice in a form that is much more willful than our Tibetan counterparts. One has only to witness, as we did, Khetsun Sangpo Rinpoche's aged sister looking at an illustrated liturgy to see the touching, heartwarming veneration that indigenous Tibetans brought up before the Chinese takeover can have for the sacred objects of their faith to realize how far most of us in the West are from this type of spiritual porosity.

An Orientation toward Perfection versus Accepting Vulnerability to Imperfection

While the seeming dichotomy between willfulness and willingness is stimulating, and it allows us to see Vajrasattva practice on a continuum between one extreme and the other, this alone does not help us appreciate in a complete way the particular values that distinguish this practice and that come into play in the question from the Western practitioner to the Tibetan Buddhist teacher. The additional noteworthy value in the practice of Vajrasattva is that it is oriented toward an image of completeness or perfection that the practitioner is expected to emulate, aspire to, and eventually achieve.

It is perhaps this orientation to become perfect with both active and receptive elements to it that is most difficult to apprehend for us in the West. The two usual pairs for us are willfulness toward perfection and a willingness to accept vulnerability. Gerald May has pointed out that willfulness toward perfection can lead to narcissistic inflation and pride, and the most prevalent instances of such a stance are seen in the civil religions of football, boxing, and professional wrestling. Whether on a global level religious life is really as willing as May portrays, or indeed, exhibits a more complex and nuanced mix of willfulness and willingness, there is certainly some sense in the larger dominant Christian culture of the West that a search for perfection is spiritually contraindicated. This is often vouchsafed with references to the idea of hubris drawn from Greek tragedy but it is also, it turns out, very much rooted in the early history of the Christian Church, where the very issue of Christ's vulnerability or perfection was hotly debated.

Elaine Pagels, in her meticulously researched *Gnostic Gospels*, points out that there was much debate in the early Church about Christ's nature, particularly his vulnerability to suffering.[57] For the early martyrs of the Church, there was a way in which they justified their misery as being of the same nature as Christ's own suffering. For example, Hippolytus, the learned Greek teacher in Rome, stated that orthodox doctrine about Christ's incarnation and passion allowed believers to endure.

> *If he were not of the same nature with ourselves, he would command in vain that we should imitate the teacher. . . .*
>
> He did not protest against his passion, but became obedient unto death. . . .
>
> Now in all these acts *he offered up, as the first fruits, his own humanity, in order that you, when you are in tribulation, may not be discouraged, but, confessing yourself to be one like the redeemer,* may dwell in expectation of receiving what the Father has granted to the Son.[58]

In a significant way that stamps orthodox Christianity, Christ's willingness to be vulnerable is assimilated to the experience of ordinary humankind, and serves as a link, then, to the historically significant suffering of the martyrs of the early Church.

The Gnostic heresy, which held that Christ was only appearing to suffer, did not carry the day, and was seen as so threatening that it was banned. This particular vision, though, is much akin to the one that eventually holds sway in the Mahayana, for example in the *Lotus Sutra* (*Saddharmapuṇḍarīka-sūtra*) where the Buddha is portrayed as manifesting his life story from an already enlightened state.

More significantly for us here, the religious goal in Mahayana Buddhism is for the individual to attain buddhahood, some form of perfection beyond suffering, a state described as omniscient (*sarvajña*), where one has completed the practice of the six perfections, and one's qualities are limitless. I think one of the hardest aspects of the Vajrasattva practice for us to grasp is that it includes a willingness to become perfect. The fact that the practice includes both active and passive aspects shows the complexity inherent in most religious systems of behavior. However, combining receptivity with an orientation to perfection brings together two orientations that fly in the face of the dominant religiosity of the West. On the other hand, the union of receptivity and perfection, while not omnipresent in Asian spiritual traditions, is certainly evident in many Tibetan practices and in the whole world of Daoist-influenced spirituality. Recently Peter Steinfels, religion writer for the *New York Times,* characterized the brew of Buddhist, Daoist, and Confucian elements that go into the martial arts as including "ascendancy through yielding."[59] It is this stance that I am calling a willingness to become perfect.

Not only does this willingness to become perfect contrast with the dominant religious model in the Christian West, the attitude toward ascendancy or completion contrasts with the perspective of psychotherapy. I was recently at a family therapy conference where Harry J. Aponte, a renowned trainer of family therapists from Philadelphia, spoke about the role of spirituality in therapy. He indicated that he was educated in the era when individuals initially felt that you would go into analysis, get over your problems, and that would be it. You would be complete. However, he and others found that sometimes ten years after analysis, some of their problems returned. For him, the ultimate solution to this was a spiritual perspective.

> To me, the self-esteem is going to come from the noble struggle, which is, I live with this, you know, I was born in a certain family, with certain craziness in my family, with certain genetics, with certain life experience, social environment, and I have things about myself that will always be a problem for me. Now, can I engage with that in a way that will lead to my growth, that requires my acknowledgement that I have the flaw that requires an awareness and an insight into the nature of my struggle with that flaw? That certainly requires my having some sort of transcendent purpose that says, you know, this will lead to something good if you engage with it in the right way.[60]

We see in Aponte's characterization of himself several elements that are helpful in understanding our modern Western approach to personal development. First of all there is the tendency to abstraction that we mentioned earlier. He takes stock of himself and finds he has "certain craziness . . . things about myself that will always be a problem"—abstract qualities that are here devoid of contextualization. He knows himself from his past, and his wisdom is evidenced by his realizing that his issues will manifest again in the future. In the mental health field, such humility with respect to one's own predispositions, which of course is an abstract judgment, is understood as a form of maturity.

Furthermore, therapy is no longer naively seen as a path to completion. Rather, for Aponte some sense of transcendent purpose is needed to serve as a container for holding our vulnerability and imperfections of affect and behavior. Indeed, it seems that one of the end results of Freud's dictum, "Where id is, there let ego be," is a tolerance for all the messiness in one's life with a sense of awareness and acceptance, and ultimately greater autonomy. For many lacking a spiritual compass, therapy provides the secular container of forgiveness and love that Aponte so eloquently wishes to assign to the transcendent. Indeed one of the most prevalent presenting problems that we as clinicians deal with is client self-hatred in the face of their human failings. Our therapeutic task is to soften and ameliorate the harshest forms of self-recrimination for imperfection, and allow our clients to tolerate their faults with some degree of acceptance. If depression is the common cold of mental health, relief of congestion often comes through acceptance of our imperfections—our angers, upsets, and griefs. One fundamental Western algorithm—driving everything in the world of personal improvement from therapy to Alcoholics Anonymous—involves an experiential identification of our human vulnerabilities (our desires, grief, envy, anger, and failings) coupled with a forgiving acceptance by ourselves, our therapist, or a Higher Power of our tendency to such vulnerabilities, all located within an encompassing attitude of improvement-but-not-perfection.

It is precisely this therapeutically supported abstract understanding of her vulnerability to imperfection that was culturally influencing the student to ask the question with which I began this discussion. (At another level, such abstract understanding of oneself, when carried to an extreme, can lead to a conceptually mediated type of distance, the Spock of *Star Trek* syndrome, which, when it presents clinically, includes a subjective sense of living life at one remove.) The Western student was wisely aware of her own predilections. I don't know her specific concerns, but for any of us it could be an issue with a predictable rage in a repetitive family situation, or a tendency to backbiting, or a repetitive problem with impulse control in the area of intoxicants, all of which are seen as nonvirtues from the Buddhist perspective. From the modern therapeutic perspective, such an understanding of our own vulnerabilities is a plus!

There is yet a further level to understanding differences in the cultural milieu between student and teacher. We in the West tend to be much more psychologically oriented than ethnic Tibetans, so that we pay great attention to the nuances of our emotional life, its ups and downs, and its unpredictable nature. In fact, the very substance of our relationships is discussion of the vagaries of our feelings and emotions.[61] In contrast, individuals in traditional Asian cultures are more oriented toward interdependence with one with another, attending to the rules and roles that govern their relationships, and relating in ways that rely on nonverbal affective attunement.[62] Our Tibetan colleagues and teachers may, if they are like their Indian and Chinese neighbors, be more prone to respond to life's stressors and the vicissitudes of experience with somatic complaints rather than emotional reactions.[63]

Our Western student who asked her question is familiar with her feelings and behavior patterns, and is aware of the ways in which they make it difficult for her to hold to certain ethical standards. In accord with our cultural norms, her way of dealing with her self-knowledge is to want to talk about her abstract propensity to such behavior. While she is oriented toward buddhahood in her practice, her everyday orientation is to the acceptance of her own imperfection.

Our Asian teacher is much more tuned to a context-specific orientation within a frame of rules and roles. He does not find obligations onerous in the way we, who are oriented toward our rights, do.[64] Rather, cultural psychologists Markus and Kitayama suggest that as an individual coming from a culture oriented toward an "obligation fulfilling social-self," he might find contentment and goodness in responding and living in accordance with norms and expectations.[65]

Unlike us, our teacher is not oriented to monitoring or reporting significant variations in his mood and emotion. He would find our preference to use abstraction to predict our potential future vulnerability to nonvirtue difficult to understand, when in the present you can make a concrete commitment not to perform such behavior and thereby satisfactorily live according to rules and norms. While the vow to certain behavior does involve projection into an abstract future, our teacher is orienting himself to the subjective immediacy of making a moral commitment. That immediate and concrete act of intentionality is what is significant and satisfying for him. He sees it as quite reasonable to be oriented toward perfection, whereas we in the West see perfectibility as a form of hubris in mythic terms, overweening pride in religious terms, or denial in psychological terms. The Western student, with her question, has come to some realization of who she is and is holding her abstract imperfections in mind with some type of perhaps hard-won psychological acceptance. These are the cultural sources of her question in the face of a liturgy that has one vowing to never again commit non-virtue.

I find myself as if wearing some form of odd, bicolored 3-D glasses from the cinema of yore. Looking through one cultural lens, everything is orange; through the other, everything bluish-gray. And yes, I sometimes open both eyes and hold both visions simultaneously. Through the orange lens, it is inspiring to imagine what we might become, to realize that my commitment today is a very concrete, real event and the future is indeed not fully predictable and therefore not faultlessly amenable to abstraction. Furthermore, there is a form of satisfaction knowing that one belongs to a tradition, and is following rules and norms that tie us into others both currently and historically. Finally, I can appreciate that I can both intend to alter my behavior but ultimately may need to rely on some power much greater than myself for spiritual progress.

At the same time through the blue lens, as a Westerner, I personally know that over-willfulness of intentionality can lead me to psychological denial and a way of being out of touch with my feelings. This in turn can lead to difficulties in my relationships and a variety of psychosomatic symptoms. One way I have of dealing with this—a way that is culturally accepted and even mandated—is in becoming ever more aware of my vulnerabilities, accepting them, anticipating they will be there in the future (abstract judgment), and being willing to share my experiences with others.

When Westerners practice, they will inevitably bring to the meditation cushion their own psychological self-understanding, their orientation toward self-reliance, and their inclination to abstraction; and, at the same time, they can train, or experiment, with emphasizing reliance on the spiritual sources of refuge in the tradition and making an immediate commitment as an aspect of the practice. Is this a neat synthesis or one that is fully at rest? Perhaps not. But then again, having access to both lenses is tremendously expansive. Insofar as we come away from this venture with a robust appreciation of both ourselves and traditional Buddhist practice, we are *hale.* To the extent we can hold in consciousness the context of both our own cultural values and those of the ancient tradition, our experience is *whole.*

In considering the interchange between student and teacher from two different cultures, there is a poignance and ultimately a compassion we feel with respect to the divides in perspective that render mutual understanding such a nuanced challenge. The immediacy that contains the immensity of the Buddhist spiritual vision and the very real predicaments of our psychological reality is a *hallowed* ground. The act of cross-cultural immersion is itself an act of healing.

Notes

1 Takamaro Shigaraki, *A Life of Awakening: The Heart of the Shin Buddhist Path,* trans. David Matsumoto (Kyoto, Japan: Hōzōkan, 2005).

2 Ibid., p. 78.

3 Ibid., pp. 87–94.

4 Ibid., p. 77.

5 Ibid., p. 109.

6 Ibid., p. 94.

7 Ibid., p. 79.

8 Ibid., pp. 104–105.

9 Tulku Thondup, *The Healing Power of Mind: Simple Meditation Exercises for Health, Well-Being, and Enlightenment* (Boston and London: Shambhala, 1996); *Boundless Healing: Meditation Exercises to Enlighten the Mind and Heal the Body* (Boston and London: Shambhala, 2000). Tulku Thondup Rinpoche made this reference to the Vajrasattva practice during the course of a private conversation in Houston, Texas, February 3, 2001.

10 Under *kailo,* as an Indo-European root related to "whole," "uninjured," "of good omen." *American Heritage Dictionary* (Boston: American Heritage Publishing Co., Inc., 1969), p. 1520.

11 Anne C. Klein, professor of religious studies, Rice University, reports that she served as a translator for a lama of the Gelukba order, Locho Rinpoche, when a Western student asked almost the identical question and received a very similar response.

12 Richard Shweder, *Thinking Through Cultures: Expedition in Cultural Psychology* (Cambridge, MA: Harvard University Press, 1991), pp. 108–110.

13 Ibid.

14 Jeffrey J. Kripal, "Psychoanalysis and Hinduism: Thinking Through Each Other," in *Vishnu on Freud's Desk: A Reader in Psychoanalysis and Hinduism,* ed. T. G. Vaidyanathan and Jeffrey J. Kripal (Delhi: Oxford University Press, 1999), p. 439.

15 See Shweder, *Thinking Through Cultures,* p. 110, for using "through" in the sense of "going toward a particular object of inquiry," and in the sense of "an action that redounds to the subject. . . ."

16 Piyadassi Thera, *The Buddha's Ancient Path* (Kandy, Sri Lanka: Buddhist Publication Society, 1974), pp. 62–66.

17 Khetsun Sangpo Rinbochay, *Tantric Practice in Nying-ma,* trans. and ed. Jeffrey Hopkins, co-ed. Anne Klein (Ithaca, NY: Gabriel/Snow Lion, 1982), pp. 86–100.

18 Ibid., pp. 144–145.

19 Ibid., p. 145.

20 Ibid.

21 Ibid., p. 21.

22 Patrul Rinpoche, *The Words of My Perfect Teacher: A Complete Translation of a Classic Introduction to Tibetan Buddhism,* rev. ed., trans. Padmakara Translation Group (New Delhi: Vistaar Publications, 1994), p. 414.

23 Khetsun Sangpo Rinbochay, *Tantric Practice,* p. 142.

24 Ibid., p. 145.

25 Ibid.

26 Ibid., p. 142.

27 Ibid.

28 Patrul Rinpoche, *The Words of My Perfect Teacher,* p. 269; Lama Tharchin, *A Commentary on the Dudjom Tersar Ngrondro: The Preliminary Practice of the New Treasure of Dudjom* (El Cerrito, CA: Pema Osel Ling, n.d.), p. 37.

29 Ibid.

30 Ibid.

31 Ibid., p. 149.

32 Ibid., p. 150.

33 Ibid., p. 151.

34 Ibid.

35 Ibid.

36 Ibid., p. 128.

37 Richard Shweder, "You're Not Sick, You're Just in Love," in *The Nature of Emotions: Fundamental Questions,* ed. Paul Ekman and Richard J. Davidson (New York: Oxford University Press, 1994), pp. 32–49.

38 See note 2.

39 Khetsun Sangpo Rinbochay, *Tantric Practice,* p. 128.

40 *Diagnostic and Statistical Manual of Mental Disorders,* 4th ed. (Washington, DC: American Psychiatric Association, 1994).

41 Jeffrey M. Schwartz, with Beverly Beyette, *Brain Lock: Free Yourself from Obsessive-Compulsive Behavior* (New York: Regan Books, 1996).

42 Jeffrey B. Rubin, *Psychotherapy and Buddhism: Toward an Integration* (New York: Plenum, 1996), p. 77.

43 See note 30.

44 Khetsun Sangpo Rinbochay, *Tantric Practice,* p. 187.

45 See note 2.

46 Tulku Thondup, *Boundless Healing,* pp. 43–44.

47 There are significant ways that we all unconsciously do this anyway, but that is a topic for extended consideration elsewhere; see Harvey B. Aronson, *Buddhist Practice on Western Ground* (Boston: Shambhala, 2004).

48 Khetsun Sangpo Rinbochay, *Tantric Practice,* p. 145.

49 Shweder, *Thinking Through Cultures,* pp. 129, 147.

[50] Ibid., p. 128.

[51] Gerald G. May, *Will and Spirit: A Contemplative Psychology* (New York: Harper SanFrancisco, 1982), p. 17. I am indebted to my colleague Michael Mauldin for this reference.

[52] Ibid., p. 13.

[53] Shweder, *Thinking Through Cultures,* p. 122. Emphasis added.

[54] Walpola Rahula, *What the Buddha Taught* (Bedford, England: Gordon Fraser, 1959), p. 138.

[55] Seigen H. Yamaoka, *Jodo Shinshu: An Introduction* (San Francisco: Buddhist Churches of America, 1990).

[56] Tulku Thondup, private conversation, Houston, Texas, February 3, 2001. His teacher took a different tack from Khetsun Sangpo, with the latter emphasizing the importance of taking on the position of strong intentionality.

[57] Elaine Pagels, *The Gnostic Gospels* (New York: Vintage Books, 1979), p. 83.

[58] Ibid., p. 89.

[59] Peter Steinfels, "Beliefs," *New York Times,* March 10, 2001.

[60] Harry J. Aponte, "Clinical Applications of Spirituality: Questions and Answers," *Texas Association for Marriage and Family Therapists 2000 Annual Conference* (Houston, TX: Sounds on Tape, 2000), no. 501.

[61] Rose Markus and Shinobu Kitayama, "Cultural Construction of Self and Emotion," in *Emotion and Culture,* ed. Shinobu Kitayama and Hazel Rose Markus (Washington, DC: American Psychological Association, 1994), p. 101.

[62] Ibid.; Richard Shweder with Joan G. Miller, "The Social Construction of the Person: How is it Possible," in Shweder, ed., *Thinking Through Cultures,* pp. 167–170; Markus and Kitayama, "Cultural Construction of Self," pp. 110–111.

[63] Shweder, *Thinking Through Cultures,* p. 319.

[64] Shweder, with Miller, "The Social Construction of the Person," pp. 167–170.

[65] Markus and Kitayama, "Cultural Construction of Self," p. 90. (Editor's note: It may be, as suggested by Corless in this collection, this is more than simply a matter of differing cultural values. Rather, at least for most Westerners, this kind of emphasis on community can serve as a healthy corrective to an overly concretized sense of being an independently existing self.)

A Tang Esoteric Manual for Rebirth in the Pure Land: *Rites for Contemplation of and Offerings to Amitāyus Tathāgata*

Charles D. Orzech
University of North Carolina, Greensboro

"I gaze upon the Marks of that Realm
which surpasses the Triple-Worlds' Way"[1]

Introduction

This essay will explore a little-known but significant commentary on the *Scripture on Contemplation of the Buddha of Limitless Life* (T. 365, *Fo shuo guan wuliangshoufo jing*, 佛說觀無量壽佛經, hereafter *Guan jing*). Along with the longer and shorter versions of the *Sukhāvatīvyūha-sūtra*, the *Guan jing* forms the canonical heart of Pure Land Buddhism in East Asia. Although catalogued as a translation by Kālayaśas (畺良耶舍, active 424–442), the text is now viewed as having been written in Chinese.[2] Its popularity owes not a little to its vivid descriptions of the Western Pure Land, descriptions that appear to have been intended as a guide to visualization which prepared the believer for the journey to the Pure Land at death. The commentary *Rites for Contemplation of and Offerings to Amitāyus Tathāgata* (T. 930, *Wuliangshou rulai guanxing gongyang yigui*, 無量壽如來觀行供養儀軌, hereafter *Wuliangshou yigui*) is designed to expedite achievement of the highest goals of the *Guan jing*: a vision of the Pure Land in this life and, on death, birth in the highest of the nine levels of rebirth in Amitābha's paradise. Long catalogued as a "translation" of the Tang dynasty esoteric master Amoghavajra (Bukong jin'gang, 不空金剛, 705–774), the *Wuliangshou yigui* played an important role in the development of Shingon in Japan.[3] There, it and another Tang esoteric manual, along with a Heian manual, form the canonical basis for the fundamental order of worship known as the "*Juhachi dō*" or "Eighteen-fold Way" (*Shiba dao*, 十八道).[4]

But it is the Tang context of the text rather than the Japanese context that I wish to explore here. An examination of the *Wuliangshou yigui* raises interesting questions with regard to esoteric Buddhism in the mid- to late Tang dynasty. Why did promoters of esoteric Buddhism write a manual to achieve rebirth in the Pure Land when the ostensible goal of esoteric Buddhism is to achieve enlightenment in this life? What does the manual tell us about the state of esoteric Buddhism in the late eighth and early ninth centuries? What, in turn, does this tell us about our notions of sectarian divisions in Tang Buddhism? And what can the way the manual is put together tell us about how esoteric Buddhism was adapted to the Chinese milieu? I argue that the *Wuliangshou yigui* exemplifies the process whereby esoteric Buddhist teachings originating in India were adapted to the religious milieu of the mid- to late Tang. Though typical of esoteric adaptations of non-esoteric material, the *Wuliangshou yigui* is unusual in the degree of integration of that material into its esoteric program. In order to understand the process by which esoteric Buddhism was adapted, and how the *Wuliangshou yigui* is exceptional, we must first examine the substance and structure of the text.

The Substance and Structure of the *Wuliangshou yigui*

The *Wuliangshou yigui* occupies approximately five pages in the Taishō canon and begins as follows:

> At that time Vajrapāṇi Bodhisattva was in the great assembly of Vairocana Buddha, and rising from his seat with hands clasped reverently, he said, "World-honored One. I will discourse on the *dhāraṇī* of Amitāyus Tathāgata on behalf of the multitude of beings whose evil karma will, in the coming age of the last period of the teaching, cause their rebirth in worlds plagued by various defilements. Through cultivation of the three esoteric gates they will be confirmed in the *samādhi* of recollecting the Buddha, [and] will attain birth in the Pure Land and entry to bodhisattvahood.[5] One cannot attain birth in that *kṣetra* by means of paltry good [deeds] and expedients lacking in wisdom. Therefore, relying upon this teaching for the correct cultivation of recollection will make certain birth in the upper category of the upper birth [class] in Sukhāvatī and attainment of the initial *bhūmi.* If a householder or a renunciant wishes to be born in the Pure Land that person should first enter the *maṇḍala* and receive *abhiṣeka.*[6] Thereafter they will receive the ritual procedures for contemplation and worship from their teacher."[7]

Having provided this authoritative charter the text plunges directly into the step-by-step ritual procedure. For convenience I place the corresponding Chinese designations for each major step from the *Wuliangshou yigui* in parentheses in the description below.

The rite begins with preparation of the site for the altar and the purification of it and of the practitioner. Whether in a special locale or in one's home, one is to clean a space and set up a square altar, decorated above with a canopy and around the sides with banners. The top of the altar is divided into an eight-section *maṇḍala,* and white sandalwood incense paste is then smeared on the positions of the deities. An image of Amitāyus in placed in the west while the practitioner is seated in the east facing the image.[8] Each day the practitioner is to bathe, put on clean clothes, and purify everything with the proper mantras. Having done so, the practitioner then purifies body, speech, and mind (*jing sanye,* 淨三業). This triple purification is the first of the steps in what will become the *Shiba dao,* or "Eighteenfold Way," which will be discussed in detail below.

Before proceeding further and entering the ritual arena, the practitioner must first visualize the Pure Land:

> Each time you are to enter the ritual arena (*daochang,* 道場) position yourself before the basic divinity (*benzun,* 本尊) [of the *maṇḍala*]. With hands clasped in "lotus flower" and eyes closed visualize him in Sukhāvatī. . . . Now, before Amitāyus Tathāgata and all the bodhisattvas, make a full prostration and visualize yourself bowing before each buddha and bodhisattva. Then chant the mantra of universal worship (*puli zhenyan,* 普禮真言).[9]

Once this process is complete, the practitioner enters the ritual arena. He confesses sins and dedicates the merit of the rite to all beings and then, on performing the *mudrā* and mantra of Amitāyus Tathāgata (Fo bu sanmeiye, 佛部三昧耶), the practitioner visualizes and distinguishes each of the thirty-two major and eighty minor marks of Amitāyus.[10] He then proceeds with the lords of the other two of the three "families": Lotus and Vajra, chanting the mantras and making the *mudrā*s of Avalokiteśvara and Vajragarbha, respectively (*Lianhua bu sanmeiye,* 蓮華部三昧耶; *Jin'gang bu sanmeiye,* 金剛部三昧耶). This accomplished, the practitioner protects himself (*beijia hu shen,* 被甲護神) and establishes a *vajra*-cordon around the ritual arena (*jin'gang que,* 金剛橛; *jin'gang zhuang,* 金剛牆). The arena is now fit for offerings, and with the aid of the mantra of Ākāśagarbha (Daxukongzang, 大虛空藏) one visualizes the offerings "as in Sukhāvatī." The practitioner visualizes a *hrīḥ* (活[紇]) in the center of the altar whose red glow illuminates the buddha lands of the ten directions. The next mantra and *mudrā* pair (*rulaiquan yin,* 如來拳印) transforms the ritual arena into the Pure Land with its jeweled earth and so forth, "as described in the [*Guan*] *jing*."[11]

At this point the practitioner visualizes a carriage "adorned with the seven jewels" (*baochelu,* 寶車輅) being dispatched to Sukhāvatī and

Amitāyus, and his retinue are invited (*qing chelu,* 請車輅) to enter the ritually created Sukhāvatī. The act of welcoming the retinue (*ying qing sheng cheng,* 迎請聖眾) results in rebirth in the uppermost level of the Pure Land. But before Amitāyus can properly "preach," all traces of defilement must be expelled. This is accomplished by Avalokiteśvara's horse-headed *vidyārāja* (*mingwang,* 明王) form, Hayagrīva (Matou, 馬頭), who expels the *māras*. The practitioner then deploys a "*vajra*-net" (*jin'gang wang,* 金剛網) above the arena and a wall of *vajra*-fire (*jin'gang huoyuan,* 金剛火院) to seal the purified ritual arena from outside influence. Now Amitāyus and his retinue can be offered fragrant water to wash their feet (*xian ejia xiangshui,* 獻閼伽香水) and lotus thrones on which to sit (*lianhua zuo,* 蓮華座). The next mantra and *mudrā* pair call forth vast clouds of offerings (*guangda bukong mani pugongyang,* 廣大不空摩尼普供養) so the deities can be properly feasted.[12] This step completes the so-called Eighteenfold Way. The worshiper then engages in a detailed visualization of Amitāyus and the assembly ("as though he were seated right before one's eyes, equipped with all of the auspicious marks"[13]), vows to be reborn in the Pure Land, and then offers a chant of praise (*Wuliangshou rulai zantan,* 無量壽如來讚歎).

The core sequence of the ritual—from the esoteric perspective—is the practitioner's immediate experience of identification with Avalokiteśvara and the Pure Land. The first element is the "Avalokiteśvara *samādhi*" (*Guanzizai sanmadi,* 觀自在三摩地) in which the practitioner visualizes a lunar disc surmounted by an eight-petaled lotus *maṇḍala.* A *hrīḥ* syllable changes into Avalokiteśvara and is identified with the worshiper.[14] One then makes the *mudrā* and recites the "fundamental *dhāraṇī* of Amitāyus Tathāgata" (*Wuliangshou rulai genben tuoloni,* 無量壽如來根本陀羅尼):

> *namo ratnatrayāya namaḥ āryāmitābhyāya tathāgatāya arhate samyaksaṃbuddhāya tadyathā oṃ amṛte amṛtodbhave amṛtasambhave amṛtagarbhe amṛtasiddhe amṛtateje amṛtavihṛṃte amṛtavihṛṃtagamine amṛtagaganakīrttikare amṛtaduṃdubhisvare sarvārthasadhane sarvakarmakramaśaskṣayaṅkare svāhā.*[15]

This is not a newly constructed esoteric *dhāraṇī* but an old one that has appeared in a range of texts with connections to the cult of Amitābha—some from pre-Tang times.[16] The *Wuliangshou yigui* says that repetition of this *dhāraṇī* results in the eradication of evil and the manifestation of *bodhi.* When the end of life is near the practitioner will see Amitāyus Tathāgata and his retinue

> gathering around to receive him, and they will comfort his body and mind. He will forthwith be born in the highest class of the highest birth in Sukhāvatī and be confirmed in the bodhisattva state.[17]

The practitioner then chants the mantra *Oṃ vajra guhya japa samaye hūṃ* to empower (加持; Skt. *adhiṣṭhāna*) his recitation, multiplying its efficacy (*lianzi nian zhu*, 蓮子念珠). This is followed by a vow (*fa yuan*, 發願) to help all beings attain *siddhi.* Specific instructions are given for chanting the above mantra while engaged in the Amitāyus *samādhi* (*Wuliangshou sanmadi*, 無量壽三摩地). During this meditation the practitioner visualizes Amitāyus on the altar complete with all his auspicious "marks." Following the instructions insures that one's practice of "recollection not be interrupted" (專注念誦不令間斷).[18] As a result of this practice one's body and mind will be purified, and whether one's eyes are open or closed one will always see Amitāyus Tathāgata.[19] The practitioner then makes the concentration *mudrā* (*ding yin*, 定印) and visualizes a full lunar disc with a *hrīḥ* syllable on it, out of which limitless rays of light appear. "Each ray of light becomes a Sukhāvatī with its retinue surrounding Amitāyus Buddha, just as described in the *Guan jing*."[20]

Having completed the aim of the ritual one makes the *mudrā* of Amitāyus (*jie benzun yin*, 結本尊印), recites the basic *dhāraṇī* (*genben tuoloni*, 根本陀羅尼) seven times, and chants the mantra of praise. At this point the core sequence is complete and the practitioner commences the exit sequence, beginning with the universal offering (*pu gongyang*, 普供養), proceeding in reverse order with each mantra-*mudrā* pair, releasing the boundaries of the arena, sending off the "guests," and then exiting the arena.[21]

On completion of the rite the *Wuliangshou yigui* further prescribes the regular chanting of the *Guan jing* as well as the recitation of certain mantras and a *dhāraṇī*.[22] Although obviously dependent upon the *Guan jing*, the *Wuliangshou yigui* does not borrow significantly from it but is content to evoke it, incorporate its recitation as a supportive practice, and go on with its own program.

The ritual laid out in the *Wuliangshou yigui* falls into three basic segments: a series of entry rites containing the so-called Eighteenfold Way, a core sequence consisting of the identification with Avalokiteśvara and the Amitāyus *samādhi*, and a series of exit rites that are a compressed and reversed form of the Eighteenfold Way. These can be further broken down into: 1) preparations of the practitioner and the ritual arena, 2) entry into and securing the boundaries of the arena, 3) initial visualization of the Pure Land and invitation of Amitāyus, 4) sealing the ritual area and worshiping Amitāyus (including a detailed visualization of him), 5) Avalokiteśvara *samādhi*, 6) *dhāraṇī* of Amitāyus Tathāgata and Amitāyus *samādhi*, 7) releasing of boundaries of the ritual arena, 8) sending off of the deities, leaving the ritual area, 9) continued chanting of

Guan jing mantras, and *dhāraṇī*. Shingon Chūinryū tradition divides the rituals into five modules: purification, construction, encounter, identification, and dissociation.[23]

Entry Rites	Preparation of practitioner and ritual arena/ visualization of "marks"
	Entry into and securing the boundaries of the arena
	Initial visualization of the Pure Land and invitation of Amitāyus
	Sealing ritual area/worshiping Amitāyus/ visualization of "marks"
Identification and Vision of the Pure Land	Avalokiteśvara *samādhi*
	Dhāraṇī and Amitāyus *samādhi*/visualization of "marks"
Exit Rites	Releasing of boundaries of the ritual arena
	Sending off of the deities, leaving the ritual area
	Continued chanting of *Guan jing* mantras, and *dhāraṇī*

For the moment I wish to call attention to one fact. The general ritual sequence is no different than that found in many other esoteric manuals from the mid- and late Tang. In all cases we see three basic modules, the nesting of a focal divinity for the particular rite, and the selection of mantras and *mudrā*s appropriate to the particular family of the divinity. In this manual the visualization from the *Guan jing* (or so we are led to believe) and the recitation of an old Pure Land mantra has been nested into the sequence just after the identification that follows on the last element of the Eighteenfold Way—the "universal offering" (*pu gongyang*, 普供養).[24] Divinities and corresponding mantras and *mudrā*s appropriate to the family of the focal divinity (Lotus family) are used. Further, the esoteric ritual technology does not displace that of the *Guan jing*. Rather, the use of the *Guan jing* continues, and the esoteric rite integrates that use and acts as a catalyst for achieving the goal of seeing the Pure Land.

Esoteric Buddhism in the Mid- and Late Tang

The *Wuliangshou yigui* did not appear in a vacuum but is one of a host of esoteric ritual manuals produced between the mid-eighth and the mid-ninth centuries. These manuals were constructed upon templates drawn from a few key texts composed as little as fifty years earlier in South Asia. Like Mahayana scriptures before them, these tantras claimed to supersede the earlier revelations, and many of the deities and rituals in them found wide and often enthusiastic reception in China. Indeed, hundreds of "esoteric" texts ("esoteric" is the term most frequently used by modern scholars to describe tantras in East Asia)[25] were translated and circulated under imperial auspices between 715–800 and 980–1078, and thousands of sculptures, temples, and grottoes were constructed.[26]

The adaptation of the tantras in China was a complex process. As one scholar put it, the tantras were "simultaneously the most politically involved of Buddhist forms and the variety of Buddhism most acculturated to the medieval Indian landscape."[27] Although many were written in the context of the volatile world of medieval Indian *sāmanta* feudalism, they were, of course, promoted as universal. Once in China esoteric teachings and rituals were often modified to fit the circumstances of their new audiences. This process was facilitated by a ritual program at once systematic and highly adaptable, as each major text lays down a ritual template with interchangeable modules.[28]

Although much of the impact of the tantras in China was diffuse—as elements of rituals, deities, and even mantras were adapted to pre-existing religious environments—there were some periods during which South and Central Asian monks were met with broad institutional support. Soon after the Indian missionary Śubhākarasiṃha (善無畏, 637–735) arrived at the Tang court in 716, Emperor Xuanzong (玄宗, r. 712–756) assigned the polymath Chan master Yixing (一行, 683–727) to help him in his work of translating and producing a commentary on the *Mahāvairocanābhisaṃbodhi-sūtra* (T. 848).[29] Along with his translation of the *Susiddhimahākara-tantra* (T. 893), Śubhākarasiṃha thus made available two of the most important esoteric texts then circulating in South Asia.[30] A few years later in 720 the monk Vajrabodhi (Jin'gangzhi, 金剛智, 671–741) arrived in the Chinese capital Chang'an and soon he and his chief disciple Amoghavajra were, if not embraced by the court, at least given the go-ahead to translate and take on disciples in exchange for performing ritual duties for the imperial house. Vajrabodhi and Amoghavajra produced the first extracts from the *Vajraśekhara-sarvatathāgata-satya-saṅgraha-mahāyāna-pratyutpannābhi-sambuddha-mahātantrarājā-sūtra* (T. 865, 866, hereafter shortened to *Vajraśekhara-sūtra*), which represented the cutting edge of esoteric Buddhism by the mid-eighth century.[31]

Amoghavajra proved himself a valuable ally to the imperial house during the An Lushan rebellion (755–763) and he gave Emperor Suzong (肅宗, r. 756–762) *abhiṣeka* or "consecration" (*guanding*, 灌頂) as a *cakravartin* or world-ruling king.[32] Under Suzong and his successor Daizong (代宗, r. 762–779) Amoghavajra and his disciples articulated an ideology of rulership with the *cakravartin* supported by his *ācārya* (religious preceptor) in a pattern remarkably similar to that found in South Asia. Amoghavajra was an ardent proponent of the teachings associated with the *Vajraśekhara-sūtra* or the *Yoga* (*Yuqie*, 瑜伽) as it was sometimes called, and under his leadership esoteric Buddhism permeated the court and was popular with the military. A ritual arena for *homa* and other practices was established in the imperial compound. Mañjuśrī cloisters were established in all official monasteries, and cloisters dedicated to Mañjuśrī and Samantabhadra were established in the Tang ancestoral seat at Taiyuan for the protection of the dynasty and the benefit of the imperial ancestors.[33]

But the assimilation of esoteric Buddhism to the Chinese milieu was nowhere more evident than in the growing production of ritual manuals to address a variety of deities and needs. Perhaps the most striking of these efforts was Amoghavajra's "retranslation" of the *Scripture for Humane Kings* (T. 246, *Renwang jing*, 仁王經).[34] The new version of this fifth-century work—a work we now know to be apocryphal—was replete with updated technical language and a long *dhāraṇī*. Amoghavajra provided two ritual manuals for the performance of esoteric rites that were at the heart of his "state-protection" Buddhism.

Typically, accounts of East Asian esoteric Buddhism jump from the death of Amoghavajra to the Japanese pilgrim Kūkai's (空海, 779–835) initiation at the hands of Amoghavajra's disciple Huiguo (惠果, 746–805). Japanese traditions credit Huiguo with fusing the lineage transmissions of Śubhākarasiṃha and Amoghavajra and creating the "dual-*maṇḍala*" system based on the *Vajraśekhara-sūtra* and the *Mahāvairocanābhisaṃbodhi-sūtra*. They then break off their treatment of China to cover developments in Japan. Yet accounts by Kūkai and other Japanese pilgrims who visited the Tang court throughout the ninth century bear witness to a flourishing of esoteric Buddhism and a plethora of esoteric manuals transmitted in lineages traced to Śubhākarasiṃha, Yixing, Vajrabodhi, and Amoghavajra. The *Wuliangshou yigui* was one of these.

The Textual Cohort of the *Wuliangshou yigui*

Were there other texts like the *Wuliangshou yigui*, and, if so, what can they tell us about the production of these manuals and the adaptation of esoteric Buddhism in the Tang? Indeed there were, and while I argue that the *Wuliangshou yigui* is atypical in some respects, it is nonetheless typical of the manner in which esoteric teachings were adapted to the Tang milieu. However, sorting out the provenance of the text and deciding what it tells us about the process of assimilation is complicated. While the proliferation of manuals attests to the success of esoteric Buddhism's assimilation to the Tang religious landscape, it also complicates the task of the historian of religions, as many manuals written in the ninth century were ascribed to Śubhākarasiṃha, Vajrabodhi, or Amoghavajra.

The Taishō canon lists Amoghavajra as "translator" (*yi*, 譯) of the *Wuliangshou yigui*.[35] The fact that a text with a very similar title, *Wuliangshou rulai niansong yigui* (無量壽如來念誦儀軌) appears in Amoghavajra's own list of works submitted to Emperor Daizong on his birthday in 771, as well as in the Zhenyuan catalogue thirteen years later, adds support to his having composed or perhaps overseen the composition of the text.[36] A look at other Tang period esoteric manuals related to Amitāyus and the Pure Land cult can help us to understand in what ways the *Wuliangshou yigui* is typical and in what ways it is not.

One attempt to sort things out was the approach taken by the editors of the Taishō canon early in the twentieth century. There ritual manuals are grouped by the deity they address. Thus, within the "esoteric" volumes of the canon (T. 18–21), texts concerning Mañjuśrī were grouped together, as were texts to Avalokiteśvara and so forth.

The Taishō editors grouped the *Wuliangshou yigui* together with three other texts: the *Jin'gangding jing guanzizaiwang rulai xiuxing fa* (T. 931, 金剛頂經觀自在王如來修行法) attributed to Amoghavajra; the *Jin'gangding jing yuqie guanzizaiwang rulai xiuxing fa* (T. 932, 金剛頂經瑜伽觀自在王如來修行法) attributed to Vajrabodhi; and the *Jiu pin wang sheng Amituo sanmadi ji tuoluoni jing* (T. 933, 九品往生阿彌陀三摩地集陀羅尼經) attributed to Amoghavajra. The logic of this grouping is apparent, as all four texts deal with the Pure Land and Amitāyus, but an examination of them reveals both continuities and fundamental differences.

Like the *Wuliangshou yigui* the two *Jin'gangding* texts (T. 931, 932) are focused on Amitāyus. Also like the *Wuliangshou yigui,* they are preached before Vairocana. The titles of the two texts also indicate a link to Mahāvairocana of the *Vajraśekhara-sūtra* cycle. The use of a five-buddha altar, the inner and outer rites of the four offerings, and the statement "Now, relying upon the *Jin'gangding jing* I will expound the essentials of the method of the Adamantine Lotus Dharma"[37] all underscore the *Vajraśekhara-sūtra* filiation of the *Jin'gangding jing guanzizaiwang rulai xiuxing fa*

(T. 931).[38] Further, the two *Jin'gangding* texts have identical openings—word for word—and some identical ritual sequences and *gāthās*, as well as a shared focus keyed to the "method of the Lotus family." However, while the text attributed to Vajrabodhi (T. 932) is considerably longer than that attributed to Amoghavajra (T. 931), it appears to be derived from the shorter Amoghavajra text, and the longer text is suspiciously absent from Buddhist catalogues of the time.[39] One important difference between the *Wuliangshou yigui* and the two *Jin'gangding* texts is in their soteriology. While the *Wuliangshou yigui* incorporates and builds upon the soteriological program of the *Guan jing*, the *Jin'gangding* texts are purely esoteric. There is no mention or even allusion to the *Guan jing*. I will return to this point below.

The *Jiu pin wang sheng Amituo sanmadi ji tuoluoni jing* (T. 933, again attributed to Amoghavajra), at less than a page in the Taishō, appears to be a fragment rather than a complete text. The "Great *Samaya* True *Lakṣaṇa* Mantra" (大三昧耶實相真言; 79c) found in the text is a portion of the fundamental *dhāraṇī* of Amitāyus Tathāgata found in the *Wuliangshou yigui* (71b11). But in all other regards it is strikingly different from the *Jin'gangding* texts and the *Wuliangshou yigui*. It describes a *maṇḍala* of the nine classes of rebirth and the twelve hypostases of Amitābha's wisdom (here styled as twelve "effulgent-buddhas," 光佛).[40] The attention given to the nine classes of rebirth also stands in contrast to the soteriological project of the *Wuliangshou yigui*, which focuses on birth in the highest class of rebirth only and doesn't even mention other classes.

All three texts are absent from Amoghavajra's list of 771, but T. 931 is attested in catalogues in 794 and 800.[41] Thus we have some evidence that a version of the *Wuliangshou yigui* could have been prepared by Amoghavajra, and that it has some affinities with the *Vajraśekhara-sūtra* cycle that he championed, and perhaps to T. 931. The text catalogued as a translation by Vajrabodhi appears to be a later composition, though based on T. 931. The provenance of the *Jiu pin wang sheng Amituo sanmadi ji tuoluoni jing* is unknown, but other than sharing a portion of a widely reproduced mantra with the *Wuliangshou yigui* it seems unrelated to the other three texts.[42]

Japanese scholars working within the fold of the Shingon and Tendai traditions have spent considerable effort in rationalizing their ritual systems, and as a result their work has highlighted structural continuities between rituals and texts that might otherwise be overlooked. Turning to the indices of Hatta Yukio's *Shingon jiten*, for instance, points us not to the texts considered above but rather to texts with similar ritual sequences (and their attendant mantras and *mudrās*).[43] The ritual sequence, beginning with the purification of body, speech, and mind and ending with a "universal offering" laid out in the *Wuliangshou yigui,* is nearly identical to that found in two other manuals. The first, attributed to Amoghavajra, is the *Guanzizai pusa ru'ilun niansong yigui* (觀自在菩薩如意輪念誦儀軌, T. 1085; hereafter *Ru'ilun*). The second, the *Shiba chi yin* (十八契印, T. 900) is attributed to Amoghavajra's disciple Huiguo, but is widely acknowledged to be of Japanese origin.[44] This is the sequence that comes to be known as the "Eighteenfold Way" (*Shiba dao;* Jpn. *Juhachi dō*) because of the eighteen *mudrā*-mantra pairs that demarcate its ritual sequence. The *Ru'ilun* is devoted to a popular form of Guanyin, and like the *Wuliangshou yigui,* the Hayagrīva *vidyārāja* is invoked to purify the ritual arena prior to sealing it off with the *vajra*-net and *vajra*-fire wall. The *Ru'ilun* and the *Wuliangshou yigui* share three lines of a four-line *gāthā.*[45] Further, the *Wuliangshou yigui* and the *Ru'ilun* share a great deal of phrasing, so much so that it is impossible that they were independently created. It is clear that these two texts are closely related and it would not be hard to imagine that Amoghavajra had a hand in the composition of the *Ru'ilun.*

This traditional view is contested by some twentieth-century scholars. That the two texts are of Tang provenance is not in doubt, but exactly when they were crafted centers upon some decidedly convoluted arguments. In short, there are two theories concerning the origin of the eighteenfold sequence found in these texts. On the one hand the sequence of rites appears to be a highly simplified version of a pattern of worship found in the *Susiddhimahākara-tantra* and its abstract, the *Suxidijielo gongyang fa* (T. 894) and in the *Mahāvairocanābhisaṃbodhi-sūtra.*[46] On the other hand it is said to be the result of a fusion of the five buddhas and four *pāramitā* bodhisattvas of the *Vajraśekhara-sūtra* with the nine chief deities of the central lotus of the *Garbha maṇḍala* depicted in the *Mahāvairocanābhisaṃbodhi-sūtra.*[47] The first theory would situate the origin of the pattern of worship found in the *Wuliangshou yigui* in the early strata of esoteric Buddhism—both in South Asia and in China—while the second theory situates it later, after the melding of the *Mahāvairocanābhisaṃbodhi-sūtra* and the *Vajraśekhara-sūtra.*

Osabe Kazuo, who has written extensively on Tang esoteric manuals, is certain that the *Shiba dao* is rooted in the tradition of *Susiddhi* and not that of the dual *maṇḍala.*[48] He regards the *Shiba dao* as a distillation of a primordial current (my term, not his) in esoteric ritual, and this is how Shingon traditions of training regard it, if not ideologically then at least practically. At the same time Osabe has argued that the *Wuliangshou yigui* shows influence from the "dual *maṇḍala*" system combining *Vajra* and *Garbha* techniques and therefore cannot be a product of Amoghavajra's "pure" (*chun*, 純) *Vajraśekhara-sūtra* teaching and must date from the later generations of Huiguo and his disciple Faquan (法全, n.d.).[49] However, Harriet Hunter's recent work on late Tang esoteric manuals associates the *Wuliangshou yigui* with the Vajradhātu ritual tradition and appears to accept its attribution to Amoghavajra.[50] Given that virtually all of the elements of the eighteenfold ritual sequence present in the *Wuliangshou yigui* and the *Ru'ilun* can be found in the *Susiddhimahākara-tantra* (translated in 726), and given the evidence from Amoghavajra's own list of scriptures, we are left to wonder how the two positions can be reconciled.

Adapting Esoteric Ritual

But perhaps there is another way to look at things, and this brings us back to the larger issue of the adaptation of esoteric ritual in Tang China and what the *Wuliangshou yigui* can tell us about the process. Osabe's dating of the text depends upon finding anachronistic elements as an aid in setting an earliest possible date for the composition of these texts.[51] But this is made difficult by two facts. First, given that the major elements of the "dual *maṇḍala*" system are present by the time of Vajrabodhi, it is hard to determine when the "dual *maṇḍala*" first arose.[52] Second, Osabe assumes that Amoghavajra promoted a kind of "pure" *Vajraśekhara-sūtra* system that then fed into the "pure" dual *maṇḍala* system of Huiguo and was distinct from other "mixed" strands of late Tang esoteric Buddhism. But such a distinction seems more and more a figment of later sectarian agendas.[53] While Amoghavajra was an unabashed proponent of the *Vajraśekhara-sūtra*, there is ample evidence that he was not exclusive or sectarian. He clearly stated that he translated and employed other esoteric teachings as well as the Mahayana.[54] Further, his disciple Zhao Qian's *Xingzhuang* recounts how Vajrabodhi transmitted to him

> the methods of the five families, the *abhiṣeka*, the *homa*—the teachings an *ācārya* should know. [He also transmitted] the *Mahāvairocana-sūtra* and the manuals of *Susiddhi*, all of the *Buddhoṣṇīṣa* divisions, and all of the mantra practices.[55]

If we have learned anything about Tang Buddhism in the last twenty years it is that things were a great deal more fluid than sectarian accounts have suggested.[56] Although I think it likely that the *Wuliangshou yigui* does date from the generation of Huiguo and Faquan, we cannot rule out Amoghavajra's having had a hand in it.

Hunter's recent work on Faquan's *Garbhakośa* manuals makes an important observation that can help us think about the process through which esoteric Buddhism was adapted to the Tang milieu. Hunter shows that Faquan purged elements of the *Vajraśekhara-sūtra* from these manuals to bring them in line with the *Mahāvairocanābhisaṃbodhi-sūtra* that he favored. But Faquan did not eliminate all elements originating from the *Vajraśekhara-sūtra* cycle—instead he kept certain ones and framed them within structures derived from the *Mahāvairocanābhisaṃbodhi-sūtra*.[57] In other words, Faquan nested certain *Vajraśekhara-sūtra* elements within an overall template derived from the *Mahāvairocanābhisaṃbodhi-sūtra*. We can understand Faquan's approach by thinking of the major ritual texts of esoteric Buddhism as presenting a basic template or ritual order consisting of a sequence of modules. Various elements, even elements from other ritual templates, can be nested into such a ritual structure. This makes for a stable but highly flexible system that can be readily adapted to local circumstances.

Thus, in the process of assimilating esoteric Buddhism to Tang China, we start with South Asian texts—the *Susiddhimahākara-tantra*, the *Mahāvairocanābhisaṃbodhi-sūtra*, and the *Vajraśekhara-sūtra*—which are more encyclopedic ritual compendia than manuals, though each has an underlying structure or ritual template. Adapting rituals for the instruction of Chinese disciples, worshipers, and patrons required the expression of these templates in considerably simplified manuals aimed at specific goals. This simplification for the sake of actual performance is the first step in the assimilation of esoteric Buddhism in China (after the act of translation itself).

We can distinguish two general types of adaptation distinguished by the amount of deviation from South Asian ritual templates and the degree of local adaptation. In the first instance we see the replication of South Asian systems in which a single ritual template predominates. A good example of this is the "Yoga teaching" of Vajrabodhi and Amoghavajra in the mid-Tang. Here we see a concerted effort to transplant the ritual system of the *Vajraśekhara-sūtra* to the Tang court. Faquan's *Garbhakośa* manuals and the *Wuliangshou yigui* would be other examples. Thus, I suggest that the *Wuliangshou yigui* as we have it is based on a template from the *Susiddhimahākara-tantra* and its abstracts into which the meditation on Amitāyus along with the old *dhāraṇī* has been nested. Appended to this structure is, of course, the injunction to continue the use of the *Guan jing* itself. The text does have some elements from the *Vajraśekhara-sūtra* cycle, but the dominant template is that of the *Susiddhimahākara-tantra*. The

Jin'gangding jing guanzizaiwang rulai xiuxing fa (T. 931) is another good example of a single dominant template, but unlike the *Wuliangshou yigui* its template is clearly that of the *Vajraśekhara-sūtra.*

More overt adaptations—those that entail combinations of ritual templates and texts regarded as separate in South Asia—mark a second form. The late Tang "dual *maṇḍala*" system that joined the two ritual programs presented in the *Vajraśekhara-sūtra* and the *Mahāvairocanābhisaṃbodhi-sūtra* that came to characterize Japanese Shingon is one example of East Asian innovation.[58] The *Jin'gangding jing yuqie guanzizaiwang rulai xiuxing fa* (T. 932) certainly incorporates elements of the dual *maṇḍala* system. Further research would be needed to determine if it is indeed structured on the basis of that template. Another example is the so-called *Susiddhi* movement of the late Tang. Apparently developed in the generation after Amoghavajra and also associated with Faquan, this system regarded the *Susiddhimahākara-tantra* as a kind of synthesis of the systems of the *Vajraśekhara-sūtra* and the *Mahāvairocanābhisaṃbodhi-sūtra.*[59]

Whether based on a single ritual template and root text or on a novel synthesis of templates, the modular structure of the esoteric ritual systems encouraged adaptation to local needs. The *Wuliangshou yigui* is perhaps the most intriguing of these adaptations. While it is typical in using a modular template, it is atypical in its preservation of a non-esoteric soteriology within its esoteric framework.

To Gaze upon that Realm

And this raises a fundamental question. For whom was the *Wuliangshou yigui* intended? The presence of the manual and of quite a number of esoteric manuals concerning Amitābha, the Pure Land, and Avalokiteśvara in the late Tang attest to the popularity of these deities, a popularity esoteric teachers obviously felt a need to address. The audience for the commentary is implied in Vajrapāṇi's statement that his discourse is intended for beings in the "age of the last period of the teaching" who have been born in "unfortunate realms." Thus,

> if a householder or a renunciant wishes to be born in the Pure Land that person should first enter the *maṇḍala* and receive *abhiṣeka.* Thereafter they will receive the ritual procedures for contemplation and worship from their teacher.[60]

We can assume from this that the writer of the *Wuliangshou yigui* regards the present time and place as less than fortunate. Further, it seems to indicate that the practice was intended for an audience both lay and monastic at a relatively introductory level. In comparison to the labyrinthine ritual detail that all but obscures the underlying structure in the *Mahāvairocanābhisaṃbodhi-sūtra,* the *Susiddhimahākara-tantra,* or even the relatively simplified "abstract" of the latter text attributed to Śubhākarasiṃha (*Suxidijielo gongyang fa,* T. 894), the *Wuliangshou yigui* gives us a straightforward and unambiguous sequence. But we should not be lulled into seeing this simplicity as a defect. The practice outlined here is basic, both in terms of its simplicity and in terms of its being foundational, and its attainment of canonical status and prescription to this day in Shingon training no doubt rests on these qualities. The production of such manuals is itself primary evidence of the adaptation of esoteric ritual practice to a broad range of practitioners.

One unusual aspect of the *Wuliangshou yigui* is that it takes as inspiration the soteriological goal of a vision of and rebirth in the Pure Land found in the *Guan jing* and integrates it into its program without denying it or erasing it. Though one "should first enter the *maṇḍala* and receive *abhiṣeka,*" one is also enjoined to chant the *Guan jing.* The recitation of the vivid descriptions of the Pure Land found in the *Guan jing* could only have reinforced the visualization at the core of the *Wuliangshou yigui.* This capacity to accommodate other forms of practice is also present in a few other Tang esoteric works. Most notably, Amoghavajra's ritual commentaries on the *Scripture for Humane Kings* carefully preserve a place for the traditional recitation of the text and its role in imperial processions. But I know of no other text where the integration is so thorough-going.

Those familiar with later Japanese Pure Land traditions might be tempted to view the *Wuliangshou yigui* more as an appropriation of Pure Land ideas than a synergistic rapprochement. After all, isn't it the case that Pure Land thinkers all the way back to Tanluan (489–554) extol the salvific superiority of "other-power" (*tali,* 他力) or the "power of the Buddha's vow" (*fo yuan li,* 佛願力) over all forms of "self-help" (*zili,* 自力)? "'The Way of easy practice,'" says Tanluan,

> means that simply by resolving to be reborn in the Pure Land, through faith in the Buddha, and by availing oneself of the power of the Buddha's vow, one attains rebirth in that Pure Land.[61]

But it is noteworthy that Tanluan

> never regards the difficult path as impossible, or the age of the five deteriorations to have begun, it just seems to him that if one were fortunate enough to hear of the easy path then it would be foolish not to choose it.[62]

As David Chappell has pointed out,

> Chinese Pure Land thinkers never went to the extreme of the Japanese Pure Land movements which actively rejected other practices as detracting from reliance on Amitābha [and Chinese practitioners of *nianfo*] always assumed that it would be supplemented by other forms of meditation and purifying practices.[63]

In the case of the *Wuliangshou yigui*, the assumption of a general compatibility of Buddhist practices was no doubt helped by certain commonalities between esoteric practice and the visionary program of the *Guan jing*.[64] Roger Corless, whose work on Pure Land topics is well known and whom this volume honors, has made some perceptive observations concerning similarities between Pure Land and esoteric traditions. Two are relevant to the *Wuliangshou yigui*. The first involves the efficacy of the invocation or calling on the Buddha's name, while the second involves the role of visualization. They are, of course, intimately linked.

Corless sets out Tanluan's understanding of *nianfo* as necessarily vocal. For Tanluan, "invocation must be truly an invocation, that is, vocalized: it is *vak-karma*. (T. 40: 835b12). Writing out the name is ineffective (T. 40: 834c25–26)."[65] Then Tanluan distinguishes two kinds of names (*ming*, 名): "names that are other than things" (*ming i fa*, 名異法) and "names that are the same as things" (*ming ji fa*, 名即法). Mantras, *dhāraṇī*, the names of buddhas and bodhisattvas, and Daoist spells are the latter.[66] For Tanluan,

> the name of Amitābha is a "spell" that works extra-samsarically ("in the inconceivable realm," *acintyadhātu*) to bring release from all suffering, whereas a spell can only liberate from particular suffering. . . . [The sound Amitābha itself is] "He of Infinite Wisdom" and its utterance effects the appearance of infinite wisdom in the darkened mind of the reciter.[67]

Whoever crafted the *Wuliangshou yigui* saw an opportunity to bring together this Pure Land notion of the power of spoken invocation with the esoteric understanding of mantra in a mutually reinforcing way. Thus the use of a supporting *dhāraṇī* to help insure "unbroken recollection" when chanting the "fundamental *dhāraṇī* of Amitāyus Tathāgata" that leads to a vision of the Pure Land.

In the *Guan jing* "recollection" (*nian*) is intimately conjoined with vision or "seeing" (*guan*). Esoteric ritual exploits the same conjunction of the oral and ocular, so it should come as no surprise that the *Guan jing* would be a target for an esoteric "makeover." Indeed, the *Wuliangshou yigui* was not the first exploration of the visionary dimensions of the *Guan jing*. Richard K. Payne has pointed out that the visualization section of the well-known *Upadeśa on the Sūtras of Amitāyus with Stanzas on the Resolution to Be Born* bears some resemblance to later esoteric practice and may reflect the influence of Yogācāra understandings of meditation.[68] Tanluan's *Commentary on the Upadeśa on the Sūtras of Amitāyus with Stanzas on the Resolution to Be Born by the Bodhisattva Vasubandhu* further unpacks the visionary dimensions of Pure Land practice, so much so that Corless remarks,

> The extensive section on visualization in the [*Lunzhu*] has nothing specifically "Pure Land" about it: were we to have only this much of the text surviving, we might assume it to be similar to the Tantric practice of visualizing Sukhāvatī as the *kṣetra* of Amitābha as a *dhyāni*-buddha in the *maṇḍala*.[69]

It is significant that for Tanluan, a key step in "recalling Amitābha Buddha" is the visualization of his "marks" (*xiang*, 相; Skt. *lakṣaṇa*), whether his "general" (*congxiang*, 總相) or "particular" marks (*biexiang*, 別相).[70] So too, the "marks" of Amitāyus play a pivotal role in the economy of recollection (*nian*) and vision (*guan*) in the *Wuliangshou yigui*, and the practitioner is enjoined to envision them no less than three times during the course of the ritual. The "fundamental *dhāraṇī* of Amitāyus Tathāgata" (*Wuliangshou rulai genben tuoloni*), which had been resurrected from older Mahayana texts connected with the Amitāyus cult, is elsewhere called the "Great *Samaya* True *Lakṣaṇa* Mantra."[71] The title is appropriate, as the practitioner is enjoined to inspect the marks of Amitāyus and vow to be reborn in the Pure Land just before entry into the Avalokiteśvara *samādhi*, and then to do so again as a part of the Amitāyus *samādhi* during which one recites "fundamental *dhāraṇī* of Amitāyus Tathāgata." Thus the *Wuliangshou yigui* primes the worshiper to experience "unbroken recollection" of Amitāyus with all his attendant marks. The aim is to "always see Amitāyus Tathāgata."[72] Successful practice thus results in a vision of the Pure Land "just as described in the *Guan jing*."[73] So too, when death nears, the worshiper will see Amitāyus and his retinue

> gathering around to receive him, and they will comfort his body and mind and he will forthwith be born in the highest class of the highest birth in Sukhāvatī and be confirmed in the bodhisattva state.[74]

I think it is clear that the rapport between the Pure Land and esoteric traditions of meditation that are joined in the *Wuliangshou yigui* go far beyond simply encouraging recitation of the older scripture. In short, it seems to me entirely appropriate that a text one might hold up as emblematic of the Chinese adaptation of esoteric Buddhism is one that takes the *Guan jing* as its inspiration, and then draws on all of the senses to produce an experience that evokes the Pure Land so that the worshiper can gaze (*guan*, 觀) "upon the marks of that realm which surpasses the triple-worlds' way."

Notes

1 From Tanluan's (曇鸞) *Commentary on the Upadeśa on the Sūtras of Amitāyus with Stanzas on the Resolution to Be Born by the Bodhisattva Vasubandhu,* T. 1819: 40.827c29; translation of Roger J. Corless, "T'an-Luan: The First Systematizer of Pure Land Buddhism," in *The Pure Land Tradition: History and Development,* ed. James Foard, Michael Solomon, and Richard K. Payne (Berkeley, CA: University of California Press, 1996), p. 118. The line refers to the *lakṣaṇa* of purity that is the overriding characteristic of Sukhāvatī, and reads: 觀彼世界相勝過三界道.

2 The text is widely believed to have been written in Chinese, but has some Central Asian links and its frame story has known South Asian parallels. Research on the topic is voluminous. For a start consult Julian F. Pas, "The *Kuan-wu-liang-shou-Fo-ching:* Its Origin and Literary Criticism," in *Buddhist Thought and Asian Civilization: Essays in Honor of Herbert V. Guenther on His Sixtieth Birthday,* ed. Leslie S. Kawamura and Keith Scott (Emeryville, CA: Dharma Publishing, 1977), pp. 194–218, and the first two chapters of the same author's recent book, *Visions of the Sukhāvatī: Shan-Tao's Commentary on the Kuan Wu-Liang-Shou-Fo Ching* (Albany, NY: State University of New York Press, 1995). Also see Kōtatsu Fujita, "The Textual Origins of the *Kuan Wu-liang-shou ching:* A Canonical Scripture of Pure Land Buddhism," trans. by Kenneth K. Tanaka, in *Chinese Buddhist Apocrypha,* ed. Robert E. Buswell (Honolulu: University of Hawai'i Press, 1990), pp. 149–173. An analysis of South Asian pericopes in the frame story of the *Guan jing* has recently been provided by Jonathan A. Silk, "The Composition of the *Guan Wuliangshuofo-jing:* Some Buddhist and Jaina Parallels to Its Narrative Frame," *Journal of Indian Philosophy* 25 (1997): pp. 181–265.

3 We have to take the term "translation" with a grain of salt, as the work is, after all, a commentary on a work produced in Central Asia and China.

4 The other Tang manual is the *Guanzizai pusa ru'ilun niansong yigui* (觀自在菩薩如意輪念誦儀軌, T. 1085) attributed to Amoghavajra, and the Heian manual is the *Shiba chi yin* (十八契印, T. 900) attributed to Amoghavajra's disciple Huiguo but widely acknowledged to be a Japanese creation. While these figured in Japanese developments, they were not the only manuals with the eighteenfold schema. Other important Tang examples are are two versions of the *Suxidijielo gongyang fa* (蘇悉地羯羅供養發, T. 894) attributed to Śubhākarasiṃha (one with and one without *siddham* mantras), and the *Achu rulai nian song gongyang fa* (阿閦如來念誦供養法, T. 921), attributed to Amoghavajra. I will treat these in a longer essay on Tang esoteric manuals.

5 The "three esoteric gates" or three esoterica (*sanmi men,* 三密門) are broadly body, speech, and mind, but have a wide range of esoteric meanings. See Mochizuki Shinkō, *Bukkyō daijiten* (Tokyo: Sekai Seiten Kangyō Kyōkai, 1974–1977), 1682c–1684a. It is notable that the text designates this a *samādhi* of recollecting the Buddha (*nianfo sanmei,* 念佛三昧), using the term *nian* which resonates with the key term in the *Guan jing*. "Bodhisattvahood" is an attempt to render *pusa zhenwei* (菩薩正位).

6 Rites of consecration, modeled on those of Indian kings, were important features of esoteric Buddhism. For a discussion of *abhiṣeka,* see Ronald M. Davidson, *Indian Esoteric Buddhism: A Social History of the Tantric Movement* (New York: Columbia University Press, 2002), pp. 121–131. Also see the entries in *Bukkyō daijiten,* pp. 811c–813c, and Ōmura Chōkaku, et al., *Mikkyō daijiten* (Kyoto: Hōzōkan, 1970), rev. and expanded ed., 6 vols., pp. 409c–410c.

7 T. 930: 19.67b–c.

8 T. 930: 19.67c.

9 T. 930: 19.68a.

10 The thirty-two major and eighty minor marks of a buddha are found in a number of texts, including the *Mahāvyutpatti* 17. For a list, see Leon Hurvitz, *Chih-I (538–597): An Introduction to the Life and Ideas of a Chinese Buddhist Monk,* Mélanges chinois et bouddhiques, vol. 12 (Bruges, Belgium: Inprimerie Sainte-Catherine, 1960–1962), appendices K and L, pp. 353–360.

11 T. 930: 19.69b5.

12 It is widely known that esoteric ritual is based on an idealized pattern of worship found throughout South Asia that revolves around inviting the gods to a banquet. The same general pattern can be seen in the sixteen traditional *upacāras* or "attendances" of household and temple *pūjā.* See Nancy E. Auer Falk, "Pûjâ," in *The Encyclopedia of Religion,* ed. Mircea Eliade (New York: Macmillan, 1987), vol. 12, pp. 83a–85a. For a detailed analysis, see Wade T. Wheelock, "The Mantra in Vedic and Tantric Ritual," in *Mantra,* ed. Harvey P. Alper. (Albany, NY: State University of New York Press, 1989), pp. 96–122.

13 T. 930: 19.70b25.

14 The text incorrectly says 日羅字 but should read 紇羅字.

15 The Sanskrit version is found in *Bukkyō daijiten* 71, and Hatta Yukio, *Shingon jiten* (Tokyo: Hirakawa shuppansha, 1985), appendix 3.

16 Osabe Kazuo (長部和雄) cites works going back to the Liu-Song dynasty, including translations attributed to Śikṣānanda, Bodhiruci, and Atigupta. These include T. 1317, 1185A, 369, 901, and 368. See *Tōdai mikkyō shi zakkō* (唐代密教史雑考) (Kobe: Kōbe shōka daigaku gakujutsu kenkyūkai, 1971), p. 102. The *Shingon jiten* contains the same list in vol. 5, p. 2148.

17 T. 930: 19.71b25.

18 T. 930: 19.72a4.

19 T. 930: 19.72a5–7.

20 T. 930: 19.72a19.

21 As in most esoteric rituals, the exit is a reversed and abbreviated version of the ritual sequence leading up to the focal portion of the rite. For a discussion of the ritual structure see Richard K. Payne, *The Tantric Ritual of Japan. Feeding the Gods: The Shingon Fire Ritual* (Delhi: Aditya Prakashan, 1991), especially pp. 90–94, on the reversal of the ritual sequence and "terminal abbreviation."

22 These are the "Heart-mantra of Amitāyus Tathāgata (*Oṃ lokeśvara-rāja hrīḥ,* Hatta, no. 884); a mantra to smash obstructions (*Oṃ amṛta-teje hara hūṃ,*

Hatta, no. 39); and the "*Dhāraṇī* That Gives Rise to the Vows of Amitāyus Tathāgata." I have as yet been unable to fully render this mantra.

23 See Payne, *The Tantric Ritual of Japan,* especially pp. 88–94. It is notable that the nesting of the identification sequence in the *Wuliangshou yigui* comes after the full eighteenfold sequence has been completed. This differs from the process detailed by Payne in contemporary Shingon practice.

24 Fritz Staal has called this process "embedding." See his "Ritual Syntax," in *Sanskrit and Indian Studies,* ed. M. Nagatomi, et al. (Dordrecht, Holland: D. Reidel Publishing Co., 1980), pp. 119–142.

25 "Esoteric Buddhism" or the "tantras" more generally have become a hotly debated academic topic. Perhaps the best treatment of the recent construction of the term is offered by Hugh B. Urban, who demonstrates that some scholars have tended to accept uncritically the recent construct "tantrism" and project it onto a variety of texts from widely ranging periods in South Asian history to anachronistically create a "tantric tradition" with Hindu and Buddhist variants. See his *Tantra: Sex, Secrecy, Politics, and Power in the Study of Religion* (Berkeley, CA: University of California Press, 2003). For a clear overview of the various sides of the definitional issue with an eye toward East Asia, see Richard K. Payne's "Introduction" in the volume edited by him, *Tantric Buddhism in East Asia* (Boston: Wisdom Publications, 2005), pp. 1–31.

26 Esoteric imagery continued to be in vogue right through the Mongol conquest, when it received a new infusion of Central Asian stimulus. For some interesting late examples connected to the complex at Baoding shan in Sichuan, see Angela Falco Howard, *Summit of Treasures: Buddhist Cave Art of Dazu, China* (Trumbull, CT: Weatherhill, 2001).

27 Davidson, *Indian Esoteric Buddhism,* p. 114. Davidson argues that mature esoteric Buddhism touted itself as "the way of secret mantras (*guhyamantrayāna*)" in a way "analogus to the [Mahayana's] self-description as the way of the bodhisattva (*bodhisattvayāna*)." It "insisted on an immutable master-disciple bond, employed royal acts of consecration, and used elaborate [*maṇḍala*s] in which the meditator was to envision himself as the Buddha in a field of subordinate [buddhas]." New scriptures were rapidly composed and "they developed rituals (particularly fire sacrifice) for the purpose of a codified series of soteriological and nonsoteriological acts and ultimately institutionalized this material in Buddhist monasteries" (p. 117). For Davidson, mature esoteric Buddhism reflects the world of medieval Indian *sāmanta* feudalism, and its *maṇḍala*s replicate the notion of the ruler as the king of kings. (See his discussion in chapter 4.) In keeping with these roots, a distinctive feature of Buddhist tantras is the prominent role played by fierce manifestations of the bodhisattvas—the *vidyārāja*s or "kings of light"—and their aid in reaching mundane objectives. The classic treatment of the *vidyārāja*s is Jean Przyluski, "Les Vidyaraja, Contribution à l'Histoire de la Magie dans les Sectes Mahāyānistes," *Bulletin de l'École Française d'Extrême Orient* 23 (1923): pp. 301–318. See also the entry in *Bukkyo daijiten,* 4779a–c; and Robert Duquenne, "Daitoku myōō," in *Hôbôgirin: dictionnaire encyclopédique du Bouddhisme d'après les sources chinoises et japonaises,* ed. Paul Demiéville and Jacques May (Tokyo and Paris:

Maison franco-japonais and A. Maisonneuve, 1929–1967), vol. VI, pp. 652–670. The best recent work is by Rob Linrothe, *Ruthless Compassion: Wrathful Deities in Early Indo-Tibetan Esoteric Buddhist Art* (Boston: Shambhala, 1999), especially the discussion on pp. 3–30.

28 For a discussion of the modular structure of esoteric ritual, see Charles D. Orzech, *Politics and Transcendent Wisdom: The Scripture for Humane Kings in the Creation of National Protection Buddhism* (University Park, PA: Pennsylvania State University Press, 1998), especially pp. 153–157.

29 There is evidence that Xuanzong's initial reception of Śubhākarasiṃha was guarded. Not only was the emperor deeply enmeshed in Daoism, but he vigorously promoted anticlerical measures as well as measures designed to stem the use of prognosticatory activities on the part of priests. In part these measures were designed to make coups more difficult. See Charles David Benn, "Taoism as Ideology in the Reign of the Emperor Hsüan-tsung (712–755)" (Ph.D. dissertation, University of Michigan, 1977), especially pp. 75–78. After the translation of one such manual he ordered the surrender of all of Śubhākarasiṃha's Sanskrit manuscripts. See *Kaiyuan shijiao lu,* T. 2154: 55. 572a14–15.

30 A translation of the first text is now available by Stephen Hodge, *The Mahāvairocana-abhisaṃbodhi Tantra with Buddhaguhya's Commentary* (London: Routledge Curzon, 2003). Rolf W. Geibel has translated the *Susiddhimahākara-tantra* (under the title *The Susiddhikara Sutra*) in *Two Esoteric Sutras* (Berkeley, CA: Numata Center for Buddhist Translation and Research, 2001).

31 Rolf W. Geibel has translated the *Vajraśekhara-sūtra* (under the title *The Adamantine Pinnacle Sutra*) in *Two Esoteric Sutras*. Amoghavajra's Chinese version of the text (T. 865), itself a translation of the first chapter of the first section of the text, was completed in 754. A full translation of the text (T. 882) was made in the Song dynasty by Dānapāla (施護, fl. 970s) under the auspices of the Institute for Canonical Translation (Yijing yuan, 譯經院). For the work of the three Tang teachers, see Chou I-liang, "Tantrism in China," *Harvard Journal of Asiatic Studies* 8 (1945): pp. 241–332. Reprinted in Richard K. Payne, ed., *Tantric Buddhism in East Asia* (Boston: Wisdom Publications, 2005).

32 The following account summarizes Orzech, *Politics and Transcendent Wisdom,* chapters 5 and 6.

33 See the discussion in Orzech, *Politics and Transcendent Wisdom,* pp. 199–200. The correspondence concerning this is found in the *Daizong chao zeng si kong da bian zheng guang zhi sanzang heshang biaozhi ji* (代宗朝贈司空大辨正廣智三藏和上表制集), T. 2120: 52.837b–838a.

34 The fifth-century version is in T. 245. It is treated in Orzech, *Politics and Transcendent Wisdom,* chapters 3 and 4. The new recension and its commentaries are treated in chapters 5 and 6, and a full translation of the text follows.

35 As in the case of Amoghavajra's ritual commentaries on the *Scripture for Humane Kings* we must interpret the term "translation" loosely. Strictly speaking, the Chinese origins of the *Scripture for Humane Kings* and of the *Guan jing* make the existence of Indic "commentaries" on these texts unlikely.

36 T. 2120: 52.839c9; T. 2156: 55.767b20; T. 2157: 55.1028c14.

37 T. 931: 19.72c.

38 Osabe, *Tōdai mikkyō shi zakkō*, p. 103.

39 It is absent both from the Kaiyuan and Zhenyuan catalogues.

40 According to the text, "If the mass of beings wish to be reborn thus in this pure land of nine classes they should respectfully approach the twelve of complete understanding (*shih-erh yuan-miao*, 十二圓妙) and day and night, at the three times, they should praise the name of the Pure Land of Nine Classes and call the names of the twelve light-buddhas" (T. 933: 19.79c). Although we have no evidence of the disposition of this *maṇḍala* during the Tang, a *maṇḍala* preserved in the *Zuzōshō* (圖像抄) orders the nine classes in the manner of the Vajradhātu *maṇḍala*, beginning in the middle and spiraling outward. *Zuzōshō*, Taishō supplement, vol. 3.

41 It appears in Yuanzhao's *Da Tang zhenyuan xu kaiyuan shijiao lu* of 794 (T. 2156: 55.754a01), and in his *Zhenyuan xin ding shijiao mulu* of 800, (T. 2157: 55.1031b03).

42 Osabe also regards the text as postdating Amoghavajra's time. See *Tōdai mikkyō shi zakkō*, p. 104.

43 Hatta, *Shingon jiten*.

44 The *Shiba chi yin* is only extant in Japanese copies and purports to be Kūkai's notes of Huiguo's oral teaching. See *Bukkyō daijiten*, p. 2359.

45 See *Ru'ilun*, T. 1085: 20.205a12–13; and *Wuliangshou yigui*, T. 930: 19.69b7–8. Also compare *Shiba chi yin*, T. 900: 18.782c16–17.

46 Its "abstracts" are two versions of the *Suxidijielo gongyang fa* (T. 894), one with and one without *siddham* mantras, listed as a translation of Śubhākarasiṃha but generally viewed as his own composition. The eighteen steps can all be found in the *Susiddhimahākara-tantra* (T. 893), although the many variations and extreme detail make doing so quite a task. They are much more apparent in the *Suxidijielo gongyang fa*. So too, most if not all of the steps in the eighteenfold sequence can be extracted from the *Mahāvairocanābhisaṃbodhi-sūtra*, T. 848: 18.46a–54c.

47 See the discussion of *juhachi dō* in *Mikkyō daijiten* 2, pp. 889c–890d; and of *juhachi geiin* in *Bukkyō daijiten*, pp. 2358a–2360b.

48 Indeed, Osabe sees these texts as evidence for a continued *Susiddhi* tradition alongside the tradition of the dual *maṇḍala* in the mid- and late Tang. See *Tōdai mikkyō shi zakkō*, pp. 102–103; his full argument on the configuration of esoteric Buddhism and its relation to *Susiddhi* in the generation of Huiguo and Faquan is on pp. 209–252. See also *Tō Sō mikkyō shi ronko* (唐宋密教史論) (Kyoto: Eiden bunshōdō, 1982), pp. 84–149.

49 Osabe, *Tōdai mikkyō shi zakkō*, p. 103 argues, among other things, that the placement of Amitāyus in the west follows the Vajradhātu method, but given the common association of the Pure Land with the west this is less than convincing.

50 Harriet Hunter, "Late Tang Chinese Handbooks for the *Garbhakośa* Rite," in *Embodying Wisdom: Art, Text and Interpretation in the History of Esoteric Buddhism*,

ed. Rob Linrothe and Henrik H. Sørensen (Copenhagen: Seminar for Buddhist Studies, 2001), p. 20 and n. 62. Both associations are more in line with traditional Shingon positions and conflict with Osabe's findings.

51 See the introduction to this project in *Tōdai mikkyō shi zakkō*, pp. 1–8.

52 Japanese traditions are heavily invested in keeping the transmission of the *Mahāvairocanābhisaṃbodhi-sūtra* and that of the *Vajraśekhara-sūtra* distinct at least until Huiguo.

53 Abé Ryūichi provides a brief but to-the-point analysis of the problems inherent in such moves, not only in treatments of Nara and Heian Buddhism but also in application to Chinese and even Indian developments. See *The Weaving of Mantra: Kūkai and the Construction of Esoteric Buddhist Discourse* (New York: Columbia University Press, 1999), pp. 152–154.

54 T. 2120: 52.840b1–5.

55 T. 2056: 50.292c8–11.

56 For a discussion of "sects" in Chinese Buddhism see T. Griffith Foulk, "The Ch'an Tsung in Medieval China: School, Lineage, or What?" *Pacific World*, n.s., 8 (1992): 18–31. Reprinted under the title "The Chan *Zong* in Medieval China: School, Lineage, or What?" in *Shin Buddhism: Historical, Textual, and Interprtive Studies*, ed. Richard K. Payne (Berkeley, CA: Institute of Buddhist Studies and Numata Center Buddhist Translation and Research, 2007).

57 Hunter, "Late Tang Chinese Handbooks for the *Garbhakośa* Rite," pp. 21–22, 30.

58 A third form of adaptation is not "esoteric" in a proper sense but rather represents the impact of the texts and practices of esoteric Buddhism *in other systems.* The widespread use of *yankou* rituals in East Asian Buddhism and the adoption of esoteric ritual elements or hermeneutics in Chan or Huayan are examples of this. In many cases we find the application of the new ritual technology to longstanding texts and rituals. Indeed, though often overlooked or relegated to a kind of secondary status, such developments had more far-reaching impact on East Asian religion than their more "systematic" cousins.

59 A good example of a text that is a full synthesis is the *Method of the Secret Dhāraṇī of the Three Types of Accomplishment That Obliterate the Hells and Convert and Expel the Karmic Obstructions in the Triple World* (T. 905, vol. 18, *Sanzhong xidipo diyu zhuan yezhang chu sanjie bimi tuoloni fa*, 三種悉地破地獄轉業障出三界秘密 陀囉尼法). Transmitted to Japan by Japanese Tendai pilgrims, it is a cornerstone of Taimitsu or Tendai esotericism.

60 T. 930: 67c6–8.

61 Tanluan, quotation from Kenneth K. Tanaka, *The Dawn of Chinese Pure Land Buddhist Doctrine: Ching-ying Hui-yüan's Commentary on the Visualization Sutra* (Albany, NY: State University of New York Press, 1990), p. 18. The original is *Wuliangshou jing yupotishe yuansheng ji Posoupantou pusa zao, zhu* (無量壽經優婆提舍願生偈婆藪槃頭菩薩造(并)註), T. 1819: 40.826b7–9.

62 Corless, "T'an-Luan," p. 124. Indeed, Tanaka, in his study of Huiyuan's commentary on the *Scripture on Contemplation of the Buddha of Limitless Life*, finds no evidence in Huiyuan's work for the widely bruited notion that eschatological

ideas were a factor in the popularity of the scripture. Tanaka, *The Dawn of Chinese Pure Land Buddhist Doctrine*, p. 111.

63 David W. Chappell, "The Formation of the Pure Land Movement in China: Tao-ch'o and Shan-tao," in *The Pure Land Tradition*, ed. Foard, Solomon, and Payne, p. 145.

64 Even the notion of "other-power" so firmly associated with Pure Land traditions has a correlate in esoteric practice. It is acknowledged that an indispensable element for "successful" practice (*chengjiu*, 成就; Skt. *siddhi*) is the empowering "grace" (*jiachi*, 加持; Skt. *adhiṣṭhāna*) of the deity being invoked.

65 Corless, "T'an-Luan ," p. 127; parenthetical text citations are in the original.

66 Ibid. The original is as follows: 名即法。有名異法。名即法者。諸佛菩薩名號般若波羅蜜及陀羅尼章句禁咒音辭等是也。(T. 1819: 40.835c06–8).

67 Corless, "T'an-Luan," pp. 127–128.

68 *Wuliangshou jing yupotishe yuansheng ji* (無量壽經優波提舍願生偈, T. 1524), attributed to Vasubandhu and catalogued as a translation of Bodhiruci. Payne has noted a similarity between the "five contemplative gates" (*wu nianmen*, 五念門) and the contemporary Shingon version of the *juhachi dō*. At minimum, I think we are seeing convergence based on a common underlying stream of meditational practice. See "The Five Contemplative Gates of Vasubandhu's Rebirth Treatise as Ritualized Visualization Practice," in *The Pure Land Tradition*, ed. Foard, Solomon, and Payne, especially pp. 242–252. For his discussion of Yogācāra, see pp. 240 ff., 252 ff.

69 Corless, "T'an-Luan," p. 125. He went on to extend these observations in "Pure Land and Pure Perspective: A Tantric Hermeneutic of Sukhāvatī," *The Pure Land*, n.s., 6 (1989): pp. 205–217. The original text of Tanluan's *Commentary* (*Wuliangshou jing yupotishe yuansheng ji Posoupantou pusa zao, zhu*) is found in Taishō T. 1819.

70 His "general" mark is that which subsumes all others, i.e., his purity, while his particular marks would be the widely understood thirty-two major and eighty minor marks of the Buddha.

71 Literally, "True Mark Mantra." This is the name given a portion of this same *dhāraṇī* found in the *Jiu pin wang sheng Amituo sanmadi ji tuoluoni jing*. See my discussion of this text above.

72 T. 930: 72a7.

73 T. 930: 72a19.

74 T. 930: 71b25.

Shinran's Secret Transmission to Nyoshin: The *Hōri hachiman chō*

James H. Sanford
University of North Carolina, Chapel Hill (Emeritus)

> [Question:] The Shingon school establishes two forms of teaching, exoteric and esoteric, that comprise all of buddhadharma. Now, to which of these does the dharma of Zen transmitted by Bodhidharma belong?
>
> [Answer:] [Shingon's] Grand Founder [Kōbō] Daishi held that because the Zen dharma was based on the words of Śākyamuni Buddha, it belonged to the exoteric class. In brief, there are three aspects to this: 1) the [sutras] relied upon, 2) the lineage, and 3) the essential teachings of the school.

Introduction

The question and answer quoted in the epigram above constitute the opening lines of the *Kaishinshō* (*Exposing the Heart*[1]), a three-chapter work by the great Shingon master, Gobō (1306–1362).[2] Gobō's text begins with the standard Shingon division of all of Buddhism into two sorts: a preliminary form called in Japanese *kengyō* (open teachings) that is available to anyone and an advanced form called *mikkyō* (secret teachings) that is accessible only to worthy aspirants by initiation. As commonly used, the term *mikkyō* includes Shingon, certain aspects of Tendai, and some odds and ends that are sometimes also referred to as *zogyō* (miscellaneous teachings). The rationale used to make the distinction between *mikkyō* and *kengyō* is not quite clear to Gobō's interlocutor, who wonders if Zen might not also be an esoteric *mikkyō* school. Since Gobō is doubtless both the author of the *Kaishinshō* and the fictive poser of this introductory question that begins it, we can be sure that it is a question that has been brought up to Gobō before, brought up often enough to need addressing. Gobō's initial response gives us some idea as to what were the major points he understood to separate *kengyō* and *mikkyō*. Even from the outset it is clear that for Gobō, Zen is decidedly not within Buddhism's innermost esoteric core.[3]

The firm distinction made between *kengyō* and *mikkyō* has had a long and healthy life both in Japanese Buddhist circles and in Western scholarship about Japan and its religions. In the first place, this division helps establish and maintain Japanese sectarian differences. Further, such institutional distinctions also align themselves with, and have been partly formed by, Western notions about a purportedly universal feature of human spirituality, namely its tendency to fall into isolated packages that can conveniently be characterized by such terms as "religions," "sects," and "denominations." However, this alleged universality is taken less seriously every year—at least in academic venues. Japanese religion seems, rather, to be characteristically interwoven and "syncretic."[4]

A related, and also increasingly untenable, belief is the idea that Japanese *mikkyō* emerged in the Heian period under the guidance of Saichō and Kūkai, but then soon went into steep decline, only to be largely replaced by the more vital "new Kamakura sects": Zen, Pure Land, and Nichiren Buddhism.[5] In point of fact, *mikkyō* not only survived the Heian-Kamakura transition institutionally and intellectually within the lasting framework of the Shingon and Tendai schools, but *mikkyō* also left deep marks on Rinzai and Sōtō Zen, on the Nichiren school, on Shintō, and even on such "nonreligious" institutions as the *iemoto* (house or family) structure of the Japanese arts.[6] This sort of secondary *mikkyō* impact extended to the Pure Land schools as well. For, in spite of its apparent close fit with certain almost normative features of Western religion—especially exclusivism and theological resistance to outside inputs—Pure Land was not immune to pressures toward amalgamation with *mikkyō* ideas and practices. I have elsewhere discussed one Shingon countermovement to normative Pure Land, the *himitsu nenbutsu* (secret nenbutsu).[7] In the brief study that follows, I look at a text from a second venue of esotericized Pure Land of a much later period, the "heretical" *kakushi nenbutsu* movement.

Both Shinran (1173–1262) and later Jōdo Shinshū figures such as Rennyo (1415–1499) warned against heretical interpretations of Pure Land doctrine.[8] Often the term *hiji bōmon* was applied to such "errors." *Hiji bōmon* literally means "the way of secret dharmas," a term that immediately suggests esoteric or *mikkyō*-ized tendencies. Among the deviations or heretical variants of Pure Land thought that appeared after Shinran were those deemed *kakushi nenbutsu* and *kakure nenbutsu.* Typically these terms are used interchangeably, or as alternative designations for *hiji bōmon.* The Japanese Buddhologist Chiba Jōryū, however, takes only *kakushi nenbutsu* to be an equivalent of *hiji bōmon.*[9]

(Linguistically, *kakushi* and *kakure* derive from the related verb forms *kakusu,* a causative form meaning "to hide," and *kakureru,* the passive "to be hidden.") Chiba allows that the usage of two terms also encompasses a historical differentiation. He posits that *kakushi* is secret in the sense of the secrets held by and passed on between members of an inner, esoteric circle, whereas *kakure* refers to groups that have been driven underground, into hiding, by external pressure from outside authorities. *Kakushi nenbutsu* comes first. *Kakure nenbutsu* does not begin until the Tokugawa era, "as a result of the prohibition of Jōdo Shinshū in the domain of the *sengoku daimyo* (warlord) Shimazu during the sixteenth century."[10] In terms of content and of practice, however, these distinctions seem a bit forced. Groups on both sides of Chiba's *kakushi/kakure* divide seem largely alike.[11]

One branch of the *kakure nenbutsu* on which we have closely detailed information is the Kagiya lineage in Kyoto that was exposed in 1775 after being infiltrated by a nun called Teigin. Her report of the secret initiation she was given in the group makes its parallels to regular Shingon procedures and notions very clear.[12] The most obvious *mikkyō*-like feature is the identity made between the initiate and Amida as the ritual unfolds in front of a scroll depicting Amida. Except that the main object of worship (*honzon*) is Amida rather than Dainichi, this appears to be virtually identical with the standard Shingon conflation of worshiper and divinity called *nyūga ganyū* (divinity enters self; self enters divinity). As was explained to Teigin during her initiation, "The *'tasuke tamae'* ("help me") that you have been reciting corresponds to the *Namu* of *'Namu Amida Butsu.'* Amida will help the person who so calls."

But help how? To attain rebirth in the Pure Land? No. The initiator goes on to tell her, "Therefore, this is called the unifying of the person and Amida Buddha." The essence of this secret Pure Land ritual is just this, the co-assimilation of the divinity and the aspirant.

Furthermore, the initiation ritual administered for Teigin concludes with that most typical of esoteric admonitions: "This should not be made known to those of other traditions." This admonition is, in fact, almost a direct embodiment of the *"mi-"* of *mikkyō.*

After her initiation was finished, Teigin's guide told her, "It took my wife four days to receive the salvation of Amida. That you should experience it so soon is rare indeed," a turn of phrase that echoes in this Pure Land context one of Shingon's central claims to superiority over exoteric forms of Buddhism, rapid salvation. (As in the classic formulation *sokushin jōbutsu,* "buddhahood achieved in this very body/lifetime.")

Finally, this Kagiya ritual places its officiating guru/guide in the position of Amida up until Teigin achieves that status herself. This too recalls a fundamental feature of tantric practice.

Kakushi nenbutsu and *kakure nenbutsu* groups trace their teachings through Shinran, just as orthodox Shinshū groups do. But their linkage back to him is of a special sort, for it follows an esoteric line of transmission. Some groups trace their beginnings to Shinran's son, Zenran, who is said to have received the true doctrine from Shinran "secretly in the middle of the night"—a claim eventually refuted by Shinran himself.[13]

Another similar claim to a special transmission is that found in the *Hōri hachiman chō* (*Guide to the Eighty Thousand Dharma Principles*), which tells of a secret transmission from Shinran not to Zenran but to Nyoshin (1235–1300), Zenran's son.[14] This text is divided into a brief initiatory formula and a series of eight points, each of which could probably have been argued separately.[15] In the treatment that follows, I translate, then provide commentary on, these segments one by one. I have also numbered each segment.

Translation

Guide to the Eighty Thousand Dharma Principles

> This is the bloodline of the heart. These words are intended for one set of ears alone. They have been written only for Nyoshin. Until life itself is given up, maintain these teachings diligently.

Commentary to the Opening Formula

"Bloodline." Here "bloodline" does double service. On the one hand, it refers to the genetic line of Shinran-Zenran-Nyoshin. At the same time, it indicates two of these same figures, Shinran and Nyoshin, linked in a typical one-to-one initiation transmission of esoteric Buddhism, a "face-to-face" transmission down a single line of fictive-kinship relatives (although here spiritual kinship and genetic kinship are wholly congruent). Each member of such a line of initiation is a vessel of the esoteric secrets transmitted from one generation to the next.

"Heart" translates that ever difficult word *shin/kokoro.* It signifies, first of all, the red bodily organ beating in the center of the human breast, but inasmuch as this physical heart is in Sino-Japanese proto-scientific venues the seat of both emotions and thoughts, the word can equally be translated "mind."

"One set of ears . . . only Nyoshin." Once again the text underlines the one-to-one nature of esoteric transmissions, and the secrecy that underlies them. The *Hōri* presents itself as far more than a simple sermon.

"Maintain these teachings diligently." The closing sentence of the passage is an esoteric pat phrase. Virtually the same words close hundreds of *mikkyō* texts.

One

> Item: Casual perspective is the *hosshō hosshin.* The elements that fill empty space are complete. He who dwells in the capital of thusness is the *hongaku* Amida. Thus, as his is a subtle body, he is called the "buddha beyond shape and form." Amida is the primordial wellspring of sentient beings and the primordial teaching buddha of all the buddhas of the three ages.

Commentary to Segment One

"Casual perspective." I am uncertain of the meaning of this compound.

"Hosshō hosshin." Hosshō hosshin is the *dharmatā dharmakāya. Dharmatā* is the underlying nature of all things, that is, of the universe made up of minimal constituents or *dharmas*, and the *dharmakāya,* the most elevated of the three bodies (or manifestations) of a buddha: *dharmakāya, sambhogakāya,* and *nirmaṇakāya.* Compounding *hosshin* and *hosshō* together may suggest the absolute identity (or nonduality) of the universe and the *dharmakāya* buddha.[16] (On this topic, see "Commentary to Segment Two," below.)

"Who dwells in the capital of thusness" is the kind of language commonly applied to Shingon's primary buddha, Dainichi (Skt. Mahāvairocana), seated at the center of his *maṇḍala* like a king in his court. But it is also an image not much different from the many Amidist paintings, such as the Taima Mandara,[17] that show Amida as monarch of the Western Pure Land.

"Hongaku." Hongaku (primordial awakening) is the position that all sentient beings—or sometimes the whole of being—are awakened from the outset, just as they are. This contrasts to the notion of *shikaku,* "acquired awakening," that allows for the development from an unawakened state to a state of awakening. This Tendai set of terms has its parallel in the Shingon pair *honne* (or *honnu*) and *shushō.* Both of these configurations stand near the nondual core of East Asian tantrism.[18]

"The three ages." These are past, present, and future; in other words, "always."

Two

The "*dharmakāya* of expedient means" emerges from the twin syllables "*A*" and "*hūṃ*." The breath of a single *yang* utterance is the breath, "*A*." From this single *yang* utterance "*mi*" is produced. Because it bespeaks the heart, it is the *dharmakāya*. The single *yin* utterance is when the utterance "*A*" is invited in as "*hūṃ*" and produces the syllable "*da*."

The place of the union of red and white is denominated as the three bodies, *dharmakāya, sambhogakāya,* and *nirmāṇakāya*. These are also the three essences—absolute, provisional, and middle. Therefore the white essence of the *vajrakoṣa* realm and the red essence of the *garbhakoṣa* realm are born of this union of *yin* and *yang*. Thus, when the duality of the noumenal *dharmakāya* and the *sambhogakāya*'s wisdom vessel merge and become absolutely one, we can speak of "Amida." Understand that the two syllables "*nan*" and "*mu*" (of "*namu*") are the twin *hun* and *po* souls, and also the antinomies, mind and thought. Thus, "*nan*" is father and "*mu*" is mother. And we can speak of the name [Amida] as father and of the shining light as mother. In this case, there is no expedient *dharmakāya* distantly separated from the *dharmatā dharmakāya*. This is called an awakened buddha. Since it is, in fact, the merciful grace of the union of cause and effect, it is the fulfillment of both self-profit and profit to others. Consider carefully how to repay this kindness and how to show gratitude for [Amida's] virtue.

Commentary to Segment Two

"The *dharmakāya* of expedient means." In a long paragraph worth quoting in extenso, Roger Corless helps us understand one fairly central Pure Land construction of the three-bodies theory:

> A minor peculiarity about the nature of Amitābha, which, however, nicely illustrates Pure Land doctrinal development, is his possession of a double *dharmakāya*. All buddhas and bodhisttvas, [Tanluan] says, have two *dharmakāya*s, an essential *dharmakāya* (Skt. *dharmatā dharmakāya;* Ch. *fa-hsing fa-shen*) and an operational *dharmakāya* (Skt. *upayā dharmakāya;* Ch. *fang-pien fa-shen*) (Note: rendered here as "expedient *dharmakāya*") which proceed from each other and are separable but not separate. . . . Śākyamuni Buddha is not explicitly tied to the double *dharmakāya* system."

Corless then points out that this "rather messy system does not fit the standard *trikāya* model," but

> Shinshū tidies it up as follows: the *dharmatā dharmakāya (hosshō hosshin)* is the *dharmakāya,* it is ineffable, nothing can be said about it, and it is not worshipped; the *upayā dharmakāya* (*hōben hosshin*) is the *sambhogakāya* and is Amitābha; Śākyamuni is the *nirmāṇakāya*.[19]

"'*A*' and '*hūṃ*,' and red and white." "*A*" and "*hūṃ*" are the seed mantras of Shingon's two grand *maṇḍala*s, the Vajradhātu/Vajrakoṣa (Vajra Realm) and the Garbhakoṣa (Womb Realm) Maṇḍalas. As Shingon in large part consists of the resolution of preliminary dualities and multiplicities into a nondual singularity, it presents a host of dual sets to encode this structure and process. These include the twin *maṇḍala*s (*ryobu mandara*), the distinction between nirvana and samsara, sentient beings and enlightened buddhas, female and male, and the twin mantras "*A*" and "*hūṃ*," correlated respectively to the Vajra and Womb Maṇḍalas. Most of these pairs are sexualized. *Vajra* in ancient Indian usage was phallic, and *garbha* can be both womb and fetus, the universe and its contents.[20]

Red and white are one more paired set. They are characteristic of tantric traditions in India, China, and Japan. They have as their primary reference male semen and female blood, whose conflation was seen as the essence of conception, the single drop of life that constitutes the beginning of a fetal being. They can be correlated with many dual sets, including, of course, the Chinese pair *yin* and *yang*.

In some ways the nenbutsu, "*Namu Amida Butsu*," seems like a mantra. It should not be too surprising, then, that in some radical Pure Land groups the easily made affinity between mantras and the nenbutsu led to a three-way identification of "*A*" and "*hūṃ*," in-breath and out-breath, and "*namu*" and "Amida." In turn, in-breath and out-breath were homologized to the in-and-out movements of sexual intercourse. By such lines of thought was Pure Land doctrine radically esotericized. Less intensely tantric readings assimilated the combined cycle of an in-breath and an out-breath to a complete nenbutsu, or the two parts of the mantra "*A-hūṃ*" to Amida and the reciter, who in the act of recitation become conjoined as one. All of this became further complicated when the Japanese Amidists utilized *kimyō* (literally, "return life") as a translation equivalent of *namu*. (More on this below.)

"Place of union of the red and white." Inasmuch as red and white encode semen and blood, this place must be the womb. Thus, it is also equivalent to the Womb Maṇḍala, to samsara and its gestating buddhas, but not to nirvana, seen as it usually is as the opposite of samsara. Shingon's central buddha, Dainichi (Mahāvairocana), also has two modes. The Vajradhātu Maṇḍala has as its *honzon* Dainichi constituted as mind. The Garbhakoṣa Maṇḍala represents Dainichi as body. Dainichi, just like the sentient beings of samsara, consists of six elements: five of body (earth, air, fire, water, and space) and one that is mind. Awakening is bodily as well as spiritual/mental.

"Nan" and *"mu"* are the syllables that begin the most common form of the nenbutsu, *"Namu Amida Butsu." Namu* transliterates the Sanskrit *namas* and has the sense of "committing oneself to" or "taking refuge in." Refuge in Amida in the case in point. A Sino-Japanese translation equivalent of *namas* is *kimyō,* whose two characters are *"ki,"* "to return," and *"myō,"* "life." The original sense here is probably "to entrust one's fate to," but esoteric speculations tie life breath, sexuality, and the nenbutsu into a single, knotted, interpretation.

The "name" is "Amida" as embedded in the nenbutsu. The shining light is the aurora of salvation radiating out from Amida to those who recite the nenbutsu. This sun and rays model would be a more natural metaphor for Dainichi, the central buddha of Shingon, whose Japanese name means "Great Sun." Amida is more conventionally likened to a solitary moon serenely floating in the sky far above this lower, dismal, world. At the same time, however, every sentient being is like a pond in that world, within which it is possible to see a reflected image of that same moon. Here, however, it is the sun, and sun and rays are nondually one. So too, probably, are Amida and Dainichi, sun and moon, buddha and sentient beings. All these beings have at their core *bodhicitta* or *bussho* (buddha-nature).

"No *dharmakāya* distantly separated" is an immanentalist denial of the orthodox Pure Land belief that Amida resides in his astronomically distant Pure Land paradise set galaxies away in the western sky. Instead, *dharmakāya* buddhahood is to be found in the here and now, in this body, just as it is. Connected to this is the fact that *"nan-mu"* (*namu*) can be understood not simply as a transliteration of *namas* but taken literally to mean "not in the south," nor, by implication, in any other direction, including even the Pure Land's usual ostensible location, the west. The whole nenbutsu then refers to "a Buddha Amida not in the north, south, east, or west," but rather wholly within the body, within the very center, within the human heart.

"How to repay this kindness." One way to repay Amida is to return one's life/trust by reciting the nenbutsu. In this case, the nenbutsu is less a call to Amida for salvation than a thankful return due for salvation already assured. This again can be seen as a *kimyō,* a "return of life."

"A" is invited in to become *"mi"* (or *"hūṃ"*). *"A"* and *"mi"* (*hūṃ*) produce *"da."* The term "invited in" suggests the invocation of a deity in a Shingon ritual. But the relation of these three syllables also seems sexual—with creation mirroring procreation. *"A"* is father, *"mi"* is mother, and *"da"* (or "Amida" as a whole) is their child. Alternatively, *"A"* is "A" and *"hūṃ"*

is "mi-da." Shingon meditation on the primal syllable *"A"* (*A-ji kan*) and the call to Amida are here fused, if not confused by their very "A"-ness, into one.

Hun and *po,* and mind and thought, give us two more dual sets. *Hun* and *po* are the twin pair of souls that the Chinese thought were the necessary prerequisites for a whole person. They join at conception, separate at death. Mind and thought seem less dual, perhaps, than mind and body—or, perhaps not.

Three

> Item: The words *"ki"* and *"myō"* comprise the return of the life of *shikaku* to the *hongaku* [A]mida. Because it is the *hongaku* [A]mida, the Buddha of the Principle of Thusness, your own heart can awaken to and contemplate the fact that your body is not [A]mida. If one returns life as a selfless *namu,* this will generate a Pure Land of mind-only and the buddha land of peace and joy will not be far off. In this way the attainment of the extremity in a singlemindedness and wholehearted trust is called "returning devotion." Because of the earnest casting aside of the foul body and returning to this singular dharma, there is a *wasan* that goes:
>
> For us in this evil world of five defilements
> *Vajra* and heart of faith are one.
> If we cast aside endless life-and-death
> We will arrive at the natural Pure Land.

Commentary to Segment Three

"Mind and body." The text takes an odd turn at this point. A purely *mikkyō* view would be to insist that the body is the locus of enlightenment/salvation—*sokushin jōbutsu* in the Shingon usage. Instead our author shifts to the claim that the locus of the Pure Land is the mind/heart. It, too, is "not far off," but it is clearly differentiated in a duality that separates mind and body. How this all relates to the mind and thought of the previous segment is not clear.

"Cast aside the foul body" is a phrase that would work in early Buddhism or in normative Pure Land, but is out of consonance with the *Hōri hachiman chō* as a whole.

Wasan are Buddhist poems written in Japanese—sometimes the word is translated "hymn." They are fairly common in the Pure Land tradition.

"Life-and-death" is the usual Sino-Japanese translation of samsara. Although it is a Buddhist technical term, the plain meaning of its component characters is never lost. In this it is like the compound *kimyō.*

A "natural" Pure Land. I am not sure of the sense of "natural" here. The term appears again in the later segments of the text.

Four

Item: "Not born, not destroyed; not going, not coming" is the heart's awakening to beginninglessness and endlessness. When one awakens to beginninglessness, this is "not born, not destroyed." When one awakens to endlessness, that is "not going, not coming." Therefore we say, *"Namu Amida Butsu."* And, since this is a natural dharma of the heart's own nature, it is the *dharmakāya* eternally beginningless and eternally endless. Thus, breath is already expended. This is a body of water. At the same time, since the moon manifests its essence in water, it is the ruler of night. In similar fashion, because the sun-essence is the ruler of daytime, [the sun] is a fire body. And then, as the passions are the tinder of the energy of fire, and as they burn up the fires of the heart, what we call *ōjō* must be taken to heart in the form of [Amida,] the Buddha of Endless Life. The Buddha of Endless Life is the body of the primal vow of empowering others. "Other-power primordial vow body" indicates the heart of a good and wise friend. By following his words, one can exit the endless doors of life-and-death (samsara). Thus we speak of *ōjō*. *"Ō"* is the birth of the unmoving tranquility body, fruit of incomprehensible explications. And *"jō,"* since it is a birthless birth, should be understood as being without beginning and without end.

When the flower of perfect awakening blossoms, we call it Amida. Because it corresponds to the buddha land, *ōjō* is proclaimed. But one need not guard one's body. One relies on the heart/mind. If you betray the heart, you also betray the body. Then the flower of perfect awakening will not bloom and the *ōjō* body will not form. Ponder this carefully.

Commentary to Segment Four

"Not born, not destroyed" are phrases sometimes used to "describe" nirvana. "Not going, not coming" is something timeless (or eternal), like the *dharmakāya.* At the same time, these words are here to set up the discussion of *ōjō* later in this segment, since its second character, *"jō,"* means "birth" or "to be born."

"Passions. . ." that "burn up the fires of the heart" seems to abruptly intrude a theme of radical Shingon, the notion that passions cannot be dispensed with but, rather, must be allowed to burst into flame until they at last consume themselves. The classic expression for this idea is the phrase *bonnō soku wa bodai,* "The passions are themselves enlightenment."

Ōjō is the most immediate goal of Pure Land practice, being reborn in Amida's Pure Land paradise, from which the attainment of nirvana is certain. The two characters of this term are "*ō*," "to go to," and "*jō*," "birth." *Ōjō* is the main topic of this entire passage.

"Primal vow." Before he was the Buddha Amida, Amida was the monk Dharmākara. At that time he foreswore his own attainment of nirvana unless all sentient beings are first able to gain access to the Pure Land. According to some traditions within Pure Land thought, all of the vows made by Dharmākara constitute the primal vow, while other traditions select specific vows, considering those to be the primal vow.

"Good and wise friend" translates *zenchishiki* (Skt. *kalyāṇamitra*), the sort of older brother figure who leads one into the Buddhist teachings and practices. In esotericized Pure Land, however, the term has a special meaning. *Zenchishiki* is the initiating guru (at times almost a shaman) who leads a local group (one is tempted to use terms like *cakra* or coven for these). The *zenchishiki* stands virtually in the place of Amida for his disciples. Chiba notes, for example, that "the adherents identify their master with Amida and his residence with the Pure Land," and further that *kakushi nenbutsu*

> was also called *fuhai hiji* (secret teaching that worship is unnecessary) . . . because they considered themselves to be identical with Amida at the moment of faith.[21]

"Birthless birth." *Ōjō* rebirth in the Pure Land is not a normal biological birth from a womb. Rather, it is a new life, in a new body, which begins seated in the heart of a lotus blossom, floating on the surface of the beautiful lake in the middle of the Western Paradise.

Five

> Item: To see the one heart move away from the taproot of life-and-death and arrive at the fruit of unsurpassed buddhahood is something that cannot be named, cannot be spoken, cannot be comprehended. The one heart abjures error, leaves the four bodies behind, and reaches the limit of the one heart. This is called the Tranquil Land. Thus, within the dream, as [Shandao] and Hōnen tell us, "The fruit of liberation from life-and-death seen in the dreams of our empty hearts must return to natural non-birth. Thus we attain *ōjō* nirvana." The heart of these lines cannot be expressed by thought or tongue. In the revered words of that saintly man, Genku (Hōnen), "I, knowing the self night after night, with acute mind enshrine dreams."
>
> To become a buddha is called [to attain] the stage of the uncreated, of complete and transparent nirvana. Therefore, to be wisely enlightened to the two characters that make up the compound "complete" is the core of

this. Likewise, if one empties the heart ever more, we can then speak of the clear Pure Land. Since the one heart manifests the primordial nonduality of male and female, it neither anchors itself in life-and-death nor abides in complete and transparent nirvana. When the one heart is clear, there will be no buddha to come forth and polish that which is not dirty to begin with nor to loath passions that do not exist. Thus the perfect awakening of the buddha and the *ōjō* of sentient beings will be a nondual unity [just] as are name and body. If one attains the *siddhi* thusly, it is called attaining the stage of fruition. Alas, existent or no, the various dharmas are the impermanent flowers of spring, bound to be scattered by the winds of birth-and-destruction. The autumn moon that follows the destruction of birth-and-destruction is obscured by the clouds of the joy of extinction. Now, within life, the accumulated doubts clear up and at this time *ōjō* becomes absolutely certain.

If already in this present life this benefit has been damaged, doubtless you will have to cast life aside and return to the land of the *dharmakāya.* If upon your arrival there, you spend a long time pondering the dharma, worshiping, fulfilling cause and effect, sitting before the altar, how will you ever again depart?

Someone asks: "Just what is this that you call the life of the *hongaku* Amida?"

I respond: "This is the doubt of the one great cause." When these words leave the lips, the buddhas of the three ages shed tears. However, Amida Tathāgata takes knowledge and kindness, dispenses compassion, and grants the boon of expedient means. Thus, the *dharmakāya tathāgata* appears. Thus, the *sambhogakāya tathāgata* appears. Thus, the *nirmāṇakāya tathāgata* appears. These are the triple forms of the *trikāya.*

In the knowledge given us about the origins of that ancient monk Dharmākara, it is said that within the forty-two emptinesses, within the precious pearl of non-attainment, a single person comes to dwell in the capital of suchness. The form of one nen[butsu] rising up constitutes the energy of the sun and the moon. This is not added to (*ka*) by the power of the practitioner. Grasping it (*ji*) as one's own thing is to break with divine protection.

Already present, in Śākyamuni's forty-nine years worth of sermons, the eighty thousand sacred teachings are devised to give knowledge of this energy. This energy is the entering and exciting wind. Wind is breath. Breath is life (*myō*). Life is Amida. When you stir up a single nenbutsu to Amida, it is the return (*ki*) of the energy of sun and moon. Just as the body is the dismal lower realm, you should know that the heart is the True Pure Land.

The heart journeys to the cloudy region of Tuṣita Heaven and sings the temper of the four directions. Just so, we speak of a Pure Land above the heavens and a Pure Land below the heavens. One should dwell in the Pure Land of non-going and never-retiring. Therefore the moon is one body, the sun is one body, and we, too, are in receipt of one body. Persons who have been awakened to this truth are deemed "one body manifoldly embodied." The life of such a person is not-born, not-destroyed, and without self. To return life to that [other?] person is to return a selfless *namu*. Thus, that person is the person who ages ago dispensed the wisdom and blessings of the primal vow as the monk Dharmākara.

The deployment of the *honzon* is as follows. The land of the Eastern Citadel is established to the rear. The land of the Western Citadel is established in the front. The left side houses being. The right side houses non-being. An eight-petaled lotus blossom must open within this house. Its sharp breath is eternal and without cessation. The sound of the bells of the golden sands of the Jambu River fills the *gohonzon* that illuminates the darkness. Therefore, the three lands of the great heart are said not to be deployed [simply] in four directions. The song of the heart says:

Return life to that ancient one,
Take joy in returning Amida's uplifting call.
Rent a dwelling on the isle of the red-and-white letter *A*.
The house of those who would return
Amida's call: a sun rising from suchness,
Stirs echoes in the resounding hills.

Commentary to Segment Five

Heart imagery has appeared all along in the text, but this segment is devoted to almost nothing else. Central here is *isshin*, "one heart." The term can mean the whole of reality seen as a single mind or entity. It also has a more limited meaning, "with the whole mind" or "wholeheartedly," as in devotion to Amida. Also implicated may be the sense in which "nenbutsu" means "to call the buddha to mind."

"The four bodies" is an expansion of the three-bodies theory, usually made by dividing the second body, the *sambhogakāya*, into two.

"Within the dream." Dreams are usually a metaphor for the illusory nature of samsara. Hereafter the *Hōri* brings up dreams repeatedly. But it is not quite clear in what sense the author wants us to take them.

"Name and body" (Skt. *nāmarūpa*) is yet one more dual set of "opposites."

Siddhi are the spiritual (or magical) "attainments" of Buddhism. Denigrated in some schools of Buddhism, they are a key component of its tantric forms.

"Clouds of the joy of extinction." The meaning of this phrase is unclear.[22]

"Within life" may be a reference to the Shingon tenet of *sokushin jōbutsu.*

The "one great cause" is the essential core of Buddhism. Different schools define it in different ways. "Doubt" may be close here to the Zen notion of the "great doubt," but this is hardly certain.

"Added" and "grasping" are the constituent elements of *kaji* (Skt. *adhiṣṭhāna*), Shingon's term for spiritual empowerment.

"Knowledge of this energy." Apparently this is the core of the eighty thousand scriptures, of the whole of buddhadharma, of Zenran's transmission to Nyoshin.

"Dismal body" and "heart." Here the conventional dualism of Pure Land thought seems to supplant esoteric readings.

Tuṣita Heaven was the abode of Śākyamuni while he awaited rebirth in our world. At this point we come closer to an esoteric view; there is a Pure Land below as well as above.

Honzon is the main image—or the central deity—of a *mikkyō maṇḍala*, ritual, or temple. So at this point we seem to have a Shingon-like image of Amida as the focus of worship—although it is not a great stretch to see Amidist paintings of Amida and the Pure Land as *maṇḍala*s of a sort. In the Kagiya initiation of the nun Teigin, she was made to sit in front of a scroll with the image of Amida and call out to him. To a degree, this seems a way a few underground adherents could set up a "portable temple" in whatever out-of-the-way site might fall to hand. The eight-petaled lotus at the center of the *maṇḍala* could be a blossom in the lake in the Pure Land, but it seems even more to recall the lotus at the center of the Womb Maṇḍala.

Six

Item: [Question:] Now, in the most ancient past, when there was no heaven, no earth, and no self, from what land did the life of the sentient beings of the three lands emerge?

I respond: Within "Immeasurable Life" was the shape of wisdom-blessing. Its light was the lotus blossom of the disc of the sun. This lotus blossom was, once again, beyond the ken of human contrivance.

[Question:] Well then, what kind of place is this "not born, not destroyed" capital?

I respond: Lotus blossoms reach two limits: the lotus of the wisdom and blessings of the "singular heaven of equal enlightenment" and the lotus blossom of the "awakening of wondrous enlightenment to suchness." The place where they meld into one is called the "heart lotus." You absolutely cannot give tidings of this heart.

Commentary to Segment Six

"Immeasurable Life" is a translation of one of Amida's full Sanskrit names, Amitāyus. Amitāyus and its alternate, Amitābha ("Immeasurable Light"), are both rendered in Japanese by the abbreviation Amida.

Seven

Item: [Question:] When you say that "return life" is to return the *shikaku* life to the *hongaku* Amida, to what place is this return made?

[Answer:] I respond: It is a return to that which is without constituents and without form.

[Question:] Well, if that is so, just what sort of place is it that you term "without constituents and without form"?

[Answer:] This phrase touches on the "one great cause." Its expression is not approached by the writing brush, nor is it easily put into spoken words. Thus the *honzon* becomes the image of *ōjō*. It is also a mirror. For the dull, ordinary person, this (note: text garbled at this point) in dreams. Therefore it is the principle of the underlying nature of immutable reality. Although we can state that it is nearby, the powers of the ordinary, unawakened person do not reach it. But the person who "uses great care to seek companions of the bloodline that transmits good belief" will attain the "one heart." Reciting the nenbutsu is like turning stones and tiles into gold. The nature of a pearl is just the same; it differs only as to whether it is or is not polished. Unpolished, it gives off no light. This lack of light is just like stones and tiles. Therefore Shandao (Zendō) said, "For companions, make yourself the intimate of 'good friends.' Draw close to such persons. Even at some distance, good friends are a treasure."

If you truly grasp the nenbutsu with faith, you will certainly arrive at the unsurpassed fruit of buddhahood. This jewel of non-attainment is beyond measure. Someone who knows this is no longer an ordinary person. With care, you can awaken to this. Alas for the foolish. They regret heaven, while even on earth the mercy [of Amida] should make us leap for joy. The source of reverence and joy? Our own heart!

Consider this and let heartfelt gratitude be engraved on your very organs. Cut yourself free from joy and free from language. Conceal this. Conceal it!

Commentary to Segment Seven

This section of the text is fairly self-explanatory. Its only notable feature is the final (and typical of *mikkyō*) admonishment to secrecy.

Eight

Item: Since this is secret, it is hard to know where to begin and where to end. We are in the middle of the dream of non-birth and non-destruction. The middle of the dream is nature. Nature is the sun and the moon. The stirring up of one nenbutsu constitutes the august *honzon.* The abiding place of the *gohonzon* is the space between *dharmatā* and *dharmakāya.* That space is where the life of the sun and moon is cultivated as a lotus blossom. This is called the "lotus blossom of the heart." When the heart abides at some distance, then the sun and the moon flee into the west and the world goes dark. This is called the wind without shape and without form.

When one arrives at the "lotus blossom *samādhi,*" the white *joro* emerges and the red *joro* emerges. When these are stirred up lifetime after lifetime, age after age, both heart and words become wondrous. This is called the "land of tranquility." In truth, it is beyond communicating. One is too few. Three is too many. This is the one great cause. If you forget it, say nothing. When breath is cut off and eyes have closed, this will be a storehouse of the *vajra*-heart.

What is written above is directed to Nyoshin alone. Writing is undone. The dream in a dream has room to store it. The order of the bloodline of the faithful can be proven by this. If, hereafter, you hold this as profound, then complete compassion will seep out and spread across the endless transmigrations of ordinary persons.

With reverence. With reverence.

Gutoku ("foolish and bald") Shinran, eighty-five years old

Commentary to Segment Eight

"Red and white *joro.*" I have a pronunciation here, but no characters. My best guess is the red and white drops of conception.

"One is too few, three is too many." I suspect this is in reference to the secret transmission. If only one person holds onto the secret, there is no transmission made. If it is shared with more than one other person, it will not be secret for long. Someone will speak it into the wrong ears. Then someone will write it down. Then it will get published. And then someone will translate it.

Notes

1 T. 2460: 77.736a.

2 Gobō was one of the "Tōji Sambō" (three masters of Tōji Temple whose names ended in "*bō*").

3 There are several key claims made by Shingon to warrant its superiority over other schools of Buddhism. Chief among these is the Shingon assertion that it alone is a revelation from the "transcendent" *dharmakāya* mode of the three kinds of manifestation of the buddha (*trikāya*) rather than an expedient expression of a lower *nirmaṇakāya* form—such as Śākyamuni, the historical buddha of our age. Features of Zen that might lead someone to consider it a form of *mikkyō* could include its one-to-one pattern of transmission, its affinity for the mantra-oriented *Heart Sutra,* and its eschewal of the verbal nature of truth. Later Japanese Zen is replete with *mikkyō*-like features that are doubtless accommodations to ambient Shingon and Tendai norms. Occasionally one encounters the term "*zenmitsu*." to describe such fusions.

4 I will stand back from the temptation to get entangled in the theological debates of postmodernism that see the use of the term "syncretism" as somehow complicit in essentialism and therefore anathema. I will only comment that I see Japanese religious notions as often being historically discrete, source-specific, and blendable, and see Japanese religion as a whole as having a notable proclivity to mix and match such elements almost at will.

5 On Kamakura Buddhism see, for example, James H. Foard, "In Search of a Lost Reformation: A Reconsideration of Kamakura Buddhism," *Japanese Journal of Religious Studies* 7, no. 4 (December 1980): pp. 274–281; and the various chapters of Richard K. Payne, ed., *Re-Visioning "Kamakura" Buddhism* (Honolulu: University of Hawai'i Press, 1998).

6 For one example of *iemoto* structure see James H. Sanford, "Shakuhachi Zen: The Fukeshū and Komusō," *Monumenta Nipponica* 32, no. 4 (1975): pp. 411–440.

7 On the *himitsu nenbutsu,* see James H. Sanford, "Breath of Life: The Esoteric Nenbutsu," in *Esoteric Buddhism in Japan,* ed. Ian Astley (Copenhagen and Aarhus: Seminar for Buddhist Studies, 1994), pp. 65–98 (reprinted in *Tantric Buddhism in East Asia,* ed. Richard K. Payne [Boston: Wisdom Publications, 2005]). Somewhat related is Kakuban's intra-Shingon adaptation of Amidism. For a key text, see James H. Sanford, "Amida's Secret Life: Kakuban's Amida Hishaku," in *Approaching the Land of Bliss: Religious Praxis in the Cult of Amitābha,* ed. Richard K. Payne and Kenneth S. Tanaka (Honolulu: University of Hawai'i Press, 2004), pp. 120–138. Chapters in the same volume by Jacqueline I. Stone, Fabio Rambelli, and Richard M. Jaffe are also relevant. Also useful on Pure Land developments is S. A. Thornton, *Charisma and Community Formation in Medieval Japan: The Case of the Yugyo-ha (1300–1700)* (Ithaca: Cornell University, 1999); see especially the critique of standard Pure Land historiography on pp. 9–14.

8 See, for example, the translation of and notes to Rennyo's "On Secret Teachings" in Minor L. Rogers and Ann T. Rogers, *Rennyo: The Second Founder of Shin Buddhism* (Berkeley, CA: Asian Humanities Press, 1991), pp. 190–192.

[9] Chiba Jōryū, "Orthodoxy and Heterodoxy in Early Modern Shinshū: Kakushi Nenbutsu and Kakure Nenbutsu," in *The Pure Land Tradition: History and Development,* ed. James Foard, Michael Soloman, and Richard K. Payne (Berkeley, CA: University of California Press, 1996), provides a number of terms used to designate Japanese Buddhist heresies: *hakarai* (personal capriciousness), *ige* (different interpretation), *i-anjin* (deviant faith), *shingi* (new interpretation), *jagi* (perverted interpretation), pp. 470–471; *hiji bomon* (secret teaching), *yachu hiji* (teaching expounded at night), p. 475; and *gedo* (non-Buddhist), p. 476. None of these is, of course, an exact match for the English (from Greek) word "heresy."

[10] Chiba, "Orthodoxy and Heterodoxy," p. 482.

[11] Other Tokugawa religious groups also had "hidden" branches, the best-known being the *kakure kirishitan,* or "underground Christians." Winston Davis, *Japanese Religion and Society: Paradigms of Structure and Change* (Albany, NY: State University of New York Press, 1992), pp. 74–75, lists several: *kakure kirishitan, kakure nenbutsu, kakure daimoku* (underground Nichirenites), and *kakure mairi* (secret pilgrims to the Shintō shrine of Amaterasu at Ise).

[12] Chiba, "Orthodoxy and Heterodoxy," pp. 477–482, records the nun's experiences.

[13] Ibid., p. 475.

[14] "Eighty thousand dharmas" is a technical term for the whole of the Buddhist teachings. Shinran's secret message purports to express the innermost core of all of them.

[15] That the introductory element plus eight segments add up to nine may not be accidental. It is likely to reflect both the nine levels of rebirth in Amida's Pure Land and the three-by-three inner court of the Womb Maṇḍala.

[16] For a discussion of the three bodies (*trikāya*) as understood by the Chinese master Tanluan, see Roger J. Corless, "Tan-luan: the First Systematizer of Pure Land Buddhism," in *The Pure Land Tradition,* ed. Foard, Soloman, and Payne, pp. 121–122.

[17] The Taima Mandara is probably an eighth-century tapestry *maṇḍala* thought to have been imported from China, and found in the Taimadera Temple. See "Taima Mandara," http://www.stolaf.edu/courses/2004sem2/Art/260/Pokie/index.htm (accessed June 21, 2006). See also "Taima Mandala," http://www.12.canvas.ne.jp/horai/con-ex.htm (accessed June 21, 2006).

[18] The fullest study of *hongaku* issues in English is Jacqueline I. Stone, *Original Enlightenment and the Transformation of Medieval Japanese Buddhism* (Honolulu: University of Hawai'i Press, 2003). Fabio Rambelli provides some telling details on radically nondual esotericism and Japanese Pure Land practices in his "'Just Behave as You Like: Prohibitions and Impurities Are Not a Problem': Radical Amida Cults and Popular Religiosity in Premodern Japan," in *Approaching the Land of Bliss: Religious Praxis in the Cult of Amitabha,* ed. Richard K. Payne and Kenneth K. Tanaka (Honolulu: University of Hawai'i Press, 2004). These are especially interesting in light of normative Pure Land's decided bent toward dualistic formulations.

[19] Corless, "Tan-luan," pp. 121–122.

[20] The fullest English treatment of the twin *maṇḍala*s is Adrian Snodgrass, *The Matrix and Diamond World Mandalas in Shingon Buddhism*, 2 vols. (New Delhi: Aditya Prakshan, 1988). For *maṇḍala*s in Japanese religion in general, the best source is Elizabeth ten Grotenhuis, *Japanese Mandalas: Representations of Sacred Geography* (Honolulu: University of Hawai'i Press, 1999).

[21] Chiba, "Orthodoxy and Heterodoxy," p. 477.

[22] Editor's note: Perhaps this is a reference to the tenth stage of a bodhisattva's progress, identified in the *Daśabhūmika-sūtra* as the *"dharmamegha-bhūmi"* or "rain cloud of dharma stage." (If this is the case then the description of these clouds as obscuring the "autumn moon that follows the destruction of birth-and-destruction" is an allusion to the tenth stage, and should not be read as indicating that the emotion of joy obscures the moon of awakening, as it seemed at first to this reader.) Sanford's text emphasizes that this happens "within life," and a tenth-stage bodhisattva is *caramabhavika*, "one who has entered supreme awakening in this life." See *The Encyclopedia of Buddhism*, 2 vols, editor-in-chief Robert E. Buswell, Jr. (New York: Macmillan Reference USA, 2004), s.v. "Bodhisattva(s)," vol. 1, pp. 58–60.

American Jōdo Shinshū Practice: A Fork in the Road

Gordon Bermant
Lecturer, Department of Psychology
University of Pennsylvania

"When you come to a fork in the road, take it."[1]

Introduction

American Jōdo Shinshū is coming to a fork on the path of practice. Causes and conditions are ripe for making the nenbutsu teaching more accessible and effective for many Americans whose current understanding is essentially zero. Ironically, these newcomers may be advantaged by their current ignorance, because they will not have to overcome habits of thought and expression that have made Shinran's message needlessly obscure.

The purpose of this essay is to describe, from this layperson's perspective, a positive picture of lay Shinshū practice. I believe that it is important for lay Shinshū followers to become more articulate and active in sharing the dharma with others. Change in this direction is now being supported within the Buddhist Churches of America (BCA) by the Ministers' Assistants Program and the increasing availability of *tokudō* training. But the necessities of our current situation require still greater participation by lay members in direct religious discussions with each other and with newcomers.[2]

The essay proceeds in three parts. The first seeks to clarify the various meanings captured in colloquial English by the word "practice." Some of the confusion surrounding what American Jōdo Shinshū "practice" should or shouldn't be arises from an incomplete agreement about what we mean when we use this deceptively complicated word. The second part relies on several authors whose approaches to lay practice have influenced me. The last part summarizes my understanding and concludes with recommendations for the practice of American newcomers to Jōdo Shinshū.

What Does Practice Mean?

It is useful to review the varieties of meaning encoded by "practice." The word can be used as a noun or a verb. As a noun, the dictionary[3] gives ten meanings; we can identify three that need to be distinguished here. First, sometimes we use "practice" as a synonym for habit or custom, as in "It is the practice of Americans to shake hands with each other rather than to bow to each other." Second, sometimes we use "practice" to refer to repetitive performances intended to acquire skill or proficiency, as in "Her violin practice required her to miss some social events." And third, sometimes we use "practice" to refer to a set of skills required for a profession or occupation, as in "He had a very active medical practice." Notice that the first use implies nothing about intentions to improve by practitioners. Used this way, our "practices" are traditional, or customary—we just do them. But the second use specifically refers to actual or intended improvement. Parents insist that their children continue the "practice" of their instruments so that the children will become competent with them and, presumably, therefore enjoy them going forward. "Practice makes perfect," we say. The third use, referring to a profession, implies that *practitioners* have become skilled enough to offer their services for the benefit of others.

The uses of "practice" as a verb tracks its uses as a noun. Sometimes we use the verb to refer to habitual or customary activities. The *American Heritage Dictionary* includes the following entry: "to follow or observe habitually or customarily: *to practice one's religion.*" This is the same sense in which we say, "She is a practicing Catholic." Used this way, the verb does not require that the practitioner be attempting to improve; it requires only that he or she be consistent. The second use of the verb, like the noun, refers directly to improvement, as in "She practiced the violin for hours each day, until her technique seemed completely natural." And third, when used in the context of the professions, the verb implies the attainment of skills from "practice" in the second sense. An example is "He practiced family law with great compassion as a result of many years of experience."

How can we apply the different uses of "practice" to the situation of Jōdo Shinshū in America? It seems to me that we can connect the three uses of "practice" to the three major groups of persons with whom we are all concerned. First, there are traditional temple members, usually Japanese Americans, whose practice is deeply customary and traditional, and who are therefore comfortable with the idea that they have "no practice." Second, there are temple newcomers, usually not Japanese Americans, who come upon Jōdo Shinshū with no prior knowledge, and therefore, must practice in the second sense of "intended improvement" in order for their participation in Jōdo Shinshū to become spiritually meaningful. Third, there are ministers, whose practice is exactly equivalent, in traditional English usage, to the "practices" of doctors and lawyers.[4] If ministers come from traditional families, they should have "professionalized" their traditional practice in order to share it with others, which is their professional responsibility.

I believe that we will not progress far in our understanding of American Jōdo Shinshū practice without making these distinctions. The distinctions lead us to ask three questions. First, how should the church serve the traditional Japanese American members in most BCA temples? This is a population that is diminishing in size but deserves great respect and concern. Second, how should the church serve newcomers to the temples? This is a population that represents an essential component of the future of Jōdo Shinshū in America. It is a population that is not defined by ethnicity or geography but only by a sincere desire to learn. And, third, how should the church develop and train new ministers to practice effectively with each of the two lay populations? Should every minister be expected to share the dharma effectively with both populations, or should ministerial training and assignments be specialized?

Here I limit discussion to the second question: what does practice entail for newcomers to Jōdo Shinshū in America?

"Laying Down a Path in Walking"[5]

K. T. Tsuji (1919–2004) was my teacher (*sensei*) in person between 1986 and his retirement in 1998, and he will always remain my teacher. In person, his lessons often came in sideways or with delayed impact, as in the following example. Shortly after I started attending Ekoji Buddhist Temple, I asked Tsuji Sensei if there was proper attire for Sunday services. His response was quick: "Don't worry about it. Come as you are." In his contribution to this collection, "The Supremacy of Amida's Vows in Rennyo" (pp. 175–187), Alfred Bloom demonstrates the central role this attitude plays in Rennyo's assertion that women are reborn in Amida's Pure Land "just as they are," that is, without requiring any transformation of gender.

The phrase "come as you are" has continued to reverberate in my mind. I had no idea at the time how Jōdo Shinshū celebrates everyday life, but as the idea opened up to me, very gradually to be sure, I experienced a relaxation that continues to ebb and flow, like a stream that sometimes courses out of sight only to surface when I am particularly thirsty. How wonderful, then, to have the colloquial Japanese phrase *sono mama* ("just as it is" or "just as you are") explained by Taitetsu Unno:

> *Sono-mama* is reality affirmed as it is without being distorted by calculative thinking. . . . Although *sono-mama* is beyond conceptual grasp, it can be manifested in a person's life. Anna Pavlova suggests something akin to this in the case of dancing; once she is said to have proclaimed, "The secret of becoming a fine dancer is to learn the theory and the technique thoroughly—then forget about it and just dance." Just dance *sono-mama,* but only after mastering the theory and technique.[6]

Unno makes explicit the analogy of dance to the practice of Jōdo Shinshū. Deep hearing and recitation of nenbutsu, he explains, are the equivalents of learning the theory and technique of dance.

> Deep hearing and recitative nenbutsu. After that everything must be forgotten and the person must "just live," but now live with awareness, sensitivity, and grace. . . . The interior practice of deep hearing, learning and forgetting, ultimately leads to a life of *sono-mama.*[7]

For members of the traditional Shin community in America, the practice of deep hearing and sincere recitation of nenbutsu have perhaps become so ingrained that explicit awareness of having learned them are "forgotten" in adulthood, so that it seems that "no practice" is required. But for the newcomer this is an impossible circumstance, just as it would be impossible for an untrained dancer to enter the *corps de ballet* on day one. The newcomer must learn what to do. The learning must be active. Passively transforming my life into a life of *shinjin* is as impossible as my passively learning to support a ballerina in a pas de deux. I must practice.

And yet, those who speak to us, as it were, from the other side of practice, tell us that the practice was not really necessary. Roger Corless has commented on this irony:

> It is notable that, although many accomplished teachers speak in terms of spontaneity, letting be, or [other-power], they do so only at the conclusion of a painful path of apparent self-power. . . . Shinran himself practiced the *nenbutsu* assiduously, but fruitlessly, for many years on [Mt.] Hiei.[8]

One must learn that there is nothing to do, and it is a very difficult lesson. It is an exceedingly difficult lesson in America, where "can-do," "never give up," "when the going gets tough, the tough get going," and similar moralistic formulae pervade the culture like dye pervades a porous fabric. Here is a homely example: I am addicted during July to watching the Tour de France on television. As I write this, Lance Armstrong is poised to win a totally unprecedented seventh Tour in a row. The preparation, skill, mental toughness, and suffering required for this accomplishment are hardly conceivable by most of us. When he is interviewed, Armstrong always sincerely compliments his team, coaches, trainers, and sponsors. He acknowledges that without them, he could not do what he is doing. But he also acknowledges that, at the end, it is going to be up to him. His performance in the grueling three weeks of racing confirms this. It would not be credible to contend that his effort is irrelevant to his accomplishment. The relationship between effort and accomplishment is something that Americans (and Japanese and virtually everyone else in the world, for that matter) understand.

It seems to the American newcomer to a BCA temple that an admonition that there is nothing to do is an unacceptable invitation to do nothing[9] or a subtle form of exclusion.[10] Very few newcomers will persevere in the face of these impressions. But this need not happen. The solution to the problem is for ministers and active laypersons to communicate clear distinctions between *effort* and *power,* and between *sincere desire for attainment* and *spiritual materialism.*

Effort and power. The importance of effort, in the form of self-reliance, is emphasized by Takamaro Shigaraki as the cornerstone of all Buddhism, just because it will finally lead to the realization of the tension that exists between our human condition and the wisdom and compassion that comprise Amida Buddha. The enlightenment of the historical Buddha eliminated that tension. Shigaraki makes this lesson clear for us, saying:

> [W]e must take responsibility and bear the responsibility for our lives resolutely; and yet, at the same time, we must be in accord with the universal principle that pervades everything in our lives. The truth is, however, that our lives are always far removed from this point of intersection. For that reason, Gautama Buddha teaches us that we must constantly strive to live at that point.[11]

Joren McDonald has emphasized the importance of keeping this distinction in the front of our minds:

> Being Jōdo Shinshū doesn't mean to stop our own effort as we rely on the [other-power] to guide us. It means we do what we can and the infinite [other-power] is always "as it is."[12]

This is an important message for a newcomer to hear again and again. It is included as well in the version of bodhisattva vows that appear in the service book used at the Ekoji Buddhist Temple in Fairfax Station, Virginia, where I met Tsuji Sensei:

> [D]espite our human limitations, let us embrace our highest aspiration for enlightenment and strive with utmost effort, in our own humble way, to follow the path of the Bodhisattva.

Aspiring with awareness of my profound limitation, and striving ceaselessly with uncalculating humility: these are the means and ends of practice. A newcomer can understand this and will respond to the challenge that it represents. The newcomer will respond to the lesson so elegantly expressed by Tsuji Sensei in his meditation on fireflies: "As for me, I am stronger, more intelligent, civilized and live longer, but I cannot give light. It makes me very humble."[13]

Desire for attainment, passivity, and spiritual materialism. The desire for attainment is presumed in the primal vow: "sentient beings who sincerely and joyfully entrust themselves to me, desire to be born in my land, and call my Name even ten times. . . ."[14] The problem for the newcomer is to understand what this means. The language is not self-explanatory. Its meaning emerges over time as the newcomer practices with it. Continued, patient practice must be supported in the newcomer by a desire that he identifies as "his own" desire. At some point, the (not-so-new) newcomer may come to understand that "his own" desire was in fact a gift of compassion from the circumstances that brought him to the vow in the first place. It seems to me that this is a definitive Shinshū learning experience.

The *correct* relocation of causality from "within me" to "outside of me" is at the core of Shin teaching. This is a delicate balancing act. If the relocation is taken too far, then passivity and apathy will result. The appropriate form of self-reliance will be lost. Roger Corless identified the problem clearly for Shinshū practitioners:

> The problem is amusingly illustrated by a (no doubt apocryphal) conversation between a parent and child who are members of the Buddhist Churches of America. "Aren't you going to get up and go to temple?" asks the parent. "Why should I?" replies the child, "If it's all *tariki* I'll just lie here in bed and let it all happen automatically (*jinen*)."[15]

Becoming apathetic is the result of losing proper self-reliance. But if the relocation of causality from "me" to "not me" is not taken far enough, the practitioner takes personal credit for his spiritual progress, mistakenly believing that his effort equates to personal power (*jiriki*).

The release, relief, and awakening that Jōdo Shinshū promises will elude this self-power practitioner. It seems that this insight is not unique to Jōdo Shinshū. It was elaborated, for example, by the late Chögyam Trungpa Rinpoche, who used the phrase *spiritual materialism:* "As long as one's approach to spirituality is based upon enriching ego, then it is spiritual materialism, a suicidal process rather than a creative one."[16]

Though this phrase does not come out of the Shinshū tradition, it communicates the risks of self-power practice in powerful, colloquial English. I think newcomers can relate to the idea of self-power practice when it is expressed using Trungpa's phrase.

Finding the correct balance through self-reflection. Shigaraki eloquently describes the practice of moving toward the delicate, profound balance that opens the mind to awakening:

> [T]he deeper we delve into our hearts and minds, while saying the *nenbutsu,* the more we will be able to perceive our defiled passions and our shadowy hearts of self-attachment. And at exactly the same time, the life and heart of the Buddha come to make themselves known to us. Here, two opposing realities reveal themselves at the same time, from completely opposite directions.... *Shinjin* is the experience in which two things which are in absolute contradictory opposition to each other, arise in simultaneous identity. In Shin Buddhism, we use the idea of *tariki* simply in order to explain this basic reality of *shinjin.* It means nothing more than that.[17]

This is not language that a newcomer can appreciate early in her practice.[18] Nevertheless, the basic message is unmistakable: the heart of practice is intense and continued self-reflection in the presence of the nenbutsu. This is just the balance betweeen willfulness and willingness discussed by Aronson in his contribution to this collection, "Vajrasattva Meditation" (pp. 3–30). Self-reflection gives deep hearing a dynamic dimension. "Hearing deeply" becomes an active process that allows total vulnerability to following the path of self-reflection wherever it takes us. This form of practice, if introduced correctly to newcomers, will engage them from the outset and sustain them as they proceed.

Conclusion: Recommendations Regarding Practice

A devout Catholic friend with whom I have been discussing religion via e-mail told me that my Buddhism made him "sad" because it seemed that I wished to replace something with nothing, rather than trying to join something lesser with something greater. Upon reflection

I could understand his viewpoint, and I realized that I had led him to this conclusion by inadequate expressions of my own. I responded to him as follows:

> No need to be sad. In fact, exactly what I seek is to replace something lesser with something greater. The referent of "emptiness" or "nothingness," which are inadequate and even misleading terms for the core of Mahayana Buddhism, is not an escape or a diminishment. It is a transformation of awareness to embrace things as they are—and aren't. What I aspire to replace is my current state of clouded consciousness and corrupted compassion with clarity and purity. Intense and continued self-reflection shows me that this aspiration is thoroughly futile through my own effort. I must rely on what is beyond my self. Accepting this, learning to appreciate the wisdom and compassion in the world coming toward me, and becoming part of it to share with others, are steps on the path of transformation. This is very slow going, and certainly beyond me during this lifetime. As to beyond this lifetime, I have no information whatsoever and feel no need to speculate. But this is a joyous and positive path, quite different in fact from the image of pessimism or escapism that Buddhism seems sometimes to project.

Perhaps five years from now, or ten, if I am still alive, I will have found other means of expression, or perhaps will have become content to remain silent. In any case, I feel comfortable that this sort of expression can be shared with others who come to our temple as newcomers who seek a practice and some description of what practice reveals. Questions of detail, such as the roles of meditation, rituals, languages used, and so on, can be negotiated and appreciated in the context of what matters at the core: intense and continued self-reflection in the context of the nenbutsu.

Notes

1 Yogi Berra, *When You Come to a Fork in the Road, Take It* (New York: Hyperion, 2001).

2 This idea is more fully developed in my essay, "Growing American Jōdo Shinshū: Are There Lessons in the Christian Missionary Model?" in *Sharing the Dharma with Others: Eleven Perspectives on Shin Buddhist Outreach,* ed. Gordon Bermant and Anna Tecson (San Francisco: Membership and Outreach Committee, Buddhist Churches of America, 2005). People who doubt the force of nenbutsu teaching to find active expression in America without "official" church support should visit the website of the Buddhist Faith Fellowship of Connecticut, http://www.bffct.orghttp://www.bffct.org/. If the report I have received is accurate, this Shin-Zen–centered, lay-run group has four hundred members!

3 *The Random House Unabridged Dictionary of the English Language,* 2nd ed. (New York: Random House, 1987).

4 The dictionary defines "learned profession" as "any of the three vocations of theology, law, and medicine, commonly held to require highly advanced learning."

5 Francisco J. Varela, Evan Thomson, and Eleanor Rosch, *The Embodied Mind: Cognitive Science and Human Experience* (Cambridge, MA: MIT Press, 1991), p. 237. In my opinion, this book represents the best effort yet to show the intimate connections between the knowledge contained in neuroscience and the wisdom of Buddhism.

6 Taitetsu Unno, *River of Fire, River of Water: An Introduction to the Pure Land Tradition of Shin Buddhism* (New York: Doubleday, 1998), p. 123.

7 Ibid.

8 Roger Corless, "Self-Power Practice with Other-Power Attitude: An Interpretation of Mind in Shin Buddhism," *The Pure Land,* n.s., 8–9 (December 1992): p. 194.

9 Roger Corless, "The Pathless Path for North America," *The Pure Land,* n.s., 13–14 (December 1997): p. 9. Corless suggests that religious permission to refrain from specific practice has a different consequence in Japan than it does in America: "The permission to be imperfect results, in Japan, in the freedom to do what needs to be done to the best of one's ability, without losing face if one is less than thoroughly successful. In North America, it may simply be a license to do nothing at all."

10 The sense of exclusion arises in a newcomer when it is accompanied by an implication that the newcomer's "Western mind" is incapable of understanding Shin (or Zen) teaching with sufficient subtlety. The resulting response of the temple newcomer is like the resentment felt by some scholars faced with apparent Japanese spiritual triumphalism. See, for example, the polemical article by Robert H. Scharf, "The Zen of Japanese Nationalism," in *Curators of the Buddha,* ed. Donald S. Lopez, Jr. (Chicago: University of Chicago Press, 1995).

[11] Takamaro Shigaraki, *A Life of Awakening: The Heart of the Shin Buddhist Path* (Kyoto: Hōzōkan, 2005), p. 6.

[12] Joren McDonald, "The Importance of Self Effort," *The Wheel of Dharma,* vol. 24, no. 7 (July 1997): p. 1.

[13] Kenryu T. Tsuji, *The Heart of the Buddha-Dharma* (Berkeley, CA: Ekoji Buddhist Temple and Numata Center for Buddhist Translation and Research, 2003), p. 63.

[14] Hisao Inagaki, *The Three Pure Land Sutras* (Kyoto: Nagata Bunshōdō, 1994), p. 243.

[15] Corless, "The Pathless Path for North America," pp. 10–11.

[16] Chögyam Trungpa, *The Myth of Freedom and the Way of Meditation* (Boulder, CO and London: Shambhala, 1976), p. 5. "Spiritual materialism" is also part of the title of a book by Trungpa, *Cutting Through Spiritual Materialism* (Boston: Shambhala, 1987).

[17] Shigaraki, *A Life of Awakening,* p. 127.

[18] Shigaraki explains at various times in his book that his interpretations do not always conform to Shin orthodoxy. His connections between *shinjin* and *tariki,* whether orthodox or not, strike this ignorant reader as a wonderful, accessible teaching.

Transmission

Yuan Hongdao and the *Xifang helun*: Pure Land Theology in the Late Ming Dynasty

Charles B. Jones
Catholic University of America, Washington D.C.

Introduction

Yuan Hongdao's (袁宏道, 1568–1610) life was one of the success stories of the late Ming dynasty. Born into a minor gentry family, he and his two brothers showed great literary promise during childhood. Hongdao and his older brother Zongdao (宗道, 1560–1600) earned the *jinshi* (進士) degree while still young; the youngest brother, Zhongdao (中道, 1570–1624), attained it in middle age; and all three had successful careers as government officials. Even while busy with public affairs, they still found time to do many of the things that constituted the good life for gentry in those days: drink wine, enjoy women, have sons, compose poetry, travel to scenic places, engage in discussions of religious and philosophical topics with good friends, and publish literary works that were well received. But alongside the triumphs, Yuan Hongdao experienced sorrow as well. Deaths in his family, the tedious rigors of official life, and serious and prolonged illnesses—all these gave him pause to reflect on the quality of his religious life and practice, and brought about a sharp change in direction toward the end of his life. Because he was introspective by nature, and possessed a great gift for writing, his extensive literary remains give us a vivid picture of a man who at the same time possessed inspired genius and an earthy humanity.

Despite these qualities, Yuan was largely ignored by both East Asian and Western scholars for a very long time. By the end of his life not much time remained for the Ming dynasty, and the Qing court that succeeded it saw in his works some anti-foreign sentiment, prompting the authorities to proscribe them for a while.[1] In the early twentieth century Chinese scholars rediscovered Yuan, but only as a literary figure, the leader of the "Gongan school" (公安派) of poetry and essay-writing, and an exponent of the "short essay" (*xiaopin wen*, 小品文) genre popular in the late Ming. In spite of the fact that his great systematization of Pure Land thought, the *Comprehensive Treatise on the West* (*Xifang helun*, 西方合論), was his longest single extant work by far, scholars ignored it, and Qian Bocheng (錢伯城) included only one fascicle of it in his critical 1981 edition of Yuan's *Collected Works.* In the 1930s the scholar Zhang Ruzhao (張汝釗) put forward the opinion that because scholars of his day sympathetic to the May Fourth Movement were hostile to religion, and figures in the government thought of Buddhism as an impediment to modernization, researchers deliberately omitted mention of Yuan Hongdao's Buddhism.[2] Following the Communist victory in 1949, it seemed Yuan Hongdao the Buddhist layman would never receive the attention he deserved.

However, interest in Yuan as a specifically Buddhist thinker began to build in the twentieth century. Mochizuki Shinkō (望月信亨) devoted three pages of his history of Chinese Pure Land thought to Yuan,[3] and in the 1970s, Araki Kengo (荒木見悟) devoted a good fifty pages to outlining the Yuan brothers' contributions to religious thought in the late Ming.[4] More recently, scholars in Taiwan and China have taken a greater interest in Yuan's Buddhist thought. In 1993, Qiu Minjie's (邱敏捷) study appeared,[5] and in 1999 Zhou Qun (周群) published his critical biography of Yuan, which included a lengthy chapter dealing exclusively with Yuan's religious thought.[6] Both of these scholars have gone on to publish further studies of Yuan.[7] Finally, Pan Guiming's (潘桂明) study of Chinese lay Buddhist history included a section on Yuan Hongdao.[8] To this date, however, Yuan Hongdao has received almost no attention from Western scholars for his contributions to the religious life of the late Ming, although some scholars have studied him as a literary figure.[9] More recently, Yuan received some attention alongside other late-Ming Buddhist figures in Jennifer Eichman's doctoral dissertation.[10]

A publishing event that greatly facilitated these studies was the appearance in 1981 of Qian Bocheng's critical edition of Yuan's *Collected Works,* which reset all the material in modern, standard type, arranged it in chronological order, and added critical notes to each individual piece on date and place of composition, textual variants in earlier editions, and explanations of references.[11] Another event that has helped propel studies of Yuan's Buddhist thought is the rediscovery of some works that had previously been thought lost. Both Qiu Minjie and Zhou Qun found archival copies of three works: the *Jinxie bian* (金屑編, *Gold Shavings*), the *Liu zu tan jing jielu* (六祖壇經節錄, *Outline of the Platform Sutra*), and the *Shanhu lin* (珊瑚林, *Coral Grove*). The first two consist of notes on other texts, and while the *Gold Shavings* does contain Yuan's own comments and thus is valuable for studying his Chan thought early in life, the real treasure of this group of texts is the *Coral Grove.* This is an anthology of essays in two fascicles compiled toward the end of his life and named after a scenic spot in his native Gongan County (公安縣), and it covers a remarkably broad range of topics. These range from Chan comments on Confucian literature, to the relationship of the "Three Teachings," to autobiographical reflections. Yuan also wrote a condensation of Yongming Yanshou's (永明延壽) *Zongjing lu* (宗鏡錄), called the *Zongjing shelu* (宗鏡攝錄) in twelve fascicles, but this work is no longer extant.

It should be clear from the above remarks that a comprehensive account of Yuan's religious thought and his contributions to the gentry Buddhism of the late Ming period would require a substantial monograph. Our goals for this chapter will therefore be more modest in scope. We will first take a look at Yuan's biography, then we will examine his contributions to Pure Land thought as seen in the *Xifang helun.* Finally, we will examine some questions and themes that arise from this text as it relates to his life and historical context.

A Brief Biography of Yuan Hongdao

To begin in the manner of most traditional Chinese biographies: Yuan Hongdao, style-name (*zi*, 字) Zhonglang (中郎), courtesy-names (*hao*, 號) Shitou jushi (石頭居士, "Layman Stonehead") and Shigong (石公), was born on the sixth day of the twelfth month in the second year of the Longqing (隆慶) era (1568), in the village of Chang'an (長安村), Gongan County, Huguang province (湖廣省) (now Mengxi village, 孟溪村, Hubei province, 湖北省), on the south bank of the Jing River (荊江). According to the biography of Yuan Hongdao composed by his younger brother Zhongdao, the Yuan family had arrived as refugees from Jiangyou (江右, in modern Jiangxi, 江西) early in the Ming dynasty.[12] While they were known locally as an educated and generous family, success in the examination system eluded them for several generations. Yuan Hongdao's father, Yuan Shiyu (袁士瑜), showed some early talent, placing first in the county examinations and becoming a *xiucai* (秀才, licentiate) at the age of fifteen, but he never placed in any subsequent examination. His father-in-law, Gong Daqi (龔大器), had earned the *jinshi* degree in 1556, and had served in a number of administrative posts before retiring to Gongan County permanently. As an official, he was capable and well liked, and in some places where he was posted people referred to him as "Buddha Gong" (Gong fo, 龔佛).[13]

After their mother's death in 1575, the boys went on to study in a series of private schools (*sishu*, 私塾) and lineage schools. The three Yuan brothers worked hard and thrived within this system. Their talent was evident: by the age of ten, Hongdao could already compose good "eight-legged essays" (*zhiyi wenzhang*, 制義文章, or *bagu wen*, 八股文), a requirement for the examinations. The eldest, Yuan Zongdao, went with his wife to study in the county seat (*xiancheng*, 縣城) in 1578, taking all the siblings with him. Hongdao and Zhongdao would later reminisce about how they would all sit together every evening while Zongdao read to them from the classics, histories, writings of the "hundred schools" (*baijia*,百家), and even stories and novels. Later, in 1583, Yuan Hongdao formed a literary society with his brother Zhongdao and others, who chose him as president by acclamation. Whenever they took a break from preparing for the examinations, they would meet to compose and share poetry. Yuan Hongdao memorialized the society in a later poem that recalled fond memories of good times, as they saw themselves as the Seven Sages of their own Bamboo Grove.[14] Thus, even from his early adolescence, we see the beginnings of Yuan Hongdao's genius, his wide-ranging literary interests, his leadership qualities, his love of good times with good friends, and his irreverence and wit.

Examination success came quickly to the two older Yuan brothers. Yuan Zongdao took the *jinshi* degree in 1586 at the age of twenty-seven *sui*, and was the *optimus* (*zhuang yuan*, 狀元) for that year. Yuan Hongdao earned his provincial degree (*juren*, 舉人) in 1588 at the age of twenty-one *sui*, and the *jinshi* degree on his second try in 1592, aged twenty-five *sui*. Yuan Zhongdao experienced more disappointment than his two elder brothers, having to take each level of the examinations multiple times, and not earning the *jinshi* degree until 1616 at the age of forty-seven *sui*, well after the deaths of both Zongdao and Hongdao. As Benjamin Elman reports, however, this was far from unusual; many men spent all of their youth, most of their middle years, and even some of their senior years living the "examination life," failing again and again in a system that passed only a small fraction of the millions of men who sat for the examinations.[15] Against this background, the achievement of the two older brothers in attaining the *jinshi* (one as the *optimus*!) while still quite young is truly amazing, and even Zhongdao's relatively late success in the examination mill still constituted the fulfillment of a dream that eluded the vast majority of aspirants for a lifetime.

Along with academic success, the civil examination system also brought Yuan Hongdao to the attention of officials and intellectuals of empire-wide standing, including fellow examinees who themselves would soon achieve eminence. These were some of the most famous scholars and officials of the period, and their names figure prominently in all scholarly studies of the Buddhist "revival" of the period: Jiao Hong (焦竑, 1541–1620), Huang Hui (黃輝, dates unknown), and Tao Wangling (陶望齡, 1562–1609), all of whom earned the *jinshi* degree in the 1589 session. (Hongdao himself failed to place, and had to wait until 1592 to earn his degree.)

It was also during the years spent in the capital that all three Yuan brothers developed an interest in Buddhism. After Yuan Zongdao attained the *jinshi* degree in 1586, he was appointed to the Hanlin Academy (Hanlin yuan, 翰林院) as a compiler (*taishi*, 太史, or *bianxiu*, 編修). Since he now had a house in the capital, both his brothers moved in with him to facilitate their preparation for the metropolitan examinations. Between 1589 and 1592, as the Yuan brothers gathered with Jiao, Huang, Tao, and others, these men introduced the Yuans to Buddhist ideas and literature. They were certainly in step with the times. The gentry had a high degree of interest in Buddhism during Yuan Hongdao's lifetime, a phenomenon that has been called a "Buddhist revival" (*fojiao fuxing*, 佛教復興) by scholars in both Chinese and Western literature. While this label is a bit misleading, implying as it does a prior decline in Buddhism, it is certainly undeniable that there was an increased interest in Buddhism among the gentry at this time, expressed in an explosion of books and pamphlets.

Beginning in 1589, Jiao Hong and Qu Ruji (瞿汝稷) gave Yuan Zongdao his first lessons in Buddhism and advised him to read the *Recorded Sayings of Dahui Zonggao* (*Dahui pujue chanshi yulu*, 大慧普覺禪師語錄, T. 1998A) and the *Recorded Sayings of Chan Master Tianmu Mingben* (*Tianmu Mingben chanshi zalu*, 天目明本禪師雜錄, *Xu zang jing* 122: 724–802). Again, this is consonant with trends among the literati at the time. Among the most popular topics and texts were those of Huayan and Chan—within Chan, Dahui Zonggao and his practice of "contemplation of the phrase" Chan (*kanhua chan*, 看話禪) reigned. As Chün-fang Yü points out, Dahui Zonggao believed strongly in the compatibility of Confucianism and Buddhism, and many of his students and patrons were literati and government officials.[16] Thus late Ming literati could imagine that Dahui's writings were meant for them.

Later in 1589, Zongdao requested permission to return to Gongan, and Hongdao, having failed the examination, went with him. Back home, they began poring through their newly acquired Chan works, and in his later memoirs, Yuan Zhongdao recounted how they spent their days studying and discussing their reading, forgetting to eat or sleep, as if drunk or ill. However, they also felt frustration at their own lack of comprehension, until one day they achieved a breakthrough so dramatic that all three brothers recorded the event in later writings. The passage that evoked their awakening came from the *Jingshan Gao chanshi fasi* (徑山杲禪師法嗣, *Dharma-lineage of Chan Master* [*Zong*]*gao of Jing Mountain*, fascicle 32). Here is the passage:

> [Da]hui said, "You officials know only that there is 'the investigation of things'; you do not know that there is 'the investigation by things.'" The official (Zhang Zishao [張子韶, 1092–1159]) was utterly nonplussed, and [Da]hui gave a great laugh. The official said, "Can the master give some instruction?" [Da]hui said, "Haven't you seen what was written in a novel? During the Tang dynasty there were some people who turned traitor with the rebel An Lushan, chief among them being Lang Shou. Now there was a painting, and when Minghuang Xingshu (i.e., Emperor Xuanzong) saw it, he flew into a rage, and ordered a courtier to take a sword and cut the image's head off. At the time, Lang Shou was in Shaanxi, and his own head suddenly fell off." The official heard this [story] and instantly grasped its profound meaning, and he inscribed this on the wall of a parked carriage: "Zishao investigates things, Miaoxi (i.e., Dahui) is investigated by things. If you wish to recognize the single thread, you'll need two five hundreds."[17] [Da]hui began giving his approval.

In commenting on this much later in his life, Yuan Hongdao wrote:

> Question: When Miaoxi said that officials only know to investigate things, but do not know to be investigated by things, what did he mean? Answer: this "investigation of things and investigation by things" is like the proverb, "I want to hit others, but I will be hit by them." People today exhaust their lives with minds desiring only to use up others without others using them up. How would this not be like being investigated by things?[18]

While Zhou Qun doubts that we can ever be sure what kind of enlightenment this passage evoked in the three Yuan brothers,[19] I believe that, based on recurrent themes in his later writings, we can make a good guess. This passage, written in 1604, shows that the story of Dahui and the official reflects themes that Yuan Hongdao still considered important fifteen years after it brought about his awakening. His later preoccupation with harmonizing all his areas of study, with Huayan teachings of the absolute non-obstruction of things and with Three Teachings thought, shows that this passage evoked his first vision of integration and interfusion. The Neo-Confucian idea of the "investigation of things" implied that a knowing subject learned about objects that remained static and had effected no change in his or her own mind. Dahui Zonggao's answer showed that engaging with the world as a knowing subject was not a one-way action but a two-way interaction, and that the world acted upon the subject as much as the subject appropriated the world.

Yuan Hongdao did not learn his Chan solely from texts and friends, however. At roughly the same time, he encountered the man who would be his master for the next ten years: the notorious official, writer, Chan practitioner, and acerbic social critic Li Zhi (李贄, 1527–1602). The two met in 1591 when Yuan Hongdao went to pay a visit to the old man in his hermitage at Dragon Lake (Long hu, 龍湖) near Macheng (麻城). Yuan was in awe of this elder statesman of layman's Chan, and Li had already read some of Yuan's writings with appreciation, so at their first meeting they each felt they had found a kindred spirit. Yuan stayed with Li for three months, and the two exchanged poems when Yuan finally set out for home.[20] After earning the *jinshi* degree in the palace examinations of 1592, Yuan went again to visit Li in 1593 prior to assuming his first official post, and they again exchanged ideas and poems.[21] Li had a great impact on Yuan's intellectual development on all fronts, from his coming literary innovations to his Chan thought, but the men would break their relationship ten years later when Yuan began turning to a form of Pure Land practice of which Li did not approve.

This awakening to the Chan of Dahui and Li Zhi was not the only significant event in Yuan's incipient Buddhist thought, however. In 1591, another event took place that impacted all three brothers, to the extent that both Hongdao and younger brother Zhongdao both wrote about it. A translation of Yuan Hongdao's account appeared in 1978 in Jonathan Chaves' *Pilgrim of the Clouds*, so here it is in Chaves' rendition:

> My friend Fang said: "I have heard the monks of Cloud Perch (i.e., Yunqi) Temple assert that if one recites Buddha's name, one may achieve birth in the Pure Land. Is this true?"
>
> I replied: "Yes. Without going into all the written accounts, let me just refer to cases I have experienced myself. Deng, the second son of my older brother Boxiu (i.e., Yuan Zongdao), became terminally ill at the age of twelve. He himself knew he had no hope of living. When he was on the point of dying, he spoke to me tearfully: 'I will die today. Is there any way to save me?' I answered: 'If you only recite Buddha's name, you will immediately be reborn in Buddha's land. The present world, with its Five Ages of Decay, is not worth yearning for. Just concentrate on Buddha with one mind and all will be well.'

> "I then had my nephew chant Buddha's name while holding the palms of his hands together in an attitude of devotion. The entire family stood around him in a circle, praising Buddha in rich tones. After a while, my nephew smiled slightly and said: 'I see a lotus flower, the color of earth, but slightly reddish.' He then continued to chant. After some more time, he suddenly spoke of the extreme brilliance of the lotus, which he said was incomparably superior to any in this world, and was now bigger than before. Still another period of time—and suddenly, he said that Buddha had arrived, the radiance of his features filling the entire room! A little later he said that there was an impure person in the room, whose presence had caused the lotus and Buddha to disappear. Boxiu looked around and noticed that a maidservant, who had just arrived, was standing in front of the folding screen. This girl, as it happened, had just had her period that evening, so Boxiu called to her to leave and had the other people encircle his son and chant Buddha's name as before. The boy then grew short of breath, and Boxiu said: 'If you just recite one character of my name, that will be enough.' The boy asked me: 'Is that all right?' and I replied: 'Yes.' But when he had chanted a few syllables more, he died, still holding his palms together."[22]

From this we see that even as he was having his first breakthroughs in Chan thought, Yuan Hongdao was also deeply touched by the efficacy of simple Pure Land practice.

In 1594, Yuan Hongdao took his first official post as magistrate of Wu County (吳縣), and went to live in Hangzhou. At this point, his life was following the most ideal script imaginable for a young man of this time. He had attained the *jinshi* degree at the age of twenty-four, and so was free of the "examination life" that bedeviled most men for decades. He had been admitted into the ranks of the government bureaucracy, and had even been posted to an urbane and prosperous area that could satisfy his craving for high culture and scenic vistas, rather than to a distant backwater. He affected a certain worldly disdain for official life, but he performed admirably as magistrate and earned the respect and love of the people there.[23]

However, he chafed under the ceaseless duties of a county magistrate, and began asking for permission to resign the following year. He finally received permission in 1597, but rather than face his father's censure for having interrupted a promising career, he went to a temporary residence in Jiangsu province with his family. From there, he did all the things he liked to do: take tours of scenic spots, write, read books, drink wine, entertain friends, and discuss philosophy. It was at this time that he had another experience that would draw him into Pure Land thought: he met with the eminent monk Yunqi Zhuhong (雲棲袾宏, 1535–1615), later honored as the eighth "patriarch" of the Pure Land tradition.

In 1597, on a pleasure expedition to the south with his friend Tao Wangling, Yuan went to the Yunqifa Temple under Five Cloud Mountain (Wuyun shan, 五雲山), where he spent time with Zhuhong. In his travel notes, he gave this assessment of Zhuhong's teaching:

> [Master] Lianchi (i.e., Zhuhong) keeps the *śīla* and *vinaya* meticulously, and although one could not say that he is most profound in the Way, neither is he lacking in what he has seen. As for his sole advocacy of the dharma-gate of *nianfo,* it is very direct, fast, and simple. Within those six words (i.e., *Namo A-mi-tuo-fo,* 南無阿彌陀佛) one turns heaven and earth. Why work so hard, rubbing one's eyes and moving even more toward crazy interpretations? Such being the case, one could say that Lianchi is "one without enlightenment," [but] this "one without enlightenment" is a real Amitābha; please go quickly to see him.[24]

In this quotation, one can see a premonition of Yuan's eventual turn toward Pure Land in his expression of admiration for Zhuhong's sole advocacy of *nianfo.* Yuan Hongdao also gave special praise to Zhuhong in an essay translated by Jonathan Chaves, where he lists the things he likes about Zhuhong. Interestingly, one is that Zhuhong, known to his contemporaries as a staunch advocate of compassion toward animals and the practice of "releasing life" (*fang sheng,* 放生), did not carp at Yuan for ordering his servant to cook meat right in Zhuhong's chamber.[25]

Two years later, Yuan lauded Zhuhong in the last fascicle of the *Xifang helun* in a passage that shows he had read the latter's *Commentary and Notes on the Shorter Sukhāvatī-sūtra* (阿彌陀經疏鈔, *Xu zang jing* 33: 326–491) prior to writing the *Xifang helun.*[26] Zhuhong thus had an influence on Yuan's Pure Land thinking. Zhuhong's *Commentary and Notes* had taken the concept of the "one mind of suchness" (*zhenru yi xin,* 真如一心) from the *Awakening of Mahayana Faith* and the idea of "clear and pure mind-only" (*qingjing weixin,* 清淨惟心) to come up with his "single, unperturbed mind" (*yi xin bu luan,* 一心不亂), a concept that made Pure Land practice a bit closer to Chan in its goals. Yuan Hongdao incorporated this concept from Zhuhong's text, and also found a way to connect Huayan thought with Pure Land's mythology and practice, as we shall see.[27]

Running out of money in 1598, he returned to the environs of Beijing to become a teacher, and during this time he formed the famous "Grape Society" (Putao she, 葡萄社), a literary club in which he advanced his innovative ideas about poetry composition and which included many of the most eminent literary figures of the time. During this period, his career got back on track: Yuan was appointed a teacher in the imperial academy, and the following year he was made the head of the Bureau of

Ceremonies (Yizhi qingli si, 儀制清吏司) within the Board of Rites.[28] Being in the center of intellectual activity, in a position that allowed him more leisure time, his work became more scholarly. He published a long essay on the *Zhuangzi* (莊子), and began delving into the great poets of the Song dynasty, allowing them to influence his own poetry. In the winter of 1599 he spent two months doing the research and writing for his major statement of Pure Land thought, the *Xifang helun.* He broke with Li Zhi by the end of the decade, feeling that in his devotion to "crazy Chan" (*kuang chan,* 狂禪), Li had failed to realize that enlightenment and practice were two sides of the same coin, and so had neglected religious cultivation. This, Yuan came to realize, represented a religious dead end.[29] However, the common assumption that Yuan Hongdao "converted" from Chan to Pure Land in 1599 turns out to be suspect when one examines his later writings. We shall examine the reasons for this suspicion shortly.

In 1600 life in the capital became less comfortable. The court was in constant turmoil due to the ineffectiveness of the Wanli emperor, the usurpation of power by palace eunuchs, and the strident efforts of "upright scholars" to set things right. The Grape Society came under attack from a prominent conservative official,[30] and Yuan Hongdao commented bitterly on the corruptions of the court in a letter to a friend.[31] When his younger brother Zhongdao failed the palace examinations in that year, all three of the Yuan brothers asked for permission to return home. Once there, Hongdao's older brother Zongdao died suddenly toward the end of the year. In response to all these developments, Yuan petitioned the court for permission to resign from office, bought some property in his native Gongan County on which he built a hermitage called "Willow Wave" (Liu lang, 柳浪),[32] adopted a vegetarian diet, and embarked on a six-year period of seclusion.

During this time, he frequently entertained his surviving brother Zhongdao, several friends both religious and literary, and many eminent monks. He composed poetry, continued to practice Chan, and went boating for recreation. One of the puzzles of this period following his composition of the *Xifang helun* is that, having apparently gotten Pure Land thought out of his system, he never returned to the subject again. The writings that date from this period largely dwell on the same themes that he explored prior to 1599. Nevertheless, because of the *Xifang helun,* Chinese Buddhist literati have always remembered him primarily as a hero of Pure Land thought.[33]

Events continued to move around Yuan. In 1602 word came that his old teacher Li Zhi had been arrested and imprisoned, and had slit his own throat rather than go on trial. The rift that had grown between the men three years earlier must have been severe; while all the other members of Yuan's circle, now recognized as the "Gongan school" of poetry, memorialized Li or helped to edit his collected works, Yuan did and said nothing to mark his former mentor's passing. The following year, Yuan Zhongdao finally passed the Shuntian provincial examinations in third place, and so won his *juren* (舉人) degree with distinction. He would not win his *jinshi* degree until after Hongdao's death.

By 1606, Yuan's letters indicate that he had grown a bit bored with the life of seclusion, and at any rate his father continued to urge him to resuscitate his public career. Thus, Yuan returned to Beijing to resume his post at the Board of Rites (which necessitated renouncing his vow of vegetarianism). While it seemed a return to his old life, many things had changed. His older brother and many members of the old Grape Society had passed away, while others were posted elsewhere. He was now an elder statesman among younger bureaucrats just starting their careers. In the autumn of that year, his wife passed away. In 1607, he was promoted to the position of Head of the Bureau of Honors (Yanfeng zhu, 驗封主) in the Ministry of Personnel (Li bu, 吏部), a job he found much more tense and demanding. His poetry at this time describes his sense of impermanence and change, of "countenances that gradually wither and decay" and "kindness and love that daily melt away."[34]

No longer the hotheaded tyro chafing under the tedium of discharging public responsibilities, as he had been as magistrate of Wu County, Yuan was now a seasoned bureaucrat who did his job conscientiously and quietly. Given the corruption in the capital, he sometimes had to take a stand against the malfeasance of his colleagues and was praised by other upright people and despised by those he openly impeached. He took his last official assignment in 1609 when he was sent to supervise the provincial examinations in Shaanxi province. He again did his job thoroughly, reading all the examination papers himself, even if preliminary readers had rejected them. True to his literary theory of direct expression, he rejected papers that depended upon style to hide a lack of substance and rewarded those that stated their case with directness and simplicity. He also took the opportunity to satisfy his craving for fine landscapes and visits with old friends while in the northwest.

When he had completed his duties in Shaanxi, he felt unwell and asked for leave to return home for a while. Finding Willow Wave under water due to heavy rains, he stayed as a guest at a friend's house. His health deteriorated rapidly, and he passed away on the sixth day of the ninth month of Wanli 38 (1610), just two days after his second wife gave birth to a son. He was forty-two years old.

This biographical sketch gives some indication of the breadth of his accomplishment. While in this chapter we are concerned primarily with his Pure Land thought, a look through his *Collected Works,* the manuscript collections now in archives in China and Japan, and his works compiled in the Buddhist canon, we see that he distinguished himself in several areas. He was a conscientious and much-loved administrator for the state. He was a highly influential (and controversial) poet and literary critic. He was an active participant in all the currents of philosophical and religious thought, writing comments and original essays on Buddhism, Daoism, and Neo-Confucianism, often relating one to the other in a way that put him into the stream of Three Teachings thought (though he paid far less attention to Daoism than others in this stream, and was never a formal adherent of the Three Teachings school). In addition to the *Xifang helun,* his literary remains include poems, "short essays" (*xiao pin wen,* 小品文), travelogues, a county gazetteer (now lost), prefaces, memorials, comments on Buddhist texts, civil examination questions and reports, and a great many letters. This is important, because to see him strictly as a Pure Land thinker, as later Chinese authors did, is to miss his complexities and the way in which he truly was a product of the exuberant literary, philosophical, religious, and cultural milieu of the Wanli period, a period that coincided closely with his life and death.[35]

But it is his Pure Land thought that will concern us here, and we now turn our attention to its expression in the *Xifang helun.*

Yuan Hongdao's Contributions to Pure Land Thought

Introduction to the *Xifang helun* and Its Significance

Yuan Hongdao has been remembered within Chinese Buddhist circles exclusively for his contributions to Pure Land thought and practice. Indeed, the most ambitious work still extant is his *Xifang helun* (*Comprehensive Treatise on the West*) in ten *juan* (卷). The fact that he completed the research and writing in only two months indicates that Hongdao worked on it at a rapid pace.[36] This work was enormously influential within Chinese Buddhist circles, as may be seen from the following five observations:

First, Ouyi Zhixu (蕅益智旭, 1599–1655), the last of the "four great monks" of the late Ming period and later honored as the ninth "patriarch" (*zu*, 祖) of the Pure Land tradition, selected the *Xifang helun* for inclusion in his anthology *Jingtu shi yao* (淨土十要, *Ten Essential* [*Texts*] *of the Pure Land*). Zhixu also wrote a special preface for it in which he praised it highly, saying "every word flows from the gate of authentic enlightenment," and criticized it mildly only for not showing a high enough regard for Tiantai thought.[37]

Second, a patron commissioned the painter Chen Hongshou (陳洪, 1598–1652) to portray the completion and initial public presentation of the *Xifang helun* in a painting, completed in 1646 or 1647. The painting, called *Elegant Gathering* (*Yaji tu*, 雅集圖), is now in the Shanghai Museum of Art.[38]

Third, the *Xifang helun* made it very quickly into a late-Ming/early-Qing anthology of Buddhist texts, the *Jiaxing da zang jing* (嘉興大藏經), whose compilation was begun in 1579 by the monk Zibo Zhenke (紫柏真可, 1543–1603) even before Yuan wrote the *Xifang helun*, and was completed in 1677.[39] These first three events reflect the very rapid acceptance of this text as authoritative within Buddhist circles.

Fourth, in later works that give biographies of Yuan Hongdao and his two brothers, the *Xifang helun* is the only composition mentioned by name, and his dubious "conversion" from Chan to Pure Land is portrayed as the defining moment of his life, in spite of the fact that the biography of Hongdao by his younger brother Zhongdao clearly lists his other works.[40]

Finally, the modern Chinese mainland scholar Guo Peng (郭朋), in his 1982 study of Buddhism in the Ming and Qing periods, devoted only five pages to Pure Land Buddhism in the Ming. Only two pages deal with the contribution of Yunqi Zhuhong; the remaining three focus on Yuan Hongdao and the *Xifang helun*.[41]

Thus, from the generation that followed right after Yuan Hongdao's death to the modern period, we see evidence that the Chinese Buddhist and scholarly communities have valued this text as a key part of China's Pure Land legacy. In spite of this, it remains largely unknown among Western academics.

Yuan's Purpose, Method, and Sources for the *Xifang helun*

In his preface to the work, Yuan explains that its purpose is to counter the overwhelming influence of the "crazy Chan" of the day, which he says ensnared him for ten years before he discovered Pure Land.[42] The problem, as he saw it, was that teachings on emptiness (*kong*, 空) and the critique of all practices as grasping that can be found in many Chan writings had become too dominant, crowding out more conventional teachings about the need for taking and keeping precepts, the reality of the goal of buddhahood, and, above all, the efficacy of the main Pure Land practice of *nianfo.* He admitted that such Chan teachings were necessary in order to cure some ills. However, to use a simile, water is useful for putting out fires, but if one applies too much water, then one causes a flood.[43] Teachings on emptiness and the provisional nature of Buddhist practice, in his estimation, had been overapplied and, like the water, were now causing problems. Therefore, he wrote the *Xifang helun* to bring balance back into the Buddhist scene.

Yuan's method of correcting the excesses of his day benefited from the highly developed state that the Pure Land tradition had reached in China by the late Ming. As Yuan explains in his preface, once he had embraced Pure Land, he began reading widely to educate himself in Pure Land thought, and he no doubt discovered what a variegated and complex literary tradition it had become by 1599. In the preface, he brings up four authors whose works he "recited solemnly" (*lisong*, 禮誦): Nāgārjuna, Tiantai [Zhiyi], Li Tongxuan, and Yongming Yanshou. These works, he said, "eliminated his doubts all at once."[44] But in addition to eliciting his faith in Pure Land and clearing away his qualms, these works also doubtless impressed him with the wide variety of beliefs and practices that they presented on a broad spectrum of topics related to Pure Land: the nature of the Pure Land, the relationship between the Buddha and the worldling, the practices that enable one to attain rebirth, and so on. The literature he read spanned one and a half millennia and two cultures, and the need to systematize and harmonize them must have struck him keenly.

Even a partial list of the works cited within the *Xifang helun* will show how widely read Yuan was at the time he composed it, and how diverse were the points of view he encountered:

Da zhidu lun (大智度論, T. 1509)[45]
Vimalakīrtinirdeśa-sūtra (維摩詰所說經, T. 475)
Lotus Sutra (妙法蓮華經, T. 262)
Awakening of Mahayana Faith (大般涅槃經, T. 1666)
Nirvana Sutra (大般涅槃經, T. 374)
Yangjuemoluo jing (央崛摩羅經, possibly a variant of T. 120 [央掘魔羅])
Fanwang jing (梵網經, T. 1484)
Pratyutpannasamādhi-sūtra (般舟三昧經, T. 417)
Questions about the Pure Land (淨土或問, T. 1972), by Tianru (天如)
Jingtu jingguan yaomen (淨土境觀要門, T. 1971)
Amituo jing tong zanshu (阿彌陀經通贊疏, T. 1758), by Kuiji (窺基)

Zongjing lu (宗鏡錄》(T. 2016), by Yongming Yanshou (永明延壽)
Treatise on the Mass of Doubts [*about the Pure Land*] (群疑論, T. 1960)
Daśabhūmika-śāstra (十住毘婆沙論, T. 1521), attributed to Nāgārjuna
Jiujing yisheng baoxing lun (究竟一乘寶性論, T. 1611)
Fozang jing (佛藏經, T. 653)
Mohe zhiguan (摩訶止觀, T. 1911), by Zhiyi
Wanshan tonggui ji (萬善同歸集, T. 2017), by Yongming Yanshou
Guan wuliangshou fo jing shu miao zong chao (觀無量壽佛經疏妙宗鈔, T. 1751), by Zhil
Treatise on Ten Doubts about the Pure Land (淨土十疑論, T. 1961), by Zhiyi
Commentary on the New Huayan Sutra (略釋新華嚴經修行次第決疑論, T. 1741), by Li Tongxuan
The Doctrine of the Mean (中庸)
The Analects (論語)

This is not an exhaustive list, but still shows how extensively Yuan cast his net. I should also point out that of all the works listed above, the one from which Yuan quotes most frequently is the *Da zhidu lun*.[46] This wide-ranging list also gave him the resources he needed to counter some of the more philosophical criticisms of Pure Land, such as charges that it fostered dualistic thinking, or that it violated Buddhist understandings of the relation of the one to the many.

Yuan's purpose in writing this text, then, was clearly apologetic, a point that will be made even more clear as we review its contents. However, as we consider the meaning of the title in the next section, we will see that Yuan did not simply intend to defend Pure Land in such a way as to seek a clear victory for it and a defeat for its detractors. His real intention was to put Pure Land into conversation with its critics in order to benefit both and fashion a more integrated Buddhist practice. Let us turn to his own explanation of the title and see.

The Title and Contents of the *Xifang helun*

The title of the text, *Xifang helun*, is actually a bit difficult to render into English because Yuan Hongdao intended it to be evocative rather than semantic in its effect. That is to say, he did not compose the title to be descriptive but to bring to mind associations of at least two kinds. The first evocation calls to mind the Huayan (華嚴) tradition. Yuan Hongdao read deeply in both the *Huayan Sutra* and in the work of its famous Tang dynasty commentator, Li Tongxuan (李通玄, 635–730). Li wrote a commentary on the "new translation" of the *Huayan Sutra* shortly after it appeared, and some time after that, his commentary was folded into the scripture itself and published under the title *Huayan jing helun* (華嚴經合論).[47] The title was clearly intended to indicate that the sutra was joined (*he*, 合) to its commentary (*lun*, 論), but Yuan's work lacks any such framework. Yuan evidently wanted the title to create an association between his text and Li's text, but not to reflect the *Xifang helun*'s actual content and structure.

Second, Yuan himself commented on the significance of the title in his later work, the *Shanhu lin*. Here he says:

> In that book *Xifang helun*, I made use of Pure Land in order to expound Chan. Because those who talk about Chan do not consider Pure Land worthwhile, and those who cultivate Pure [Land] do not expend any effort on Chan, I brought them together and discussed them.[48]

This statement will be very significant later when we assess Yuan Hongdao's religious orientation, but for now we will simply note the light it sheds on both the title and the purpose of the book. Yuan evidently intended it to convey the sense that the book represented a joint discussion of many issues under the general rubric "Pure Land." As noted at the end of the last section, it also indicates that Yuan's purpose was not to mount arguments in favor of Pure Land to defeat or displace Chan, but to initiate a conversation between the two that could improve the practice of the latter and correct its followers' excesses. Any English translation of the title will, therefore, be somewhat arbitrary, and so we leave it untranslated in this chapter.

Now to the contents: Within each fascicle, Yuan discusses discrete topics under various headings, making use of various methods. In some sections, he does almost nothing but provide citations from sutras and treatises, while in others, he writes original essays with almost no citations from authoritative texts. In these latter instances, he uses his own reasoning, exhortations to practice, and anecdotes from his own interactions with Buddhist clergy and laity to make his points.

The text consists of ten fascicles (*juan*):

Fascicle 1: On Buddha Lands (第一刹土門)

In this fascicle, Yuan attempts to systematize various understandings of any land that a fully enlightened buddha inhabits, not just Amitābha's Pure Land in the west. He begins at the most abstract level, drawing on Huayan thought to explain the land inhabited by the Buddha Vairocana.

At this level of understanding, one sees no distinctions between anything whatsoever. Vairocana pervades all things, so there is no "buddha" and "buddha land." Following this, Yuan explains concepts of the Pure Land as found in various scriptures, such as "mind-only Pure Land" (*weixin jingtu*, 惟心淨土) as found in the *Vimalakīrti-sūtra*, and "manifesting-by-transformation pure land" (*bian xian jingtu*, 變現淨土) found in the *Lotus Sutra*. He proceeds in this vein so that the reader gains a sense of the wide variety of ways in which the relationships between buddhas, buddha lands, impure beings, and impure lands may be conceived. However, in the tenth category, "the inconceivable pure land that receives sentient beings of the ten directions" (*sheshou shifang yiqie youqing bukesiyi jingtu*, 攝受十方一切有情不可思議淨土), he returns to a Huayan understanding of total integration, but this time centered on Amitābha's Pure Land rather than Vairocana's. Amitābha's Western Pure Land, unlike Vairocana's rather abstruse land, contains particular features, such as birds that preach the dharma and jeweled trees. These exemplify, as opposed to merely assert, the relationship between the particular and the universal, and so by encompassing both poles instead of just one, Amitābha's Pure Land is superior to Vairocana's.

Fascicle 2: On Conditioned Origination (第二緣起門)

This fascicle explains the human predicament and its cure. The first section describes the lives of unenlightened beings as a mass of suffering, and the following sections explain how and why salvation from this situation is possible. For example, section 7, "On Superior Expedient Means" ("*Sheng fangbianzhe*," 勝方便者), explains why it is that even a single recitation of Amitābha's name can bring about effects wholly out of proportion to the devotee's own effort. Yuan stresses that this practice is not something that the practitioner does alone; indeed, the power of the practice belongs primarily to Amitābha, manifesting in the practice. Yuan uses several metaphors to illustrate this. One is the reed sail of a boat that enables the boat to transport a heavy cargo. The reed sail itself has no power, but it is a device that makes use of the great power of the wind.[49] In this example, the reed sail is the devotee's recitation of the name, and Amitābha's power to save is the wind. Yuan also deals with many commonly raised objections to Pure Land in this fascicle, such as: Why should a new bodhisattva want to go to the Pure Land rather than remain in the world to do good? Since beings are inherently enlightened, why should they want to go to a Pure Land to "become" a buddha? Why should literate people engage in a practice that is really just for the ignorant masses? Yuan responds to these objections and challenges his literate readers to take up Pure Land practice.

Fascicle 3: On Sections and Categories (第三部類門)

This fascicle arranges Buddhist scriptures into four categories depending upon their emphasis (or lack of emphasis) on the Pure Land and the practice of *nianfo.* The four categories are described in terms of the metaphor of warp and weft threads on a weaving loom: first, the warp within the warp (經中之經), meaning scriptures whose exclusive or main theme is the story of Amitābha and his Pure Land and which discuss it extensively; second, the weft within the warp (經中之緯), indicating works that discuss Pure Land topics to the exclusion of others but are short and incomplete; third, the warp within the weft (緯中之經), meaning scriptures that discuss Pure Land topics but include other subjects as well, such as the *Huayan Sutra,* the *Lotus Sutra,* and the *Śūraṅgama-sūtra,* among many others; and, fourth, the weft within the weft (緯中之緯), or scriptures and texts that make only passing references to Pure Land topics and thus contribute nothing of substance to one's understanding or practice.

Fascicle 4: On Doctrinal Characteristics (第四教相門)

Within this section, Yuan sets forth a scheme of doctrinal classification (*panjiao,* 判教) very similar to that established by Fazang for the Huayan school. This scheme includes six categories: the pure teaching of existence (*chun you jiao,* 純有教), the teachings that lead to quiescence (*qu ji jiao,* 趨寂教), the incomplete teaching (lit., "teaching with remainder," *you yu jiao,* 有餘教), the complete teaching (lit., "teaching without remainder," *wu yu jiao,* 無餘教), the teaching of sudden enlightenment (*dun wu jiao,* 頓悟教), and the ultimate teaching (*yuan ji jiao,* 圓極教). Very quickly, the first five outline a graded path for practitioners of varying capacities. The first is simple ethical teachings for those mired in bad habits; the second is the Hinayana teachings; the third represents a proto-Mahayana that realizes the emptiness of both persons and phenomena, but lacks compassion as it denies the capability of *icchantika*s, *śrāvaka*s, and *pratyekabuddha*s to attain full buddhahood, showing that it does not understand the truth of universal buddha-nature. (This clearly represents the Faxiang [法相] school.) The fourth appears to correspond to Tiantai (天台), since it recognizes the One Mind in all things, but the section is too brief to be certain of this. The fifth is related explicitly to the Chan school, but Yuan concludes the section by saying that Pure Land in some form qualifies here as well. The sixth and final section is very long, and goes to great lengths to show that no matter what standard one uses to determine the matter, Pure Land teaching represents the highest truth of Buddhism. It also makes great use of Huayan thought to press its points. For example, Yuan says that because Amitābha is an emanation of Vairocana, he can both be located in the Pure Land and pervade everywhere, because all the lands of the ten directions are but a single realm of wisdom.[50] This shows that Pure Land practice not only does not conflict with the highest philosophy within Chinese Buddhism but positively depends upon it to work. In this way, Pure Land can be the highest teaching because it puts abstract philosophical notions into concrete operation.

Fascicle 5: On Principle and Truth (第五理諦門)

In this fascicle, Yuan delineates a way of looking at ultimate reality that both accords with the most profound insights of Buddhist thought and allows the reader to understand how Pure Land practice can work without violating them. This fascicle has four sections: the "characteristics [of all things] are this very mind" gate (*ji xiang ji xin men*, 即相即心門), the "this very mind is the characteristics [of all things]" gate (*ji xin ji xiang men*, 即心即相門), the "neither mind nor characteristics" gate (*fei xin fei xiang men*, 非心非相門), and the "neither 'is' nor 'is not'" gate (*li ji li fei men*, 離即離非門). I will present only the argument of the fourth section here to illustrate Yuan's way of thinking.

In this fascicle, Yuan discusses the relationship between the devotee's practice and the Buddha's power. He begins by quoting Zhiyi, who says that the relationship is mysterious and inconceivable; one cannot pin it down by saying that the practice is effective because of the Buddha's power, the devotee's power, both together, or neither. Yuan illustrates the point with two metaphors. He notes that a certain kind of tree produces a flower when it comes in contact with a woman, and repeats a belief that an elephant's tusk produces a flower when thunder sounds. The tree has no eyes, the tusk has no ears, and yet somehow they detect and respond to the woman and the thunder in a way that cannot be explained. All dharmas are inconceivable, and one can never fully understand how causes produce effects. However, this does not mean that the effects are not produced. Thus, one may perform *nianfo* even as an unenlightened being who does not know the true nature of the world as mind-only, or of the Pure Land as empty, or of the Buddha's *dharmakāya* as free from all characteristics (the main points of the preceding three sections, which I have not summarized). The effect, whether a vision of the Buddha in this life or rebirth in the Pure Land in the next, still comes about.

In all four sections of this fascicle, Yuan is pursuing his apologetic task. For centuries, critics had castigated Pure Land advocates for their lack of understanding and their dualistic views. Here, Yuan turns the tables and shows that it is the critics who have only a partial understanding of Buddhist truth. If they really understood the principles of mind-only, emptiness, and the two truths, then they would see that the Pure Land, like any other phenomenon that appears to the deluded mind, is provisional, but not by that token false. If it were true that one needed to awaken to reality before one could be saved, then this would lead to the conundrum that one would have to be able to adopt the fully enlightened viewpoint before being enlightened—a vicious circle, in Yuan's estimation. The Buddha, however, knows how to make use of the delusions of the unenlightened in order to move them in the right direction, and thus Pure Land shows how all can be liberated from suffering and ignorance by the Buddha's use of expedient teachings.

Fascicle 6: On Pointing to the Nature (第六稱性門)

This fascicle is concerned with issues of practice in accordance with a Pure Land understanding, and consists of five sections: "Practicing the Mind of Faith" (*"Xinxin xing,"* 信心行), "Practicing Meditation" (*"Zhiguan xing,"* 止觀行), "Practicing the Six Perfections" (*"Liudu xing,"* 六度行), "Practicing the Compassionate Vows" (*"Beiyuan xing,"* 悲願行), and "Practicing in Accordance with Dharmas" (*"Chengfa xing,"* 稱法行). However, Yuan does not exclude the apologetic task from his exhortations to a full program of Buddhist practice. Once again responding to the charge that Pure Land thought and practice lack sophistication and are only for the simpleminded masses, he explains how Pure Land fulfills the three contemplations of the Tiantai:

> As for the three contemplations existing in the word *nian,* one repetition of the buddha's name leads to the penetration of the reciting subject's substance being empty and the recited object being without characteristics. This means that the recitation includes the "contemplation of emptiness." The buddha that is recited (or contemplated) is the *sambhogakāya,* meaning that the mind breaks through the delusions of views and thoughts. Even though the substance of the reciting subject is empty and the object of recitation has no characteristics, this does not prevent the subject from discriminating the appearance of the object. Thus, recitation includes the "contemplation of the provisional." The buddha being recited (or contemplated) is a reward body, meaning that the mind has broken through the delusions of sense perception. Right at the moment that the subject and object are empty, the

> subject and object appear. Right at the moment that the subject and object appear, the subject and object are quiescent. Therefore "emptiness" and "the provisional" mutually co-inhere, and recitation includes the "contemplation of the middle."[51]

In a similar vein, he also shows how the practice of *nianfo* fulfills all the six perfections. In all the sections of this fascicle, Yuan demonstrates that even a simple person who recites Amitābha's name orally, while pursuing a program of morality and compassion in daily life, accords with Buddhism's most profound insight automatically.

Fascicle 7: On Attaining Rebirth (第七往生門)

The seventh fascicle takes up the subject of rebirth in various realms as a result of religious cultivation. The problem Yuan faces here is that different scriptures present vows and practices that lead to rebirths in places other than Amitābha's Western Pure Land, such as another human rebirth, rebirth in one of the heavens of the formless realm, rebirth in Tuṣita Heaven with Maitreya, or rebirth in another buddha's buddha land. Yuan brings up these alternatives and tells why each is an inferior destination compared to Amitābha's Pure Land. For example, some Buddhists vow to take rebirth in Tuṣita Heaven where Bodhisattva Maitreya is awaiting his final rebirth. This is defective because it is not really a pure land, only a conventional heaven within samsara. Those reborn there may not even find Maitreya, since the heaven is so immense, and they will be easily distracted by the pleasures of divine life and lose their resolve.[52]

The final two sections of this fascicle shift the focus somewhat. Yuan counsels all neophyte Buddhists to generate the true spirit of bodhisattva compassion in *bodhicitta,* the vow to attain full enlightenment in order to save all other sentient beings. While Yuan explores several side issues connected with this, such as the question of whether the attainment of buddhahood requires three incalculable eons or is instantaneous, in the end he declares that those who generate *bodhicitta* should immediately vow to be reborn in Amitābha's Western Pure Land, the "incubator" of all buddhas. As he says at the end of this fascicle:

> For this reason, a gentleman who arrives at awakening should decide to seek rebirth in the Pure Land and practice in accordance with the teachings. One avoids backsliding, waits until one's power of endurance is firm and solid, and then enters the world to benefit living beings. Because after all, only this is the fruit of buddhahood.[53]

Fascicle 8: On the Snares of [False] Views (第八見網門)

In this fascicle, Yuan explores ten types of misunderstanding that impede progress toward buddhahood or toward rebirth in the Pure Land. They are: the pitfall of annihilationism (*duanmie duo,* 斷滅墮), the pitfall of timidity caused by doubts (*qielie duo,* 怯劣墮), the pitfall of attachment to words (*suiyu duo,* 隨語墮), the pitfall of lunacy and lack of restraint (*kuangzi duo,* 狂恣墮), the pitfall of dilettantism (*zhili duo,* 支離墮), the pitfall of delusive emptiness (*chikong duo,* 癡空墮), the pitfall of [merely] following conditions (*suiyuan duo,* 隨緣墮), the pitfall of mind-only (*weixin duo,* 唯心墮), the pitfall of sudden enlightenment (*dunwu duo,* 頓悟墮), and the pitfall of perfect reality (*yuanshi duo,* 圓實墮). These are all very interesting for the way they shed light on Yuan Hongdao's perceptions of the contemporary Buddhist scene and its problems.

Of particular interest are the fourth and fifth sections, because in them we find Yuan's analysis of and objections to the "crazy Chan" tendencies of his day. The fourth pitfall, that of "lunacy and lack of restraint," seems to be aimed at Yuan's associates in Buddhist studies, Li Zhi in particular. He says:

> There are some who are devils who specialize in showing off "crazy wisdom." Unwilling to keep the precepts or engage in religious cultivation, they spout off quotations that sound scriptural such as "the vexations are wisdom" or "lewdness, anger, and ignorance are *brahma*-conduct." From words they produce an understanding, and from this understanding they produce poison.[54]

Evidently, the rationale for this is that one should not grasp at the concept of "guilt," because it is nondual with "no-guilt." Yuan opposes this with citations from both the *Da zhidu lun* and Yongming Yanshou's *Zongjing lu* (宗鏡錄) that condemn such attitudes and say that only at the highest levels of realization can one know when it is skillful to break precepts for the good of living beings. For all others, precepts and morality are absolutely essential for progress on the Way. He ends by quoting Nāgārjuna, who said, "A thousand days of study and understanding do not compare to one day of keeping the precepts."[55]

The fifth pitfall, that of "dilettantism" (lit., the "pitfall of fragmentation and scatteredness," 支離墮), can be quickly summarized by noting that it refers to people who glance through some scriptures and develop pride in their knowledge and abilities in debate without ever really putting their knowledge into action. In their pride they also disparage Pure Land practice, especially oral invocation of the Buddha's name.

Yuan recounts his own experiences in discussing Buddhism with clever monks and laypeople who had great pride in their knowledge and abilities but no real accomplishments in the Way. In Yuan's words, they suffer from "lecture-mat sickness" (講席之病). We note that this section contains far fewer quotations than other parts of his work, and appears to present his own account of the problems afflicting lay and monastic Buddhism in his day.

Fascicle 9: On Practice and Maintaining [Precepts] (第九脩持門)

This fascicle continues the presentation of the problems of late Ming Buddhism and Yuan's recommendations. Whereas most of the difficulties, or "pitfalls," of the last fascicle had to do with mistaken beliefs and misconstruals of Buddhist concepts, this one deals mostly with conduct. Yuan presents strongly worded recommendations that his readers take on the whole panoply of traditional Buddhist practice: generating faith, taking vows, receiving and keeping the precepts, finding a pure place to live and practice, consorting with pure companions, and the like.

Each of the fascicle's ten headings has an introduction of varying lengths, followed by a list of ten suggestions for implementation. Yuan's blueprint for the Buddhist life is very detailed and not easy to summarize, and so we will say only that it constitutes a very conventional set of practices and vows. However, one detail that is of interest, as it casts light on some possible ambivalence that Yuan felt toward his own lifestyle, is that in the seventh section, the "Gate of Pure Precepts" (*"Jingjie men,"* 淨戒門), Yuan specifically advises the reader to stay away from wine, women, and poetry gatherings. These are all pleasures that he enjoyed in abundance both before and after composing the *Xifang helun*. Was he expressing guilt over his inability to reform his own life, or was this intended as tongue-in-cheek? It is difficult to say.

Fascicle 10: On Explaining Discrepancies (第十釋異門)

The last fascicle of the *Xifang helun* brings the work to a close by discussing discrepancies between one Pure Land text and another on various points. There is no particular order to these questions, and one example will serve to show what Yuan seeks to accomplish here. The second question concerns the size of Amitābha Buddha's body and the size of the land in which he dwells. A certain scripture, the *Sheng wang jing* (聲王經),[56] describes the Pure Land as being a certain size, while the *Meditation Sutra* (觀無量壽佛經, T. 365) describes Amitābha's body as being so large that the whole land could not even hold one of his eyes if he were as large as the first scripture described him. Yuan settles this by appealing to a commentary called the *Haidong shu* (海東疏),[57] which says that Amitābha has many cities of different sizes to suit various sorts of denizens. One should not be too concerned about the size of the city.

Major Themes and Contributions of the *Xifang helun*

As it would require a lengthy monograph to explore all of the contents of the *Xifang helun,* we will examine only three themes here: first, how Yuan addresses criticisms of Pure Land from Chan partisans; second, Yuan's introduction of Huayan thought into the Pure Land tradition to elucidate the relationship of the ultimate to the provisional; and third, the question: Is this really a Pure Land text?

Addressing Chan criticisms. Yuan clearly intended the *Xifang helun* to serve an apologetic purpose. He was evidently quite concerned about the denigration of Pure Land that he encountered in Chinese Buddhist literature and heard firsthand from monks and friends. This kind of writing dates back to the very beginnings of Pure Land in China, as early authors such as Daochuo (道綽, 562–645), author of the *Anle ji* (安樂集, T. 1958), strove to answer various criticisms of Pure Land. By Yuan Hongdao's day, Pure Land thought had gone in two distinct directions that altered the conditions of the debate. The first, called "mind-only Pure Land," held that Amitābha and his Pure Land were constructions of the mind, and that, as the *Platform Sutra* and the *Vimalakīrti-sūtra* said, one needed only to purify one's own mind and realize one's own inherent buddha-nature, and the Pure Land, being nothing but the present world seen correctly, would manifest right then and there. This was the point of view espoused by Yuan's former Chan teacher Li Zhi in his work on Pure Land thought, the *Jingtu jue* (淨土決).[58] This conception of Pure Land practice was very easy to harmonize with Chan thought, and so provoked no challenge.

The other kind of Pure Land was called either "western-direction Pure Land" (*xifang jingtu,* 西方淨土) or "other-direction Pure Land" (*tafang jingtu,* 他方淨土). This type presented more of a problem for Chan thinkers and late Ming dynasty intellectuals. According to this stream of thought, the Pure Land and Amitābha Buddha really did exist outside of the believer's mind, and by either visualizing the Buddha or chanting his name, he would actually come to meet one at the moment of death and guide one to rebirth in the Pure Land. To critics, this entailed many kinds of dualism: pure versus impure, this *sahā* world versus the buddha land, Buddha versus worldling, and so on. It thus appeared to violate fundamental Mahayana thought. For example, the Chan school held to the idea that all beings inherently had buddha-nature, and so were already the equal of all buddhas. In addition, Huayan thought held that all things, times, and places mutually pervaded without obstruction (*shishi wu ai,* 事事無礙), and were all perfectly incorporated into the fundamental principle (*lishi wu ai,* 理事無礙). To say that one could not become a buddha in this present world, that one had to leave it and journey to a distant buddha land, and that one then had to spend eons practicing to become a buddha, all indicated that Pure Land practitioners who inclined toward the "western-direction" model did not understand that they were already buddhas, that the Pure Land is already present to the enlightened mind, and that past, present, and future all collapsed in a single moment. Therefore, critics regarded it as an simplistic practice not worthy of practitioners with any degree of intellectual capacity.

This bothered Yuan Hongdao. When his nephew died, he saw firsthand how effective this simple practice could be, and so, when he turned his mind to Pure Land in 1599, he applied his intellectual energy to explaining how the "western-direction" model not only did not violate the highest principles of Buddhist philosophy, but in fact fulfilled them in a way the Chan critics had failed to appreciate and could not rival. To do this, he had to articulate the connection between ultimate reality as seen by an enlightened mind and ordinary reality as seen by worldlings. Throughout the pages of the *Xifang helun,* Yuan does this from a number of perspectives. From within the Huayan framework, he showed how the mutual pervasion of all things by all other things does not negate their existence as particulars. From a mind-only perspective, he demonstrates that the ultimate existence of all things as mental constructs does not negate their subsistence outside of the individual's mind. From the Mādhyamika point of view, he showed that ultimate truth (*zhen di,* 真諦) does not negate conventional truth (*su di,* 俗諦). Thus, in the second fascicle, we find him arguing:

> All sentient beings have this pure nature, just like fine gold, which is always fine gold whether fashioned into jewelry or bedpans. The bedpan is only an implement; its impurity comes from its being a bedpan, not from its being made of gold. Sentient beings are also like this. They all have the pure [buddha-]nature; they only differ as jewelry and bedpans; their nature is not different.[59]

Thus, the ultimate truth holds: unenlightened beings are indeed nondual with buddhas.

But the problem with the critics of Pure Land is that they only realized half of this truth. In their zeal to establish the identity of jewels and bedpans on the basis of their ultimate nature as gold, they forgot that jewels and bedpans, even though merely conventional realities, are still distinguishable without error as jewels and bedpans. Conventional truth is still truth in Mādhyamika. In addition, by chastising Pure Land practitioners for not realizing ultimate truth, they merely point out the trivial fact that the unenlightened are not enlightened, and it is simply tedious to criticize the unenlightened for not adopting an enlightened viewpoint. Yuan points out that, after rebirth in the Pure Land, devotees will ultimately become fully enlightened buddhas, and *then* they will realize that they were no different in nature from buddhas all along, that this *sahā* world was the Pure Land, and that everything around them was a construction of the mind. But until then, they remain in the dark.

That is why buddhas use expedient means such as Pure Land practice to reach people. In two or three places within the *Xifang helun*, Yuan points out that buddhas, knowing that people are unenlightened, use whatever means they can to entice them and move them in the right direction. Here is a sample:

> If one wants to please children, one uses cakes and fruits; if one wants to please women, one uses beautiful silks. What all people value are gems and jade, clothing and food. Thus, [in the Pure Land] there are the seven natural gemstones, and in the inner palace fine and marvelous clothing, drink, and food. It is like the children in the burning house (a parable of the *Lotus Sutra*)—had it not been for the goat-cart, the deer-cart, and so on, they never would have come out. Now Śākyamuni the Tathāgata, in accordance with people's feelings and views, preached about the seven-jeweled Pure Land of Amitābha. This was only to catch them where they were. Once they achieve rebirth there, they will come to realize that the jewels are just so much brickbats and rubble, and that the real purity of the land was indescribable. It is like when a minister of state arrives at a new post. He explains the splendors of the emperor's palace to the locals in terms of the things that they value most, knowing that a straightforward description would be about as useful as describing forms to one born blind.[60]

In much Buddhist literature, to call a certain teaching an "expedient means" (*fangbian*, 方便) was to denigrate those who followed it as being somewhat deficient. In many instances, one calls an opponent's teaching "expedient means," while one's own teaching is direct and aimed at those of sharp minds and good roots. Yuan combats this tendency by asking his opponents if they are really so enlightened that they can see the truth directly and thus do not need expedient teachings themselves:

> You say, "Only purify your own mind, and then what need is there to discriminate?" If you enter a latrine, could you remain there long? Go into a charnel-house where the air is filthy with black smoke. Could you refrain from holding your nose? Could you share your dishes and bed with someone who has scabrous sores oozing pus and blood? If not, then this is a sign that you detest the five defilements. If you still need a clean room and sanitary companions, then this is a sign that you would delight in the Pure Land.[61]

In summary, one of the accomplishments of the *Xifang helun* is that in it, Yuan Hongdao balances ultimate and conventional perspectives as defined within a number of Buddhist schools to demonstrate three points. First, that literal conceptions of Amitābha, his Pure Land, and the process of attaining rebirth and eventual buddhahood there do not violate the highest truths of Buddhism. Second, these truths, in fact, are the key to understanding how Pure Land thought and practice save unenlightened worldlings. And, third, that buddhas, realizing the plight of ignorant beings, can use provisional teachings effectively to save worldlings and give them a chance to become buddhas as well.

Use of Huayan thought. Modern scholars who have studied the *Xifang helun* have commented that one of its special characteristics is its use of Huayan thought to explain Pure Land concepts and practices. Qiu Minjie points out that Yuan Hongdao spent time researching the *Huayan Sutra* and Li Tongxuan's commentary on it, as evidenced by his multiple references to and quotations from Li's works throughout the *Xifang helun*,[62] and believes that the ten-fascicle structure of the text, with each fascicle named a "gate" (*men*, 門), was based on the "ten gates" of Huayan thought.[63] Zhou Qun notes that few Pure Land thinkers at that time did this. Most great writers on Buddhism in the late Ming, he says, talked exclusively in terms of Chan and Pure Land. A few, such as Ouyi Zhixu might also write on Tiantai but not Huayan.[64] Yunqi Zhuhong did use Huayan concepts in his Pure Land writings, and may have influenced Yuan Hongdao to do so,[65] although Yuan had certainly studied Huayan on his own.[66] Yuan, therefore, was among the few who used Huayan thought and concepts to explain Pure Land, something consistent with his demonstrated interest in Huayan as evidenced in his letters and other writings.[67]

One certainly does see many references to Huayan ideas in the *Xifang helun*. The first section of the first fascicle opens with a discussion of the "Pure Land of Vairocana" (毘盧遮那淨土), describing how all of reality and all living beings are already in it. Roughly paraphrasing, Yuan says that this pure land is the entire *dharmadhātu* in which all things co-inhere: purity and defilement, buddhas and beings, all perfectly interfused. This is the true, resplendent recompense of all sentient beings, and is the straight dharma, not an expedient teaching. Ordinary beings are benighted and cannot perceive this, thus hungry ghosts die of thirst by the water's edge. They do not see that, whether they be in heaven or hell, it is all the product of their originally enlightened mind. Vairocana pervades everywhere and everything. This being the case, one cannot ultimately distinguish him from either Śākyamuni or Amitābha, but neither do they collapse into absolute identity either. From Śākyamuni's point of view, he pervades everything; Amitābha is one of the phenomena he pervades. From Amitābha's perspective, he pervades everything; Śākyamuni is one of the phenomena he pervades. Even on the human level, "self" cannot exist without "other" and vice versa.[68]

The last section of the first fascicle places Amitābha's Western Pure Land on the same level as this, or even slightly higher. The presentation of the "Pure Land of Vairocana" given above is highly abstract, and requires great intelligence and achievements in meditation to understand. Amitābha's Pure Land, on the other hand, in its very concreteness, wealth of detail, and specificity, gives a better illustration of the relationship between the universal and the particular as conceived by Huayan thinkers. It is the "Inconceivable Pure Land that Receives Sentient Beings of the Ten Directions" (攝受十方一切有情不可思議淨土), and by reflecting on it, practitioners get a chance to examine the relationship between its conventional and ultimate aspects. Whereas in the first section, one merely asserts that all beings are emanations of Vairocana, here one looks at relationships between things such as Amitābha and his Pure Land, cause (religious practices leading to rebirth) and effect (attainment of rebirth), past and present, and the specific features of the land and its general nature. Looking at all these apparent dualities and differences, one sees that within them is the "inconceivable" nature, and that apart from these conventional particulars, there is no ultimately existent essence to be found. In this way, Amitābha's Pure Land, with its highly developed and specific imagery of buddhas, lotus ponds, jeweled trees, birds that sing the dharma, and so on, becomes the vehicle for realizing the deepest truths of Huayan thought.[69]

Yuan also brings up a theme that will serve later Pure Land apologists well. In various places, he notes that the *Huayan Sutra* itself recommends Pure Land practice. For example, he notes that the southward journey of the youth Sudhana, in the course of which he visits fifty-three teachers, both begins and ends with Pure Land teachings. His first teacher, the monk Deyun (德雲比丘), advises him to seek rebirth, and in the final fascicle of the sutra, the great Bodhisattva Samantabhadra (普賢菩薩) and all his companions utter the "ten great vow-kings" (*shi da yuan wang*, 十大願王), one of which is that they will all seek rebirth together in the western Land of Utmost Bliss.[70] This served to show that Pure Land practice was not only for ignorant people, since even a celestial bodhisattva like Samantabhadra actively pursued the goal of rebirth in Amitābha's Pure Land. It also located support for the practice in one of the most revered scriptures in Chinese Buddhism, a fact that later masters, such as Yinguang (印光, 1861–1947), utilized.[71]

Despite the prominence of Huayan reasoning and citations from the *Huayan Sutra* and its commentaries, we should be cautious before ascribing too great or too central a role to Huayan thought in the *Xifang helun*. It may be true that Yuan Hongdao, along with Zhuhong, was one of the first thinkers in Chinese Buddhism to make use of Huayan concepts and literature in defending "western-direction Pure Land," but, as noted prior to our summary of the work, he cites many scriptures and treatises throughout its pages, and Huayan references, while numerous, are not in the majority. There are many more citations from the *Da zhidu lun;* would this make the *Xifang helun* a Sanlun (三論) text? Maybe not.

A more balanced assessment of the text's diverse doctrinal affiliations could be made by reiterating the point made in the previous section: one of the text's major concerns is to counter Chan critics who accuse Pure Land, in its "western-direction" interpretation, of violating Buddhism's understanding of ultimate reality by introducing dualisms and false distinctions. To do this, Yuan uses materials from a multitude of schools to show that, no matter how one construes the difference between reality as it is and as perceived by unenlightened beings, the deepest understanding of the relationship between the conventional and the ultimate remains the same. In other words, no matter whether one approaches Pure Land's vision of the cosmos from a Sanlun, Weishi (consciousness-only; also known as Faxiang), Tiantai, or Huayan perspective, one finds ultimate truth directly within that world's particularities and distinctions; realization of ultimate truth does not obliterate individuality. The gold in the jewelry and bedpans shines through without the objects losing their identities as jewelry and bedpans. If one destroys them as particular objects to arrive at nothing but the gold, one has only a shapeless mass of gold, devoid of any particular identity and function.

If one adopts a Huayan approach, then realizing that Amitābha, his land, Śākyamuni, the present world, and all living beings are emanations of Vairocana does not erase their particular identities. Vairocana is found right in these things, not by looking beyond them or by homogenizing them. If one adopts a Sanlun perspective, then to collapse all false distinctions between pure/impure, past/present/future, worldlings/buddhas, and so on does not reduce them all to a single substance; one sees ultimate truth not by doing away with conventional truth but simply by realizing that it is conventional truth. Yuan makes similar moves with mind-only and Tiantai thought as well. The point is that he does not restrict himself to Huayan ideas in explaining Pure Land. His main aim is to show that Pure Land practice finds support in all of the philosophical schools of Buddhism.

When we take all of Yuan's arguments into account, then, it appears that the *Xifang helun* cannot be construed as a Huayan-Pure Land text. Rather, Yuan mines all the available schools of Chinese Buddhist thought in order to prove their compatibility of Pure Land practice. By doing this, he sought to defend "western-direction Pure Land" from its detractors' charge of propounding false dualisms.

Is this a Pure Land text? Having just asked whether the *Xifang helun* is really a Huayan-Pure Land text, I want to raise another question now: Is the *Xifang helun,* strictly speaking, primarily a Pure Land text? The answer, it will turn out, is "yes," but it is still useful to raise the question, as it allows us to qualify this "yes" appropriately.

The first reason for raising this question has to do with the quotation given above (p. 104) from Yuan's *Shanhu lin* regarding his motivation for writing the *Xifang helun.* As the reader will recall, Yuan stated that his purpose was really to put Chan and Pure Land in conversation. Based on this, Zhou Qun has suggested that this work is *not* a Pure Land text, or at least not *just* a Pure Land text. Rather, it represents Yuan's attempt to reform what he saw as the excesses of the style of Chan that he himself had pursued during the ten years prior to its composition. Zhou Qun notes that Yuan did not give up his Chan practice but continued to sit in meditation and discuss Chan with lay and monastic friends while in retirement at Willow Wave, where he moved after publishing the *Xifang helun.*[72]

Thus, in the end, we can say that the *Xifang helun* is indeed a Pure Land text, insofar as its ostensible subject matter is the Pure Land, but we must understand this correctly. It is not a Pure Land text in the sense that it sets up Pure Land as a separate "school" and tries to steer Buddhists into it and away from other "schools." Rather, it uses Pure

Land as a tool to open a broader discussion about what it means to be a Buddhist of any kind. Pure Land becomes a lens through which one may see and understand all other aspects of Buddhism, from the most basic practices such as the taking of the five lay precepts up through Chan meditation and enlightenment and the philosophies of Tiantai and Huayan. Pure Land illustrates, explains, focuses, and unifies all of these. The text is Yuan's description of how to be a serious Buddhist, and not just a dilettante or "crazy Chan" follower.

This may also shed some additional light on the question, raised in the biography of Yuan above, as to whether he actually "converted" from Chan to Pure Land. In that section, we argued against this simply from his biography and later writings, but here we must examine the presuppositions behind the question. The question itself assumes that these were two opposing "schools" in late Ming China, and one had to belong either to one or the other. If we understand that Yuan's real intention in the *Xifang helun* was not to oppose Chan as if it were a competing school but simply to oppose a corrupting tendency in the kind of Chan practiced within his own social and intellectual circles, then it becomes easier to see that he was not opposed to Chan at all, nor did he abandon it.[73] He was a reformer of Buddhism, not a proselytizer for one school of Buddhism against others. This being the case, his failure to refer to Pure Land in his post-1599 writings is easier to understand. To put it another way, if one believes that in 1599 Yuan abandoned Chan altogether in order to "convert" to Pure Land, then one would expect that he would remain loyal to his new "school" after completing the *Xifang helun* and continue to write about it exclusively. If one makes this assumption, then the fact that he did not do so would indeed be a puzzle. On the other hand, if we see that his intention in composing the *Xifang helun* was simply to reform Buddhism in general, or at least among his gentry peers, then the fact that in the 1604 *Shanhu lin* he returns to composing explanations of Chan teachings and commenting on texts of other schools is much less difficult to understand.

Conclusions

The popularity of the *Xifang helun* among subsequent generations of Chinese Buddhists has created an odd dichotomy in the way we must approach Yuan Hongdao and his most famous work. After its publication, the text took on a life of its own and was read, studied, anthologized, and commemorated as a great landmark in the advance of the

Pure Land dharma gate. As Yuan's other works on religion and literature either fell out of circulation or were banned by the Qing government, the *Xifang helun* remained in the Chinese Buddhist canon. Because of this, Yuan came to be identified as a great Pure Land Buddhist; an informant in Taiwan once told me that had Yuan been a monk rather than a layman, he probably would have been added to the roster of Pure Land "patriarchs." As it is, his biography in the *Sages and Worthies of the Pure Land* and the *Biographies of Buddhist Laymen* note his involvement in Pure Land to the exclusion of all else.

However, when we turn our attention to Yuan Hongdao's life and work as a whole, we see a man who was very much a product of the religious and cultural trends of the Wanli period. Except for a two-month period in late 1599, his philosophical, religious, and literary efforts went into poetry and literary theory, Chan thought and meditation, the use of Chan thought in commenting on passages from Confucian classics, travelogues, short essays, and politics. Within this context, his composition of the *Xifang helun* presents us with something of a mystery. Why write one large work on Pure Land and then abandon the topic altogether?

It may well be that, even in this, Yuan was a representative of the gentry Buddhism of his time. Since, as we have seen, thinkers of this period did not separate Pure Land out as a "school" distinct from other schools, but as a "dharma gate" that provided one among many possible entry points into Buddhism, Pure Land was simply one aspect of the total Buddhist picture of the late Ming. Other writers, while primarily committed to Chan, wrote on Pure Land; we noted above that Li Zhi had his own contribution in this field, and Ven. Dr. Shengyan (釋聖嚴), in his survey of Pure Land literature of the Wanli period, lists several others.[74] Even Chan masters such as Hanshan Deqing (憨山德清) wrote on Pure Land.[75]

What distinguishes Yuan Hongdao's efforts in this area is his serious engagement with the "western-direction" branch of Pure Land thought at a time when writers primarily adopted the "mind-only Pure Land" position and explained it in Chan terms. Perhaps it was the death of his nephew that impelled Yuan to defend this more literal interpretation, or perhaps he was swayed by his contacts with Zhuhong. Whatever initially evoked his interest, the result was a work in which he discovered that the most literal interpretation of Pure Land, one that took its mythology at face value and engaged with a practice and set of concepts available even to those on the lowest rungs of the social and educational ladder, provided the perfect window through which to see the deepest truths of

Buddhism. While the "mind-only Pure Land" position allowed one to declare facilely that "all is one," the "western-direction Pure Land" point of view forced one to grapple, at a deeper level, with the relationship of the universal to the particular, the pure to the impure, and the worldling to the Buddha. As he himself said, Chan and Pure Land needed to have a conversation, and in writing the *Xifang helun,* Yuan Hongdao hoped to get the discussion going.

Notes

1 The Qing documents asking that Yuan's works be "pulled and burned" (*chouhui*, 抽燬) are reproduced in *Yuan Hongdao ji jianjiao* (*The Collected Works of Yuan Hongdao with Annotations*), ed. Qian Bocheng, 3 vols. (Shanghai: Guji chubanshe [古籍出版社], 1981), vol. III, pp. 1682–1684. Hereafter, citations from this work will be noted as CWYH, followed by the volume and page number(s).

2 Zhang Ruzhao, "Yuan Zhonglang de Foxue Sixiang" (袁中郎的佛學思想, "Yuan Zhonglang's Buddhist Thought"), *Renjian shi* (人間世) 20 (January 1935): p. 20.

3 Mochizuki Shinkō, *Chūgoku jōdō kyōri shi* (中国淨土教理史, *A History of Chinese Pure Land Thought*) (Kyōtō: Hōzōkan, 1978), pp. 484–486.

4 Araki Kengo, *Myōmatsu shukyō shisō kenkyū* (明末宗教思想研究, *Studies in Religious Thought at the End of the Ming*) (Tokyo: Sōbunsha, 1979), pp. 421–471.

5 Qiu Minjie, *Can chan yu nianfo: Wan Ming Yuan Hongdao de fojiao sixiang* (參禪與念佛: 晚明袁宏道的佛教思想, *Chan Practice and Buddha-Recitation: The Buddhist Thought of Yuan Hongdao in the Late Ming*), Zongjiao wenhua cong shu, vol. 3. (Taibei: Shang Ding [商鼎], 1993).

6 Zhou Qun, *Yuan Hongdao ping zhuan* (袁宏道评传, *A Critical Biography of Yuan Hongdao*) (Nanjing: Nanjing University Press [南京大学出版社], 1999).

7 Zhou Qun, *Ru-Shi-Dao yu wan Ming wenxue sixiang* (儒释道与晚明文学思潮, *Confucianism, Buddhism, Daoism, and Late-Ming Literary Thought*) (Shanghai: Shanghai Bookstore Publishing [上海书店出版社], 2000); Zhou Qun, "Lun Yuan Hongdao de foxue sixiang" (論袁宏道的佛學思想, "A Discussion of Yuan Hongdao's Buddhist Thought"), in *Chung-Hwa Buddhist Studies Studies* (中華佛學研究) 6 (2002): pp. 383–417; Qiu Minjie, "Yuan Hongdao de 'Xifang helun' de jingtu sixiang" (袁宏道《西方合論》的淨土思想, "The Pure Land Thought of Yuan Hongdao's 'Xifang helun'"), in *Diguan* (諦觀) 73 (1993): pp. 73–98.

8 Pan Guiming, *Zhongguo jushi fojiao shi* (中国居士佛教史, *A History of Chinese Lay Buddhism*), 2 vols. (Beijing: China Social Studies Press [中国社会科学出版社], 2000) vol. 2, pp. 747–759.

9 Ming-shui Hung, "Yüan Hung-tao and the Late Ming Literary and Intellectual Movement" (Ph.D. dissertation, University of Wisconsin, 1974); Jonathan Chaves, *Pilgrim of the Clouds: Poems and Essays from Ming China by Yüan Hung-tao and His Brothers* (New York: Weatherhill, 1978); Chih-ping Chou, *Yüan Hung-tao and the Kung-an School* (Cambridge: Cambridge University Press, 1988).

10 Jennifer Lynn Eichmann, "Spiritual Seekers in a Fluid Landscape: A Chinese Buddhist Network in the Wanli Period (1573–1620)" (Ph.D. dissertation, Princeton University, 2005).

11 Yuan Hongdao, CWYH.

12 Yuan Zhongdao, *Kexue zhai qianji* (珂雪齋前集, *Earlier Anthology from Kexue Studio*), 5 vols. (1618; Taibei: Weiwen [偉文], 1976, reprint), p. 1699.

13 Zhou Qun, *Yuan Hongdao ping zhuan*, p. 34.

14 The society was called the "City South Literary Society" (Chengnan wen she, 城南文社). See Zhou Qun, *Yuan Hongdao ping zhuan,* p. 35. Yuan's poem, called "Instructing Members of the Society" ("Shi sheyou," 示社友), is in CWYH I, pp. 40–41.

15 Benjanim A. Elman, *A Cultural History of Civil Examinations in Late Imperial China* (Berkeley, CA: University of California Press, 2000), pp. 140–141.

16 Chün-fang Yü, "Ta-hui Tsung-kao and Kung-an Ch'an," *Journal of Chinese Philosophy,* v. 6 (1979): p. 229.

17 A *guan* was a string used to hold one thousand copper cash; thus, the official's poem means that his own "investigation of things" and Dahui's "investigation by things" are seamlessly connected, like the one thousand coins strung on a single string; the two teachings are represented by five hundred of the coins.

18 問:妙喜言諸公但知格物不知物格,意旨如何? 答: 格物物格者,猶諺云 "我要打他, 反被他打" 也. 今人盡一生 心思欲窮他而反被他窮倒.豈非物格耶? CWYH III, p. 1284.

19 Zhou Qun, *Yuan Hongdao ping zhuan,* p. 39.

20 Ibid., p. 40.

21 Ibid., pp. 42–43. Yuan and Li's poems are reproduced in CWYH I, pp. 73–78.

22 Chaves, *Pilgrim of the Clouds,* pp. 82–83; romanization adapted for consistency. Original in CWYH I, pp. 476–477. Yuan Zhongdao's account is in his *Kexue zhai jinji,* pp. 1655–1656. It is from Zhongdao's account that we know the date of this incident.

23 Zhou Qun, *Yuan Hongdao ping zhuan,* pp. 43–44.

24 CWYH I, p. 437.

25 Chaves, *Pilgrim of the Clouds,* p. 76; original in CWYH I, pp. 465–466.

26 近則雲棲和尚。 所著小本疏鈔。 條分類析。 精宏淵博。 真照夜途之長炬。 截苦海之輕舟。*Xifang helun,* T. 1976: 47.417a2022–2024.

27 Zhou Qun, *Yuan Hongdao ping zhuan,* p. 159.

28 Ibid., p. 56.

29 This is a good place to alert the reader that Li Zhi's identification as a proponent of "crazy Chan" has been refuted by Jiang Canteng (江燦騰) in a recent book. He claims that the sayings and incidents in Li's life upon which this charge was based were grossly distorted by his enemies, and in fact his own religious life and practice were far more conventional than his rhetoric would lead one to assume. See Jiang Canteng, "Li Zhuowu yu wan Ming fojiao sixiang yi ji dui 'kuang chan' de piping" (李桌吾與晚明佛教思想以及對'狂禪'的批評, "Li Zhuowu and Late-Ming Buddhist Thought and a Critique of 'Crazy Chan'"), in *Zhongguo jindai fojiao sixiang de zhengbian yu fazhan* (中國近代佛教思想的诤辯與發展) (Taibei: Nantian Shuju [南天書局], 1998), pp. 323–399.

30 Zhou Qun, *Yuan Hongdao ping zhuan,* p. 57.

31 CWYH II, pp. 704–705.

32 Yuan gave it this name because of the hundreds of willow trees that surrounded the house, which gave the appearance of waves on the sea when the wind blew.

33 See, for example, Peng Jiqing's (彭際清, 1740–1796) entry on the three Yuan brothers in his *Jushi zhuan* (居士傳), which records the *Xifang helun* but no other work from Yuan Hongdao's hand. Peng Jiqing, *Jushi zhuan* (*Biographies of* [*Buddhist*] *Laymen*), in *Wanzi xu zang jing* (卍字續藏經) (Taibei: Xinwenfeng, 1978), vol. 149, pp. 966–967.

34 容顏漸朽謝, 恩愛日銷亡. From a poem Yuan wrote upon parting with his brother Zhongdao. See CWYH III, p. 1351. Translations mine.

35 A good general description of Wanli-era gentry culture may be found in Timothy Brook, *The Confusions of Pleasure: Commerce and Culture in Ming China* (Berkeley, CA: University of California Press, 1998).

36 Yuan describes the writing process in the text itself. See *Xifang helun*, T. 1976: 47.388b21.

37 "西方合論十卷字字從真悟門流故絕無一字蹈襲又無一字杜撰雖台宗堂奧尚未詣極而透徹禪機融貫方山清涼教理無餘矣." Ouyi Zhixu, "Xifang helun xu" (西方合論序, "Preface to Comprehensive Treatise on the West"), in Ouyi Dashi Quanji (蕅益大師拳集, *The Collected Works of Great Master Ouyi*), 21 vols. (Taibei: Fojiao chubanshe [佛教出版社], 1989, reprint), vol. 17, p. 11195.

38 That this painting represents this event is the theory advanced by by Ts'ai Hsing-li in her Ph.D. dissertation on the painting. See Hsing-li Ts'ai, *Ch'en Hung-shou's 'Elegant Gathering': A Late Ming Pictorial Manifesto of Pure Land Buddhism* (Ph.D. dissertation, University of Kansas, 1997).

39 See the timeline on publication of this anthology (嘉興大藏經刻藏年表) given in Fan Jialing (范佳玲), *Zibo dashi shengping ji sixiang yanjiu* (紫柏大師生平及思想研究, *A Study of the Life and Thought of Master Zibo*). *Fojiao lun cong* (佛學論), no. 28 (Taibei: Chung-hwa Institute of Buddhist Studies, 2001). http://www.chibs.edu.tw/publication/LunCong/028/028-10.htm#10.

40 See, for example, the two works by Peng Jiqing dealing with biographies of Buddhist laymen (*Jushi zhuan*) and of Pure Land practitioners (*Jingtu shengxian lu*, 淨土聖賢錄). One example is the entry on the three Yuan brothers in the *Jushi zhuan, wanzi xu zang jing*, 居士傳卍字續藏經, vol. 149, p. 967a.

41 Guo Peng, *Ming-Qing fojiao* (明清佛教, *Buddhism in the Ming and Qing*) (Fuzhou [福州]: Fujian Renmin chubanshe [福建人民出版], 1982), pp. 162–166.

42 *Xifang helun*, T. 1976: 47.388b14-388b15: "余十年學道墮此狂病。 後因觸機。 薄有省發。遂簡塵勞。歸心淨土。"

43 *Xifang helun*, T. 1976: 47.388a29–388b01: "滅火者水。水過即有沈溺之災。"

44 *Xifang helun*, T. 1976: 47.388b15–388b16: "禮誦之暇。 取龍樹天台長者永明 等論。細心披讀。忽爾疑豁。既深信淨土。"

45 It seems doubtful that Yuan Hongdao read all one hundred fascicles of this work. Almost every citation is from fascicle 38.

46 As a side note and a pointer to possible future research, it is of interest that the list does not include some of the most influential authors and texts of the early Chinese Pure Land tradition, such as Tanluan (曇鸞, 476–542), Daochuo (道綽, 562–645), and Shandao (善導, 613–681). Their absence might be a sign

that they were not as important to the developed Chinese Pure Land tradition as previously thought.

47 Li's commentary is called *Xin Huayan jinglun*, 新華嚴經論 (*Discussion of the New Huayan Sutra*), T. 1739.

48 西方合論一書乃借淨土以發明宗乘因談宗者不屑淨土修淨者不務禪宗故合而論之. Yuan Hongdao, *Shanhu Lin* (*Coral Grove*) I: 26b3–4. A photocopy of this book was kindly sent to me by Prof. Qiu Minjie, who obtained a copy from the Naikaku Bunko (内閣文庫) in Kyoto (from the Kanshomon [漢書門], shelf 10, box 73, accession number no. 10043).

49 *Xifang helun*, T. 1976: 47.393b28ff: 又如一葉之葦席。 能運萬斛之舟。 是風之 力。非葦力故。

50 *Xifang helun*, T. 1976: 47.401b22–40123: 阿彌陀佛。 即本師盧舍那。 猶屬情量。 何以故。十方世界。惟一智境無別佛故。

51 *Xifang helun*, T. 1976: 47.405a14–405a21: 則純以念佛一聲。 入三觀門。 言念存三觀者。如一聲佛。遂了此能念體空所念無相。即念存空觀。所念之佛即應身。即心破見思惑也。雖能念體空所念無相。不妨能念分明所念顯然。即念存假觀。所念之佛即報身。即心破塵沙惑也。正當能念所念空時。即能念所念顯然。正當能念所念顯時。即是能念所念寂然。空假互存乃念存中觀。

52 *Xifang helun*, T. 1976: 47.406c22–407a4.

53 *Xifang helun*, T. 1976: 47.408b26–408b27: 是故悟達之士。 決當求生淨土。 如法修 行。免致退墮。俟忍力堅固。入世利生。方為究竟佛果故。

54 *Xifang helun*, T. 1976: 47.410c11–410c16: 有等魔民。 專逞狂慧。 不肯持戒修 行。 妄引經中相似語言。如煩惱即菩提婬怒癡即梵行之類。隨語生解。隨解發毒。果如彼說。迦文悟道。應親寶女。阿難婬舍。何須提[牿/女]。六祖初隨獵人。尚未受戒。何苦但食肉邊菜也。

55 *Xifang helun*, T. 1976: 47.411a23–41124: 故千日學解。不如一日持戒。

56 Full title: *Amituo guyin sheng wang tuoluoni jing* (阿彌陀鼓音聲王陀羅尼經), T. 370.

57 I have not yet been able to identify this text. It does not appear (at least not under this title) in Ono Gemmyo, and online searching reveals only that another work in the Taishō, the *Qixin lun shu bi xiao ji* (起信論疏筆削記, T. 1848: 44), also quotes it.

58 Li Zhi, *Jingtu jue*, in *Wanzi xu zang jing* 108: 357–382.

59 *Xifang helun*, T. 1976: 47.393a20–393a24: 一切眾生。 皆有如是淨性。 譬一精金。 冶為釵釧及溺器等。金性是一。溺器者是器。具穢非金穢故。若加銷治。為種種玩好等物。金亦不易。生佛亦然。同一淨性。但以釵釧溺器。而有差別。非是性異。

60 *Xifang helun*, T. 1976: 47.393b01–393b11: 謂樂兒童者。 當以餅果。 樂婦女 者。 必用綺羅。一切眾生所重。惟寶玉衣食。是故有自然七寶。及與樓閣妙麗衣服飲食等事。譬諸火宅諸兒。非羊鹿等車。決不肯出。出已純與大車。今釋迦如來。順眾生情見。說阿彌陀七寶淨土。秖為眾生見境如是。合如是說。眾生生已。各各自見細妙淨相。無可比喻。方知琉璃[王車]璖瑪瑙。猶如瓦礫。如達官貴人。向田舍兒。說王宮精嚴。姑就彼人所極珍異者為比。向非情量所及。如對生盲說色。亦無所用其方比矣。

61 *Xifang helun*, T. 1976: 47.412c16–412c20: 汝言心淨土淨不須分別者。 引汝入 廁室 中。能久住不。入死屍場。穢氣熏灼。不掩鼻不。與疥癩膿血之人。能同應器及床褥不。若不能者。此相即是厭五濁相。若居住尚須淨室。同遊尚宜淨侶者。此相即是忻淨土相。

62 Qiu Minjie, *Can chan yu nianfo,* pp. 67–68.

63 Ibid., p. 69.

64 In fact, as mentioned above, Zhixu criticized Yuan Hongdao for emphasizing Huayan over Tiantai in the *Xifang helun.*

65 Zhou Qun, *Yuan Hongdao ping zhuan,* p. 159.

66 For example, in a letter written in 1596 to a friend, Yuan laments his own lack of progress in Chan, but then explains that both "progress" (*jin,* 進) and "regress" (*tui,* 退) are both instantiations of principle (*li,* 理), demonstrating the Huayan idea of the mutual interpenetration of principle and phenomena (*li shi wu ai,* 理事無礙). Again, the particular phenomena of "progress" and "regress" pervade one another, showing that phenomena interpenetrate without obstruction (*shi shi wu ai,* 事事無礙). See "To Cao Luchuan" (曹魯川), in CWYH I, pp. 253–254.

67 Zhou Qun, *Yuan Hongdao ping zhuan,* pp. 57, 139, 146.

68 *Xifang helun,* T. 1976: 47.390a11–390b10.

69 See *Xifang helun,* T. 1976: 47.390a10–392a27.

70 *Xifang helun,* T. 1976: 47.408a03–408a05: 如善財初發心悟道時。德雲比丘。教以憶念一切諸佛法門。及入彌勒閣後。普賢菩薩。為發十大願王。導生極樂。This episode does not actually occur in the Taishō version of the *Huayan Sutra.*

71 For Yinguang's use of this argument, see *Yinguang Dashi quanji* (印光大師拳, *The Collected Works of the Great Master Yinguang*), rev. and expanded ed., 7 vols., ed. Shi Guangding (釋廣定) (Taibei: Fojiao Chubanshe, 1991), vol. 1, p. 360.

72 Zhou Qun, *Yuan Hongdao ping zhuan,* p. 60.

73 Zhou Qun, *Yuan Hongdao ping zhuan,* p. 163.

74 See the chart in Shengyan, *Mingmo fojiao yanjiu* (明末佛教研究, *Studies in Late Ming Buddhism*), Zhihui hai (智慧海) 9 (Taibei: Dongchu Publications [東初出版社], 1992), pp. 105–108.

75 As one example among several, see the essay "Shi xiu jingtu famen" (釋示修繕淨土法門, "Expounding the Practice of the Pure Land Dharma Gate"), in Hanshan Deqing, *Hanshan Laoren meng you ji* (憨山老人 夢遊集), 4 vols. (Taibei: Xinwenfeng [新文豐], 1993, reprint), pp. 436–440. This was originally printed in Jiangbei (江北) by the Jiangbei Scriptural Press (江北刻經處) in the spring of Guangxu 5 (1879).

Spiritual Kinship and Lineage in Major Buddhist Traditions[1]

Charles S. Prebish
Religious Studies Program, Utah State University

Introduction

In an interesting discussion article published in the online *Journal of Buddhist Ethics,* Paul Numrich recounts the famous Theravāda dialogue between the Buddhist monk Mahinda and King Devānampiya Tissa of Ceylon (present-day Sri Lanka) concerning Buddhism's establishment on the island kingdom. The king wants to know precisely when this new religion's roots may be considered to be firmly established on the island. Mahinda's reply:

> When a young man, born of Ceylonese parents on the island of Ceylon, having gone forth on the island of Ceylon and learned the monastic discipline in this same island of Ceylon, when he will recite that discipline on the island of Ceylon—then, Great King, will the roots of the religion indeed be deep.[2]

Numrich then cites Michael Carrithers's often quoted remark: "No Buddhism without the *Sangha* and no *Sangha* without the Discipline."[3] Thus, the growth of Buddhism into countries beyond its Indian birthplace, and its survival in those countries, required and was predicated upon the establishment of the sangha and its implementation as the basis of Buddha's spiritual family. This paper explores the development of Buddha's spiritual family and the role played by spiritual kinship in the growth of the buddhadharma in, and beyond, Asia.

The Buddhist Sangha

Despite the fact that the term *sangha* is used today in a more extended and comprehensive fashion than originally, referring to almost any community loosely associated with Buddhism, in the time of the Buddha the term was used in a radically different fashion. The Sanskrit word *sangha* simply connotes a number of people living together for a certain purpose. In the midst of many religious sanghas in the general wanderers' (*parivrājaka*) community, the Buddha's followers appropriated the term in a rather distinct fashion, one that gave their fledgling community a clear and unique identity. While outsiders may have referred to the Buddha's first disciples as *Śākyaputrīya-śrāmaṇa*s or "mendicants who follow the Buddha," the original community referred to itself as the *bhikṣu-sangha,* or "community of monks." Later, when the order of nuns was founded, they became known as the *bhikṣuṇī-sangha,* and the two units were collectively known as the *ubhayato-sangha,* the "twofold community." In Theravāda countries, this quite narrow usage of the term sangha has remained the predominant meaning of the word, as is pointed out by most modern scholars writing on the Buddhist community. Occasionally, in the early literature, the Buddha uses the term *cātur-disa-sangha,* or "sangha of the four quarters," but it seems clear from his usage that he still means the monastic sangha exclusively. Eventually, however, as the eremitical lifestyle deteriorated in favor of settled monasticism, the term "sangha of the four quarters" took on a new and wider meaning, but it is clear enough that only the Buddhist monastic assemblies are its constituent members.

Early Buddhist history records that the Buddha also admitted lay members into his community, and that they eventually became a vital, symbiotic part of that community. Nevertheless, the lay community was initially considered autonomous to, and even distinct from, the monastic community. Thus, "the four groups of Buddhists were not referred to collectively as a single order (*saṅgha*)."[4] How did this transformation from two distinct and autonomous groups (i.e., monastic and lay members) to a "fourfold sangha" of *bhikṣu*s (monks), *bhikṣuṇī*s (nuns), *upāsaka*s (laymen), and *upāsikā*s (laywomen) evolve? The importance of the laity, or what Reginald Ray calls "the second normative lifestyle" of Indian Buddhism, cannot be minimized in the process.

> The laity practiced a compromised Buddhism and, in so doing, acted as a kind of buffer between the authentic Buddhism of the monks and the non-Buddhist environment of larger India.[5]

Although the goal of the lay Buddhist is *puṇya* or "merit," while the monastics' goal is arhatship or "liberation," the two communities are clearly interdependent, united in their spiritual kinship to the Buddha. To think otherwise, and especially so in the West, would be incorrect. It is not hard to see, then, how the fourfold sangha of monks, nuns, laymen, and laywomen came to interpenetrate and become coincident with the sangha of the four quarters. In other words, it is possible to use the word *sangha* in the broadest sense, to include all Buddhists. Étienne Lamotte summarizes both the result and process:

> The sangha or Buddhist community consists of four assemblies (*pariṣad*): mendicant monks (*bhikṣu*), nuns (*bhikṣuṇī*), laymen (*upāsaka*), and laywomen (*upāsikā*). The religious are distinguishable from the lay followers through their robes, discipline, and ideal and religious prerogatives. At the risk of being misunderstood . . . [a]lthough both the sons of the Śākya, the monks and the laymen represent divergent tendencies which, without coming into direct opposition, were to be asserted with increasing explicitness: on the one hand the ideal of renunciation and personal holiness and, on the other, active virtues and altruistic preoccupations.[6]

The Earliest Spiritual Kinship: *Kalyāṇamitra*s

The most overarching reference in the entire Buddhist tradition denoting spiritual kinship is that of the *kalyānamitra,* or "spiritual friend." In a well-known passage in the *Saṃyutta-nikāya,* the Buddha is questioned by Ānanda regarding the status of the state of spiritual friendship (*kalyāṇamitratā*). Ānanda suggests that this state is half of the holy life, and is immediately reprimanded by Buddha for his faulty understanding, who instructs:

> Not so Ānanda; not so Ānanda. This association with spiritual friendship, association with virtuous companionship, association with goodness *is the whole of the holy life.*[7]

The Buddha immediately goes on to suggest that he himself is the highest *kalyāṇamitra,* and it is because of his function in this capacity that beings subject to birth and rebirth are able to free themselves from old age, sickness, and death—and, indeed, from *duḥkha* itself.[8]

With Buddha established as the highest spiritual friend, he necessarily becomes the archetypal model for all subsequent spiritual kinship relationships in his spiritual family. As a result, a hierarchy is postulated in one's search for the proper *kalyāṇamitra* beginning with a buddha. This hierarchy is maintained throughout the Pāli Canon. Since it is the *kalyāṇamitra* who functions as the spiritual guide of the Buddhist practitioner, it is critical to explore how this most important relationship developed in the *nikāya,* Mahayana, and Vajrayana Buddhist traditions. Nathan Katz says as much:

> The *kalyāṇamitta* is the Buddhist *guru,* and all forms of Buddhism—Theravāda, Mahayana, or Tantrayana—are single in affirming his crucial position.[9]

Lineage and Spiritual Kinship in the Major Buddhist Traditions

In the earliest Buddhist tradition, the role and function of the *kalyāṇamitra* or spiritual friend was immediately and intimately associated with the process by which ordination into the Buddhist sangha was established. Admission into the Buddhist monastic community was initially rather simple and straightforward. It required only Buddha's exhortation for the individual to come forth into the monastic life, with no essential distinction made between the novitiate (*pravrajyā*) and full (*upasaṃpadā*) ordination. Later, when a distinction was made between the novitiate and full ordination, and Buddha allowed monks other than himself to confer these ordinations, additional requisites were added, including the shaving of one's head, taking on yellow robes, and repeating the threefold "refuge formula" (*triśaraṇa*). Moreover, the novice monks—called *śrāmaṇera*s—were required to observe ten principles of training called *śikṣāpada*s. To normalize the relationship between newly ordained junior monks and their senior colleagues, and to assure that proper social decorum was maintained, each prospective junior monk was required to select two individuals to serve as his spiritual mentors: his ordaining monk (known as the *upadhyāya*), and his teacher (called his *ācārya*). The primary function of the *upadhyāya* (or preceptor) involved his ability to teach the novice monk proper discipline and observance of the rules, while the *ācārya,* who was often a dharma master, officiated in the absence of the *upadhyāya.* In this way, the young monk would be properly trained in both the doctrine and the discipline of the Buddhist community. The obligations of the *śrāmaṇera* to his *upadhyāya* and *ācārya* are clearly spelled out in the Pāli *Mahāvagga* (I.25.1–24) which explicitly states:

> Monks, I allow a teacher. The teacher, monks, should arouse in his pupil the attitude of a son; the pupil should arouse in his teacher the attitude of a father.[10]

Alongside the spiritual kinship that developed between preceptors and their disciples, the ongoing preservation of the doctrine and discipline mandated that some additional relationships needed to be established to sustain the dharma and the vinaya intact. To accomplish this a tradition of "vinaya masters" (*vinaya-dharas*), "dharma masters" (*dharma-dharas*), and "abhidharma masters" (*mātṛkā-dharas*) developed. In addition, a tradition of "text reciters" (or *bhāṇakas*) developed as well. These masters and reciters learned their respective textual and doctrinal traditions by heart, and passed on their literary and spiritual legacy to their own line of spiritual heirs. No doubt, these individuals contributed as well to the spiritual lineages found in various Buddhist traditions today, and can be considered as precursors to the traditions discussed below.

Yet it was not just the monastic community that was enjoined to facilitate spiritual kinships in the early tradition. No text in early Buddhism provides a better, or clearer, statement of lay ethics than the famous *Sigālovada-sutta* of the *Dīgha-nikāya*. The text describes a series of familial and social relationships emphasizing the duties and responsibilities of husband and wife, friends, servants and workpeople, duties associated with one's livelihood, and teachers and pupils.[11] Clearly, the standards of teacher-student interactions are substantially parallel to those of the other familial relationships outlined in the text. And it is not only in the Theravāda or other *nikāya* Buddhist traditions that familial associations are emphasized. Throughout Indian Mahayana literature, where both lay and monastic bodhisattvas become the ideal type of practitioner, bodhisattvas of both genders are referred to as being either a "son of a good family" (*kulaputra*) or "daughter of a good family" (*kuladuhitṛ*), where the "family" is unmistakably Buddha's overarching spiritual family. Here too, preachers of the Mahayana dharma were referred to as *dharma-bhāṇakas*, were often lay bodhisattvas, and occasionally were women, thus suggesting a continuing emphasis on spiritual kinship and the importance of Buddhist lineage traditions.[12]

Even after Buddhism extended beyond India, the profoundly religious spiritual kinships were maintained. In China, for example, when a member of the laity decided to deepen his commitment to the Buddhist tradition by renouncing lay life and taking his initial, preliminary entry or "tonsure" into the monastic tradition, he was given the surname Shih, which corresponds to the first syllable of Śākyamuni (*shih-chia-mou-ni* in Chinese). In so doing, he was considered to be *fo-tzu*, "son of the Buddha." Moreover, his tonsure names reflected his tonsure Buddhist family. Holmes Welch, in his classic book *The Practice of Chinese Buddhism 1900–1950*, notes that

> A Chinese could only "leave the home" by accepting a monk as his master. That monk became his "father." Fellow disciples became his "brothers." Not only were the kinship terms borrowed from lay life, but family

> institutions and attitudes were borrowed too. A disciple often inherited his "father's" temple and was expected to look after his grave and soul tablet like a filial son.[13]

An enormous scholarly literature has developed that traces the various spiritual lineages in the Chinese, and particularly Chan, Buddhist traditions. Lineage trees have been established that begin with the first Indian patriarch, Mahākāśyapa, and proceed through the twenty-eighth Indian and first Chinese Chan patriarch Bodhidharma; and then expand to include the various meditation school lineages in Korea, Japan, and Vietnam.

Robert Buswell's research on the Korean Zen tradition demonstrates a similar result. He reports that postulants (*haengja*s in Korean) are assigned a "beneficent master" (*ŭnsa*) who sponsors the postulant for ordination "as does the 'vocation father' in Catholic monasticism."[14] Buswell goes on to note:

> Competition is especially keen among the postulants to have the Sŏn master as their *ŭnsa*. The Sŏn master is quite choosy in accepting new disciples and accedes only to a limited number of requests from the *haengja*. Monastic "families," like their secular counterparts, maintain the earlier Chinese emphasis on the primacy of the senior line within the lineage.[15]

The same circumstance can be found throughout the Zen tradition in Japan. William Bodiford argues that

> The Zen school places great importance on the master-disciple relationship. According to modern descriptions of this discipleship, the master's goal is to cause his disciple to recreate through his own training the same intuitive cognition of reality that the master himself experiences. . . . Traditionally referred to as the "transmission" of the teacher's mind to the disciple, this technique has been termed the crucial "pivot of the Zen teaching method."[16]

Transmission is the "pivot" because it affirms the authentic status of the spiritual kinship between the student, his spiritual parent, and the Buddha himself. Bodiford says as much:

> According to Zen adherents, "This acknowledgment implies the recognition of the disciple as an authentic heir not only of the Dharma of his master and his master's line but of the Dharma of the continuous line of Zen teachers reaching back to Bodhidharma, and thence to [Śākyamuni] Buddha."[17]

In Sōtō Zen, the acknowledgment of attainment is referred to as *inka shōmei,* while the ritual process of confirmation into the dharma lineage of his master is known as *shihō*, processes that are maintained today throughout the modern world of Zen.

In all likelihood, no Buddhist tradition has ever placed more emphasis on lineage and spiritual kinship than that of Tibetan Buddhism. Unlike Mahayana, in which some schools, such as Pure Land, seem not to emphasize the role of lineage and transmission in their practices and rituals, the entirety of the Vajrayana tradition turns on the role and function of spiritual kinship. As such, it becomes the exclusive, basic mechanism of the relationship that exists between student and dharma teacher. Moreover, lineage becomes the cornerstone of each of the four traditional schools of Buddhism in Tibet. In the aftermath of the Tibetan holocaust, the maintenance of the Tibetan Vajrayana lineages in the numerous diaspora communities becomes critically important for the ongoing survival of the entire tradition. Public awareness of these lineages has recently been enhanced by the development of a number of websites that record the various lineage trees in each of the four schools. For example, nalandabodhi.org offers a complete lineage of the Kagyu lineage, from Buddha through Tilopa, Nāropa, Marpa, Milarepa, Gampopa, and each of the seventeen Karmapas, beginning with the first Karmapa Dusum Khyenpa (1110–1993), and concluding with Ugyen Trinley Dorje, the current seventeenth Karmapa.[18] The nalandabodhi.org website, at the outset of its materials on Buddhist schools, notes, "It is indeed the trasmission of this living quality of wisdom which is the essential quality of Tibetan Buddhism today."[19] It is especially interesting to note that within the Gelug tradition, a monk who successfully completes his monastic and academic training, and passes all the appropriate examinations, is referred to as a *geshe* (Tib. *dge bshes*), the Tibetan equivalent word for the Buddhist Sanskrit term *kalyāṇamitra*, or "spiritual friend," identified above as the earliest and highest expression of spiritual kinship in Buddhism.

The Spiritual Shift to America

Few would disagree that the 1893 World Parliament of Religions in Chicago changed the religious landscape for the development of Buddhism in America.[20] Especially significant for Buddhism was the fact that Anagarika Dharmapala delivered the concluding address of the opening ceremonies, and placed the event squarely in a Buddhist context by asserting that the Parliament "was simply the re-echo of a great consummation which the Indian Buddhists accomplished twenty-four centuries ago."[21] By the third day of the Parliament, nearly all of the Japanese delegation had been introduced, including members of the Jōdo Shinshū, Nichiren, Tendai, Shingon, and Zen traditions.

Among the participants at the parliament was Shaku Sōen, who was to return to America a decade later and promote the school of Rinzai Zen. Sōen returned to America in 1905, and established a basic ground for the entry of Zen. Later, three of his students were selected to promote the Rinzai lineage in America. The first of Sōen's students, Nyōgen Senzaki, came to California in the first decade of the twentieth century. Sōen's second disciple, Shaku Sōkatsu, lived in America from 1906–1908, and again from 1909–1910, but eventually returned to Japan without having made much impact. By far Sōen's most noted disciple was Daisetsu Teitaro Suzuki. Suzuki worked for Open Court Publishing Company in LaSalle, Illinois, from 1897–1909. He visited America again from 1936 until the beginning of World War II, and eventually returned for a final time from 1950–1958, lecturing frequently in American universities and cities.

The Rinzai lineage was not the only one to develop in America. The Sōtō tradition began to appear in America in the 1950s. By the mid-1950s, Soyu Matsuoka Rōshi had established the Chicago Buddhist Temple, and Shunryu Suzuki Rōshi arrived in San Francisco in 1959, founding the San Francisco Zen Center shortly thereafter. The dharma successors to Suzuki Rōshi have continued the Sōtō lineage, while other teachers in this lineage have also appeared.

In addition to the traditional forms of Rinzai and Sōtō Zen, still another form of Zen has appeared in America, one that attempts to harmonize the major doctrines and practices of each school into a unified whole. Proponents of this approach included Taizan Maezumi Rōshi (arriving in 1956), Hakuun Yasutani Rōshi (who visited the United States first in 1962, and thereafter regularly until his death in 1973), and Philip Kapleau, an American by birth who first learned about Japanese religion and culture while serving as a court reporter in 1946 during the War Crimes Trials held in Tokyo. Maezumi Rōshi and Kapleau Rōshi have been enormously successful. Maezumi Rōshi established the Zen Center of Los Angeles, where he resided until his death in 1995. He left a dozen dharma heirs, many of whom have developed their own vital, creative communities. Kapleau Rōshi too was quite successful, having built a stable Zen community in Rochester, New York that was notable for its attempt to develop an American style for Zen practice. Also significant are Robert Aitken Rōshi, who founded the Diamond Sangha in Hawai'i in 1959; Eidō Shimano Rōshi, who first came to the United States as a translator for Yasutani Rōshi; and Joshu Sasaki Rōshi, who founded the Cimarron Zen Center in Los Angeles in 1966 and the Mt. Baldy Zen Center five years later.

As early as 1964, Madihe Pannaseeha Thera, a visiting emissary from Sri Lanka, noticed that there was much interest in Buddhism in the United States, but no center available for presenting the Theravāda viewpoint. The following year Ven. Bope Vinita Thera was sent from Vajirarama Temple in Sri Lanka to take up residence in what came to be known as the Buddhist Vihara Society in Washington, DC. In 1967 Ven. Vinita Thera was succeeded by Mahāthera Dickwela Piyananda, and later, Mahāthera Henepola Gunaratana took up residence in the *vihāra.* In many respects Wat Thai fulfilled a similar function on the West Coast, where in 1972 five Thai monks began to establish an extensive series of programs for both Asian and non-Asian Buddhists. Recently, Paul Numrich postulated a conservative estimate of between 500,000 and 750,000 Theravāda Buddhists in the United States in 1990, the vast majority living in urban environments.[22] In addition, Numrich counted 142 Theravāda Buddhist temples in 1996, all but the Washington Buddhist Vihara having been built after 1970.

Over against the presence of largely ethnic Theravāda communities, however, is the development of the *vipassanā* movement. It is clearly Theravādin in origin but almost exclusively a Euro-American Buddhist phenomenon. The leader of the *vipassanā* movement was Mahāsi Sayādaw, a Burmese monk who devised a methodology for eliminating the *samatha* or "calming" practice in Theravāda meditation, and moving directly into the "insight" or *vipassanā* phase. His teaching method was brought to the United States primarily by Joseph Goldstein, Jack Kornfield, Sharon Salzberg, and Ruth Denison. The various centers affiliated with this initial venture constitute a formidable network for *vipassanā* training on the North American continent.

The Tibetans were one of the latest of the Asian Buddhist communities to arrive in the United States. The earliest notable figure to appear was the Gelug teacher Geshe Ngawang Wangyal (1901–1983), who arrived in February 1955. He also eventually brought Geshe Lhundrup Sopa, Lama Kunga, and two other lamas to America. Within a short time, Geshe Wangyal had attracted Robert Thurman, Jeffrey Hopkins, and Christopher George, three Harvard students interested in Buddhism. They learned Tibetan, and in turn, taught the other lamas English.

Not long after Geshe Wangyal had arrived in New Jersey, Deshung Rinpoche traveled to the University of Washington to work on a research project sponsored by the Inner Asia program. He arrived in 1960, along with H. H. Jigdal Dagchen Sakya, and stayed more than twenty-five years. One of the very earliest Sakya centers in the United States was founded by Lama Thartse Kunga, originally brought to the United States in 1962 by Geshe Wangyal. He established the Ewam Choden Tibetan Buddhist Center in 1971. Like many Tibetan centers in the United States, Ewam Choden maintains close ties with the Tibetan community in India.

Not long after the founding of Ewam Choden, the Sakya Monastery of Tibetan Buddhism was founded in 1974 in Seattle by H. H. Jigdal Dagchen Sakya, H. H. Ngawang Trinley Sakyapa, and Deshung Rinpoche. On the other coast are two additional important Sakya facilities: the Sakya Center for Buddhist Studies and Meditation (Sakya Sheidrup Ling) in Cambridge, Massachusetts, and the Sakya Phuntsok Ling Center for Tibetan Buddhist Studies and Meditation in Silver Springs, Maryland.

The earliest and best known Nyingma teacher in the United States is Tarthang Tulku Rinpoche. He arrived in the United States in 1968, settling in Berkeley, California, the following year. He established the Tibetan Nyingma Meditation Center in March 1969, and in 1973 the Nyingma Institute. Two years later he began the highly ambitious project to establish Odiyan Retreat Center on 900 acres in Sonoma County, and in 1975 started the Tibetan Aid Project and Tibetan Relief Foundation to assist in the resettlement of Tibetan refugees. More recently, another Nyingma teacher known as Sogyal Rinpoche has become extremely active and popular on the North American continent. In 1981 he founded the Rigpa Fellowship, which now has a major center in Santa Cruz, California.

There can be little doubt that the most famous Tibetan Buddhist in the West has been Chögyam Trungpa Rinpoche (1939–1987). He became a novice monk at age nine, and received full ordination in 1958. Eventually he was forced to flee Tibet, traveling to India where he studied English with Freda Bedi (also known as Sister Kechog Palmö). In 1969 he gave up his monastic vows and later moved to the United States to take up residence at "Tail of the Tiger" (later renamed Karmê-Chöling) in Barnet, Vermont. Within a decade, he had built an impressive international network of religious centers, organized under an umbrella-like institution known as Vajradhatu, and a series of secular ventures, organized as part of the Nalanda Foundation. Following his death in 1987, responsibility for his complex community fell to Ösel Tendzin (Thomas Rich, 1944–1990), Trungpa's Vajra Regent. Although he was the first Westerner to receive empowerment in the Karma Kagyu lineage, he died of AIDS slightly more than a decade following his empowerment. Responsibility then fell to Trungpa's eldest son, Mipham Rinpoche, who now administers the renamed Shambhala International organization. Trungpa was strongly influenced by H. H. Sixteenth Gyalwa Karmapa (1923–1981), who was recognized early as the new incarnation of the head of the Karma Kagyu lineage. The North American seat of H. H. Gyalwa Karmapa was established at the Karma Triyana Dharmacakra, founded in Woodstock, New York in 1978.

Spiritual Kinship in American Buddhist Communities

There is a rich literature in the discipline of Buddhist studies documenting Buddhism's slow but progressive acculturation into the various countries of Asia during the centuries following Buddha's death. Most generally, the process took at least a half-millennium in each new culture it encountered. However, because Buddhism has been present on American soil for barely a hundred and fifty years, the process and the results of acculturation remain necessarily complex and preliminary, thus complicating the issue of assessing the role of spiritual kinship in American Buddhist communities. In 1979, I wrote:

> Throughout this study, I have made much of the fact that there is a singular relationship between Buddhism's degree of acculturation in its new American environment and its potential future role in American religious life.[23]

Twenty years later, Richard Seager devoted the entire final chapter of his book *Buddhism in America* to the topic of "Making Some Sense of Americanization." In other words, the struggle of acculturation continues to be a defining issue. Seager says that "One key issue for convert Buddhists is maintaining the authenticity of the dharma for future generations."[24] For American Buddhist communities, both immigrant and convert, the key to maintaining that "authenticity of the dharma" rests on preserving carefully those aspects of the tradition which emphasize the core value of spiritual kinship present in the Buddhist tradition from the outset—and that involves an impeccable concern for the procedure by which entry into Buddha's spiritual family is preserved and by which spiritual leadership is affirmed.

No doubt one of the most influential, beloved, and *earliest* of all Sōtō Zen teachers in American Buddhism was Shunryu Suzuki Rōshi. His book *Zen Mind, Beginner's Mind*[25] remains perhaps the singular staple product for beginning Zen students in America. Moreover, David Chadwick's stunning biography, *Crooked Cucumber: The Life and Zen Teaching of Shunryu Suzuki*,[26] provides a moving and compassionate picture of this most influential master who helped to shape the nature of American Zen. Suzuki Rōshi's biography is significant because it offers the potential prototype for Asian Buddhist teachers in America. The Japanese word *rōshi* means "old master," and Suzuki Rōshi was unquestionably the venerable spiritual father of the San Francisco Zen Center (SFZC). As such, he was especially careful in making sure that *shihō,* dharma transmission, and *inka shōmei,* the "seal of approval," would be properly performed when he selected Richard Baker as his first, and only, Western dharma heir. Although he had ordained Baker as a Zen monk in 1966, and conferred the formal transmission ceremony on him on December 4, 1970 in Japan, Baker's transmission ceremony was reenacted and his installation as SFZC's second abbot took place on November 21, 1971, complicated by Suzuki Rōshi's failing health and imminent death. Around 3:00 A.M. on December 4, 1971, Shunryu Suzuki died. That turmoil followed under Baker's tenure as abbot of SZFC is almost beside the point. What is not beside the point is that Baker became the first Western student of an American Zen master to be certified as an "old master," or *rōshi,* as well as abbot of a major American Buddhist community, thus extending the Sōtō Zen lineage in America and maintaining the spiritual kinship of Buddha's family in his role as *kalyāṇamitra* in a new setting.

In his role as abbot and master, Richard Baker Rōshi was now, as a first-generation dharma heir in America, able to extend Buddha's spiritual kinship by performing two kinds of Zen ordination, each of which marks membership for the disciple in Buddha's spiritual family: *jukai,* lay ordination; and *tokudō,* monastic ordination. In the former ordination, often translated as "receiving the precepts," the individual generally takes refuge in the Three Jewels, affirms the three pure precepts, and accepts the ten grave precepts. Along with affirming the precepts, he or she receives a new "dharma name," marking entry into the new spiritual family. In the latter ordination, as a monastic the initiate affirms a more rigorous practice and code of conduct, but is again welcomed into Buddha's spiritual family. It is also significant to note that Baker Rōshi has conferred dharma transmission to a number of his own second-generation spiritual heirs.

Initially, SFZC had two obvious methods of extending its dharma family and Suzuki Rōshi's branch of the Sōtō Zen lineage: 1) internally, by creating affiliate centers in new locations; and 2) externally, through the work and centers founded by Baker's second-generation spiritual heirs.[27] The former method was accomplished by the acquisition of Tassajara Hot Springs in 1966, which was established as a monastic center; and by the opening of Green Gulch Farm in 1972. Nonetheless, SFZC has not expanded aggressively as some other Zen communities have done. The latter method was truncated by Baker's resignation as abbot in 1983. While Baker later established Zen communities in New Mexico and Colorado, his relationship to SFZC remains somewhat unclear.

One community that has successfully expanded both internally and externally is the Zen Center of Los Angeles (ZCLA), founded by Taizan Maezumi Rōshi. Maezumi Rōshi came to Los Angeles in 1956, one year after having received dharma transmission from Hakujun Kuroda Rōshi. In addition, he received *inka* from Koryu Osaka Rōshi and Hakuun Yasutani Rōshi, making him a dharma heir in three different Zen lineages. While he initially served as priest at Zenshuji Temple, the United States headquarters of Sōtō Zen, he established ZCLA in 1967. Before his untimely death in 1995, Maezumi Rōshi had built an impressive community that included the Kuroda Institute (founded in 1976), as well as the White Plum Sangha, which is an association of Maezumi Rōshi's dharma successors.

Unlike SFZC, Maezumi expanded his dharma family both internally and externally. During his lifetime, he worked to help his closest disciples establish six temples in the United States and Europe, each of which was formally registered with the headquarters of Sōtō Zen in Japan. Many of these centers now have their own affiliates as well. In addition, more than fifty groups in the Americas and Europe are affiliated with ZCLA. Perhaps more importantly, Maezumi Rōshi offered dharma transmission to twelve of his disciples. Prior to his death, Maezumi Rōshi conferred *inka* on Bernard Glassman, who was his most senior disciple. Most importantly, many of those who were transmitted by Maezumi have become certified as *rōshi*s in their own right, and have in turn transmitted Maezumi's lineage to a large number of their own second-generation Western dharma heirs. As a result, the spiritual kinship fostered by the White Plum Sangha has expanded exponentially, both numerically and geographically. Never lacking in creative approaches to expanding his dharma family, Glassman has conferred dharma transmission to a number of individuals with formal religious affiliations outside of, and in addition to, Buddhism. In 1991, he transmitted Robert Jinsen Kennedy, a Jesuit priest and theology professor. Kennedy, in turn attained *rōshi* status, and created his own dharma lineage, having transmitted several teachers in his own right. Glassman also transmitted Rabbi Don Ani Shalom Singer. This circumstance has fostered what Seager calls "a state of creative ferment,"[28] while yielding not only an intra-Buddhist dialogue but also an interreligious dialogue as well, witnessed by the foundation of organizations such as the Society for Buddhist-Christian Studies.

As noted above, no Buddhist tradition places higher emphasis on the role of lineage and spiritual kinship than that of Tibetan Buddhism. That the role of the spiritual teacher (or guru) is preeminent in traditional Tibetan Buddhism can be verified by the establishment of the figure of the guru as a fourth "refuge," added to the traditional three of Buddha, Dharma, and Sangha. According to John Powers,

> Guru yoga purifies one's awareness through practices that involve visualizing the teacher as an embodiment of the pure, exalted wisdom of buddhahood.[29]

The Tibetan Buddhist tradition is filled with magnificient stories of the patriarchs of the various lineages, and tales of their incarnations in an unbroken chain of *tulkus* (Tib. *sprul sku*) in each lineage. Previously, the tradition of incarnate lamas had been confined to Inner Asia, but in the more recent period of Buddhism's globalization, *tulkus* have begun to appear, and be identified as such, in the West. The phenomenon was first brought to the public's eye by Bernardo Bertolucci's film *Little Buddha,* but many other cases have come to light in subsequent years.

Perhaps the primary means for extending spiritual kinships and widening Western dharma families in the various lineages of Tibetan Buddhism is through the propitious use of "empowerments." These ritual initiations, called *abhiṣeka* in Sanskrit and *dbang* in Tibetan, are essential for certain practices because they create a karmic "link" between the practitioner and the practice. Some of the most famous and important empowerments, like that of the *Kālacakra,* were once limited to highly experienced and accomplished practitioners, but are now routinely performed in Western lands, and often by the Dalai Lama himself. Like the Zen tradition, Tibetan Buddhism has gradually spawned a series of Western students of Asian masters who have become highly visible and provocative teachers in their own right; these have begun to build their own spiritual families in the West.

Two additional, innovative means of developing spiritual kinship relationships have developed in some Western communities of Tibetan Buddhism. On August 22, 1976, Chögyam Trungpa, perhaps the most visible and well-known Tibetan Buddhist to have established residence in the West, empowered one of his students, Thomas F. Rich, as Vajra Regent, and gave him the Buddhist name Ösel Tendzin. Previously, Rich had been executive vice president of Trungpa's primary communities, Vajradhatu and the Nalanda Foundation. He assumed leadership of Vajradhatu in 1977, and thereafter, when his teacher went on a yearlong retreat. His empowerment was confirmed in 1977 by Gyalwa Karmapa as the first Western student to be empowered in this way. Rich died of AIDS in 1990, three years after the death of his teacher, and control of Trungpa's communities was entrusted to Trungpa's eldest son Ösel Rangdröl Mukpo, born in 1962. Eventually identified as an incarnation of Mipham Rinpoche, he was installed as Sakyong, or leader of the now-named Shambhala International, in May 1995. Shortly thereafter he presented another innovative device for extending spiritual kinships within his worldwide organization by identifying nine of the community's most senior students as *"acharyas,"* or teachers. Overall, the combination of both traditional and innovative techniques for spreading spiritual kinship relationships in Vajrayana Buddhism has been profoundly successful in the West.

Unlike the Mahayana and Vajrayana schools present in the Western world, Theravāda Buddhism manifests an altogether different circumstance with respect to spiritual kinship relationships in a Western setting. In the first place, immigrant Theravāda Buddhism in the United States is almost entirely a post-1965 development, resulting from the 1965 amendments to the Immigration and Nationality Act of 1952. Paul Numrich has estimated that within a quarter-century there were between one-half and three-quarters of a million immigrant Theravāda Buddhists in the United States in 1990,[30] and the number is likely much larger now. While Numrich acknowledges that generalizations are difficult in the immigrant Theravāda community, due in part to the ethnic diversity of that group, he does note that

> In an important sense, the temples of this study prefer to import foreign monks for the role they play in transmitting traditional Asian Theravāda in an American context.[31]

In other words, immigrant Theravāda Buddhism seeks not so much to effect an Americanization process in its temples as it does to maintain traditional Asian Buddhist values. As a result many, if not most, Theravāda temples in the United States maintain some institutional affiliation with a parent community in Asia, even if that affiliation is informal. In a sense, the spiritual kinships in Western Theravāda communities are perhaps best categorized as backward-looking, rather than expressing a concern for establishing new roots. This suspicion is supported by the fact that traditional Theravāda Buddhism has been perhaps the least attractive to the convert Buddhist community, and, among the Theravāda converts, their association with the immigrant Theravāda community is utterly minimal. This phenomenon has resulted in what Numrich has labeled "parallel congregations," in which ethnic, immigrant Theravādins and convert Theravādins might occupy the same geographic temple space, most often at different times, while engaging in vastly different activities.

At the outset of this paper, we learned that the primacy of the monastic community was paramount in early Buddhism, and that emphasis has remained profoundly intact in Asian Theravāda countries. Unfortunately, the Theravāda monastic community in the West remains tiny, further limiting the possibility for strong spiritual kinship ties to develop in the new setting.

Summary and Conclusions

One of the most profound developments in the globalization of Buddhism is that the various traditions, once so distinct in their respective Asian homelands, now find themselves in close proximity—for the first time in the history of Buddhism—to one another in their new Western settings. It is not unusual for Theravāda, Mahayana, and Vajrayana groups to find themselves neighbors in the same country, city, and even neighborhood. No doubt one can argue that this represents a great prosperity for the Buddhist tradition, but it also presents serious challenges and even liabilities as well. Is it possible to make some sense out of the seemingly conflicting emphases of these diverse Buddhist traditions, sects, and schools? Is it possible to find some unifying principle or basis by which the huge diversity of global Buddhism might reestablish the sense of spiritual kinship among all Buddhists that prevailed in Buddha's original sangha of the four quarters?

On November 12, 1987, the American Buddhist Congress was formed, with a carefully stated policy of goals, objectives, and activities. At the core of their goals is an attempt to

> Serve as a major representative of member Buddhist organizations and individuals in expressing their collective voice in matters of Buddhist interests at all levels.[32]

Speaking with a "collective voice" represents a major attempt to facilitate an American Buddhist tradition that reflects and represents the spirit of the Buddha's original family, while encompassing the totality of the Buddha's diverse community of *kalyāṇamitras*. This does not mean to presume that global Buddhism will present "one dharma," as Joseph Goldstein's popular book *One Dharma: The Emerging Western Buddhism*[33] suggests, but rather as one vast but diverse spiritual family.

Notes

1 This essay was originally published in *Religious Studies and Theology,* vol. 22, no. 1, pp. 27–43.

2 See Paul David Numrich, "Vinaya in Theravāda Temples in the United States," *Journal of Buddhist Ethics* 1 (1994): pp. 23–32. The passage appears in the *Samantapāsādikā* I, 102; *Mahāvaṃsa* 126; *Dīpavaṃsa* chapter 14, verses 20–24; and *Vinaya-nidāna* 103.

3 See Michael B. Carrithers, "'They Will Be Lords Upon the Island': Buddhism in Sri Lanka," in *The World of Buddhism: Buddhist Monks and Nuns in Society and Culture,* ed. Heinz Bechert and Richard Gombrich (New York: Facts on File, 1984), p. 133.

4 Akira Hirakawa, *A History of Indian Buddhism: From Śākyamuni to Early Mahayana,* trans. and ed. Paul Groner (Honolulu: University of Hawai'i Press, 1990), p. 60.

5 Reginald Ray, *Buddhist Saints in India: A Study in Buddhist Values and Orientations* (New York: Oxford University Press, 1994), p. 21.

6 Étienne Lamotte, *History of Indian Buddhism: From the Origins to the Śaka Era,* trans. Sara Webb-Boin (Louvain: Institute Orientaliste de l'Universit, Catholique de Louvain, 1988), p. 54.

7 *Saṃyutta-nikāya* XLV.2.2ff. See, for example, M. Leon Feer, ed., *Saṃyutta Nikaya* (1884–1894; London: Luzac & Company, Ltd., 1960, reprint), vol. 5, pp. 2–3; and F. L. Woodward, trans., *The Book of the Kindred Sayings (Saṃyutta Nikāya)* (1884–1904; London: Luzac & Company, Ltd., 1956, reprint), part V, pp. 2–3.

8 *Saṃyutta-nikāya* III.2.8ff. See, for example, Feer, ed., *Saṃyutta Nikaya,* vol. 1, pp. 88–89; and Woodward, trans., *The Book of the Kindred Sayings (Saṃyutta Nikāya),* part I, pp. 112–115.

9 Nathan Katz, *Buddhist Images of Human Perfection: The Arahant of the Sutta Piṭaka Compared with the Bodhisattva and the Mahāsiddha* (Delhi: Motilal Banarsidass, 1982), p. 190.

10 *Mahāvagga* I.32.1. See Hermann Oldenberg, ed., *The Vinaya Piṭakaṃ,* vol. 1 (London: Luzac & Company, Ltd., 1964, reprint), p. 60. The translation is from I. B. Horner, trans., *The Book of the Discipline* (1952; London: Luzac & Company, Ltd., 1962, reprint), vol. 4, p. 79.

11 See J. Estlin Carpenter, ed., *The Dīgha Nikāya* (1911; London: Luzac & Company, Ltd., 1960, reprint), vol. 3, pp. 189–190 (XXXI.29).

12 Hirakawa, *A History of Indian Buddhism,* p. 308.

13 Holmes Welch, *The Practice of Chinese Buddhism 1900–1950* (Cambridge, MA: Harvard University Press, 1967), p. 247.

14 See Robert Buswell, *The Zen Monastic Experience* (Princeton, NJ: Princeton University Press, 1992), p. 82.

15 Ibid., pp. 82–83.

16 William M. Bodiford, "Dharma Transmission in Sōtō Zen: Manzan Dōhaku's Reform Movement," *Monumenta Nipponica* 46, no. 4 (Winter 1991): p. 423.

[17] Ibid.

[18] See "The Kagyu Lineage," http://www.nalandabodhi.org/kagyu2.html (accessed May 29, 2002); also see the general website of the Mahabodhi Society of USA, http://www. mahabodhi.org (accessed May 29, 2002).

[19] See Nalandabodhi, "The History of Buddhism in Tibet," http://www.nalandabodhi.org/tibet_buddhism.html (accessed May 29, 2002). Another valuable website on lineages is Simhanada, "The Lineages of Buddhism," http://www.simhas.org/lineages./html (accessed May 29, 2002) and the additional links to individual lineages in the Tibetan and Chinese Buddhist traditions.

[20] For important reading on the World Parliament of Religions, consult Richard H. Seager, *The World's Parliament of Religions: The East-West Encounter, Chicago, 1893* (Bloomington, IN: Indiana University Press, 1995).

[21] Anagarika Dharmapala, "Opening Address," cited in *The World's Parliament of Religions. An Illustrated and Popular Story of the World's First Parliament of Religions, Held in Chicago in Connection with the Columbian Exposition of 1893*, ed. Rev. John Henry Barrows, 2 vols. (Chicago: The Parliament Publishing Company, 1893), pp. 95–96.

[22] Paul Numrich, *Old Wisdom in the New World: Americanization in Two Immigrant Theravada Temples* (Knoxville, TN: University of Tennessee Press, 1996), pp. xix–xx.

[23] Charles Prebish, *American Buddhism* (North Scituate, MA: Duxbury Press, 1979), p. 192.

[24] Richard H. Seager, *Buddhism in America* (New York: Columbia University Press, 1999), p. 243.

[25] Shunryu Suzuki, *Zen Mind, Beginner's Mind,* ed. Trudy Dixon (New York: Weatherhill, 1970).

[26] David Chadwick, *Crooked Cucumber: The Life and Zen Teaching of Shunryu Suzuki* (New York: Broadway Books, 1999).

[27] Suzuki Rōshi's premature death makes it impossible to determine whether he would have conferred *inka* on additional disciples, thus leaving Richard Baker as his sole Western dharma heir.

[28] Seager, *Buddhism in America,* p. 231.

[29] John Powers, *Introduction to Tibetan Buddhism* (Ithaca, NY: Snow Lion Publications, 1995), p. 270.

[30] See Numrich, *Old Wisdom in the New World,* p. xix.

[31] Ibid., pp. xix, 45.

[32] See a full statement on the background, goals, objectives, and activities of the American Buddhist Congress at http://americanbuddhistcongress.org/aboutus.html (accessed June 10, 2002).

[33] Joseph Goldstein, *One Dharma: the Emerging Western Buddhism* (New York: HarperCollins, 2002).

How Not to Talk about Pure Land Buddhism: A Critique of Huston Smith's (Mis)Representations

Richard K. Payne
Dean, Institute of Buddhist Studies, Berkeley

Preface

Unfortunately, I only came to know Roger Corless as anything more than an academic colleague late in his life, after his retirement from Duke University and eventual relocation close enough to the Institute of Buddhist Studies that he could teach for us on a regular basis. Indeed, the last time I saw Roger was at the opening of our new offices in Berkeley, California. Despite the advanced state of the illness that would eventually kill him, he was happy—no, enthusiastic—to see the new facility now devoted to the propagation of Pure Land Buddhism. The frontispiece is a photograph of Roger taken that day and evidences his joyful attitude.

As described by Gordon Bermant in his preface to this volume, "Appreciating Roger" (pp. xi–xviii), the Roger Corless that I came to know encompassed many distinct identities. In addition to other things, he was both a Shin Buddhist and a Catholic, and, as I only learned after his death, he was involved with Nichiren Buddhism as well.

In the present popular culture this kind of religiously plural identity is perhaps not uncommon. It seems, however, that the autonomy of each element within a personal plurality is often blurred into a kind of vague and diffuse "spirituality." With Roger, however, I never had the sense that he equated the various religious commitments that constituted his life, much less confusing them with one another.

Introduction

In contemporary American culture, Huston Smith is widely recognized and esteemed as a leading scholar of religious studies. His *World's Religions* (originally, *The Religions of Man*)[1] has sold millions of copies and is still used as a textbook in introductory courses across the nation. Even people who do not recognize his name hold views about religion that have been deeply informed by his teachings and writings. Through his writings, teaching, television appearances, and works in other popular venues, Smith has played a formative role in developing the contemporary American understanding of religion. When I first met him, through a class offered by the University of California Extension, Santa Cruz, sometime in the late 1970s, I found him to be very charismatic, a quality that in itself made his vision of religion convincing. His view that religion is a central part of personal existence has been part of a more general social development toward an individualized understanding of religion, moving away from institutional forms of religion toward something more personally relevant.[2] In addition, he has provided an alternative to rejecting the unknown religious Other as a threat. Smith has spoken reassuringly to a society confronted by the reality of religious diversity as happening in our own towns and cities, if not on our own streets. In contrast to views of religions that see them as competing—sometimes violently—over irreconcilable claims regarding truth and value, Smith presents a view of religious diversity as forming a harmonious whole in which each complements the other.

It is noteworthy, then, when in his recent *Buddhism: A Concise Introduction*[3] he turns his attention, after years of neglect, to Pure Land Buddhism. For these reasons, how Smith represents Pure Land Buddhism not only reflects widespread conceptions about the nature of religion generally, and Buddhism per se, but may also have a lasting influence on how Pure Land is received more widely. There are, however, three problematic aspects of Smith's treatment of Pure Land Buddhism specifically, and of Buddhism generally.

The first of these is that he uncritically perpetuates a particular image of Buddhism, that known as "Buddhist modernism." The second problem with Smith's treatment of Shin and of Buddhism is his use of Christian religious concepts and categories as if they were universal. The final problem is Smith's own theological commitment to Traditionalism, which informs his late representations of Buddhism, forcing it to fit with his own theology. After discussing each of these three problems in Smith's representations of religion and Buddhism, we will examine his representations of Pure Land and Shin Buddhism. First, however, it is worth considering the historical development leading up to Smith's treatment of Pure Land, as this history itself reveals important limitations that create specific distortions in its representation of Buddhism.

History of Smith's Pure Land "Afterword"

Published under joint authorship with Philip Novak, *Buddhism: A Concise Introduction* is divided into two sections. Except for one new chapter, the first section largely repeats the Buddhism chapter of Smith's previous work, *Religions of Man/World's Religions.* The second section by Novak discusses the movement of Buddhism to the West. This second section is followed by the Afterword written by Smith dealing specifically with Pure Land Buddhism—a topic of which he claims special knowledge because of his experiences as the child of Christian missionaries growing up in China.

The first section has had two previous incarnations. First, there is the chapter as it appeared in the original *Religions of Man,* published in 1958. In 1991, thirty-three years later, *Religions of Man* was reissued in a revised edition under the title *The World's Religions: Our Great Wisdom Traditions.* This revision comes after his "discovery" of Traditionalism in the 1969–1970 academic year, an event that may explain his choice of subtitle for the new edition. Other than minor editorial changes, the only significant change to the Buddhism chapter was the addition of a section treating Tibetan Buddhism. Similarly, the difference between the chapter in its second incarnation in *The World's Religions* and its third incarnation as the first part of *Buddhism: A Concise Introduction* is for the most part relatively minor. Beyond minor editorial changes, in the process of converting the sections into separate chapters they are expanded by the addition of apposite stories. The only significant change to this third incarnation of the first section is a new chapter on Theravādin *vipassanā*—the meditation practice followed by the work's coauthor, Novak, and hence probably from his pen.

Thus, between 1958 and 2004, the section by Smith has only been revised to the extent of having two sections added: one on Tibetan Buddhism and one on Theravāda. But other than these two new chapters—what might be referred to as a purely aggregative change—no rethinking of the content, no revision of the understanding of Buddhism as it was known in the 1950s, was undertaken. This lack of any significant revisioning between 1958 and 2004 ignores a huge body of research on Buddhism that had been published in the intervening years.

While evidencing the limitations of Smith's scholarship, I believe it reveals more than that. Dismissing more than four and a half decades' worth of research on the very topics on which Smith continued to publish is not simply a matter of a lack of awareness or interest, but rather appears to be the consequence of a presumption regarding the nature of religion.

This is the presumption that every religion has an essential core that remains unchanged, no matter what additional information becomes available. It seems that as far as Smith is concerned, he determined the essence of Buddhism and adequately described it in 1958. Therefore, there has been no need to reconsider his characterization of Buddhism—even after almost half a century, during which time hundreds of publications about Buddhism have appeared. The essence that Smith used to structure his representation of Buddhism is that image promoted by Buddhist modernism.

Uncritical Perpetuation of Buddhist Modernism

Buddhist modernism presents a version of Buddhism that was created during the latter part of the nineteenth and first part of the twentieth centuries in response to assaults on Buddhism by Christian missionaries. In an attempt to assert the value of Buddhism, Buddhist apologists—both Euro-American and Asian—created a representation of Buddhism that itself reflected the religious ideas and values of liberal Protestantism.[4] Indeed, some authors have felt it appropriate to use the term "Protestant Buddhism" for this modern interpretation of Buddhism.[5] Three of these religious ideas seem to have been particularly formative for the modernist reinterpretation of Buddhism.[6]

These ideas were, first, that religion should be a rational system of personal self-development—which has as its corollary an opposition to superstition and ritualism. Second, that the religions important in the modern world all have an historical founder whose self-appointed task was the purification of a decadent religious system. Third, in keeping with the social gospel of nineteenth-century liberal Protestantism, Buddhist modernism also emphasized social reform as a more general expression of its purification of a decadent religious system. This reformist program included emphasizing the role of the laity in decision-making; extending practices and standards previously only undertaken by monks, such as meditation, to the laity; and asserting a congruence between Buddhism properly understood and modern science. As Sarah Levine and David N. Gellner have put it,

> Buddhist modernists mark a radical departure from traditional Buddhist revivalists, because they seek to monasticize the laity as well, that is, to bring

> the laity up to a level of Buddhist virtue that had previously been thought possible and appropriate only for monks. Modernist revivalism is frequently combined with social reform, and usually consists in viewing the religion in question as scientific or at least as compatible with modern science.[7]

Thus, the rejection of supposedly irrational practices, such as ritual, and superstitious beliefs was motivated by the desire to portray Buddhism as a rational system of self-development. In this process, individual meditation practices were promoted as paradigmatic of Buddhism—part of the "monasticization" of the laity.[8]

As noted above, despite its recent publication date (2004), the substantive core of Smith and Novak's *Buddhism: A Concise Introduction* dates to the mid-1950s, when the Buddhist modernist representation of Buddhism was the one most easily accessible. Smith perpetuates its claim to authority as "original" Buddhism uncritically, and has continued to perpetuate it as such without change. It is the Buddhist modernist portrayal of Buddhism that informs Smith's representations of the essence of Buddhism.

That Smith essentializes Buddhism in accord with the self-representations of Buddhist modernism means that his representation of Buddhism is structured in two specific ways. First, as discussed above, Buddhist modernism selectively highlights those religious values that appeared to be congruent with late nineteenth- and early twentieth-century liberal Protestant theology. Second, it fits the history of Buddhism into the mold of Protestant conceptions of the universal pattern of religious history. Protestant religious historiography imposes a cyclic pattern of a founder who teaches an originally pure, rationalistic morality that gradually decays, is reformed back to its original purity, only to be followed by another cycle of decay and reform.

This liberal Protestant revisioning of the essence of Buddhism is presented by Smith when he states that the Buddha preached a religion that was "without authority, ritual, theology, tradition, grace, and the supernatural."[9] Immediately thereafter, Smith goes on to characterize "original Buddhism"[10] in positive terms as empirical, scientific, pragmatic, therapeutic, psychological, egalitarian, and individualistic.[11] Doing so, he emphasizes exactly those qualities that a mid–twentieth-century liberal Protestant audience would find acceptable—and indeed, hardly a more concise summary of the Buddhist modernist representation of Buddhism can be found.[12]

Smith has set up this characterization of the "original" teachings of the Buddha as part of the Buddha's being a figure of reform—modeled precisely on Protestant historiography's understanding of Jesus as a reformer of temple Judaism, which is in turn itself the basis of the images of Martin Luther and John Calvin as reformers of medieval Catholic Christianity. Making the history of Buddhism fit into this mold, Smith characterizes the religion of India at the time of the Buddha as "corrupt, degenerate, and irrelevant, matted with superstition and burdened with worn-out rituals."[13] At the same time, by portraying the Buddha's teachings in this manner, Smith manages to set up the future of Buddhism—when rituals, speculative philosophy, appeals to authority, and appeals to the power of buddhas and bodhisattvas become evident—as a process of decline and decadence.[14] This dynamic comes into play when he presents Hōnen and Shinran as the founding figures of Japanese Pure Land Buddhism.

While Smith is not responsible for creating the Buddhist modernist representation of Buddhism (or for creating the Protestant historiography of religion), he is responsible for perpetuating it. This perpetuation is itself evidence of a second set of presumptions that Smith expresses when he describes his own purposes in writing *The Religions of Man* originally. He models his presentation on music appreciation, asserting that he is not interested in a balanced, historical approach but rather a presentation of the best of religions—their values.

> Probably as much bad music as good has been written in the course of human history, but we do not ask that a course in music appreciation give it equal space. Time being limited, we expect no apology for spending it with the best. I have taken a similar position with regard to religion.[15]

What is implicit in such an approach is the presumption that Huston Smith is himself in a position to judge what is "best" in any and all religions, as well as the presumption that it is only what he considers to be "the best" that people need to know about a religion. Thus, what we have is not "original Buddhism," as Smith claims, but *Smith's* Buddhism—his judgment as to what is best about Buddhism and his selective representation of Buddhism according to that judgment. The rhetorical strategy of cloaking the representation of Buddhism that Smith himself has created in raiment of "original Buddhism," replete with all the weight of authority such a phrase brings with it, is an instance of bad faith.[16]

Universalizing Christian Categories and Concepts

Not only has Smith chosen to ignore all of the advances in Buddhist studies scholarship that have taken place over the last four and a half decades, but as a work in religious studies his text similarly fails to note advances in that field as well. One of the key issues for religious studies in the English-speaking world has been an increasing awareness of the problems involved in raising familiar concepts and categories to the status of universal concepts and categories. Although these familiar concepts and categories are (almost by definition) Christian, if not more specifically modern Protestant, once abstracted from that context they are commonly treated as context-neutral and universal. Once considered to be context-neutral and universal, it is assumed that they can be applied without regard to historical period or sociocultural setting. From this assumption it follows that the same concepts and categories employed, for example, in the study of late nineteenth-century American Protestantism can be applied universally—that these same concepts and categories will apply equally well to all religions, no matter whether one is studying such widely divergent religions as early medieval Indian Buddhism or postcolonial Afro-Brazilian Candomblé.[17]

One example of the difficulties produced by the tendency in religious studies to universalize Christian concepts and categories is the use of the concept "soteriology." Although employed in its Latinate form, this refers to salvation, which in the Christian context implicates a three-part narrative structure: salvation from sin by a savior. Yet, the human condition as defined by Buddhism is arguably one of ignorance, not sin. The three-part narrative structure for Buddhism would instead be: awakening from ignorance by following the eightfold path. To universalize soteriology is, then, to at least implicitly define Buddhism as a religion of salvation, and in doing so to misrepresent its most fundamental teachings.

While it may be understandable that a work on religious studies published in the mid-1950s would have made the assumption that Christian concepts and categories could be universalized, to perpetuate that assumption into the treatment of Buddhism in 2004 is much more problematic. Like the uncritical perpetuation of Buddhist modernism, the unreflective universalization of Christian concepts and categories also constitutes a distorting factor in Smith's representations of Buddhism.

Another example of Smith's unreflective universalization of Christian concepts and categories is the use of "grace" in his representation of Buddhism. (Smith also equates "other-power" [*tariki*] with the Christian concept of "grace,"[18] which will be discussed below in our examination of the problems with Smith's treatment of Pure Land per se.) He introduces grace into his representation of Buddhism in the chapter in which he discusses the differences between Theravāda and Mahayana. There he claims that Theravāda asserts that "self-reliance is our only recourse. . . . For Mahayana, in contrast, grace is a fact."[19] The closest he comes to defining his use of the term "grace" in a Buddhist context is to reference the Mahayana "doctrine of cosmic help (grace)."[20] This hardly explains which *Buddhist* concept he intends.

The idea of grace is not context-neutral. It is part of a complex of ideas, the entirety of which is at least implicitly entailed by its use. Taking as one example, a Catholic encyclopedia explains that

> Christian grace is a fundamental idea of the Christian religion, the pillar on which, by a special ordination of God, the majestic edifice of Christianity rests in its entirety. Among the three fundamental ideas—sin, redemption, and grace—grace plays the part of the means, indispensable and Divinely ordained, to effect the redemption from sin through Christ and to lead men to their eternal destiny in heaven.[21]

In its native Christian context, grace is identified as an integral part of the description of the human condition as one of sin, and in need of salvation, which is attained through grace. An unnuanced use of the term "grace" in reference to Buddhism implicitly introduces this entire complex of ideas.

Also typical of Smith's universalizing is his claim that the traditional worldview is one committed to a "great chain of being" metaphysics.[22] The "great chain of being" was given name by Arthur Lovejoy, but the idea originated with Plotinus' adaptation of Platonic thought, in what is now known as Neoplatonism. The idea of the "great chain of being" is that the phenomenal world, the world of our experience, is derivative from a higher reality. This is also known as "emanationist metaphysics," in that being or existence emanates out from the ultimate source, progressively creating lesser forms of being, including human existence. The metaphor of the chain is used to convey the idea that there is a dependence of the lower upon the upper, but in Neoplatonism the lesser is not only derivatively dependent upon the higher, it is less real. The identity of the real with the good in Neoplatonic thought also gives a moral ranking to the levels of reality—the higher levels being of greater goodness, the lower being increasingly evil. In this system, that which is purely evil is the purely nonexistent.

Smith's particular version of the great chain of being is Kabbalistic in character. Kabbalah is also an emanationist metaphysics, one in which the ultimate source of being is known as the "Ein Sof." By describing

Smith's view as Kabbalistic I mean that in his conception the source of being is inherently unknowable for humans; it exists behind a mystical "cloud of unknowing." The source of being in Smith's theology is unknowable just as the Ein Sof of Kabbalistic thought is. This presumption of the limits of human knowledge is in direct opposition to the Buddhist goal of wisdom as knowledge of impermanence.

One of the consequences of emanationist metaphysics is a belief that there is a hierarchical order of being—that some things are more real than others, and that the less real derive from the more real. In another of his recent works, *Why Religion Matters*, Smith argues that hierarchy is not only one metaphysical system among others and is spiritually better than any other, but makes the extraordinary—and unsubstantiated—claim that it is the sole metaphysical system of all religions.

> Etymologically, *hierarchy* comes close to being a perfect word for joining the two virtues—holiness, *heiros*, and sovereign power, *arkhes*—which, conjoined, announce religion's central claim.[23]

That a theocratic politics would follow from acceptance of such a claim is passed over in silence by Smith. And, as will be discussed further below, as an empirical claim, this universal generalization is simply false.[24]

Universalizing religious concepts and categories involves treating them as if they were unproblematically applicable to all religious traditions, without regard to historical or social location—as context-neutral. Smith universalizes both broadly Christian concepts and categories, such as grace, as well as his own theological ideas, such as emanationist metaphysics and the hierarchical view that is its corollary. Doing so, however, misleads readers into thinking that they understand something, such as Buddhism, when in fact they are being led to something quite different—Smith's own theology. In such a case the assertion of a fundamental unity of religions obscures rather than clarifies.

Smith's Soft Traditionalism

Traditionalism: perennialism + anti-modernism. To adequately grasp the problematic character of Smith's Pure Land "Afterword" requires that we see it within the larger context of Smith's own ideological commitments. This broader context goes beyond his specific treatment of Shin, and even his treatment of Buddhism in its entirety, to include his overall Traditionalist project—a personal commitment he has explicitly embraced. This, however, means that we will need to first understand Traditionalism as a system of thought.

Roughly speaking, Traditionalism combines perennialism and anti-modernism. From perennialism it takes the notion that there is a single, universal, ultimate religious truth that is variously manifest in the different religious traditions. The mystics are the ones who have accessed this single, universal, and ultimate truth, and they are, therefore, the source and definition of that which is authentic and valuable in any religious tradition.

The anti-modernism of the Traditionalists is rooted in Romanticism, historically the intellectual background for Traditionalism. Much of the rhetorical appeal of Traditionalism is found in its prophetic decrying of the modern condition. In light of this diagnosis of the current condition of humanity, it prescribes an abandonment of modernity and a return to traditional social organization and traditional religion. The common human propensity for nostalgia about an idealized past is here converted into a religious—and, in fact, social and political—program.

Mark Sedgwick has been instrumental in identifying Traditionalism as a coherent and influential—albeit largely unrecognized—system of religious thought. Sedgwick distinguishes between "hard Traditionalists" who are explicit in their commitment to Traditionalism, and "soft Traditionalists" who use Traditionalist ideas but who do not make their commitments explicit. Smith is a somewhat ambiguous case. His most popular and successful works make no reference to Traditionalism or to the founding Traditionalist figures, such as René Guénon (1886–1951) and Frithjof Schuon (1907–1998). Yet in an autobiographical tone, he has written repeatedly about the revelatory quality of his encounter with the writings of Schuon.[25] In a tale clearly benefiting from frequent retelling, we are given a vision of a miraculous discovery of three of Schuon's works explaining Buddhism and Shintō, Vedānta, and Islam at exactly the right moments in a year-long around-the-world study tour in 1969–1970. Not only did these books miraculously appear at just the right moment, but they led Smith to reconsider Schuon's *The Transcendent Unity of Religions* and resolve thereby his own personal theological quandary regarding the unity and diversity of religions.

Smith's implicit Traditionalism becomes evident when he asserts in *Why Religion Matters* that he can "use the terms *traditional* and *religious* interchangeably, for all traditional societies were religious."[26] This kind of apparently purposeful terminological confusion is endemic to Smith's writings, and makes it possible for him to imply certain conclusions without arguing for them. In this case, the unexpressed implication of this formulation is a dualistic opposition. If traditional and religious are coterminous, then modern is necessarily irreligious. Under such an implication the ideas of a modern religion or a traditional secularism are simply oxymorons, despite the existence of both.

The concept of "tradition" is central to Traditionalism, but is itself deployed rhetorically without clear definition—as an empty signifier it is much more powerful and, therefore, more useful. Having established this rhetorical grounding, Smith goes on to assert that all religions, presumably including Buddhism, share five characteristics. While this characterization of all traditional religion under these specific five characteristics seems to be unique to Smith,[27] it is important as a clear expression of Smith's own theological precommitment to a perennialist view regarding the unity underlying the appearance of diversity.

The five characteristics that Smith asserts apply to all religions are, first, that "*spirit is fundamental and matter derivative*"; second, that "human beings are *the less who have derived from the more*"; third, that there is a "*happy ending*"; fourth, since the world is the intentional creation of a perfect being, it is meaningful; and, fifth, that people belong in the world.[28] (He has given other such lists of characteristics elsewhere.[29])

Although Smith presents these five characteristics of traditional religion as unproblematic, each of them is in fact highly contentious. The claim that "spirit is fundamental and matter derivative" only works within those religions that first of all make the spirit-matter distinction. Daoism might, for example, be offered as an instance of a religion in which such a distinction is not made. The closest analogy might be the relation between the Dao and the "ten thousand things," but the Dao is not "spirit," nor are the ten thousand things "matter"—and indeed, in some understandings, the Dao and the ten thousand things do not differ from one another. Second, the notion of human beings as the less which derives from the more is an expression of Neoplatonic emanationism (and perhaps, Anselm's ontological proof), and would hardly apply to religions that do not accept an emanationist metaphysics. Those forms of Hinduism that embrace a cyclic cosmogony would seem to have no such emanationist metaphysics. Not all religions believe in a "happy ending." Certainly the examples of classic Greek religion, as well as the Norse conception of Ragnaröok demonstrate the falsehood of this claim. Likewise, the Hebrew Sheol is not a happy ending either.

That the world is the intentional creation of a perfect being is also not found in Buddhist (or Hindu) cosmogonies, where the cosmos simply has always been, though cycling through periods of creation, decay, and quiescence before reemerging in a new cycle. There are also Native

American mythologies in which the world is the creation of twins, one good and one evil. Finally, the question of whether we humans belong here in this world is only an issue for religions in which the idea has been asserted that we do not—a view perhaps only asserted by Gnosticism. Thus, we find that far from being an empirically based generalization about traditional religions, Smith's five characteristics are in fact an expression of his own theology—an assertion of what religion should be, instead of what it is. Rather than claiming his constructive role in creating this theology, however, he commits an act of bad faith—asserting its objectivity and universality, and claiming the authority of "tradition" for it.

It is in this fashion that Traditionalist thinkers construct a hegemonic metanarrative about religion. Typically the Traditionalist metanarrative combines perennialism, with its own implicit Neoplatonism, and antimodernism. Traditionalism seemingly invariably portrays the history of religion as a process of decay from an idealized past (*gemeinschaft,* or "community" in the romantic sociology of Ferdinand Tönnies[30]) in which communities are portrayed as unified by shared commitments to traditional ways of life. The cause for this decay, this decline from this ideal(ized) past, is identified with the rise of modern society (*gesellschaft,* or "society"), particularly with science and technology, relativism and materialism. From this diagnosis of the contemporary human condition, the prescription is a return to the past, abandoning modernity for a supposedly simpler life, one fully in harmony with the natural and supernatural (hierarchical) order of being.

Having discussed the three distorting lenses through which Smith projects his representation of Buddhism generally, we can now turn our attention specifically to his treatment of Pure Land.

Smith's (Mis)Representations of Pure Land Buddhism

At two points in his "Afterword," Smith explicitly equates Pure Land with Christianity, more particularly with Protestant Christianity. At the start of this chapter, he explains having overlooked Pure Land on the grounds that the focus of general public interest was on Zen at the time he wrote *Religions of Man.* This explanation is itself emblematic of the problems with Smith's approach to religious studies—he is self-consciously not attempting to produce a balanced or comprehensive historically informed work in comparative religions. Instead, it is evident that the interest Anglo-Americans had for Zen was more important for his intended audience, despite the fact that "the largest sect in Japanese Buddhism is Shin Buddhism."[31] Smith's diagnosis for the lack of interest in Pure Land Buddhism is that it did not appear to offer an alternative to Christianity, that it did not have the exotic appeal of Zen.[32] However, rather than exploring the contours of difference between Pure Land and Christianity (much less the problematics of the appeal of the exotic Other[33]), Smith then suggests that it is this very appearance of familiarity that provides the best gateway to understanding the Pure Land tradition.

The first comparison Smith makes is between Pure Land and the Christianities of Paul and Luther, but without any explanation. What he does specifically point to is the soteriological dynamics of evangelical Christianity—as exemplified in the revivalism of George Whitefield and the program of Alcoholics Anonymous—in which grace comes to those who accept their own utter powerlessness and accept their total dependence on a higher power. This is a misleading and utterly superficial understanding of Pure Land thought. Within Pure Land thought itself, dependency on Amida's vow is in fact limited to the question of the eventual attainment of awakening. It in no way extends to a fatalistic abnegation of personal will, as expressed in the saying, "Not mine, O Lord, but thy will be done."

Not only is the Christian concept of grace not universalizable, as discussed above, but if one understands Pure Land thought in its own Buddhist context, Amida is not available as an intercessor. As a buddha *tathāgata*, Amida no longer exists. What is effective is the vow; it is the continuing karmic efficacy of the vow of Amida that anyone thinking of him, even as few as ten times, is assured birth in Sukhāvatī.[34] Smith, however, attributes to Buddhism what can only be seen as a version of the Catholic conception of a Treasure House of Merits accumulated by the saints—

> a storehouse of salvific energy personified by [buddhas] and bodhisattvas who dwell in innumerable ethereal realms. From these luminous, heavenly beings, faithful Buddhists can request and receive, not just some help or help that matches their own efforts, but unlimited help. It is a Cosmic Resource that is not of human making, but from which mortals need only ask in order to receive.[35]

Within the context of Pure Land thought, however, what the vow assures is not assistance with one's marital problems, or with having one's child accepted to the right college, or with getting a raise at work, but only birth in Sukhāvatī, which, while it is a very nice place, is only a stepping-stone—though the final one—on the path to awakening.

Indicative of the way in which Smith simply universalizes Christian concepts, we find embedded in this quotation—without qualification or comment—the phrase "faithful Buddhist." What it means to be a faithful Christian is relatively clear—exclusive and unwavering adherence to a specific set of doctrinal claims, such as the divinity of Jesus. This has its roots in the Hebrew Bible's emphasis on exclusive adherence to Yahweh as the one true God, an emphasis that indirectly reveals the pluralistic reality of ancient Near Eastern religion. But nowhere in its entire history has Buddhism developed a concept like "being faithful" in this sense.

It is also the case that fitting Shin Buddhism into the category of religion as defined by Smith entails undesirable consequences. For example in his other recent work, *Why Religion Matters,* Smith sets up an agonistic dichotomy between science and religion—a move consistent with Smith's increasingly evident commitment to a kind of Kabbalistic Neoplatonist soteriology and cosmology discussed above. If we accept that Buddhism fits into this understanding of religion, then of necessity Buddhism is also set in opposition to science. Yet, as at least suggested above, religion is not a natural but rather a social category—one that we create and maintain through use. Hence, there is no necessary reason either that science and religion should be antagonistic, nor is there any necessary reason that Buddhism be classed as a religion—particularly not as that category is defined by Smith.[36]

As discussed in the second section above, Smith universalizes Christian concepts and categories, applying them uncritically to all religions. One of the Christian conceptions that Smith universalizes in his representation of Pure Land Buddhism is "faith." He does this without any evidence of having reflected on the propriety of using a term so heavily laden with Christian meaning in a Buddhist context—without considering, in this instance, the possibility of differences between the Pure Land concept of *shinjin* and Christian faith. And indeed, in contemporary works this term is frequently glossed as "faith"—a rendering Smith invokes by giving his Afterword the subtitle "The Flowering of Faith." The equation of faith and *shinjin* is not, however, an unproblematic one.

The appropriate way to translate *shinjin,* or even whether it is best left untranslated, has long been a contentious issue among Shin scholars, apologists, and interpreters—the proverbial oceans of ink having been expended on this hotly contested issue. The importance of attending to the religious connotations of such key terms—that these considerations are not simply matters of intellectual posturing—is particularly evident in this case.

The term "faith" as it exists in contemporary Western popular religious discourse necessarily entails two contrastive connotations. The first is the "works versus faith" debate that marked the Reformation. In other words, one cannot use the term "faith" today without it implicitly introducing the concept of works as its contrastive marker. A second connotation entailed by the use of the term "faith," prominent in American religious history, is the contrast between faith and knowledge (or reason).[37] Following the Second Great Awakening (ca. 1800–1840) American Protestant religion took on a distinctly anti-intellectual emphasis, rejecting knowledge as an impediment to faith. The denial that reflective thought serves any religious value corresponds to the Romantic emphasis on the irreducible and veridical character of personal experience—a rhetorical claim often repeated in perennialist assertions regarding the nature of mystical experience, and its privileged epistemological position. The two connotations—faith versus works, and faith versus knowledge—are necessarily entailed in any use of the term "faith" in contemporary American religious culture, whether made explicit or not. The failure to reflect on those connotations explicitly and to bring into discussion the radically different semantic contexts of "faith" in modern American religious culture and *shinjin* in Pure Land Buddhism simply conflates the two. This, then, necessarily leads to a misrepresentation of the meanings intended by the term *shinjin.*

Put briefly, the Sanskrit roots for the term *shinjin* are themselves complex, being both *śraddhā,* the characteristic of confidence in the efficacy of the teachings necessary to engage in practice, and *cittaprasāda,* the mental equanimity attained at a very advanced stage of the path. In a fashion typical of the thought of medieval Japanese Buddhism, medieval Buddhists such as Shinran perform what Paul Groner has referred to as the "shortening of the path," that is, the equation of the beginning of the path with the end.[38] Another very important aspect of the meaning of *shinjin* is that throughout his major work, the *Kyōgyōshinshō,* Shinran equates *shinjin* with *bodhicitta,* the intent to awaken, a central theme running throughout the entirety of Mahayana Buddhism. Smith's failure to indicate to the reader that there are any relevant nuances distinguishing *shinjin* and faith simultaneously binds Pure Land thought to a Christianized conception of it, and unnecessarily obscures its continuity with the rest of Mahayana Buddhism.

As alluded to above, another one of the concepts that has been raised to universal status is mysticism as definitive for all forms of religion. This idea is central to perennialism, a view of religion made popular by Aldous Huxley. According to this view, all religions are based upon, founded upon some mystical experience, and all of these mystical experiences are "ultimately" the same; that is, any differences between the records of these experiences is explained away as "merely cultural." (The reductionist character of this approach does not seem to bother Smith and many others who object to other kinds of reductionisms.) Thus we find Smith claiming that

> Mystics are people who have a talent for sensing places where life's carapace is cracked, and through its chinks they catch glimpses of a world beyond.[39]

He then cites several examples, such as Isaiah, Christ, Arjuna, John, Saul, Augustine, St. Francis, St. Ignatius, and Jacob Boehme. Included in this list is "The Buddha finding the universe turning into a bouquet of flowers at the hour of his enlightenment." First, which description of the Buddha's awakening is he referring to? Second, other descriptions do not fit into Smith's generality about mystics—the Buddha did not see through the "carapace" of life to some "world beyond." He simply saw the way things actually work, understanding that this is different from how we want them to work. This is not access to a transcendent realm—despite the tendency of authors influenced by perennialist assumptions to reduce all founding narratives to reports of a unitary and universal mystical experience.

When we consider Smith's interpretation of Hōnen and Shinran we find that it is itself based on another author's work (see below, "Appendix: Smith's Plagiarism"[40]), one which presents an interpretation of Hōnen and Shinran as if they were German Idealists, thereby according them an appearance close to the Romantic-Traditionalist view to which Smith is himself committed. Taking representative selections from this section of Smith's description of Shin and Pure Land Buddhism, Smith begins by describing Hōnen and Shinran as "world-class metaphysicians who hear in the formula ["*Namu Amida Butsu*"] reverberations of eternity."[41] He then goes on to assert that Shinran claims that

> Ultimately all religions are paradoxical. . . . Our "abysmal sinfulness" is identical with the Unthinkable Power that saves us. The "I" in the I-Thou relationship is identical with the "Thou" and the finite "I am" is identical with the "Eternal I Am. . . ." Our dying to our finite selves is our rebirth in the Universal Self.[42]

Smith claims that this is "Shinran's voice," yet, the description is loaded with anachronisms of the worst kind. Smith's unthinking assertion of anachronisms is evidence of the dehistoricized character of his approach to religion—he doesn't care about understanding a religion in terms of its own time and place, but only as an instantiation of what he conceives to be the singular and universal religious tradition.

To call Hōnen and Shinran, or any Buddhist thinker, a "metaphysician" is to impose a category that is effectively absent from Buddhist thought. The closest Buddhist analogue to metaphysics is abhidharma, which is itself highly psychological in character, and which does not propound any notion of a transcendent absolute. Not only is Buddhist thought distinctly different from Western philosophical metaphysics; an adequate understanding of the significance of Smith's attribution of the title "metaphysician" to Hōnen and Shinran entails a digression through the thought of Frithjof Schuon, noted above as having been formative for Smith's religious views after 1969–1970. Schuon begins his book *The Transcendent Unity of Religions* by making a three-way distinction. Philosophy, according to Schuon, derives from reason—"a purely individual faculty"[43]—and is the lowest of his three epistemological categories. Higher than philosophy is religious faith, which, although it "proceeds from Revelation," is an "indirect and passive participation" in the divine through the vehicle of symbolic representations. Metaphysic (Schuon seems to imply that there is only one by using the singular form) surpasses religion, because it is "a direct and active participation in divine Knowledge."[44] Because an individual's "innermost essence . . . is not distinct from his Divine Principle," one capable of direct intellectual intuition of the divine has an absolute certainty, and is able to perceive the higher truths through the veils of religious symbolism and dogma.[45] Thus, Smith's ascription of the title "metaphysician" to Hōnen and Shinran has very specific Traditionalist significance, but which he avoids making explicit.

Continuing then with the other anachronistic features of Smith's portrayal of Shinran, while "reverberations of eternity" has a nice poetic ring to it, the idea of eternity per se does not play the same religious role in Buddhist thought as it does in Christian thought, where it is tied into discussions regarding the doctrine of creation and God's role as creator. The notion of "all religions" is certainly not one that Shinran could have possibly concerned himself with, as the idea had not yet been formulated anywhere at that time—not in Japan, but also not in Europe. While "paradox" is central to Neoplatonic conceptions of how one achieves direct insight into the nature of the One, it is actually not part of Buddhist thought regarding the path—despite the existence of misleadingly Neoplatonic interpretations of *kōans* and Indian logic.

"Unthinkable power" is another nice-sounding phrase, one pointing toward the Kabbalistic character of Smith's emanationist metaphysics. It is a phrase, however, that entirely misrepresents Shinran's thought. Central to all Pure Land Buddhism, including the forms propagated by Hōnen and Shinran, is the practice of nenbutsu (Ch. *nianfo;* Skt. *buddhānusmṛti*), which means to hold the Buddha in mind, either through visualization of an image or through recitation of the name. If Amida is "unthinkable," as Smith asserts, then the entire structure of Shin doctrine is based on a fallacy—for we are constantly assured that it is by thinking about Amida—that is, nenbutsu—that one is assured of birth in Sukhāvatī.

The formulation of "I and Thou" is from Martin Buber, a twentieth-century Austrian Jewish mystical theologian. How could Shinran, working several centuries earlier, have made the assertion that "I" and "Thou" are identical? And Buber's distinction between an "I-Thou" and an "I-it" relation is itself based on Kantian philosophic conceptions postdating Shinran by several centuries, and located in an entirely different philosophic discourse. Similarly the "I Am" movement was started in California in the 1930s, and so assertions about the identity of the "finite 'I am'" with the "'Eternal I Am'" are equally anachronistic, inaccurate, and misleading. Finally, the idea of being reborn in "the Universal Self" is incoherent in a Buddhist context, as there is no "universal self." Even if Smith were to assert a loose and entirely misleading equation between Amida and the "universal self," this would not accurately represent Shin thought, as one is not born into an identity with Amida but rather born in his presence in Sukhāvatī.

An accurate understanding of the thought of the Pure Land lineage-holders requires that they be understood in the context of the Indo-Sinitic Buddhisms that had been transmitted to Japan, and which had been developing there for over seven centuries by the time of Hōnen and Shinran. This is what they were thinking of, and to fail to place them in this context will necessarily lead to misunderstanding them and the religious significance of the Pure Land teachings.

Conclusion

One straightforward way to summarize our critique of Huston Smith's representation of both Pure Land specifically and Buddhism generally is to ask: What does an author conceive the function of religion to be? Is the function of religion conceived to be reassurance, comfort, or disturbance? As mentioned already, religion is, of course, not a natural category but rather a socially constructed or intersubjective category. As such, the preconceptions an author holds about the function of religion will deeply structure the way in which that author represents religion.

More specifically, we can identify four different problems with Smith's representations of Buddhism. First, Smith's representation of Buddhism in general is a version of Buddhist modernism set within the narrative structure of Protestant historiography—an essentialized, ahistorical, and elitist representation. Second, the claim to represent "tradition" is a matter of bad faith; that is, it is not an accurate representation of any particular tradition, nor is it a generalization based on examination of actual traditional religions, but rather a modern construct, created on the basis of Romantic notions, perennialist thought, and anti-modernism. Third, Smith's Traditionalism asserts its own religious view as a hegemonic metanarrative, imposing theist, absolutist, dualist, and emanationist thought onto all religions, and giving epistemological privilege to mystical experience. Fourth, these are not the characteristics of Buddhism taken as a whole, nor are they the characteristics of Pure Land Buddhism in particular—though by overcoding by means of selection and interpretation, a representation of Pure Land that fits these universalized claims about religion can be constructed.

The proper application of comparison as a tool for understanding at the very least includes the necessity of not only stating in what ways two things are alike but also stating how they are different.[46] Huston Smith, in contrast, simply ignores inconvenient differences. The proper use of comparison is an issue related to the study of religion generally, and runs through all of the topics just considered. No doubt some would excuse these misrepresentations of Shinran's thought on the grounds that Smith is trying to make Shin Buddhism accessible to a Western audience. However, given the extent of his imposition of Western ideas onto Shinran's thought, it seems that what has happened instead is that Smith has represented Western religious conceptions under the guise of Pure Land Buddhism—Traditionalist perennialism and anti-modernism dressed in Buddhist robes.

Popular wisdom has it that some people think in terms of similarities and other people think in terms of differences.[47] To whatever extent this may be true, when—as in Smith's presentation of Shin Buddhism—the similarities obscure the differences, then the representation becomes a misrepresentation. In turn this would suggest that any such natural biases of thought need to be controlled for by principled scholarship.

To my mind, and I believe that Roger Corless would agree with me, there is an important difference between Buddhism and other religions, a difference that makes choosing to be a Buddhist, or choosing to remain a Buddhist, a choice that has consequences—a choice that is meaningful and significant in a person's life. This would not be the case were it true that all religions—or spiritualities, if one prefers—are ultimately the same.

Appendix: Smith's Plagiarism

Smith gratefully acknowledges the assistance of Taitetsu Unno in writing his "Afterword."[48] He then goes on later in the chapter to pay Unno the ultimate compliment of plagiarizing him. Having discovered plagiarism in another of Smith's works (*Why Religion Matters*),[49] I was not surprised to find him engaging in a paraphrase so thinly reworded as to seem, to this reader, to be problematic (the standard I am using is, "Would I find such an instance problematic in the work of a student?" And the answer in this case is "Yes"). One of the issues making this problematic is the length of the parallel sections—were they shorter, it would not be so clearly a case of stepping over the edge into plagiarism. In this case, however, the sections are extensive and it is clear that he is presenting the work of another as his own, without even acknowledging that it is a paraphrase from Unno. It is his failure to even acknowledge the source he is so closely paraphrasing that I find crosses the bounds into intellectual dishonesty.

That the reader may judge for him- or herself, the two relevant sections are quoted in full, first from Smith:

> Ultimately all religions are paradoxical. . . . The towering paradox that religion confronts us with is its insistence that the opposites that texture the world we normally experience are, when rightly understood, actually one. This is the famous doctrine of the *concidentia oppositorum,* the coincidence of opposites. Addressing this point, Shinran argued that we have not gotten to the root of things until we perceive the Absolute Unity that is their foundation. The consequences of this perception (as Nāgārjuna saw) are momentous, for if we take them seriously they pull us up short with realizations like these: Our "abysmal sinfulness" is identical with the Unthinkable Power that saves us. The "I" in the I-Thou relationship is identical with the "Thou" and the finite "I am" is identical with the "Eternal I Am." We utter the Nembutsu but really Amida utters it through us. Our longing to become eternal is actually

Amida's longing that we become so. Our love for Amida is his love for us. The indwelling Light in our hearts is His Holy Light. Our dying to our finite selves is our rebirth in the Universal Self. Our passivity is Tireless Activity working within us. This sordid world is the Pure Land. And on and on, with every dichotomy collapsing into—what shall we call it? Amida's Infinite Light and Compassion? The Primal Vow? The Nembutsu? Eventually words give out and we are left with the wordless apprehension that we are always already free. Life's trials have been surmounted and we are at peace.[50]

And now, from Taitetsu Unno's introduction to Kenryo Kanamatsu's work *Naturalness: A Classic of Shin Buddhism:*

[I]t must be noted that at their deepest point, all religions transcend reason; in short, ultimately religions are paradoxical. For example those phenomena that stand in logical opposition to each other are declared to be One; that is, in a state of "coincidence of opposites. . . ."

In brief, he (i.e., Kanamatsu) refers to . . . man's "abysmal sinfulness" and its Oneness with the "Unthinkable Power" that save that abysmally sinful man. He writes of the Oneness of the "I" and the "Thou." Of the finite "I am" and the Eternal "I Am." Of our utterance of the Nembutsu and Amida's utterance of the Nembutsu. Of our longing to become Eternal and Amida's longing for us to become so. Of our love and His Everlasting Love. Of the indwelling light and Amida's Light. Of absolutely dying unto the self and the absolute rebirth of the self in the Universal Self. Of forms and the Formless. Of passivity and Activity. Of this world and the spiritual world, i.e. the Pure Land.[51]

Smith also plagiarizes from Hiroyuki Itsuki's work *Tariki: Embracing Despair, Discovering Peace,* though he confuses the situation by attributing the characteristics described to Shinran, while Itsuki is speaking of Rennyo. First Smith, then Itsuki:

[P]reaching to people who started working when the stars were still shining in the skies and continued long after dark to return to collapse like exhausted beasts of burden on beds of straw.[52]

[Rennyo] was telling these people, who started working when the stars were still shining in the skies and continued long after dark, only to return to their homes and collapse like exhausted beasts of burden on a bed of straw. . . .[53]

Notes

1 Huston Smith, *The Religions of Man* (New York: Harper and Bros., 1958); and *The World's Religions: Our Great Wisdom Traditions* (San Francisco: Harper SanFrancisco, 1991).

2 See Wade Clark Roof, *Spiritual Marketplace: Baby Boomers and the Remaking of American Religion* (Princeton, NJ: Princeton University Press, 1999) for a sociological examination of this process.

3 Huston Smith and Philip Novak, *Buddhism: A Concise Introduction* (San Francisco: HarperSanFrancisco, 2004).

4 Sarah LeVine and David N. Gellner note that Henry Steel Olcott's 1881 *A Buddhist Catechism* (London: Theosophical Publishing Society, 1904), which is still in print and considered authoritative in some circles, "took for granted Olcott's own anticlerical and antiritual Protestant background and specifically attacked 'ceremonialism,' 'rites,' and 'priests.'" LeVine and Gellner, *Rebuilding Buddhism: The Theravada Movement in Twentieth-Century Nepal* (Cambridge, MA and London: Harvard University Press, 2005), p. 5.

5 See LeVine and Gellner, *Rebuilding Buddhism*, p. 7.

6 The term "Buddhist modernism" has come to be used to refer to a variety of not entirely congruent concepts. Here I am referring specifically to the programmatic efforts to reform Buddhism according to what was understood to be "modern" in the latter half of the nineteenth century. This is distinct from any sociohistorical discussions of the effect of modernization on Buddhist societies.

7 LeVine and Gellner, *Rebuilding Buddhism*, p. 11.

8 The "monasticization" of the laity is itself not unique to Buddhist modernism. It was part of the early modern development of Christianity, thus contributing to the model of what a modern religion ought to be that was accepted by Buddhist modernists. On the monasticization of the laity in Christianity, see Jean Delumeau, *Sin and Fear: The Emergence of a Western Guilt Culture 13th–18th Centuries*, trans. Eric Nicholson (New York: St. Martin's Press, 1990).

9 Smith, *Religions of Man*, p. 97 (*World's Religions*, p. 96) and Smith and Novak, *Buddhism: A Concise Introduction*, p. 28, are virtually identical, except that "without. . ." has been changed to the more qualified "critical of. . . ."

10 Smith and Novak, *Buddhism: A Concise Introduction*, p. 29.

11 Smith, *The World's Religions*, p. 98 (*Religions of Man*, pp. 96–97); Smith and Novak, *Buddhism: A Concise Introduction*, pp. 29–30.

12 For recent critiques of Buddhist modernism, see Ngakpa Traktung Yeshe Dorje and A'dzom Rinpoche, "Ignore the Man Behind the Curtain," http://www.damtsig.org/articles/traktung.html (accessed Tuesday, April 10, 2007); Stephen Prothero, "Boomer Buddhism," *Salon*, February 26, 2001, http://archive.salon.com/books/feature/2001/02/26/buddhism/print.html (accessed Tuesday, April 10, 2007). Each of these includes important critical reflections on the topic, but they are not without their own problems. The first expresses an anti-academic prejudice that ignores the importance of the

contributions to the study of Buddhism that originate in academia, while the second asserts that the only legitimate form of Buddhism is monastic.

13 Smith and Novak, *Buddhism: A Concise Introduction*, p. 23.

14 The pervasive quality of this historiographic pattern of decay and reformation is evidenced by the characterization of the Kamakura Buddhist "founders" as reformers.

15 Smith, *Religions of Man*, p. 5 (*World's Religions*, p. 4).

16 We are using the term here as described by Jean-Paul Sartre—willfully remaining ignorant of one's own choices, that is, treating oneself as unfree (a being-in-itself), in order to avoid the responsibility of free choice (a being-for-itself).

17 Reflection on the categories as identified in this sentence, which locate the topic in both cultural time and place, point to the very difference being suggested—"Buddhism" as distinct, for example, from "early medieval Indian Buddhism."

18 Smith and Novak, *Buddhism: A Concise Introduction*, p. 188.

19 Ibid., p. 67.

20 Ibid., p. 65.

21 *The Catholic Encyclopedia*, "Sanctifying Grace," http://www.newadvent.org/cathen/06701a.htm (accessed Thursday, March 22, 2007). Similarly, Wikipedia explains in the entry titled "Divine Grace," http://en.wikipedia.org/ wiki/Divine_grace (accessed Thursday, March 22, 2007):

> In Christianity, divine grace refers to the sovereign favour of God for humankind—especially in regard to salvation—irrespective of actions ("deeds"), earned worth, or proven goodness.
>
> More broadly, divine grace refers to God's gifts to humankind, including life, creation, and salvation. More narrowly but more commonly, grace describes the means by which humans are saved from original sin and granted salvation. This latter concept of grace is of central importance in the theology of Christianity, as well as one of the most contentious issues in Christian sectarianism.

22 Huston Smith, *Why Religion Matters: The Fate of the Human Spirit in an Age of Disbelief* (New York: HarperCollins, 2001), p. 226.

23 Smith, *Why Religion Matters*, p. 225.

24 Smith makes several fallacious moves in defending the idea of hierarchy. First, he claims that "reckless assaults on the word ["hierarchy"] from what Frederick Crews has called the eclectic left have all but ruined it by building oppression into its very definition" (*Why Religion Matters*, p. 225). This sentence alone contains two fallacies. The first is a *petitio principii* circularity, by characterizing whatever has been said—which we don't know, because Smith fails to cite any examples so that we cannot judge for ourselves—about hierarchy as "reckless assaults." The second is an *ad hominem* fallacy in the vaguely abusive term "eclectic left," which is also left undefined and unspecified and is, therefore, as it is used here, at least simply a wonderfully vague catch-all term that allows the reader to project whatever negative associations he or she might have onto it. A third issue is the reference to Frederick Crews, who

seems to be cited as a validating authority, but without any justification as to his authority on this issue, or even the relevance of the phrase Smith appropriates to the issue of hierarchy—beyond that perhaps of having created a slogan useful for Smith's rhetoric.

Smith next introduces the idea of "empowering hierarchies," saying that the idea that hierarchies are inherently oppressive makes an empowering hierarchy an oxymoron, when in fact there are "chains of command that are legitimate and enabling" (*Why Religion Matters,* p. 225). He then gives examples of empowering hierarchies, "A loving family with small children is an empowering hierarchy, as is a well-run classroom. The definitive example of a benevolent hierarchy is God's relation to the world" (*Why Religion Matters,* p. 225).

Although this might initially appear either as an argument by analogy (something like: [1] Loving families and well-run classrooms are alike in being empowering hierarchies, and [2] God's relation to the world is also a benevolent one; therefore, God's relation to the cosmos is hierarchical) or as a fallacious extension of a particular claim ("Some hierarchies are empowering") to a universal claim ("All hierarchies are empowering"). As is frequently the case with Smith's writing, however, the argument is so poorly presented that it seems impossible to convert to a clear form. Indeed, as it stands it is nothing more than a simple assertion that God's relation to the world is a benevolent one. Clearly, this is a theological claim and indeed one that is highly controversial. Even within Christian theological discussions, there are those who find the Christian God to be rather authoritarian, arbitrary, judgmental, and punitive.

More relevant to our considerations here, from a Buddhist perspective, there is no God and there is no presumption that the world is a benevolent one. (At the same time, this is not to say that the world is inherently evil, either. The Buddhist cosmos is morally neutral.)

25 This tale appears in Smith's introduction to the reissue of Schuon's *The Transcendent Unity of Religions,* rev. ed. (Wheaton, IL: Quest Books, 1993), as well as in David Ray Griffin and Huston Smith, *Primordial Truth and Postmodern Theology* (Albany, NY: State University of New York Press, 1990).

26 Smith, *Why Religion Matters,* p. 34.

27 Mark Sedgwick, personal communication, January 18, 2008.

28 Smith, *Why Religion Matters,* pp. 34–38.

29 Smith has offered a rather more detailed definition of religion in an article called "The Universal Grammar of Religion," *Religion East and West* 5 (2005): pp. 1–5. In this article he sets out fourteen points that he claims constitute the "universal grammar of religion upon which all religions stand" (p. 1). His use of the term "universal grammar" is supposedly a borrowing of the idea from Noam Chomsky, but so misrepresents that idea that it seems little more than an attempt at appropriating Chomsky's name and terminology for the sake of its authority. Smith offers these fourteen points as defining what *religion* is, and should, therefore, be true of *all instances of religion.* Closely paraphrasing, these fourteen points are:

1. Reality is infinite.
2. The infinite includes the finite.
3. The contents of the finite are hierarchically ordered in a "great chain of being."
4. Causation is from the top of the hierarchy downward.
5. The infinite is singular, and when it descends into the finite it becomes multiplicity.
6. In ascent, distinctions merge into the simplicity that is the infinite.
7. The simplicity that is the infinite is absolutely perfect.
8. The external hierarchy is reflected internally.
9. Human knowledge is finite and cannot therefore know the infinite completely, but can receive partial revelations of the infinite.
10. Such revelations require interpretation and explanation.
11. Fundamentalist literalism makes the mistake of believing that human knowledge can encompass the infinite.
12. There are two kinds of knowing—rational and intuitive—and religious knowledge is intuitive, not rational.
13. All religions have exoteric and esoteric aspects, the difference depending on ability to deal with abstractions: the esoteric is more abstract, the exoteric more reified.
14. Because we are limited and finite, the infinite will always remain a mystery to us.

The reflective reader will no doubt note that many of these ideas are quite contrary to fundamental Buddhist teachings, and therefore, the claim that these are characteristics of religion per se is quite evidently not a generalization based on any evidence but rather part of Smith's universalizing rhetoric.

30 Michael Löwy and Robert Sayre, *Romanticism Against the Tide of Modernity* (Durham, NC and London: Duke University Press, 2001), pp. 70–71.

31 Smith and Novak, *Buddhism: A Concise Introduction*, p. 186.

32 Ibid., pp. 186–187. Personally, I think that Smith is correct in this diagnosis. Tibetan lamas in red robes and with shaved heads get much more media attention than do Shin priests who are only rarely shaved and commonly wear business suits.

33 For a treatment of this issue, see Richard K. Payne, "Hiding in Plain Sight: The Invisibility of the Shingon Mission to the United States," in *Buddhist Missionaries in the Era of Globalization*, ed. Linda Learman (Honolulu: University of Hawai'i Press, 2005).

34 It should be noted, however, that there are different modes of engagement with Pure Land thought, in some of which Amida is indeed treated as an intercessor. This is not in accord with Pure Land doctrine, however, and at least in Western forms may be suspected of revealing the influences of Christian models of religiosity.

35 Smith and Novak, *Buddhism: A Concise Introduction*, p. 189.

36 The difficulty of using the category of religion in relation to Buddhism is reflected in the extensive qualifications that some scholars feel are necessary when doing so. See for example, Michael von Brücke, *Einführung in den*

Buddhismus (Frankfurt am Main and Leipzig: Verlag der Weltreligionen, Insel Verlag, 2007), pp. 18–19.

37 Stephen Prothero, *Religious Literacy: What Every American Needs to Know—and Doesn't* (San Francisco: HarperSanFrancisco, 2007), pp. 87–92. It would seem that because religious commitment has been structured around this oppositional dualism, which is itself in no way a natural one, it has contributed to the kinds of conflicts seen in contemporary American society. The resolution of these would seem to be in recognizing their correlation with one another, rather than siding with one pole of the opposition or the other.

38 Paul Groner, "Shortening the Path: Early Tendai Interpretations of the Realization of Buddhahood with This Very Body," in *Paths to Liberation: The Mārga and Its Transformation in Buddhist Thought*, ed. Robert Buswell and Robert Gimello (Honolulu: University of Hawai'i Press, 1992).

39 Smith, *Why Religion Matters*, p. 29.

40 That Smith is plagiarizing here is no excuse for his repetition of these anachronisms; see my "Appendix: Smith's Plagiarism," pp. 166–167.

41 Smith and Novak, *Buddhism: A Concise Introduction*, p. 194.

42 Ibid., pp. 194–195.

43 Ibid., p. xxix.

44 Ibid., p. xxx.

45 It may be worth noting that one of the differences between Smith and Schuon is that while the tone of the former's religious epistemology is a kind of Kabbalistic mystical a-gnosticism, the latter's epistemological tone is distinctly Gnostic.

46 See Jonathan Z. Smith, *Drudgery Divine: On the Comparison of Early Christianities and the Religions of Late Antiquity* (Chicago: University of Chicago Press, 1994) on the proper use of comparison as a method in the study of religion.

47 This is a very loose expression of the difference between feeling types and thinking types in Jungian theory.

48 Smith and Novak, *Buddhism: A Concise Introduction*, p. 185, note.

49 See my review in *Theology and Science*, vol. 5, no. 1 (March 2007): pp. 109–117.

50 Smith and Novak, *Buddhism: A Concise Introduction*, pp. 194–195.

51 Taitetsu Unno, introduction to Kenryo Kanamatsu, *Naturalness: A Classic of Shin Buddhism* (Bloomington, IN: World Wisdom, 2002), pp. xii–xviii.

52 Smith and Novak, *Buddhism: A Concise Introduction*, p. 196.

53 Hiroyuki Itsuki, *Tariki: Embracing Despair, Discovering Peace* (New York: Kodansha America, 2003), pp. 115–116.

Interpretation

The Supremacy of Amida's Vows in Rennyo: The Case of Women

Alfred Bloom
Institute of Buddhist Studies, Berkeley and University of Hawai'i (Emeritus)

Introduction

This essay examines the soteriology of Rennyo, and its application to the issue of the salvation of women. Shin Buddhist soteriological principles were established by Shinran (1173–1263). However, it is safe to say that Rennyo (1415–1499) did not add to those principles substantively but nuanced them differently, while he brought the teaching to the masses.

Through his letters, Rennyo made Shinran's teachings simpler and more accessible to the ordinary person. It is clear from a cursory comparison of Shinran's writings with Rennyo's letters that Shinran's thought was more scholarly, and more elusive for the ordinary person to grasp and appreciate fully. Shinran did, however, attempt to reach the masses, requesting that his letters be read to the members, and making copies of texts or translating *kambun* texts such as the *Kyōgyōshinshō* to Japanese. He averred that he was writing for the unlettered common person.[1] Nevertheless, it was Rennyo who successfully interpreted Shin teaching for the masses.

We get support for this view when we observe the succeeding history of Shin Buddhism until Rennyo (1415–1499). After Shinran the Shin Buddhist movement divided into several branches, traditionally said to be ten, of which the Hongwanji was one. Despite efforts in propagation and copying texts by the seven succeeding abbots (*monshu*, 門主, lit., "master of the gate") of the Hongwanji prior to Rennyo, the Hongwanji languished in poverty.[2] When Rennyo became the eighth abbot, however, there was a dramatic turnabout in the fortunes of the movement. He labored to expand the movement through teaching tours, letters, and by having the *Shōshinge* (*Hymn of True Faith*)[3] printed. This block-print version was used as a ritual text, while effectively offering a summary of the teaching. He strenuously opposed deviant Shin teachings and advocated the superiority of Shin Buddhism over other traditions. Though he emphasized that all traditions should be respected, he also asserted that they not be followed. Consequently, he has been called the "Restorer of Shin Buddhism" or "Second Founder."[4]

More recent modern evaluations suggest that he was an innovator because of changes he made in propagation, ritual, and organization. There is, therefore, a clear contrast between Rennyo and his predecessors, and this contrast has left its mark on the development of Shin Buddhism. Through his varied activities Shin Buddhism emerged from obscurity into a well-organized, powerful religious and social institution.

Shinran and Rennyo

As with Kakunyo (1270–1351, third abbot), and the succeeding abbots, Rennyo inherited the conviction that only the Hongwanji branch represented the truth of Shin Buddhism in the face of the rivalry of other branches and other Buddhist sects as well. Though Rennyo purports to transmit Shinran's teaching, there are significant contrasts in their personalities and approaches to religion resulting from their differing historical, social, and religious contexts.

Shinran was more introverted and self-reflective. Wracked by an intense sense of personal defilement, he experienced the corruption of the age as his own. Sharing the scholarly tradition of Tendai Buddhism, Shinran explained and clarified the basis for his understanding of Buddhist and Pure Land tradition through the prism of his religious despair and his association with Hōnen. His writings are interpretive and complex, as the *Kyōgyōshinshō,* his major scholarly work, demonstrates.

Shinran unintentionally created a movement, while being more individually oriented. He viewed himself as simply transmitting the true understanding of Hōnen's teaching, but his interpretations inspired the formation of a movement, which took several forms, and in the Hongwanji the movement became an institution that was headed by his hereditary descendants.

Rennyo, on the other hand, inherited the movement that Shinran inspired. It had already become institutionalized through the efforts of previous abbots. Rennyo's early experience with dire poverty, as well as his devoted effort along with his father to propagate the faith, led him in his teenage years to commit himself to the mission of reviving the fortunes of the Hongwanji. Following the ideal of the third abbot, Kakunyo, he sought this goal by uniting all the branches of Shin Buddhism under the wing of the Hongwanji.

Rennyo's personality was more outgoing. His poverty and the circumstances surrounding his birth, and his difficulties in becoming abbot, as well as his encounters with impermanence and sorrow in the loss of four wives, his eldest son, and six daughters, enabled him to identify with ordinary people and their suffering in that time of upheaval. However, unlike Shinran, he tells little about his own religious change or development. He consciously accepted the role of teacher or leader of an emerging movement, though he was not a scholar like Shinran. Further, he had to deal with the problems of religious power and authority that accompanied his status. His position as a teacher must be considered in the light of his enormous influence, for which there is little comparison among other medieval teachers. As a consequence of the commemoration of the five-hundredth anniversary of his death (1998), together with changed historical and social conditions, Rennyo is being examined as a man of his times, rather than being measured by standards of a later age.

The Basic Features of Shinran's Soteriology

There have been many scholarly and popular discussions of Shinran's teachings—teachings that are the foundation of Rennyo's work. Suffice it to say that Shinran emphasized absolute other-power in all aspects of religious faith and activity. No matter how evil a person may be, he or she is never beyond the embrace of Amida. Shinran had a vision of Amida Buddha's all-encompassing compassion and wisdom in which every feature of religious life is grounded in directing of virtue (*ekō*, 回向) of Amida Buddha's vows (*praṇidhāna*). The experience of trust endowed through Amida's vow involves a transformation of the self-striving mind to the mind of reliance, the one moment of true entrusting (*shinjin ichinen*, 信心一念).[5] All subsequent efforts are responses of gratitude for, and commitment to, Amida's compassion, which is supremely represented in his name, *Namu Amida Butsu*. The assurance of final enlightenment that one receives through true entrusting (*shinjin*) liberates one from the many religious fears and superstitions common to Japanese society,[6] fears that also appear to be universal. Finally, the goal of religion, according to Shinran, was to return to the world as a bodhisattva or in oneness with Amida Buddha to work for the awakening and nirvana of all beings.

The Characteristics of Rennyo's Soteriology

Rennyo shared Shinran's vision of Amida's all-encompassing compassion and wisdom. Since he was born within an already existing institutional system, he assumed that it faithfully transmitted the truth of Amida's vow as interpreted by Shinran. However, he simplified Shinran's complex teaching, holding to the principle that in teaching, you select one hundred from a thousand things that might be offered, and from one hundred, you choose ten. Finally, from the ten, you select one. As a consequence of his approach to teaching, focusing on the essentials and propagation, his emphases differed from those of Shinran. Bereaved of wives and children, as well as witnessing the violence of the age, Rennyo was keenly aware of the impermanence, unpredictability, and violence in life. In view of the brevity of life and depth of our human evil, the afterlife became of the greatest importance for him (*goshō no ichidaiji*, 後生の一大事),[7] in contrast to Shinran's stress on the reception of faith and assurance of rebirth in this life and the paradoxical character of birth (*ōjō*, 往生) which takes place in the moment of faith and at the end of life.

Rennyo drew a clear distinction between this world and the next. Where Shinran focused on the deceitfulness of this world, Rennyo concentrated on its impermanence. The human realm is a place of uncertainty. The land of utmost bliss is one of eternity, and should be the object of our aspiration and the decisive settling of mind. For Rennyo the most important thing was the afterlife.

For Rennyo, just as for Shinran, faith is fundamental and is the source of nenbutsu. Faith "is granted by Amida Tathāgata . . . this is not faith generated by the practicer, . . . it is Amida Tathāgata's Other-Power faith."[8] The term *shinjin* is taken by Rennyo to be Amida's other-power true mind, which displaces the believer's mind of self-striving.[9] An alternative term for faith is *anjin* (安心) or *yasuki kokoro* (やすき心), which was rarely used by Shinran. For Rennyo, it has essentially the same meaning as *shinjin*,[10] but with emphasis on the aspect of the peace or tranquility that attends receiving faith. It is the settled mind that witnesses to the oneness of the person and the buddha (*ki hō ittai*, 機法一,[11] oneness of beings and dharma). Rennyo interprets the phrase *Namu Amida Butsu* as evidence of the reality of that oneness when it is evoked in trust and gratitude. *Namu* refers to foolish beings, while *Amida Butsu* is the reality of the Buddha's compassion, which unconditionally embraces all beings.[12]

It is important to note that the inward and spiritual nature of *shinjin-anjin* (信心安心) renders external, adventitious appearances, or varying outward conditions, such as the status or roles of people in life, irrelevant in attaining trust. On receiving the settled mind, one carries on a normal life, whether it is as a samurai, hunter, fisherman, or tradesman. After faith or settled mind is established, nothing is taboo.[13] Settled faith, however, means to honor the laws of the state and fulfill public obligations[14] and to be discreet in offering the teachings to others. Rennyo calls his followers to self-responsibility.

The relation between Buddhism and the state or society is a key issue in Rennyo's thought, but it must be viewed in the light of his historical situation. Rennyo's idea of the parallel relation of secular law and buddhadharma is reminiscent of Jesus' idea of "rendering unto Caesar what is Caesar's and unto God what is God's." Rennyo also encouraged his followers to be respectful of the gods and buddhas, as did Shinran, reminding them that Amida is the primal teacher, while other spiritual beings are his manifestations. They are compassionate means (Skt. *upāya,* Jpn. *hōben,* 方便) to guide people to the buddhadharma.

With respect to religious life, the hallmark of Rennyo's teaching is his emphasis that the nenbutsu is only for gratitude, arising spontaneously from the settled mind of faith. He rails against the perfunctory, mechanical, conformist recitation of the name without understanding its essential meaning. He calls for discussion and questioning in meetings in order to confirm settled faith. While the arising of faith is completely a matter of Amida's compassionate working or other-power, Rennyo strongly upholds and emphasizes the principle of karma as the basis for encountering the teaching.

The process of deliverance is outlined by Rennyo in five conditions,[15] which must to be present in order for a person to attain truly settled faith. First there is the unfolding of good karma from the past. This dimension explains the varying conditions for people to encounter the dharma. Second there is the meeting with a good teacher. There must be a mode in which the dharma is transmitted. Third is receiving Amida's light. This aspect suggests the moment when the teaching grasps the person and there is the realization of its truth. We speak of the truth dawning. Fourth is attaining faith, the instant that true entrusting arises. And fifth is the urge to say the name of the Buddha Amida in thankfulness. We can view these five elements as a simultaneous moment in which we have the good fortune to encounter a teacher who opens the truth to us, as is evidenced by Gordon Bermant's encounter with K. T. Tsuji, recounted in his essay in this collection, "American Jōdo Shinshū Practice" (pp. 77–86). In that moment we attain trust in the vow, reject sundry practices, and recite the name of Amida Buddha in the form of the phrase *Namu Amida Butsu* in gratitude. It is altogether the one moment of entrusting and realizing of truly settled faith.

Shinran's and Rennyo's approach to faith are similar in being inward, requiring a definite turn of the mind in trust in Amida's vows. It is expressed in grateful recitation of the nenbutsu. There is a common emphasis in both teachers on the absolute other-power foundation of deliverance. They understand that Amida is a power within the heart and mind of the person, bringing about a spiritual transformation, as well as it is enshrined as the essence of the nenbutsu itself. Rennyo's term *anjin* or *yasuki kokoro,* settled mind, however, appears within an institutional setting of community and, as in some Christian communities, one may take it as a sign of their salvation that they are born within the faith community. There were observances such as daily recitation of the *Shōshinge* and the annual *Hōonkō* (報恩講, service of thanksgiving for the teaching), which commemorates Shinran's death, reinforcing Shin beliefs and community. An important feature of expressing one's settled faith is grateful recitation of the nenbutsu, while keeping one's eye on the goal of rebirth in the Pure Land. The communal character of faith is also expressed through obeying the various regulations that Rennyo set down as a means of avoiding conflicts and obstacles to the teaching in society or maintaining order within the sect. In all, a good Shin Buddhist for Rennyo was not only one who witnessed to settled faith, but one who also lived in an appropriate manner in society.

Perhaps no issue highlights more the distinctive character of Rennyo's thought than his focus on the issue of the salvation of women. His argument for the supremacy and truth of Shin Buddhism rests in great measure on the importance of the salvation of women, which is a major subject throughout his letters.

The Salvation of Women in Rennyo's Thought

Rennyo's soteriology is well exemplified in its application to the situation of women. The topic of the salvation of women or women's role in religion has contemporary relevance because ancient social and religious views about women as either inferior or subordinate still persist in attitudes and practices throughout all cultures, East and West, including

Shin Buddhism. In the West, the story of Adam and Eve in the Bible casts a woman as the catalyst for the emergence of sin in the world, while in Buddhism women are obstacles to men's progress to awakening.

To place Rennyo's view in perspective we should take note that Buddhism began with awakening being equally available to men and women. However, over time women were placed at a disadvantage, particularly in the Mahayana monastic tradition, through the mythological portrayal of a buddha as possessing the thirty-two major and eighty minor marks of a great being. One of these thirty-two marks was the possession of the male genital organ. Consequently, to become a buddha one clearly had to be a male. Under the influence of such beliefs and the patriarchal orientation of Hindu culture in the background, the view was widespread that women, because of the nature of their bodies, are unable to attain the status of Brahma, Indra, *cakravartin* (universal monarch), king of demons, or buddha. These were known as the five obstacles, which became well entrenched in Buddhism around the first century B.C.E.

In addition, the *Laws of Manu* in India and Confucianism in China stipulated that a woman must observe three subordinations to father, husband, and sons. These relationships denied women any possibility for social or spiritual leadership. Despite the existence of texts that offer a positive portrayal of the spiritual accomplishments of women, texts such as the *Lotus Sutra*[16] and the Pure Land sutras, which were understood to declare that a woman had to transform into a man before attaining buddhahood or entering Amitābha's Pure Land, became widely accepted. According to the thirty-fifth of Amida's vows in the *Larger Pure Land Sutra* (*Sukhāvatīvyūha-sūtra*), in addition to faith in the teaching, a woman must renounce her body in order to avoid rebirth as a woman and attain birth in the Pure Land. This renunciation suggests the denial of sexuality and femininity in women. Nevertheless, all Pure Land teachers advocated the salvation of women based on this vow.

Shinran had great respect for women, particularly his wife Eshin-ni. Though he mentioned the five obstacles and the transformation of women based on the thirty-fifth vow in his poems on the great teachers, he did not specially focus on the issue. In his *Hymns of the Pure Land* (*Jōdo wasan*)[17] he declared that the goal is buddhahood for women. Generally, he is following Shandao's view, which he relates in his "Hymns of the Pure Land Masters."[18]

However, in the famous passage on the "Great Ocean of Faith" in his *Kyōgyōshinshō*,[19] Shinran specifically asserted that there is no distinction between male and female when it comes to reception of *shinjin,* which is the key soteric moment in his thought. While Shinran recognized the traditional view of women in Pure Land teaching, he also held a broader perspective, suggesting the complete equality and nondiscrimination of women in deliverance. In *Hymns of the Pure Land,* Shinran wrote:

> In the land of happiness, *śrāvaka*s, bodhisattvas,
> Human beings, and *deva*s all possess luminous wisdom,
> And their bodily features and adornments are all the same;
> Different terms are used for them only in accord with the forms of existence in other worlds.
>
> Their countenances, dignified and wonderful, are beyond compare;
> Their bodies, delicate and subtle, are neither human nor *deva.*
> Theirs is the body of emptiness, the body of boundlessness,
> So take refuge in Amida, the power of nondiscrimination.[20]

In "Hymns of the Pure Land Masters" Shinran indicates:

> Although initially there are nine grades of beings,
> Because birth attained through Amida's pure Primal Vow is birth that is no-birth,
> The Pure Land is free of such discriminations.[21]

Zonkaku (存覺, 1290–1373; son of the third abbot of the Hongwanji, Kakunyo, 覺如, 1270–1351) devoted a short text on the rebirth of women, the *Nyōnin ōjō kikigaki* (*Notes on the Rebirth of Women*).[22] Largely dependent on Hōnen's work, Zonkaku depicts the plight of women, employing traditional social stereotypes of women and religious discrimination by major Buddhist institutions in order to promote Pure Land teaching. He maintained that the major function of the thirty-fifth vow was to ensure the deliverance of women as the primary object of Amida's salvation.

Rennyo is distinctive, however, in referring to women some forty-three times in the 221 authentic letters. Numerous letters focus on the issue of their deliverance. As the frequency of his references indicate, he had deep interest in and sympathy for women. This was doubtless because of the many women in his own life, including his mother, stepmother, five wives, and fourteen daughters among his twenty-one children, as well as the ministers' wives and many women followers with whom he associated.

Rennyo refers to women generally with the designation "women with five obstacles and three subordinations" (*goshō sanshō no,* 五障三従の女人), together with the more general phrase "common mortal with five major sins and ten evils" (*jūaku gogyaku no bonbu*, 十悪五逆の凡夫). These phrases are used to depict the profound corruption of both men and women.

Rennyo amplifies the deep defilements of women when he states that "We must realize that unbeknownst to others, all women have deep evil karma; whether of noble or humble birth, they are wretched beings. . . ."[23] He also declares that women exceed men in their defilement.[24] However, he never characterizes women in the negative terms of earlier Buddhist writings such as those indicated in Zonkaku's text, which suggest that women are full of envy, are vain, or are obstacles to men on the path to enlightenment. It is said that the self-centeredness and spiritual defilement of women come about because of their worldly concerns for their family and their devotion to the gods. The background of the criticism of women stems from the monastic situation where monks, having rejected worldly concerns, looked upon women's devotion to the welfare of their families as attachment to the world. Women might resort to various gods seeking benefits, safety, and good fortune for their children and families. The image became entrenched in tradition. However, Rennyo counsels women that, despite their great evils, "they should not be concerned about the depth and weight of their evil karma,"[25] since it is through their faith and other-power that they are delivered.

The institution of married clergy in Shin Buddhism, where wives became helpmates, rendered the ancient derogatory descriptions inappropriate and useless. While Rennyo, however, clearly continues the tradition that women are very corrupt, he employs it to emphasize that they can only truly be delivered by Amida Buddha's nondiscriminating vow, in contrast to all other buddhas who are incapable of emancipating women by their own power.[26] According to him, all buddhas have abandoned women, except Amida who has made the thirty-fifth vow for them.[27]

As other previous teachers, Rennyo assumes the traditional view of the thirty-fifth vow, which was specifically made to relieve the doubts of women concerning their rebirth, but he only once refers to the idea of transformation from female to male.[28] Further, while he believes that everyone is a common foolish being (*bonbu*, 凡夫) and stands in need of Amida Buddha's compassion, women are the most clear illustration of the Buddha's capacity to save.

In order to highlight the supremacy of Amida's vow and Shin Buddhist teaching over other sects, Rennyo asserts that in the age of *mappō* (末法), the last age in the demise of the dharma, the gods and buddhas have no power to deliver evil men or women or have abandoned them. He indicates that women, on their part, should single-heartedly and earnestly take refuge in Amida's vow and give up mixed practices or praying to other gods. They are to consider themselves as evil persons who trust in the wondrous buddha-wisdom of Amida's primal vow, which was made for such superficial women, described as people who deeply doubt, think abominable things, and are devoted to children and worldly prosperity.[29]

Women who have attained *shinjin* are in the rightly established state or the company of the truly assured (*shōjōju*), and are destined for nirvana without retrogression. They have the position equal to the awakened, and to Maitreya or Vaidehī. These are all conditions that Shinran declared were signs of the immediacy of the assurance of birth in Amida's Pure Land given in this life in the one moment of *shinjin*. This assurance of birth negates the need for the welcome of Amida Buddha at the moment of death, or *raigō/raikō* (来迎), a belief prominent in medieval Japanese Pure Land teaching as the means of assuring rebirth in the Pure Land.

The message Rennyo gave to women is essentially what he gave to all people he met, but when he takes special note of women it is clear that, despite employing discriminatory language derived from the larger Buddhist tradition, he respects them greatly and particularly wished to encourage them. Women are not obstacles to men's salvation but objects of Buddha's compassion. Rennyo was more interested in offering hope and assurance than he was in denying women their sexuality or femininity, as the tradition suggested.

We should note here in connection with the question of whether there are women in Amida's Pure Land, that Shinran and his successors consoled the bereaved with the hope that they will meet their loved ones there. Despite the specifics of doctrine, religious traditions tend to accommodate to human sentiment and hope, ignoring technical doctrinal formulations. More than just accommodation to sentiment, Shin Buddhism holds that with settled faith one enters into the company of the truly assured in this life, attaining rebirth in principle, while at death one immediately becomes a buddha and attains nirvana where all personal distinctions are transcended. Consequently, an implication of Rennyo's reiteration of Shin principles of salvation, in accord with Shinran's teaching in the *Kyōgyōshinshō,* means that women attain birth in the Pure Land just as they are (*sono mama*), an idea discussed by Bermant in his essay. Since everyone, man or woman, attains the truly assured state in this life with true entrusting (*shinjin*) and immediate buddhahood on death, Rennyo never mentions the idea of gender transformation, which is closely associated with meeting Amida Buddha at the end of life (*raigō/raikō*) in the thirty-fifth vow. The absence of any such mention can be understood as suggesting that women are not saved at the expense of their femininity or sexuality, and that they attain the highest realization on the same basis as men.

Conclusion

In his own way, Rennyo's soteriology carried on Shinran's intention to convey Amida's compassion to ordinary people in a comprehensible fashion. Despite changed circumstances, Rennyo maintained the spirituality and inwardness of Shinran's teaching. He proclaimed the superiority of Shin Buddhism, using the issue of the salvation of women. He showed that women were included within the vision of Amida's absolute compassion without negating their femininity, as implied in the concept of five obstacles and the transformation to male in the thirty-fifth vow. Nevertheless, Rennyo's use of traditional negative descriptions of women as even more corrupt than men tended to support or reinforce traditional social stereotypes of women's inferiority. They remained subordinated to the patriarchal order, reinforced, for example, by Rennyo's counsel to obey Confucian principles prescribed by the royal dharma (*ōbō,* 王法), or secular law, while nurturing the buddha-dharma (*buppō,* 佛法) in their hearts. Rennyo's concern with the afterlife also limited his view of the status of women in this life. He never discussed the three subordinations as part of the salvation offered by Amida, though it always appears linked with the five obstacles. The task of Shin Buddhism in the future is to complete the work of Shinran and Rennyo in promoting full social and spiritual equality for all people in this life as well as the next.

Notes

[1] See the *Collected Works of Shinran,* hereafter CWS (Kyoto: Jōdo Shinshū Hongwanji-ha, 1997), "Notes on 'Essentials of Faith Alone,'" CWS I, p. 469; also "Notes on Once-Calling and Many-Calling," CWS I, p. 490.

> That people of the countryside, who do not know the meanings of written characters and who are painfully and hopelessly ignorant, may easily understand, I have repeated the same things over and over. The educated will probably find this writing peculiar and may ridicule it. But paying no heed to such criticisms, I write only that ignorant people may easily grasp the meaning.

[2] Daigan Matsunaga and Alicia Matsunaga, *Foundation of Japanese Buddhism,* vol. 2 (Los Angeles and Tokyo: Buddhist Books International, 1976), pp. 116–117.

[3] This text appears in the *Kyōgyōshinshō* at the end of the "Practice" volume. It presents a concise poetic summary of Shinran's understanding of the teachings of the seven great teachers whom Shinran determined as his lineage.

[4] Ibid., p. 117.

[5] "True Teaching, Practice, and Realization," CWS I, pp. 110–111, no. 60. Rennyo's definition of *shinjin,* Minor L. Rogers and Ann T. Rogers, *Rennyo: The Second Founder of Shin Buddhism* (Berkeley, CA: Asian Humanities Press, 1991), p. 167, *Gobunshō* I-15. (Alternative reading for *Gobunshō* is *Ofumi.*)

[6] "A Record of Lament of Divergences [*Tannishō*]," CWS I, p. 665. See also "True Teaching, Practice, and Realization," "Chapter on Transformed Buddha-Bodies and Lands," CWS I, p. 255, nos. 81–84; p. 258, no. 86.

[7] Rogers and Rogers, *Rennyo: The Second Founder of Shin Buddhism,* pp. 38–39, n. 88. See "Notes on 'Essentials of Faith Alone,'" CWS I, p. 455, for Shinran's view of the immediacy of birth.

[8] Rogers and Rogers, *Rennyo: The Second Founder of Shin Buddhism,* p. 190.

[9] Ibid., p. 167, *Gobunshō* I-15.

[10] Ibid., *Gobunshō* II-15.

[11] There are several terms by which Rennyo makes reference to this relationship. In *Gobunshō* II (Rogers and Rogers, *Rennyo: The Second Founder of Shin Buddhism,* p. 184), Rennyo refers to the oneness of the Buddha's mind and the believer's ordinary mind, *busshin* (仏心) and *bonjin* (凡心). The accompanying note explains that *butsu-bon-ittai* (仏凡一体) indicates the moment that *shinjin* arises, while *ki-ho-ittai* (機法一体) is the state of having attained *shinjin.*

[12] Ibid., *Gobunshō* IV-14.

[13] Ibid., *Gobunshō* I-9.

[14] Ibid., pp. 215–216, *Gobunshō* III-13.

[15] Ibid., pp. 186–187, *Gobunshō,* II-11.

[16] Bunno Kato et al., trans., *The Threefold Lotus Sutra* (New York and Tokyo: Weatherhill/Kosei, 1973), pp. 212–214; Hisao Inagaki, trans., *The Three Pure Land Sutras* (Kyoto: Nagata Bunshōdō, 1994), pp. 246–247. The thirty-fifth vow of Amida Buddha in the *Larger Pure Land Sutra:*

If, when I attain buddhahood, women in the immeasurable and inconceivable buddha lands of the ten quarters who, having heard my name, rejoice in faith, awaken aspiration for enlightenment and wish to renounce womanhood, should after death be reborn again as women, may I not attain perfect enlightenment.

17 "Hymns of the Pure Land," CWS I, p. 341, no. 60.

So profound is Amida's great compassion
That, manifesting inconceivable Buddha-wisdom,
The Buddha established the Vow of transformation into men,
Thereby vowing to enable women to attain Buddhahood.

Shinran here expresses the traditional view common in his time.

18 Ibid., p. 377, no. 64.

19 Ibid., p. 107, no. 51.

20 Ibid., p. 330, nos. 222–223.

21 Ibid., p. 372, no. 46.

22 *Shinshū Shōgyō Zensho*, vol. 3 (Kyoto: Kōkyō Shoin, 1957), pp. 109–118.

23 Rogers and Rogers, *Rennyo: The Second Founder of Shin Buddhism*, p. 253, *Gobunshō* V-14.

24 Ibid., p. 247–248, *Gobunshō* V-7.

25 Ibid., p. 254, *Gobunshō* V-15.

26 Ibid., p. 247, *Gobunshō* V-7.

27 Ibid., p. 160, *Gobunshō* I-10.

28 Masamaru Inaba, ed., *Rennyo Shōnin Ibun* (Kyoto: Hōzōkan, 1972), no. 17, 5:8, 28, pp. 86–87.

29 Rogers and Rogers, *Rennyo: The Second Founder of Shin Buddhism*, p. 171, *Gobunshō* II-1.

Shinran's Pure Land Buddhism as a Way of Being Religious: Some Twenty-first–century Tasks for Shin Buddhist Theology

Ruben L. F. Habito
Perkins School of Theology, Southern Methodist University

Can the religious teaching of a thirteenth-century Japanese Buddhist founder bear any relevance for a post-Enlightenment, postmodern, globalized society such as our twenty-first–century world? This essay, offered as a tribute to Roger Corless, a respected scholar of Pure Land Buddhism and leading figure in Buddhist-Christian dialogue, addresses this question.

Inspired by Shinran's life and teaching, reinterpreting his message for every successive generation has of course been an ongoing task of adherents of the Shin Pure Land Buddhist community. Such a task falls under what can be called "Shin Buddhist theology." Without going into the arguments on the use of this term, here I take "Buddhist theology" in the broad sense as "intellectual reflection within a religious tradition" (following David Tracy), which thus entails

> critical reflection upon Buddhist experience in light of contemporary understanding, and critical reflection upon contemporary understanding in light of Buddhist experience.[1]

Taitetsu Unno, prominent Shin Buddhist scholar and interpreter of this tradition, has outlined three important areas to consider in this regard.

> First, it must respond to the deepest existential and spiritual yearnings of people who seek but cannot find answers to the perennial questions of life and death. . . . Second, it must respond to the intellectual, social, and cultural challenges of postmodernity without losing its critical perspective. . . . And third, it must offer alternative solutions to concrete problems, ranging from conflict situations in everyday life to global concerns for the survival of the planet.[2]

This essay is offered in this vein by an outsider to the Shin Pure Land Buddhist community, yet also one who continues to receive inspiration from Shinran's life and teachings, as well as receiving the gift of long-standing friendships with and valuable support from many members of this religious community.[3]

The first part sketches an approach toward understanding Shinran's religious message, adapted from a framework developed by my late colleague Frederick J. Streng, detailed in his *Understanding Religious Life*.[4] On this basis, the second part highlights areas wherein Shinran's message may have significant bearing on the needs of our own time, and then outlines the tasks of a Shin Buddhist theology that follow from such an analysis.

Shinran's Way of Being Religious

By "way of being religious," I refer to a framework that involves a fourfold set of elements that various religious traditions share. First, a religious tradition takes as its point of departure a view of the problematic nature of human existence. Second, a religious tradition presents a view of ultimate reality and human ultimate destiny that is understood as a resolution of the human problematic. Third, a religious tradition prescribes concrete steps and practices to the realization of that ultimate reality and human ultimate destiny in an individual's life. Fourth, the community of adherents of a given religious tradition cultivates and develops forms of social expression of the way to ultimate reality and human ultimate destiny. The "way of being religious" as manifested in a particular tradition refers to the actual content of these four features in an integrated structure. Let us now examine this content in Shinran's Shin Pure Land Buddhist teaching.

The Problematic of Human Existence

In his writings, Shinran repeatedly emphasizes the utter powerlessness of human beings to attain ultimate liberation through their own efforts. Behind this view of the human inability to realize one's ultimate destiny is Shinran's unquestioning acceptance of the then-prevalent notion of the "latter days of dharma" (*mappō*).[5]

This notion presupposes a tripartite system wherein the first period, usually identified with the first five hundred years immediately following the Buddha's entry into nirvana, is considered the "age of true dharma." During this period, teaching, practice, and enlightenment flourished, and were readily accessible to those who sought them. The subsequent period was called the "age of semblance dharma," wherein teaching and practice were still accessible but enlightenment was rare. In the third period, both practice and enlightenment are now beyond the reach of ordinary human beings. During this period, aptitude, motivation, and the capacity for, as well as the environment conducive to, practice and the attainment of enlightenment are no longer to be found. In thirteenth-century Japan, it was widely held that the world had already entered this third, degenerate period, and that it was only the teaching of the Awakened One that can serve as a lifeline to ultimate liberation.

For Shinran, this was the teaching contained in the three Pure Land sutras, which told of the primal vow of the Buddha Amida to bring all sentient beings to Sukhāvatī. Without this teaching, human beings are rendered bereft of any prospect of finding liberation from this cycle of suffering and endless birth and death, and are consigned to wallow in the muddy waters contaminated by the three poisons of greed, anger, and ignorance.

The following passages from Shinran's writings provide us with a glimpse of the human problematic as he understood it.[6]

> It is now more than two thousand years
> Since the passing of Śākyamuni Tathāgata.
> The right and semblance ages have already closed;
> So lament, disciples of later times!
>
> Now, amid the five defilements in the last dharma age,
> Sentient beings are incapable of practice and realization;
> Hence the teachings that Śākyamuni left behind
> Have all passed into the *nāga*'s palace.
>
> During the right, semblance, and last ages,
> Amida's Primal Vow has spread.
> At the end of the semblance and in this last dharma age,
> Good practices have all gone into the *nāga*'s palace. . . .
>
> Ignorance and blind passions abound,
> Pervading everywhere like innumerable particles of dust.
> Desire and hatred arising out of conflict and accord
> Are like high peaks and mountain ridges.[7]

On the one hand, Shinran's view of the human condition can be construed as pessimistic and negativistic, unflattering to the human, disclaiming the aptitude and capacity of humans for ultimate self-realization.

This is undoubtedly key to Shinran's religious view throughout his career, ever since the momentous religious experience that led him to leave the monastery at Mt. Hiei to become a follower of Hōnen. This view was understandably generated, and also bolstered and confirmed, by the situation of Japanese society and time, wherein many were pushed to the brink of despair in the chaotic and turbulent conditions that characterized thirteenth-century Japan.

However, this view of utter human powerlessness was only one side of Shinran's central religious message. It is simply a prelude to his teaching that the primal vow of Amida has brought forth a dynamic power that permeates throughout the universe, opening the path of realization to all sentient beings. This is no other than Amida's compassion, inviting all beings to simply acknowledge and accept it. In short, rather than being a pessimistic view of the human condition, Shinran's is a proclamation of the infinite capacity of the human being, grounded in his or her understanding of the primal vow of Amida.

Shinran's View of Ultimate Reality and Human Ultimate Destiny

The primal vow of Amida is the cornerstone of Shinran's view of ultimate reality and human ultimate destiny. Following the entire Pure Land tradition that began in India and found wide acceptance in East Asia, Shinran affirms that it is the efficacious nature of the primal vows of Amida that Śākyamuni Buddha sought to convey to all, as the very ground for his appearance in human history. The following and similar passages resonate with this singular message.

> The true and real benefit is Amida's Vow. Thus, the reason that the [buddhas] appear in the world age after age is that they desire to bless and save all sentient beings by teaching the power of Amida's Vow. Since they take this as their fundamental intent, the Vow is called the true and real benefit. Further, it is termed "the direct teaching for which all [buddhas] appear in the world."[8]

The figure that occupies the central place in this message is none other than the Buddha Amida (Skt. Amitābha, Immeasurable Light, or Amitāyus, Immeasurable Life).

> From this treasure ocean of oneness form was manifested, taking the name of Bodhisattva Dharmākara, who, through establishing the unhindered Vow as the cause, became Amida Buddha. For this reason Amida is the

"Tathāgata of fulfilled body." Amida has been called "Buddha of unhindered light filling the ten quarters." This Tathāgata is also known as *Namu-fukashi-gikō-butsu* (Namu-Buddha of inconceivable light) and is the "dharma-body as compassionate means." "Compassionate means" refers to manifesting form, revealing a name, and making itself known to sentient beings. It refers to Amida Buddha. This Tathāgata is light. Light is none other than wisdom; wisdom is the form of light. Wisdom is, in addition, formless; hence this Tathāgata is the Buddha of inconceivable light. This Tathāgata fills the countless worlds in the ten quarters, and so is called "Buddha of boundless light." Further, Bodhisattva Vasubandhu has given the name "Tathāgata of unhindered light filling the ten quarters."[9]

In this and related passages Amida Buddha is extolled as the embodiment of ultimate reality, the "Tathāgata of the fulfilled body." Amida is the locus of the storehouse of infinite merit generated by the primal vow, who dispenses this merit in overabundance to all sentient beings who call upon his name.

Truly we know that without the virtuous Name, our compassionate father, we would lack the direct cause for birth. Without the light, our compassionate mother, we would stand apart from the indirect cause of birth. Although direct and indirect causes may come together, if the karmic-consciousness of *shinjin* is lacking, one will not reach the land of light. The karmic-consciousness of true and real *shinjin* is the inner cause. The Name and light—our father and mother—are the outer cause. When the inner and outer causes merge, one realizes the true body in the fulfilled land. . . .[10]

Human ultimate destiny is thus construed as the attainment of rebirth in Sukhāvatī where Amida Buddha dwells as a king of dharma (*dharmarāja*), and where all beings realize the fulfillment of their own buddha-nature.

Tathāgata is none other than nirvana;
Nirvana is called buddha-nature.
Beyond our ability to attain it in the state of foolish beings,
We will realize it on reaching the land of peace.[11]

Shinran connects these central Buddhist notions, each with its own particular philological, philosophical, and historical content—*tathāgata,* nirvana, buddha-nature, land of peace—as terms referring to human ultimate destiny. It is the marvelous working of Amida Buddha's all-pervading compassion that opens this realm to all sentient beings.

The Way to Ultimate Reality and Human Ultimate Destiny in Individual Expression

Having disclaimed the possibility for human beings to attain ultimate realization by virtue of their own efforts and merit, Shinran turns to the power of saying the name of Amida Buddha as the efficiacious cause of birth in Sukhāvatī.

> Reverently contemplating Amida's directing of virtue for our going forth to the Pure Land, I find that there is great practice, there is great *shinjin*. The great practice is to say the Name of the Tathāgata of unhindered light. This practice, embodying all good acts and possessing all roots of virtue, is perfect and most rapid in bringing about birth. It is the treasure ocean of virtues that is suchness or true reality. For this reason, it is called great practice. This practice arises from the Vow of great compassion, which is known as "the Vow that all Buddhas extol the Name," "the Vow that all Buddhas say the Name," and "the Vow that all Buddhas praise the Name."[12]

These opening lines of the second chapter of his masterwork, *The True Teaching, Practice, and Realization of the Pure Land Way* (*Kyōgyōshinshō*), lay out Shinran's view of the way to the realization of human ultimate destiny in an individual's life, encapsulated in the phrase "great practice." It is also notable that at this very juncture, on the same breath and in the same line, he emphasizes "great *shinjin*."[13]

This juxtaposition serves to emphasize that the "great practice" of saying the name of Amida, the "Tathāgata of Unhindered Light" (an alternative rendering of the Sanskrit Amitābha) is inseparable from that entrusting mind that simply finds vocal expression in saying the name. In other words, for Shinran, "great practice" and "great *shinjin*" are two sides of the same coin, which is none other than the individual's opening of his or her entire being to the power of Amida's compassion in enabling one to go forth into the Pure Land.

> Reverently contemplating Amida's directing of virtue for our going forth, I find there is great *shinjin*. Great *shinjin* is the superlative means for attaining longevity and deathlessness. It is the wondrous way to awaken aspiration for the pure and rejection of the defiled. It is the straightforward mind directed to us through the selected Vow. It is *shinjin* that actualizes Amida's profound and vast benefiting of others. It is true mind that is diamondlike and indestructible. It is pure *shinjin* by which a person easily reaches the Pure Land where no one goes. It is the mind that is single, realized by the person who is grasped and protected by the compassionate light. It is great

> *shinjin,* rare and unsurpassed. It is the quick path difficult for people to accept. It is the true cause of attaining great nirvana. It is the white path by which all virtues are fulfilled instantly. It is the ocean of *shinjin* that is itself suchness or true reality.[14]

In the above passage, the original term *shingyō* is rendered in the English translation as *"shinjin." Shingyō* is a compound of the characters for "entrusting" and "joy," and can alternatively be rendered as "joy-in-entrusting." In short, an individual who entrusts one's entire being to the compassion of Amida finds joy in being assured of entry into the Pure Land, not just as a future promise but as an experienced reality. This is a theme that is quite notable in Shinran's Pure Land teaching, in contrast to that of his own teacher, Hōnen.

For the latter, frail and fallible human beings need to frequently recite the name of Amida, lest at the hour of death, when such recitation is deemed most crucial, one's mind should be distracted and thus neglect the recitation at that precise time. This is based on the understanding that Amida's vow is about transporting those who recite the name of Amida at the point of death from this land of sorrows to Sukhāvatī.

For Shinran, however, an individual who with a sincere and single-minded entrusting mind recites the name but once is instantaneously assured of entry into the Pure Land. This assurance brings forth inner peace and joy, and empowers a human being to live in the light of Amida's compassion.

> When one realizes true and real *shinjin,* one is immediately grasped and held within the heart of the Buddha of unhindered light, never to be abandoned.
>
> "To grasp" (*sesshu*) means to take in (*setsu*) and to receive and hold (*shu*). When we are grasped by Amida, immediately—without a moment or a day elapsing—we ascend to and become established in the stage of the truly settled; this is the meaning of *attain birth.*[15]

Shinran also strongly emphasizes that this "great practice" of saying the name of Amida (nenbutsu) with a deeply entrusting mind is not an act that arises out of an individual human being's own power and capacity. Rather, it is the very working of Amida's compassion upon that individual that makes such a practice possible. "Concerning the nenbutsu, no working is true working. For it is beyond description, explanation, and conceptual understanding."[16]

The only true and efficacious practice for the realization of human ultimate destiny is the recitation of the name with a sincere and entrusting mind. Such a singular practice already assures them of entry into the Pure Land, and thus into final nirvana.[17] Thus, for the followers of Shinran's teaching, there is no need for any special rituals or practices in preparation for an individual's death. Deathbed rituals, which had been a feature of Pure Land belief and devotion since its inception in China and the rest of East Asia, understood as ways of preparing for Amida's coming to welcome the individual into the Pure Land, no longer found a place in their religious life and worldview.

> The idea of Amida's coming at the moment of death is for those who seek to gain birth in the Pure Land by doing various practices, for they are practicers of self-power. The moment of death is of central concern to such people, for they have not yet attained true *shinjin.* We may also speak of Amida's coming at the moment of death in the case of those who, though they have committed the ten transgressions and the five grave offenses throughout their lives, encounter a teacher in the hour of death and are led at the very end to utter the nenbutsu.
>
> The practicer of true *shinjin,* however, abides in the stage of the truly settled, for he or she has already been grasped, never to be abandoned. There is no need to wait in anticipation for the moment of death, no need to rely on Amida's coming. At the time *shinjin* becomes settled, birth too becomes settled; there is no need for the deathbed rites that prepare one for Amida's coming.[18]

Social Expression of the Way to Ultimate Reality and Ultimate Destiny

If an individual finds complete assurance of entry into the Pure Land through the singleminded recitation of the name with a sincere and entrusting mind, how do the followers of Shinran's teaching find social expression of this way to ultimate human destiny?

It is here that another cardinal teaching of Shinran's Pure Land Buddhism comes into play. This is the teaching of the twofold direction of Amida's compassion. The first direction is one of "going forth" (*ōsō*) into the Pure Land, and the second is the "returning to this world" (*gensō*) and transferring of merit to others.

> Amida's directing of virtue to beings through the power of the Primal Vow has two aspects: the aspect for our going forth to the Pure Land and the aspect for our return to this world. Regarding the aspect for going forth, there is great practice, there is pure *shinjin.* . . .[19]

One is set in the direction of going forth with the great practice of reciting the name, grounded in *shinjin,* an attitude of a sincere and entrusting mind. With this, an individual experiences deep inner peace and quiet joy, with the assurance of entry into the Pure Land. As such, one no longer needs to be anxious about attaining one's ultimate destiny and, for all practical purposes, has "arrived."

What does a person in this state of mind thereby do henceforth? First and foremost, the significance of the recitation of Amida's name undergoes a radical transformation from this point on. Here nenbutsu is no longer practiced as a way of seeking entry into the Pure Land, since one is already assured of that. Rather, the recitation of the name is now continued as an expression of gratitude for Amida's infinite compassion.

> Through the compassion of Śākyamuni and Amida,
> We have been brought to realize the mind that seeks to attain buddhahood.
> It is by entering the wisdom of *shinjin*
> That we become persons who respond in gratitude to the buddhas' benevolence.[20]

Having accomplished the first direction of "going forth," a person who has experienced the inner peace and joy of *shinjin* now makes the turn of "returning to the world"—

> Those who reach the Pure Land of happiness
> Return to this evil world of the five defilements,
> Where, like the Buddha Śākyamuni,
> They benefit sentient beings without limit.[21]

A person who has now experienced this second movement of "returning to the world," now becomes a vehicle of Amida's compassion toward others. Such a person will be present in the world and engage in action for the benefit of others, but in a way that is not through his or her own efforts but precisely as a vehicle of Amida's compassion. Shinran makes this important distinction regarding works of compassion on behalf of others.

> Concerning compassion, there is a difference between the Path of Sages and the Pure Land Path. Compassion in the Path of Sages is to pity, commiserate with, and care for beings. It is extremely difficult, however, to accomplish the saving of others just as one wishes. Compassion in the Pure Land Path should be understood as first attaining Buddhahood quickly through saying the nenbutsu and, with the mind of great love and great compassion, freely benefiting sentient beings as one wishes. However much love and pity we may feel in our present lives, it is hard to save others as we

> wish; hence, such compassion remains unfulfilled. Only the saying of the nenbutsu, then, is the mind of great compassion that is thoroughgoing.[22]

The question of how a person of *shinjin* is to relate to others comes to the fore. Shinran's own attitude is reflected in the following comments, recorded as the fifth entry in his disciple Yui-en's well-known tract, *A Record of Lament of Divergences* (*Tannishō*).

> As for me, Shinran, I have never said the nenbutsu even once for the repose of my departed father and mother. For all sentient beings, without exception, have been our parents and brothers and sisters in the course of countless lives in the many states of existence. On attaining Buddhahood after this present life, we can save every one of them.
>
> Were saying the nenbutsu indeed a good act in which I strove through my own powers, then I might direct the merit thus gained toward saving my father and mother. But this is not the case.
>
> If, however, simply abandoning self-power, we quickly attain enlightenment in the Pure Land, we will be able to save, by means of transcendent powers, first those with whom we have close karmic relations, whatever karmic suffering they may have sunk to in the six realms through the four modes of birth.[23]

How are we to understand this startling statement, that Shinran "never said the nenbutsu even once for the repose of [his] departed father and mother"? In a society as deeply influenced by Confucian values as Japan, taking care of one's parents, including praying for their well-being in this life and the next, are considered to be any human being's primary duty. How can such a person steeped in Pure Land piety as Shinran confess such neglect of this primary duty?

Shinran offers his own explanation: such intentions and actions on behalf of one's parents, as well as for others in general, laudable as they may be, are in the end by themselves ineffectual. This is because no human effort is sufficient to assure anyone of entry into the Pure Land, not even the effort of reciting Amida's name, insofar as this is construed only as human effort.

Thus, rather than prescribing that his followers engage in what he already knows to be fruitless effort, Shinran counsels them to turn to the great practice, with deep entrustment, thereby assuring that they would attain buddhahood. It is upon this attainment, and only then, that one can be able to truly "save" all beings, beginning with one's own parents.

Here it is clear that it is not one's efforts that effect this salvation but rather the power of Amida's compassion, which has now become the power that runs through an individual's entire life. The "transcendent powers" referred to are those that come to be activated upon attaining buddhahood, powers which can now be directed in the work of Amida's compassion.

This caution about falling into the delusion of self-power in performing acts of compassion, however, does not preclude cultivating intentions for the benefit and well-being of others. For example, the following is how Shinran advises his followers to relate to those who revile them.

> Those people, described here as such, perform deeds that will bring about the suppression of the nenbutsu and act out of malice toward people of the nenbutsu. In this regard, without bearing any ill will toward such persons, you should keep in mind the thought that, saying the nenbutsu, you are to help them.[24]

The greatest compassion one can offer to others is that of extending to them the compassion of Amida that one has accessed through *shinjin* and the recitation of the name.

> True and real *shinjin* is the diamondlike mind. The diamondlike mind is the mind that aspires for Buddhahood. The mind that aspires for Buddhahood is the mind to save sentient beings. The mind to save sentient beings is the mind to grasp sentient beings and bring them to birth in the Pure Land of peace. This mind is the mind aspiring for great enlightenment. This mind is the mind of great compassion. . . .[25]

For Shin Pure Land Buddhists, the greatest act of compassion one can offer to all sentient beings, more than any temporal assistance in their various kinds of needs or suffering in this impermanent world, is to enable them to enter into the Pure Land. And since this itself cannot be accomplished through human effort but through Amida's compassion alone, the only assured way to extend this act of compassion to others is by letting Amida's power envelop one's own being, through one's earnest recitation of Amida's name, and thereby letting this compassion flow out of oneself where it will. As such, in principle, acts of charity to help one's neighbors in their temporal needs are not regarded as an inherent aspect of the Shin Buddhist religious worldview.

There is an important facet in the social expression of Shinran's message that one may not find explicitly laid out in his writings. This refers to the formation of a tightly knit religious organization among the community of his followers, with spiritual leadership given to a direct heir of Shinran through successive generations. This organization developed through the centuries and is now among the largest and most powerful religious institutions in Japan today. This is of course none other than the Jōdo Shinshū, jurisdictionally divided into the Higashi (Eastern) and Nishi (Western) branches of the Honganji temple complex, with headquarters located in Kyoto.[26]

The establishment of Jōdo Shinshū as a community of believers and as a hierarchically structured religious institution is itself somewhat of an historical irony, as Shinran himself disclaimed having any disciples. The fact that a well-knit and highly organized religious organization developed after his death, however, has assured the continuing transmission and propagation of his message through history. Since the nineteenth and twentieth centuries, Jōdo Shinshū's influence has gone beyond Japan, with communities of followers and temples now located in many different parts of the world, as for example the Buddhist Churches of America in the continental United States.

I have presented Shinran's Pure Land Buddhist teaching as a "way of being religious," that is, in the format of a fourfold structure. This involves his view of the human problematic, his view of ultimate reality and the ultimate destiny of human existence, his prescription for an individual's way to the attainment of that ultimate destiny, and the social expressions of that way.[27] This fourfold schema allows us to set Shinran's religious message in fresh relief in the context of a postmodern, religiously pluralistic, twenty-first–century global society, beset by enormous problems that now cast a shadow on the very survival of humanity itself. The question that looms in this regard is this: Can Shinran's religious message have bearing for our twenty-first–century world?

Reinterpreting Shinran's Message for Our Time

With the rough sketch of the religious structure of Shinran's teachings given above in the foreground, I would like to take up three points raised by Taitetsu Unno in his essay outlining tasks of "constructive Buddhist theology,"[28] and offer tentative—and hesitant—reflections on each. Tentative, because my understanding of Shinran's teaching has largely been informed by my own reading and reflection over the past three decades, and not from the standpoint of a professed adherent or scholar of Shin Buddhism. I must hasten to add, though, that my appreciation of Shinran has been enhanced and inspired by significant exchanges and ongoing friendships with members of the Jōdo Shinshū community, and it is with them in mind that this is offered.[29] Hesitant, for related reasons, that I remain an outsider to this community of Shinran's followers, albeit, as declared above, a thoroughly sympathetic one. In the interests of full disclosure, in undertaking critical and constructive theology I locate myself in the Roman Catholic and Zen Buddhist traditions. My hope is that these reflections on Shinran's religious message may be taken in a spirit of interreligious friendship, toward mutual challenge and learning, by my colleagues in the Jōdo Shinshū community as well as in the academy.[30]

Shinran and the Spiritual Yearnings of Our Age

How can Shinran's teaching respond to "the deepest existential and spiritual yearnings of people who seek but cannot find answers to the perennial questions of life and death"?[31] It goes without saying, of course, that this has been an ongoing task of thinkers of the Shin Buddhist community through the ages—that is, to present Shinran's message in a way that responds to these deep-seated and timeless human questions of each epoch.[32]

Inspired by Rennyo (1415–1499, eighth abbot of Honganji), the Honganji was revived in the sixteenth century. Since that time Shinran's followers have constituted one of the largest religious groups in Japan.[33] Given this fact, one can find volumes of literature presenting Shinran's message in different forms and with varying degrees of reception in Japanese society. These include didactic or systematic expositions of Shin Pure Land Buddhist belief for members of the religious community, devotional tracts, personal accounts of religious experience, and literary pieces (short stories, novels, poetry), not to mention scholarly writings on Shinran's life and thought, placed in the context of Japanese religious history, culture, and society.

Of those who took on the task of reinterpreting Shinran's message during the so-called modernization period of Japan—beginning with the Meiji Restoration in the 1860s and continuing into the postwar period—among the more prominent are Kiyozawa Manshi (1863–1903), Soga Ryōjin (1875–1971), and Kaneko Daiei (1881–1976). Tanabe Hajime (1885–1962), noted philosopher of the Kyoto school, also produced major writings that were profoundly influenced by Shinran's religious message.[34] In his later years Daisetsu T. Suzuki (1870–1966)—best known in the West for his voluminous writings on Zen Buddhism—also devoted his research and writings to Shin Pure Land Buddhist thought. This was especially the case following his appointment to Ōtani University, which has historical and administrative links to the Eastern branch of the Honganji community.[35] And needless to say, there is a long list of those who are known in Japan for their works on many aspects of Shinran and Pure Land Buddhist thought.

Selecting material from the vast corpus of writings in Japanese and making these available in translation would putatively be an ongoing task for those who seek to bring Shinran's message beyond Japan's shores. Such translations would serve to fill in some lacunae, and promote better understanding of this major stream of Buddhism in the Western hemisphere, making Shinran's teachings more accessible to people struggling with fundamental questions of life and death in our world today.[36]

Shinran's Message in a Religiously Pluralistic World

A second point raised by Taitetsu Unno as included among the tasks of constructive Buddhist theology relates to the intellectual, social, and cultural challenges of postmodernity.[37] I will not presume to be able to elaborate fully on this point here, but will simply note one facet. This concerns the task of critical and constructive reflection on one's own religious tradition in the context of a religiously pluralistic world.

In a globalized society characterized by a diversity of religious views among different sectors of our human community, and wherein these religious differences serve to set groups at odds with one another, the task of finding a place for the religious Other within the framework of one's own religious worldview becomes a pressing task for members of any community. This would enable members of a given religious group to at least relate in constructive and mutually cooperative ways with those from other communities, instead of simply writing them off, or even demonizing them or regarding them in inimical ways or else as less than worthy of respect as fellow human beings.

Interreligious dialogue and cooperative ventures in the context of dialogue are now among activities encouraged and undertaken on many levels of our global society, and members of the Shin Pure Land Buddhist community have also been part of this endeavor, both in Japan as well as in the international scene.

As is the experience of anyone who engages in interreligious activity, a possible outcome of such engagement is an enhanced, and perhaps even a transformed way of regarding and understanding one's own religious tradition.[38] A question that arises in this regard is this: In what way can the self-understanding of Shin Buddhists, and concomitantly, their understanding of Shinran's religious message, be enhanced or transformed through such interreligious encounters?

To an outsider like myself, some particular theological questions come up in the light of the above. Given that for Shin Buddhists, entry into the Pure Land is assured in and through the recitation of the name of Amida, and not through human effort nor through ethical action, will those who belong to other traditions and have different belief systems, and thereby do not believe in Amida nor take on this practice, be "left behind"? In short, will Pure Land devotees meet only other Pure Land devotees when they finally arrive at that place? A corollary question would be: Is the Pure Land to be regarded as a "place" after all, or is it a spiritual state or mode of being? In either case, are there alternative ways of getting there without the formal recitation of the name of Amida, such as for those born in cultures without historical connections to Shin Pure Land Buddhism? In short, can there be those who, without formally knowing about Amida or of the practice of reciting Amida's name, assume a similar or analogous religious attitude as the "entrusting mind" (*shinjin*) but, say, recite the name of Jesus, Allah, Krishna, or some other religious figure, and thus (anonymously) receive the merit of entry into Amida's Pure Land?

Many scholars have already pointed out resonances and points of intersection between Shin Buddhist and Christian doctrines and themes.[39] Just as the Christian thinkers who have engaged in this dialogue with Shin Pure Land Buddhist thought have arrived at profound insights and new horizons of understanding regarding their own Christian tradition as a fruit of this engagement with Pure Land Buddhism, in what way can encounters with Christianity, or with Judaism or Islam, for example, bring about new insights and enhanced understanding of Pure Land teaching on the part of Shin Buddhists? These are questions that may only be answered by those who take such steps of interreligious engagement while being committed to their own faith tradition.

Shinran's way of being religious, in the structure presented above, can provide a helpful grid and a set of useful reference points for engaging in dialogue with other traditions. This fourfold structure includes the human problematic underscoring human powerlessness insofar as ultimate realization is concerned, the optimistic view of human ultimate destiny with the assurance of entry into the Pure Land of Amida, the prescription of the way to the realization of that ultimate destiny in the clear and simple practice of reciting the name of Amida with a totally entrusting mind, and the social expression of the Pure Land way in a life of compassion.

Each of the items in this fourfold structure of Shinran's religious message in itself calls for deeper reflection and deserves treatment in greater detail in a way that can highlight Shinran's contribution to world culture and religious thought.

On the first item, Shinran's view of human powerlessness for ultimate realization can be compared and contrasted with differing views of human nature presented by thinkers throughout history and across cultures. Shinran's view of the human predicament can be considered in the light of ever-recurrent questions as to whether human beings are "intrinsically good" or "intrinsically evil," or "a mixture of both," or "neither," and so on. In this vein, comparisons with Christian views of human nature as "fallen" or "sinful," as a backdrop for understanding the central message of the Christian gospel, readily come to mind.[40] Comparisons with views of the human condition in other religious or philosophical traditions remain ongoing tasks.

On the second item, there is indeed a great variety of and divergence in views of ultimate reality and of human ultimate destiny among the different religious and philosophical traditions of the world, and Shinran's view invites particular reflection in this context, in comparison with theistic or monotheistic views, noting the distinctive aspect that Amida Buddha is not regarded as creator of the universe, as is the case with monotheism. In this regard, how the notion of Amida Buddha as a figure representing ultimate reality relates to the Buddhist notion of emptiness is a theme that deserves ongoing investigation and reflection.[41]

Shinran's prescription for religious praxis can also be further considered in comparison with prescriptions toward the realization of ultimate destiny in an individual's life as taught or prescribed in other religious traditions. Shinran's view that the very practice of reciting the name of Amida is not a matter of human effort, but is itself a "given" through the power of Amida's compassion, is a significant point to ponder in this regard. Here again, comparisons with Christian themes readily come to mind, and call for further elaboration.[42] On this point, the question of whether ultimate realization is through "other-power" (*tariki*) or "self-power" (*jiriki*) has been a theme of ongoing debate and discussion not just in Buddhist but also in wider religious circles, and a dialectical way that overcomes this apparent opposition and integrates them into a broader and more intricately textured framework for understanding religious praxis awaits further reflection and elaboration.[43]

Such dialogue between adherents of Shin Pure Land Buddhism and members of other religions, as well as other Buddhist traditions, on the level of doctrine and individual religious praxis can be a significant impetus to the development of American Shin thought. Additionally, however, dialogue and interaction from a standpoint of social praxis also presents a significant challenge to Shin Buddhist self-understanding, and can throw fresh light on Shinran's religious message. We turn now to the fourth item in the fourfold religious structure, namely the social expression of the way to ultimate realization in Shinran's teaching.

Can Shin Pure Land Buddhism Contribute to Global Healing?

Do members of the Shin Pure Land Buddhist community have anything to offer, from the standpoint of their religious vision and message, in addressing the pressing tasks faced by all of us as a global community? These include tasks of healing the widening rift between the haves and the have-nots of the world, tasks of reconciling conflictual and often violent modes of interaction between segments of our human community, and tasks of healing our ecological malaise that is at a point of being a threat to our survival. In other words, can Shinran's message be reinterpreted in ways that can ground his followers' engagement in the sociopolitical realm, and if so, how?

First of all, it can be pointed out that the social component or dimension in Shinran's teaching still awaits more thorough elaboration by interpreters of this tradition. Historically, ever since the death of Shinran, guidelines for living in society for his followers have been issued in general terms, including injunctions against speaking ill of people of other religious practices, denigrating religious objects or symbols of other traditions, or behaving in ways harmful to others or to society as a whole.[44] More recently, some Shin Buddhist thinkers have been addressing the question of a Shin Buddhist social ethics, seeking to carve out the concrete implications of Shinran's teaching in our day-to-day life in the world.[45]

I have been privileged to meet and interact with Shin Buddhist priests and lay devotees in Japan who are challenging the conventional interpretation of Shinran's message as one mainly directed to individual religious praxis. They have been engaged in the task of rereading Shinran's writings precisely in the attempt to discern the implications of his teaching for those in situations of socioeconomic and political oppression. They are temple priests and lay devotees who happen to live in an area threatened with environmental destruction through the establishment of a nuclear power plant in the vicinity, and who are considering some form of protest action in this regard. They are devoted Shin Buddhist followers who have been sensitized to and seek to redress the patterns of discrimination against certain groups by virtue of their birth, social status, or ethnic origin, a pattern of discrimination that is still prevalent in Japanese society. They are Shin devotees who have begun to reflect on their socioeconomic and political situation in the context of Japan's role as economic oppressor vis-à-vis other Asian societies. They are spouses of temple priests and their allies who have come to question the inequities in the religious hierarchy based on gender and other factors. From their concrete social locations, and as devoted followers of Shinran, they earnestly turn to Shinran's writings for guidance on how to respond to the problems they experience in their particular situation. There are some who have formed study and reflection groups to read Shinran's texts together, discussing the relevance of the texts to their particular social situation and seeking ways of responding to the situation in this light.[46]

Reading Shinran's texts together in small groups, and reflecting on the socioeconomic, cultural, and political contexts in which the members of the group find themselves, brings up a scenario akin to that of the grassroots communities in Central and Latin America and the Philippines. In much the same way that Shin adherents have been reading Shinran's writings, these people read the Bible together in small groups, and it was here in these small groups of lay adherents reading and reflecting together that the seeds of liberation theology sprouted and blossomed.[47]

In this regard, an essay by Uehara Senroku (1899–1975), noted post-World War II intellectual historian and religious thinker, provides a set of methodological guidelines in reading and understanding Shinran's message for contemporary times. This essay, entitled "Shinran-ninshiki no hōhō" (translated roughly as "A Hermeneutic of Shinran"), outlines five kinds of approaches in the study of Shinran. First, there is the traditional approach of sectarian studies (*shūgakuteki hōhō*); second, Western methodological approaches (*seiyogakuteki hōhō*); third, the approach from the perspective of world history (*sekaishigakuteki hōhō*); fourth, an "empathetic" approach (*Shinran-teki hōhō,* literally, "approaching Shinran by way of Shinran himself"); and fifth, approaches from the perspective of ethno-national tasks as Japanese (*kokuminteki hōhō*).

The first two denote approaches to Shinran taken by those within the Shin Pure Land Buddhist community, wherein the authors' as well as readers' acceptance of the authoritativeness of Shinran's teaching is presupposed. The second, which can be taken either by those within or outside of the Shin community, employs an "objective and detached" stance taken vis-à-vis the material for study. The bulk of what is known as "Shinran studies" in Japan would fall under one or the other category described above.

It is in the third, fourth, and fifth approaches outlined by Uehara that new horizons in our understanding of Shinran may be opened, whether or not one professes religious affiliation with the community of his followers. I have addressed this in a previous essay,[48] and will only briefly summarize the key points here.

The approach to Shinran from the perspective of world history is one that Uehara had previously applied in the study of Nichiren. He situated Nichiren and his religious ideas by reference to the events of his day—including the Mongol attempts to invade Japan in 1268 and 1271, the turmoil in Japanese society at the time, and parallel events going on in different parts of the world—all of which provide a bigger picture in looking at the religious figures of the Kamakura period of Japanese history. Uehara, offering a disclaimer that he himself is neither a devotee nor scholar of Shin Pure Land Buddhism, unfortunately does not go into detail as to how this proposed approach can throw new light on Shinran and his thought, beyond making the suggestion for others to pursue this line of investigation, that is, of "Shinran in the context of the world events of his time." One example that could be given of a view of Shinran along these lines is that found in work of the late Tamura Yoshiro, who examined the thought of the four major figures of Kamakura Buddhism (Hōnen, Shinran, Dōgen, and Nichiren) in the context of their particular ways of reacting or relating to the notion of original enlightenment (*hongaku shisō*), a tendency in Buddhist doctrine and praxis that originated in Chinese Tiantai thought and found flowering in Japanese Tendai Buddhist circles.[49]

Superficially, the "empathetic approach" to reading Shinran may be considered as asking the question "What would Shinran do?" within the context of concrete situations calling for a response or decision. But on a more profound level, this approach would be analogous in many ways to the kinds of reading of biblical texts that are done by those seeking wisdom and discernment in addressing situations where the Bible itself may not provide a clear answer. In other words, it is a way of reading that seeks to uncover the spirit, rather than just the letter, of the text, fathoming the basic orientation of the biblical message and applying it to situations not specifically laid out in detail in the biblical text itself. In reading Shinran, for example, the fact that he lived and walked with those in the margins of the society of his time, notably those that were discriminated against by mainstream society, those who were pronounced "evil" in this world and thereby had no hope for salvation, and privileging them as the most immediate recipients of Amida's compassion, is a "hermeneutical device" that contemporary readers seeking a socially liberative message in Shinran's teaching have employed.[50]

Approaches to Shinran from the perspective of Japanese ethnonational tasks, in Uehara's thinking, are not about cultivating ethnocentric or nationalistic sentiments, but about reading Shinran while asking the basic questions that Japanese people need to ask themselves in the light of their role in global society. Uehara's emphasis is precisely on the urgent need for his fellow Japanese to see and think beyond their ethnic and national boundaries, and to see themselves from a global perspective. The questions that arise in this regard inevitably have to do with issues of survival and coexistence with other peoples, of equality and freedom, of human rights, of justice for all.

Taking Uehara's hint and extending the horizon of concerns beyond his own time and particular location (i.e., postwar Japan, and the Japan of the economic boom of the 1960s and early 1970s), and bringing it to our contemporary world—the global ecological crisis, the escalating conflicts in global society, the increasing gap between the haves and the have-nots of the world on a global scale—all loom within the horizon of issues to be considered in reading Shinran and seeking to understand his message for our times.

The "hermeneutical key" that may open up fresh insights in this regard is Shinran's teaching on the "returning back to the world" (*gensō-ekō*) of the Pure Land devotee empowered by Amida's compassion. In other words, Amida's compassion is the power to which a Shin Buddhist who has experienced assurance of entry into the Pure Land has totally entrusted him- or herself. Given this, the question to be asked, as we confront the global issues the human community faces at this point of our history, is this: How can Amida's compassion work through the Shin Buddhist devotee in a way that empowers the latter to engage herself or himself in these issues facing our contemporary world? This becomes a matter of sharpening one's vision of what the world needs now, and focusing one's discernment on concrete tasks at hand. This would involve cooperation with others in the continuing study of and reflection on various aspects of the state of the world, mapping out the areas of need and the various manifestations of suffering, investigating their causes, and seeking ways to address these causes.

In short, details and directions for developing the contents of social ethics and tasks of social engagement in Shin Buddhism can be laid out as followers remain faithful to their central religious praxis of reciting the name of Amida, experiencing the power of compassion at work in and through them, and letting this power carry them on toward engagement in the concrete tasks of global healing. Once again, the emphasis here is not on what the Shin Pure Land Buddhist devotees can do individually or collectively, but on how their earnest praxis effects a transformation in their very being, and enables them to become vehicles of Amida's compassion in this twenty-first–century world of ours. The practical details involved in these tasks of social engagement toward global healing need to be worked out in cooperation not just with members of one's own religious community but in a way that transcends religious and other boundaries, to include "all men and women of good will" who bear the woundedness of Earth, and who together comprise our global sangha, the Earth Community.[51]

In this essay I have sought to lay out a format for understanding the structure of Shinran's Shin Pure Land Buddhist teaching, and have suggested some areas for further study and reflection on reinterpreting Shinran's message for our twenty-first–century world. It is presented in honor of Roger Corless, and also in gratitude to and deep appreciation for all my Shin Buddhist friends and colleagues in Japan and North America, with the hope that the suggestions offered especially in the second part, outlining some tasks in Shin Buddhist theology, may be taken in a spirit of collegiality, as shared tasks we can continue to work on in the years to come.

Notes

1 See Roger Jackson and John Makransky, eds., *Buddhist Theology: Critical Reflections by Contemporary Scholars* (Surrey, UK: Curzon Press, 2000), p. 18.

2 Taitetsu Unno, "Constructive Buddhist Theology: A Response," in Jackson and Makransky, eds., *Buddhist Theology*, p. 387.

3 Among those to whom I would like to express a deep debt of gratitude are Professors Shigaraki Takamaro, Ueyama Daishun, and Nakamura Hisashi, mentors and former colleagues at Ryūkoku University, Kyoto, Japan, for their guidance and support through the years, and especially for their invitation to join their Faculty of Intercultural Communication (1998–2000); Dennis Hirota, now with this faculty at Ryūkoku; Most Ven. Ohtani Koshin, *"sempai"* and friend since student days at Tokyo University's Graduate School Department of Indology and Buddhist Studies; Robert Rhodes and colleagues at Ōtani University, who invited me to the International Symposium commemorating the five-hundredth anniversary of Rennyo's death in 1999; Rev. Sugiura Myodo and the late Rev. Suzuki Ryowa, Rev. Isetani Isao and Isetani Kuniko, Rev. Tamamitsu Junsho and Tamamitsu Katsuko, Shin Buddhist priests who have taught me and also inspire others to read Shinran from the perspective of those marginalized in society; Dr. Kawahashi Noriko and her colleagues, for their inspiring work on women's rights in Japan; Kenneth K. Tanaka and Kimie Tanaka, friends since graduate school days; and, in North America, most especially Alfred Bloom and Taitetsu Unno, among others, for their inspiring and insightful work on Shinran and Pure Land Buddhism in a contemporary context.

4 Frederick J. Streng, *Understanding Religious Life* (Belmont, CA: Wadsworth, 1985).

5 For a highly acclaimed study of this notion and its different versions as transmitted through Asia, see Jan Nattier, *Once Upon a Future Time: Studies in a Buddhist Prophecy of Decline* (Berkeley, CA: Asian Humanities Press, 1991).

6 I have referred to Alfred Bloom's *Essentials of Shinran* (Bloomington, IN: World Wisdom Press, 2006), as a handy guide to locating key texts of Shinran. The translations are based on the two-volume work, *The Collected Works of Shinran*, hereafter CWS (Kyoto: Shin Buddhism Translation Series, Jodo Shinshu Hongwanji-ha, 1997). In each passage cited in the text, the English title of Shinran's treatise, volume number, and page located in CW are given at the end of the citation.

7 *Pure Land Hymns of the Dharma Ages*, CWS I, pp. 399, 400, nos. 2, 3, 4, 8. See also *Notes on "Essentials of Faith Alone,"* CWS I, p. 466, and *Gutoku's Hymns of Lament and Reflection*, CWS I, pp. 421–422, nos. 94–99.

8 *Notes on Once-Calling and Many-Calling*, CWS I, p. 485. See also *True Teaching, Practice, and Realization of the Pure Land Way* (*Kyōgyōshinshō*, hereafter KGSS), CWS I, p. 8, no. 3, from the *Larger Sutra; Hymns of the Pure Land*, CWS I, p. 340, no. 54; *A Collection of Passages Revealing the True Teaching of the Pure Land Way*, CWS I, p. 7, no. 2. See also *Passages on the Pure Land Way*, CWS I, pp. 295–296; and *A Collection of Passages on the Types of Birth in the Three Pure Land Sutras*, CWS I, p. 639; and KGSS, CWS I, p. 10, no. 7.

9 *Notes on Once-Calling and Many-Calling,* CWS I, pp. 486–487. See also *The Virtue of the Names of Amida Tathāgata,* CWS I, pp. 657, 656; chap. 5 of KGSS, CWS I, p. 177, no. 1; *Notes on the Inscriptions on Sacred Scrolls,* CWS I, p. 501.

10 Chap. 2 of KGSS, CWS I, p. 54, no. 72. See also letter 22 of *Lamp for the Latter Ages,* CWS I, p. 555.

11 *Hymns of the Pure Land,* CWS I, p. 350, no. 93.

12 Chap. 2 of KGSS, CWS I, p. 13, no. 1.

13 The latter term, *shinjin,* is now the preferred way of rendering a key term in Shinran's works, normally written with two characters meaning "entrusting" and "mind."

14 Chap. 3 of KGSS, CWS I, p. 79, no. 1.

15 *Notes on Once-Calling and Many-Calling,* CWS I, p. 475. See also chap. 2 of KGSS, CWS I, pp. 110–111, no. 60; *Notes on Once-Calling and Many-Calling,* CWS I, p. 474; *Notes on "Essentials of Faith Alone,"* CWS I, p. 453.

16 *A Record of Lament of Divergences,* CWS I, p. 666, no. 10. See also letter 22 of *Lamp for the Latter Ages,* CWS I, p. 555.

17 There have been ongoing debates among Shin Pure Land thinkers on the relationship between entry into Pure Land and the realization of final nirvana. A widely accepted view holds that entry into Pure Land is the penultimate stage wherein entry into final nirvana will inevitably follow once the karmic lifespan in the Pure Land has been exhausted. In contemporary terms, this can perhaps be likened to having one's ticket confirmed and stamped with an assigned seat on a plane, and one is now in the pre-departure area awaiting take-off.

18 Letter 1 of *Lamp for the Latter Ages,* CWS I, p. 523.

19 *Passages on the Pure Land Way,* CWS I, p. 296.

20 *Hymns of the Dharma-Ages,* CWS I, p. 407, no. 34. See also *Hymns of the Pure Land,* CWS I, p. 348, no. 85; and *Hymns of the Dharma-Ages,* CWS I, p. 406, no. 30.

21 *Hymns of the Pure Land,* CWS I, p. 329, no. 20. See also *Passages on the Two Aspects of Tathāgata's Directing of Virtue,* CWS I, p. 635; and *Passages on the Pure Land Way,* CWS I, pp. 301–302; chap. 4 of KGSS, CWS I, p. 158, no. 14 and p. 174, no. 18. Also, *Treatise on the Pure Land* [Vasubandhu], chap. 4 of KGSS, CWS I, p. 155, no. 7.

22 *A Record of Lament of Divergences,* CWS I, p. 663, no. 4.

23 Ibid., p. 664, no. 5.

24 Letter 5 of *A Collection of Letters,* CWS I, p. 566; and letter 8, p. 570.

25 Chap. 3 of KGSS, CWS I, p. 113, no. 66. See also *The Sutra of Great Compassion,* chap. 3 of KGSS, CWS I, p. 119, no. 992.

26 James Dobbins, *Jodo Shinshu: Shin Buddhism in Medieval Japan* (Honolulu: University of Hawai'i Press, 2002, reprint).

27 I have previously used this fourfold schema as an approach to understanding Nichiren's Buddhist teaching. See my essay, "Nichiren's Way of Being

Religious: A Case Study in East Asian Buddhism," in Sueki Fumihiko, et al., eds., *Kimura Kiyotaka Hakase Kinen Ronshu* (*Commemoration Volume in Honor of Dr. Kiyotaka Kimura*) (Tokyo: Shunjūsha, 2001).

28 See note 2.

29 I have offered some reflections on Shinran's teaching and some resonances with biblical texts in my *Shinran to Seisho no Yomikata* (*Reading Shinran and the Bible*) (Tokyo: Akashi Shoten, 1989).

30 James Fredericks has written about the significance and transformative impact of what he terms "interreligious friendships." See his essay "Masao Abe: A Spiritual Friendship," *Spiritus* 3, no. 2 (2003): pp. 219–230. See also his "Inter-religious Friendship: A New Theological Virtue," *Journal of Ecumenical Studies* 35, no. 2 (Spring 1998): pp. 159–174.

31 Taitetsu Unno, "Constructive Buddhist Theology," in Jackson and Makransky, eds., *Buddhist Theology*, p. 387.

32 For a helpful historical account, see Galen Amstutz, *Interpreting Amida: History and Orientalism in the Study of Pure Land Buddhism* (Albany, NY: State University of New York Press, 1997).

33 See Mark Blum and Yasutomi Shin'ya, eds., *Rennyo* (New York: Oxford University Press, 2005).

34 See Tanabe Hajime, *Philosophy as Metanoetics*, trans. Takeuchi Yoshinori (Berkeley, CA: University of California Press, 1986); see also Taitetsu Unno and James Heisig, eds., *The Religious Philosophy of Tanabe Hajime* (Berkeley, CA: Asian Humanities Press, 1990).

35 For well-chosen representative samples of writings on Shinran's thought by Kiyozawa, Soga, Kaneko, and Suzuki, see Alfred Bloom, ed., *Living in Amida's Universal Vow: Essays in Shin Buddhism* (Bloomington, IN: World Wisdom, Inc., 2004).

36 A noteworthy example of a translated work in English that conveys Shinran's message to our contemporaries through personal narratives and anecdotal accounts in beautiful prose is *Tariki: Embracing Despair, Discovering Peace* (Tokyo: Kodansha International, 2001), a volume that draws upon the spiritual journey of the author, acclaimed novelist Hiroyuki Itsuki, who has several bestselling works to his name.

One can of course find any number of acclaimed literary masters and intellectuals whose works in Japanese drawing upon Shinran's religious thought and the Shin Buddhist spiritual path have been widely received, and these deserve consideration for possible English translation. Among those awaiting translation, I would like to cite the work of Korean-Japanese essayist and poet Ko Sa Myun. Especially noteworthy is the collection of short essays entitled *Hitotsubu no Namida wo Idakite: Tannishō to no Deai* (*Embracing One Teardrop: My Encounters with the Tannishō*) (Tokyo: Mainichi Shinbunsha, 1977), wherein he describes his experience of near-despair upon the death by suicide of his own twelve-year-old son, and the solace he received in an experiential encounter with the compassion of Amida Buddha. Such a work, among many others, would certainly address what Taitetsu Unno describes as "the deepest existential and spiritual yearnings of people" of our time, in the various situations we find ourselves in this contemporary world.

Among the prominent authors who have published works in English that introduce and expound on Shinran's thought and Pure Land Buddhist teachings are Alfred Bloom, Takeuchi Yoshinori, Taitetsu Unno, Dennis Hirota, Ueda Yoshifumi, Kenneth K. Tanaka, Takeda Ryusei, and others. See the following as examples of their work: Alfred Bloom, *Shinran and the Gospel of Pure Grace* (Tucson: University of Arizona Press, 1965); Ueda Yoshifumi and Dennis Hirota, eds., *Shinran: An Introduction to His Thought* (Kyoto: Hongwanji International Center, 1989); Takeuchi Yoshinori, *The Heart of Buddhism: In Search of the Timeless Spirit of Primitive Buddhism,* ed. and trans. James W. Heisig (New York: Crossroad, 1991); Kenneth K. Tanaka, *Ocean: An Introduction to Jodo-Shinshu Buddhism in America* (Berkeley, CA: WisdomOcean Publications, 1997); Taitetsu Unno, *River of Fire, River of Water: An Introduction to the Pure Land Tradition of Shin Buddhism* (New York: Doubleday, 1998). The International Association of Shin Buddhist Studies, an academic group that holds biennial conferences, gives established as well as younger scholars a forum to present their ideas. Its members, both those who profess adherence to the Shin Buddhist community as well as those who do not, continue to engage in the task of reinterpreting Shinran's message for our contemporary world, in ways that would respond to the spiritual yearnings of people of our twenty-first century. *The Pure Land: Journal of the International Association of Shin Buddhist Studies* and *Pacific World: Journal of the Institute of Buddhist Studies* are two academic journals devoted to studies in Shin Pure Land Buddhism.

37 See Frederic B. Burnham, ed., *Postmodern Theology: Christian Faith in a Pluralist World* (New York: Harper and Row, 1989), for a collection of essays on how "postmodernity" presents particular challenges to religious communities. The authors, Christian theologians, offer reflections and proposals for their own tradition that may be applied in analogous ways to the Shin Buddhist tradition.

38 See John B. Cobb, Jr., *Beyond Dialogue: Toward a Mutual Transformation of Christianity and Buddhism* (Philadelphia: Fortress Press, 1982), for a now-classic exposition of this theme of mutual transformation in interreligious encounters. Cobb devotes sections of the book to Shinran's thought and its resonances with themes in the Christian tradition.

39 See, among others, Paul Ingram, "Faith as Knowledge in the Teaching of Shinran Shonin and Martin Luther," *Buddhist-Christian Studies* 8 (1988): pp. 23–36; and Jan van Bragt, "Does Jodo Shinshu form a Bridge between Jodo Shinshu and Christianity?" *Japanese Religions* 18, no. 1 (1993): pp. 47–75. For a recent and insightful study, see Sharon Baker, "The Three Minds and Faith, Hope and Love in Pure Land Buddhism," *Buddhist-Christian Studies* 25 (2005): pp. 49–65.

40 See Gerhard Schepers, "Shinran's View of the Human Predicament and the Christian Concept of Sin," *Japanese Religions* 15, no. 2 (July 1988): pp. 1–17.

41 On this and related points, see the essays in the collection edited by Dennis Hirota, *Toward a Contemporary Understanding of Pure Land Buddhism: Creating Shin Buddhist Theology in a Religiously Plural World* (Albany, NY: State University of New York Press, 2000).

[42] See Kenneth Lee, "Comparative Analysis of Shinran's Shinjin and Calvin's Faith," *Buddhist-Christian Studies* 24 (2004): pp. 171–190.

[43] This is also a theme for intra-Buddhist reflection, besides being one for inter-religious conversation, recalling the traditional distinction made among the Buddhist traditions between those that espouse meditative praxis as "self-power" as opposed to the devotional practice that places reliance on "other-power."

[44] See Dobbins, *Jodo Shinshu*, p. 67.

[45] See Ama Toshimaro, "Toward a Shin Buddhist Social Ethics," and Kenneth K. Tanaka, "Ethics in American Jodo Shinshu: Trans-ethical Responsibility," in Bloom, ed., *Living in Amida's Universal Vow*, pp. 173–188, and 197–213, respectively.

[46] I acknowledge my profound debt of gratitude to my Shin Buddhist friends and colleagues who have invited me to join them in their group studies and visits to their communities, and have shared with me their struggles and aspirations in this regard. In particular, I would like to express gratitude to the members of the circle around Maruyama Teruo, himself a Nichiren priest but who has gathered around him a group of activist Buddhists from different traditions, including Shin Pure Land Buddhists such as the late Rev. Suzuki Ryowa and Rev. Sugiura Myodo, Rev. and Mrs. Tamamitsu Junsho and Katsuko, Rev. and Mrs. Isetani Isao and Kuniko, and Dr. Kawahashi Noriko. Each one, in various ways, helped me with new insights into Shinran's vision for liberation.

[47] I describe some of these encounters in *Shinran to Seisho no Yomikata;* see note 29.

[48] See my essay, "Uehara Senroku's Hermeneutic of Shinran: Prospects for Shin Studies," *The Pure Land*, n.s., 8–9 (December 1992): pp. 47–63.

[49] Tamura's studies, enshrined in his award-winning *Kamakura Shin-bukkyō Kenkyū* (Kyoto: Hōzōkan, 1969), and presented in many of his other works published in Japanese, have spawned reactions, both appreciative and critical, from other scholars of Buddhism, and have generated debates about *hongaku shisō* and its influence on Japanese Buddhism. My monograph, *Originary Enlightenment: Tendai Hongaku Doctrine and Japanese Buddhism* (Tokyo: International Institute for Advanced Buddhist Studies, 1996), examines Tamura's work and outlines some of the key critical points raised by Matsumoto Shiro and Hakamaya Noriaki in the wake of Tamura.

[50] Again, I refer to my *Shinran to Seisho no Yomikata* for further elaboration of these points.

[51] For a delineation of what some of these practical tasks may involve, see David Korten, *The Great Turning: From Empire to Earth Community* (San Francisco: Berrett Koehler Publishers, 2006).

Amida and Pure Land within a Contemporary Worldview: From Shinran's Literal Symbolism to Figurative Symbolism

Kenneth K. Tanaka
Musashino University, Tokyo

Preface

One of the major challenges facing contemporary Shin Buddhists is to find more meaningful ways of understanding Amida and Pure Land, which are difficult to grasp on account of their "transcendent" nature. Of course, this has been an ongoing challenge faced by numerous Shin scholars and writers before me, but I would like to offer my views building on what others have proposed and what I have previously published.[1] It is my hope that my endeavor will be a way of honoring Roger Corless, who, as will be seen below, has also offered some valuable perspectives on this topic.

I realize that Amida and Pure Land have separate doctrinal origins in early Indian Buddhist development, but we are treating them as *a set*, for they appear together as integral components of the narrative that makes up the core teaching as articulated in the Pure Land sutras. Further, they continued to serve that function for subsequent Pure Land Buddhists in East Asia, including Shinran and Shin Buddhists up to the present.

The "challenge" we are about to tackle has been well articulated in the following set of questions posed by Gordon Kaufman, a noted Christian theologian and former professor at the Divinity School at Harvard University. As someone outside the Shin tradition, he is, perhaps, afforded a vantage point for a more objective evaluation of Shin Buddhist claims. Speaking at a symposium at Ryūkoku University in 1989, he asked:

> How now are we today to understand this Pure Land? Is there really some special place other than this world to which we may go after death, a Pure

> Land of joy and peace? Many religious mythologies have spoken this way; but, in the light of modern scientific cosmology and our modern knowledge of the grounding of human existence in the evolution of life and the earth's ecology, it is difficult to make much sense of this kind of thinking. . . . Perhaps sophisticated Buddhists, following the lead of Shinran, understand that the Pure Land is not a real place at all, but basically a symbol for a different state of mind; but would such notion be attractive and acceptable to ordinary practicers of Shin Buddhism? . . . My second set of questions has to do with Amida's Vow. First, of course, one wonders who—or what—is Amida Buddha? Is Amida some sort of "cosmic person," a kind of god? If so, how are we to conceive this sort of being today?[2]

Here Kaufman distinguishes two types of understanding with regard to Pure Land, the first of which he refers to as "some special place other than this world to which we may go after death" and the second as "a symbol for a different state of mind." Perhaps we can thus refer to these two kinds of understanding as substantialist and symbolic, respectively. The same can be applied to Amida, since a substantialist understanding would make Amida "some sort of 'cosmic person,'" while a symbolic understanding would render Amida a representation or personification of a deeper reality.

Kaufman suggests that while sophisticated Shin Buddhists might find the symbolic understanding attractive, "ordinary" Shin Buddhists would find the substantialist understanding more acceptable. It is difficult to determine who would qualify as "ordinary," but the survey that I conducted of American Shin Buddhists revealed that virtually all embraced a symbolic understanding.[3]

Conversely, the substantialist understanding was discernibly weak. While this group cannot be representative of all Shin Buddhists today, I believe they represent a cohort that is seriously attempting to incorporate the Shin teachings into their spiritual lives. Moreover, it is my evaluation that most Shin Buddhists today, whether in Japan or in the United States, would not take a substantialist view of a Pure Land of bejeweled trees located billions of buddha lands to the west and presided over by Amida and bodhisattvas. Thus, contrary to Kaufman's perception, most "ordinary" Shin Buddhists would subscribe to a symbolic understanding.

Shinran's Understanding

Now, let's move on to Shinran's understanding, which Kaufman saw as being symbolic, based on his comment, ". . . *following the lead of Shinran,* [sophisticated Buddhists would] understand that the Pure Land is not a real place at all, but basically a symbol for a different state of mind." As we attempt to determine the accuracy of Kaufman's portrayal, I have decided to focus on Shinran's understanding of Amida and Pure Land as expressed in his *Notes on "Essentials of Faith Alone,"* which constitutes Shinran's clearest and most succinct explanation on this subject.

> *The land of bliss is the realm of nirvana, the uncreated. The land of bliss* is that Pure Land of happiness, where there are always countless joys and never any suffering mingled with them. It is known as the land of peace. It was Master [Tanluan] who praised and called it "Land of Peace." Also, the *Treatise on the Pure Land* describes it as "the lotus repository world" and as the uncreated. . . .
>
> Since it is with this heart and mind of all sentient beings that they entrust themselves to the Vow of the dharma-body as compassion, this *shinjin* is none other than Buddha-nature. This Buddha-nature is dharma-nature. Dharma-nature is the dharma-body. For this reason there are two kinds of dharma-body in regard to the Buddha. *The first is called dharma-body as suchness and the second, dharma-body as compassionate means. Dharma-body as suchness has neither color nor form; thus, the mind cannot grasp it nor words describe it. From this oneness was manifested form, called dharma-body as compassionate means.*
>
> *Taking form, the Buddha proclaimed his name as Bhikṣu Dharmākara and established the Forty-eight great Vows that surpass conceptual understanding.* Among these Vows are the Primal Vow of immeasurable light and the universal Vow of immeasurable life, and to the form manifesting these two vows Bodhisattva Vasubandhu gave the title, "Tathāgata of unhindered light filling the ten quarters." This Tathāgata has fulfilled the Vows, which are the cause of that Buddhahood, and thus is called "Tathāgata of the fulfilled body." This is none other than Amida Tathāgata.[4]

The Two Traditions Forming Shinran's Understanding

Based on Tanluan's *Commentary on the Pure Land Treatise,* Shinran recognizes two kinds of dharma bodies. We are drawn to the line, "For this reason there are two kinds of dharma-body in regard to the Buddha." One is the dharma body as suchness, and the other is the dharma body as compassionate means. The former "has neither color nor form; thus, the mind cannot grasp it nor words describe it." And the latter is Amida, which took form out of oneness.

This set of two bodies is quite well known and can be said to be drawing from the doctrine of the two levels of body, one of dharma and one of form (*rūpa*), that originated hundreds of years earlier in Indian

Buddhism. However, what I wish to emphasize is that these two kinds of dharma body actually represent two "developments" within pre-Mahayana and Pure Land Buddhist thought.

The dharma body as compassionate means—that is, Amida—is found in the Pure Land sutras (both the so-called *Larger* and *Smaller Sukhāvatīvyūha-sūtras*), which are estimated to have been compiled in the first century C.E. In the *Larger Sutra,* we find the narrative of Bhikṣu Dharmākara making the vows and eventually becoming Buddha Amitābha (i.e., Amida), which comes to serve as the foundation on which the Pure Land teachings and practices developed.

On the other hand, the dharma body as suchness is not explicitly found in the Pure Land sutras but was introduced into Pure Land discussion by Tanluan in his *Commentary on the Pure Land Treatise* completed in the sixth century. Tanluan must have acquired this concept while he was involved in the study of Indian Mahayana texts centered on the Yogācāra tradition prior to his legendary conversion to the Pure Land way.

As alluded to above, Buddhist texts have long articulated a two-bodies theory of the form body (*rūpakāya*) and dharma body (*dharmakāya*) in its various meanings and connotations. And Tanluan knew about one version of the two-bodies theory, dharma body as suchness and dharma body as compassionate means. Soon after, in the latter half of the sixth century, Zhingying Huiyuan (523–591) applied the prevailing three-bodies theory (*dharmakāya, sambhogakāya,* and *nirmāṇakāya*) to explain Amitābha, thus furthering the doctrinal move to reconcile Amitābha of the Pure Land sutras with the buddha-body theory in Mahayana Buddhism current at the time. However, Tanluan, by means of his two-bodies theory, is the earliest known writer to reconcile the two traditions.

What needs to be borne in mind in this discussion is that the Pure Land sutras present a clearly substantialist portrayal of Amida and the Pure Land. This tradition goes back, in part, to the doctrine of past and future buddhas that began as early as the third century B.C.E. Within a hundred years after that, we see the emergence of the concept of transcendent contemporary buddhas of the other world-realms within the Mahāsaṃghika and Lokottaravādin schools. The proponents of this view actually thought of these buddhas as "beings" who resided in "actual objectively existent realms" in ways similar, if not the same, to how we today look at the planets and stars. Then when the Pure Land sutras appeared in the first century C.E., they identified one of the numerous contemporary buddhas as Amitābha dwelling in one of the buddha lands called Sukhāvatī.[5]

It is vital that we acknowledge this substantialist stream within the Pure Land tradition that existed in sixth-century China and right up to the time of Shinran and even today. We cannot, therefore, quickly dismiss this element based on our understanding that Shinran, following Tanluan's lead, "demythologized" the Pure Land narrative. Tanluan did not eliminate the narrative, as we shall now see below.

Tanluan's Reconciliation of the Two Traditions

In this respect, Tanluan is clearly a pivotal figure in Pure Land Buddhist development, for he sought to reconcile the two streams of thought. For this reason, he is often described as the "demythologizer" of the Dharmākara-Amitābha narrative. However, I feel it is more correct to see Tanluan as "reconciler" of two discrete developments, for he did not eliminate the narrative but set it within the framework of Mahayana doctrine of the two bodies, informed by the truth of emptiness as well as the two truths of the ultimate and the conventional.

For example, he characterizes the mode of existence of the Pure Land as "subtle" (*wei*) and explained, "Though it is extra-phenomenal, it exists."[6] So, it does exist but not in the ordinary way. I believe the same message is found in his well-known description, "That [Pure] Land is the Realm of Non-birth."[7]

Tanluan's attempt to reconcile the two can further be seen in his idea of the "interpenetration of the expanded and the essential" (*guanglüe xiangru;* Jpn. *kōryaku sōnyū*). The "essential" refers to "one dharma phrase" (*ifazhu;* Jpn. *ichihokku*), which constitutes another term for the ultimate truth. The "expanded" refers to the seventeen decorated forms of the Pure Land, Amitābha, and the two bodhisattvas described in the *Treatise on the Pure Land* attributed to Vasubandhu. The decorated forms of Pure Land (expanded) and the ultimate truth (essential) are mutually dependent. The former emerges based on the latter, while the latter is expressed through the former.[8]

The decorated forms must be rooted in ultimate truth, but the ultimate truth cannot be understood by ordinary beings. Hence, ultimate truth expresses itself through the decorated forms, which are in accord with the emotional and intellectual capacity of the unenlightened. Here we see Tanluan's recognition that the form is necessary to fulfill the needs of ordinary beings.

It is in connection with this relationship between ultimate truth and decorated forms that Tanluan discusses the two kinds of dharma bodies, which, as we saw above, Shinran quoted in articulating his own understanding. Between the two dharma bodies, the dharma body as compassionate means serves as "representation" or "symbol" for the dharma body as suchness, as noted in Shinran's passage, "From this oneness (i.e., the dharma body as suchness) was manifested form, called dharma body as compassionate means." Since dharma body as compassionate means is Amida, this passage has come to serve as one of the bases for Amida being regarded as "symbol," evidenced in Kaufuman's understanding as well.

There are other doctrinal bases for Shinran's understanding. The most well-known is found in Shinran's short tract *On Jinen Hōni,* written at the age of eighty-eight:

> As the essential purport of the Vow, [Amida] vowed to bring us all to become supreme Buddha. Supreme Buddha is formless, and because of being formless is called *jinen.* Buddha, when appearing with form, is not called supreme nirvana. In order to make it known that supreme Buddha is formless, the name of Amida Buddha is expressly used; so I have been taught. Amida Buddha fulfills the purpose of making us know the significance of *jinen.*[9]

Here, too, we find a clear expression of Shinran's understanding of Amida as representation or symbol in the last line, "Amida Buddha fulfills the purpose of making us know the significance of *jinen.*"

So, it appears safe to regard Shinran as having understood Amida as representation or symbol of the dharma body of suchness (*Notes on "Essentials of Faith Alone"*) or of supreme buddha (*On Jinen Hōni*).[10]

Applying Paul Tillich's Definitions of Religious Symbols

In examining Shinran's understanding of Amida and Pure Land from a contemporary perspective, I propose to apply a rudimentary definition of religious symbols as put forth by the noted Protestant theologian Paul Tillich. He saw four characteristics that comprise a religious symbol, which can be summarized as 1) acceptability, 2) innate power, 3) perceptibility, and 4) figurative. These characteristics are by and large accepted by other writers of religious symbols and myth. Allow me to apply each of the four characteristics to Shinran's description cited above.

The first characteristic of "acceptability" points to the social nature of a symbol, as Tillich explains:

> This implies that the symbol is socially rooted and socially supported. Hence it is not correct to say that a thing is first a symbol and then gains acceptance; the process of becoming a symbol and the acceptance of it as a symbol belong together.... The individual can devise signs for his own private needs; he cannot make symbols. If something becomes a symbol for him, it is always so in relation to the community which in turn can recognize itself in it.[11]

Shinran in this regard had inherited a rich and long Pure Land tradition that went as far back as the early as the first century C.E., when the Pure Land sutras were compiled. His selection of the lineage of seven masters headed by the eminent Mahayana proponent Nāgārjuna reveals Shinran's respect for the authenticity of the Pure Land lineage. The seven masters were in fact part of a greater lineage, whose origins went back to Amida Buddha, wherein even the historical Buddha Śākyamuni was relegated to the role of a messenger. For Shinran, the Amida narrative was an unquestionable component of the tradition and informed his historical outlook and worldview. His doctrinal formulation is embedded in the Pure Land tradition and reveals no hint of questioning the basic paradigm that he inherited.

The second characteristic points to the "innate power" that the symbol contains, particularly in contrast to a mere sign:

> It gives to the symbol the reality, which it has almost lost in ordinary usage, as the phrase "only a symbol" shows. This characteristic is decisive for the distinction between a sign and a symbol. The sign is interchangeable at will. It does not arise from necessity, for it has no inner power. The symbol, however, does possess a necessary character.[12]

Tillich maintains that symbols, unlike signs, possess an ability to convey meaning with an inherent power of their own. But through time, with the gradual shift from a mystical to a technical view of the world, they have lost that power—though not completely.

For Shinran, the name (*myōgō*) *"Namu Amida Butsu"* and its cognates was more than a name designating Amida Buddha but constituted Amida itself. There is no buddha independent of the name, for Amida Buddha is none other than the name. Further, the name also possessed all the necessary virtues to enable the person of *shinjin* to be assured of eventual full and complete enlightenment. However, the seeker must engage the name by *reciting* the name. In this way, the name would exhibit the "inner power" (Tillich's term) for actualizing the soteriological needs of the seeker.

Tillich describes the third quality of symbol "perceptibility" as follows:

> This implies that something which is intrinsically invisible, ideal, or transcendent is made perceptible in the symbol and is in this way given objectivity.[13]

The same point is made by Mircea Eliade, who saw that without the symbol ultimate reality would remain elusive, since it is by nature imperceptible.[14]

The Pure Land tradition, as discussed earlier, has long made it its hallmark to make the profundity of dharma accessible to seekers of ordinary abilities or circumstances. As early as the seventh century, Daochuo explained the soteriological process by means of an ingenious metaphor of fire and ice: "It is like lighting fire on top of ice. As the fire intensifies, the ice melts. When the ice melts, then the fire goes out."[15]

The fire and ice refer to the ignorant, passion-ridden people who aspire to be born in an existent, objective Pure Land. The melting of the ice refers to the soteriological process of their singleminded resolve to be born in a substantialist Pure Land, which eventually leads them to the attainment of wisdom. This attainment automatically extinguishes the fire of the false notion that the aspirant actually is born in a substantialist Pure Land. Shinran does not deviate from this basic understanding of the tradition, for he states:

> Know, then, that although they neither seek nor know the indescribable, inexplicable, and inconceivable virtues of the Pure Land of happiness, those who entrust themselves to the Primal Vow are made to acquire them.[16]

It's important to bear in mind that a person of *shinjin* would not directly perceive Amida or the Pure Land in this life but would undergo a life-transforming experience, in which one feels assured of birth in the Pure Land upon death.

The fourth characteristic of a symbol is its "figurative" quality. The symbol itself denotes an intrinsic reality, for the symbol is merely a representation. It, therefore, should not be taken literally.

> This implies that the inner attitude which is oriented to the symbol does not have the symbol itself in view but rather that which is symbolized in it.[17]

It is with this last point that Shinran's interpretation, in my view, fails to adhere to Tillich's definition. How is this so?

As we saw above, Shinran certainly understood Amida (and Pure Land) as a representation of oneness, which was expressed, "From this oneness was manifested form, called dharma-body as compassionate means." However, this manifestation was realized *when the narrative took place innumerable* kalpas *ago*, at which time dharma body as compassionate means entered "history." For Shinran, the narrative actually took place in this *sahā* world in an extremely distant past.

Hence, for Shinran the narrative was not figurative, because when he thought about Amida or the Pure Land, he did not see them as merely a symbol but as carrying reality in and of itself. Yes, they were the manifested forms of oneness, but that manifestation had taken place *kalpa*s earlier, and *he saw them to be true historically.*

Having thus applied Tillich's four characteristics of symbol to Shinran's understanding, we found that all but the fourth characteristic applied. Hence, we will have to qualify Shinran's understanding and refer to it in this paper as "literal symbolism." In contrast, an understanding that fulfills all four will be referred to as "figurative symbolism." I contend that most of us living in the twenty-first century would adhere to figurative symbolism. We can understand the difference by considering that Shinran lived in a different worldview, one that no longer exists today.

The Inevitable Gap between the Worldviews of Shinran and the Contemporary World

Shinran's worldview is in concert with those of pre-modern people who generally did not make any distinction between mythic narrative and historical fact. John Yokota makes this same point when he states:

> For Shinran, however, the Amida story is historically true, and it was important for him to anchor Amida in the historicity of [Śākyamuni]. . . . This story of Amida, in particular the establishing of the Vows, has historicity for Shinran.[18]

For Shinran, the Amida narrative was real in the sense that "it actually took place" in the incalculably distant past, which included Bodhisattva Dharmākara becoming Amida ten *kalpa*s ago and currently residing in Sukhāvatī Pure Land. Thus, that Amida took form out of oneness ("From this oneness was manifested form, called dharma-body as compassionate means") does not negate its "historicity" for Shinran, so that for him the Bodhisattva Dharmākara *actually lived in this* sahā *world in the distant past.*

The next logical question to be asked would be, "*When* did Shinran think that the dharma body as compassionate means took form out of oneness?" *It would have to be in the innumerable distant* kalpas *ago,* at which time the king (the future Bodhisattva Dharmākara/Amida) was inspired by Buddha Lokeśvararāja. It was then that the formless took form or entered history. The great distance in time probably did not concern Shinran as much as it has concerned us (for it can no longer be reconciled with our knowledge of history, which of course was not available to Shinran). What was important for Shinran was not the actual length of time but that the narrative refers to what actually happened as described in the sutras.

As Shinran's writings discussed above have shown, Shinran knew conceptually of the *provisional* nature of Dharmākara and Amida. But regarding this, I wish to stress the point that this form or dharma body as compassionate means was provisional in relation to the formless oneness or dharma body as suchness, but *not* provisional in relation to Shinran himself or the human side. This is a subtle but an important point, one that I rarely see other contemporary writers make.

As a passion-filled foolish being (*bonnō guzoku no bonbu*), Shinran saw himself as capable only of accepting the teachings of Amida and Pure Land as presented to him by Hōnen. Shinran's attitude can be seen in the well-known passage in the *Tannishō:*

> But I am incapable of any other practice, so hell is decidedly my abode whatever I do.
>
> If Amida's Primal Vow is true, [Śākyamuni's] teaching cannot be false. If the Buddha' teaching is true, [Shandao's] commentaries cannot be false. If [Shandao's] commentaries are true, can Hōnen's words be lies? If Hōnen's words are true, then surely what I say cannot be empty.
>
> Such, in the end, is how this foolish person entrusts himself [to the Vow].[19]

Shinran saw no other way but to humbly accept the teachings. This, I argue, led him not to be so presumptuous as to regard Amida or Pure Land *only figuratively.* He does not claim to comprehend "oneness" or the "mechanism" by which oneness manifested as form provisionally. Shinran saw himself simply affirming the teachings as presented. In fact, he did not claim even to experience Amida (let alone, oneness) *directly,* for, as we saw above, it was in the name *"Namu Amida Butsu"* itself that Amida manifested directly in his life. Thus, Amida and the Pure Land were not provisional for *him.* Further evidence for this can be found in Shinran's letters, where he makes the statement:

> My life has now reached the fullness of its years. It is certain that I will go to birth in the Buddha Land before you, so without fail I will await you there.[20]

One may argue that Shinran in these letters was carrying out a more pastoral function, in which he resorted to provisional and skillful means to speak to those whose abilities could only grasp a more literal and substantialist Pure Land. In other words, he personally did not believe in such a literal Pure Land but taught it to his disciples simply as an appeasement. However, I have found no compelling evidence to think that he took such an approach.

Now, I realize that there can be a way of understanding this issue in which history is "collapsed" or "transcended" in the moment of *shinjin*. Yokota also recognizes this point, as he explains:

> That is, it is not totally impossible that Shinran thought of the Amida myth and of Dharmākara raising the Vows in the existentialist-like manner of the collapsing of time in the now-moment of faith, and in his writings there are suggestive passages that lend themselves to such an understanding: "Pondering the mind of true entrusting of oneself to Amida, this mind of entrusting has one-moment. One moment expresses the moment of entrusting as being the ultimate point of time."[21]

I realize that this "one-moment as ultimate point of time" way of understanding Shinran's view of history is in vogue among Shin thinkers. For example, Furusawa Katsuhiko writes about "absolute time" (*zettaiteki jikan*) based on a "synchronic" (*enkan teki*) perspective, which differs from "linear time" (*chokusen teki*). The moment of *shinjin* is regarded as an absolute, synchronic time, in which one experiences a different order of time. Furusawa sees three qualities in this order of time: "severance of time" (*toki no danzetsu-sei*), "simultaneity with the eternal" (*ei'en to no dōji-sei*), and "reversibility of time" (*jikan no kagyaku-sei*). Specifically in regards to the narrative, he writes:

> In the one moment when one rides on the power of the Vow, he transcends both the past of innumerable *kalpa*s of transmigration as well as the future that afforded no possibility of escaping [transmigration based on self-power].[22]

Reconciling the Difference

I believe these two seemingly conflicting understandings of time and history can be reconciled, for I see them to be the two modes of engagement operating at *two distinct "stages"* respectively on the Shin spiritual path, which I shall refer to as "pre-*shinjin*" and "post-*shinjin*." These two correspond, in many ways, to the two modes of conception of and engagement with the transcendent proposed by Dennis Hirota, "teleological" and "interpersonal."[23]

In the pre-*shinjin* stage, Shinran found himself in the literal symbolic understanding of the narrative. The narrative is understood literally as referring to actual events. The substantialist Pure Land lies in the distant western direction, where Amida presides. Thus, Shinran finds himself relating to Amida and Pure Land in a dualistic manner. He is *here* and Amida and Pure Land are *out there.*

However, in the post-*shinjin* stage, Shinran found himself no longer relying only on the narrative, for he now rested in the true reality that has emerged in the experience of *shinjin.* The dualistic outlook has given way to the nondual. He came to realize the relative nature of linear historical time, which has been superseded by the absolute nature of synchronic time experienced in the moment of *shinjin.* And in this mode, he comes to regard Amida and Pure Land in a figurative manner, which is why he was able to speak of Amida in more deliteralized expressions as "Buddha of Infinite Light" and Pure Land as the "Realm of Immeasurable Light."

However, this does not mean that the narrative of Amida and Pure Land *disappeared;* it took on new meaning for him. I believe that in his post-*shinjin* stage, he maintained *both modes* of understanding, though his nondual, figurative understanding probably became more fundamental than the dualistic, literal understanding. But the latter continued to function in his mind, especially since the common people with whom he worked were steeped in the worldview that was more consistent with the literal understanding of the narrative.

Plus, even in a post-*shinjin* mode for such a spiritually gifted person as Shinran, it is my belief that he probably shifted from one mode to the other in the course of a day or even an hour. When "we are in control" we find ourselves better able to be more conceptual and theoretical within our figurative outlook, but in moments of mental weakness we tend to seek the more personal or literal expressions. That is in the character of ordinary, foolish beings (*bonbu*). And Shinran, by his own admission, was a *bonbu.*

In concluding this segment, I want to reiterate the point that Shinran maintained a literal symbolic understanding (especially in his pre-*shinjin* mode) to a greater degree than is generally acknowledged by contemporary writers. This poses a dilemma for contemporary Shin Buddhists, who live in a world very different from Shinran's.

Our Inevitable Departure from Shinran

As argued already, our knowledge of history and worldview have changed drastically even in just the past century and a half, making it difficult for most of us to understand the narrative as referring to a historical event or to accept it as literal symbolism. This constitutes a dilemma for Shin Buddhists today, for on this point we find ourselves deviating from Shinran, who as founder should be our primary reference point. We are thus called to clarify the role that Shinran plays in our understanding of Shin teachings.

Speaking personally, the centrality of Shinran is clear as the primary reference point for me, but there are different ways in which I can regard him. One way is to regard Shinran's views as absolute "gospel." From this perspective, there would be no leeway for reinterpretation.

Another way is to regard Shinran as one among many luminaries in the wider Pure Land path, albeit the most important one for Shin adherents. In other words, he becomes for me the "eighth patriarch" in the Pure Land lineage that ultimately goes back to Śākyamuni. In the former approach, I would, metaphorically speaking, be facing Shinran, who is facing *toward me* as object of my unquestioned reverence. In contrast, in the latter approach I face Shinran, who is facing *the other way.* We are both facing the same direction toward Śākyamuni, although Shinran is much farther ahead than me. I follow Shinran as my exemplar but not as object of worship.

This approach probably would not sit well with those who stress that element of the Shin tradition, which I believe is partly rooted in the "cult of Shinran veneration," from the earliest period of the Shin institution. I, too, revere the Shin tradition, but there can and should be various approaches to tradition. If tradition means, as some undoubtedly would have it, accepting Shinran's views exactly without any room for interpretation, then I cannot with any honesty remain part of that tradition.

Another Dilemma

There have been many contemporary writers on Shin teachings before me who have argued in the same vein and then proposed their interpretation for their audience. And I contend that many among them sought to present Amida and the Pure Land, whether consciously or not, in a figurative symbolic mode. This has been made possible by the efforts of contemporary scholars such as Paul Tillich and Joseph Campbell, who helped many people today appreciate the nature of ancient mythic narratives. Many now understand the mythic narratives as not true "factually" but true in conveying a deeper meaning about reality and human existence.

However, herein lies another dilemma. In the Shin Buddhist context, the figurative symbolic understanding of the narrative is *not* of the same order as that of Shinran in his post-*shinjin* stage. On account of his spiritual transformation, Shinran came to regard Amida and Pure Land in a *nondualistic* manner. On the other hand, for contemporaries in the pre-*shinjin* stage, their figurative symbolic understanding is still *dualistic* in nature, where they regard the narrative primarily in a *conceptual* mode. Hence, we have two kinds of figurative symbolic understanding, *nondualistic* (Shinran in his post-*shinjin* mode) and *dualistic* (contemporary seekers in their pre-*shinjin* mode).

With this in mind, I would now like to summarize some of the representative interpretations as resources in formulating a contemporary understanding.

Interpretations by Contemporary Writers

In order to gain a better handle on the wide range of interpretation, I have chosen to categorize them into nine different types. Typologies have their limitations, but I believe they help us gain a bird's-eye view of the range of available interpretations.

Rationalist: Nonomura Naotarō

From a rationalist perspective informed by the humanist movement of the 1920s, this controversial Ryūkoku University professor (later to be relieved from the faculty) rejected the idea of birth in an otherworldly and mythological Pure Land as an anachronism and a deviation from the true intent of Buddhism. In his view, the bejeweled, paradise-like Pure Land was an unfortunate Indian accretion, which in Japan was perpetuated in order to serve the needs of a feudalistic society.

He, however, applauds Shinran's this-worldly orientation for its spirit of humanism in its capacity for spiritual transformation—*shinjin*—in this very life. This view rejects the substantialist, other-power dimension, while extolling human capability.[24]

In my view, his effort to "modernize" is commendable, but he went too far when he eliminated elements such as other-power and the Pure Land, which appealed to religious sentiment and provided the distinctive quality of Pure Land Buddhism.

Mental: D. T. Suzuki

D. T. Suzuki, perhaps the most effective transmitter of Zen Buddhism in the West during the twentieth century, spoke of the Pure Land in the following manner:

> The Pure Land is not many millions and millions of miles away to the west. According to my explanation, the Pure Land is right here, even in this very hall (New York Buddhist Academy in the spring of 1958). Amida is not presiding over a Pure Land beyond our reach. His Pure Land is this dirty earth itself.[25]

This kind of understanding about the Pure Land is often maintained within the Zen tradition, along with what can be referred to as the "Pure Land as nothing but the pure mind" perspective. A Chan protagonist from eighth-century China expressed this latter understanding:

> There is a group of monks and nuns and laymen and laywomen who truly believe that the Pure Land really exists. [However,] the Pure Land is none other than the time when the mind is pure. Where does the Western Pure Land exist separate [from the mind]?[26]

While this kind of portrayal appeals to the modern mind, particularly in the West, Shin orthodox tradition has consistently rejected this view, labeling it as "mind-only Pure Land." In doing so, the tradition has pointed to Shinran's writing, which refuted this type of understanding primarily in order to discourage any vestige of religious self-righteousness that can incorrectly inflate the ego. Shinran says:

> However, priests and laymen of the Declining Age and masters of these days, sunken in the idea "that one's true nature is Buddha" and "that the Buddha's Pure Land exists in one's mind," degrade [belief in] the True Enlightenment in the Pure Land.[27]

Comparative: John Cobb, Jr. and Masao Abe

The two leading scholars in the Buddhist-Christian interreligious dialogue have shown a keen interest in Shin doctrine. Both writers identify the role of Amida Buddha in Shin doctrine with that of Jesus in Christianity. Cobb remarks:

> The feature of the totality to which Pure Land Buddhists refer when they speak of Amida is the same as that to which Christians refer when we speak of Christ.[28]

Masao Abe also sees Amida and Christ on a similar level, as he writes:

> Amida is the mediator between Dharma and human self as the fulfillment of vow in the trans-historical realm. Amida is personal with invisible form and color. . . . Christ is the mediator between God and the human self as the incarnation of the Son of God in history. Godhead is impersonal without any form and will.[29]

In my view, the juxtaposition of Jesus and Amida is problematic, since Amida is not historical in the modern sense. Śākyamuni would be the more appropriate equal to Jesus than Amida, since Śākyamuni and Jesus are both clearly historical figures. This exemplifies the inherent limitations of the comparative approach, for one is often left wanting when a doctrinal element from one tradition is applied to explicate an element in another tradition.

Mahayana Philosophy: Ishida Mitsuyuki, Ueda Yoshifumi and Dennis Hirota, Hoshino Genpō, Alfred Bloom, Taitetsu Unno, John Ishihara Yokota, David Eckel, and Others[30]

The authors grouped together here constitute only a small percentage of a large number of writers who have attempted to place Shin teaching within broader Mahayana doctrine, for example, the bodhisattva spirit exemplified in Dharmākara's career, the triple-body (*trikāya*) concept that provides an undergirding for the nature of Amida, and the two-truths theory. In so doing, they have helped to dispel the unwarranted but common perception of Pure Land Buddhism as simply a folk religion or even a Buddhist aberration. Their approach is indispensable for contemporary Shin thinkers who are concerned about the broader framework from which to interpret and present the Shin teachings, particularly of Amida and Pure Land. We will discuss two of these authors as examples of this approach.

The most recent within this group of writings is the one by David Eckel, who, as a well-recognized scholar of Indian Mahayana tradition, has provided an immensely valuable set of materials for Shin thinkers to utilize for rethinking their tradition. Another important resource, containing a wealth of valuable views, was compiled by Alfred Bloom in a collection of essays by notable modern and contemporary writers.[31] Many of the essays address the very issues that I have raised in this paper. My regret is that I was not able to incorporate them in this paper as fully as I would have wished, but it will be certain to be part of my project in the immediate future.

Affirmation of Form: Roger Corless

Roger Corless recognizes two forms of experiencing dharma: a mysticism of darkness and a mysticism of light. The former is adopted by the Mādhyamika school, where the realized true reality (*śūnyatā*) is not expressed in words. Corless, in his creative way, calls this mode "apohic" from the Sanskrit word *apoha*, meaning "taking away." The Mādhyamika proponents "take away" words and philosophical positions, for they are deemed ultimately inconsistent with and inadequate for expressing the true reality.

The mysticism of light, on the other hand, is represented by the Yogācāra and Pure Land schools and found expressed in the *Avataṃsaka-sūtra* and the Pure Land sutras. Corless refers to this mode of expression as "alamkaric," from the Sanskrit word *alaṃkāra,* meaning "ornament." Here, *śūnyatā* is described "as full, brilliant, and sparkling." Concerning the Pure Land tradition, Corless cites Tanluan, who helped to affirm the ornaments or the arrays of Pure Land as an alamkaric expression. Thus, Corless argues effectively on behalf of the often-maligned expressions of form and posits form (alamkaric, or "with form") on an equal footing with that of the formless (apohic, or "without words").[32]

Religious Meaning: Ōhara Shōjitsu

Ōhara recognizes three modes of existence: physical existence (*butsuriteki jitsuzai*), conceptual existence (*kannenteki jitsuzai*), and religious existence (*shūkyoteki jitsuzai*). Pure Land exists in the third mode of existence, but not in the first two. The sutra passages from the *Larger* and *Smaller Sutras* describe, in Ōhara's view, the Pure Land's transcendence of the physical realm as indicated by the fact that it "surpasses" or "distances this [world]" by millions of buddha lands to the west. The Pure Land cannot be subject to the limitations and impermanence of conditioned existence.

Secondly, what he calls "conceptual existence" lacks clarity, in my view, but appears to mean the symbol for an ideal human world that Ōhara rejects on account of what he sees as extreme subjectivism and privatization at the expense of losing the universal and objective quality of Pure Land.

Ōhara's advocacy of the Pure Land as a religious meaning rests on the fundamental Buddhist position of viewing the world as the result of one's karma or mind. This being the case, the anguish and impermanence experienced by humans in this *sahā* realm is due to their karmic evil. However, the very realization of the relative, anguish-laden nature of the *sahā* realm constitutes a religious awakening, which paves the way for a greater appreciation of the opposite qualities of permanence and happiness established as the result of the purified karmic activities of Amida.[33]

This interpretation perhaps represents the most common type of explanation by Shinshū teachers in Japan. Its strength lies in avoiding the pitfalls of the prior two "extremist" positions, and in showing that the Pure Land and Amida are of a reality that differs, in its nature, from the scientific and idealistic/ethical modes of existence. However, it falls short in presenting a palatable and sensible explanation for ordinary seekers with little or no Buddhist or, more specifically, Shinshū background. It offers little in terms of motivating them to inquire further into the teachings. This type of interpretation requires a whole set of "aftercare service" for motivating and nurturing seekers in their religious aspirations.

Poetic Language: Ōmine Akira

Here, the Dharmākara-Amida narrative is not taken as historical fact but as a mythopoetic expression of true reality that defies grasping by everyday or conceptual language. The mythopoetic language opens up a channel through which a seeker is allowed to come in touch with the reality that otherwise would elude him. According to Ōmine, this mythopoetic language differs from mysticism:

> All forms of mysticism are characterized by the continual negation of linguistic expression with regard to reality. . . . But such literature is the linguistic expression of an experience which has already been attained; the experience itself is not attained by means of words. . . . In contrast myth and poetry (the mythopoetic) plumb the interior depths of language itself, and is created through the purification of the horizon of language. . . . Mysticism, which is based on the extrication of words, is an experience in letting go. Contrary to this, myth grasps the bottom of the depth by following words as they are born from that place where there are no words.[34]

Then later, at the level of internalizing the mythopoetic language, one experiences, in its quintessential form, a profoundly deepened appreciation of the name *"Namu Amida Butsu."* As attested by Shinran, the name is none other than Amida itself. Ōmine speaks of this name as the pure language that arose from ultimate reality:

> The Name, Namu Amida Butsu, as conceived by Shinran, can be thought of as the horizon of pure language. Pure language is that which it expresses. In this standpoint everything exists within the words and nothing exists without. There is no Buddha apart from the Name, Namu Amida Butsu. The formless remains itself in the very midst of form while taking on form.[35]

The core of Shinran's Pure Land thought lies in the dharma body as compassionate means, in other words, in the inconceivability of the name. This is the standpoint that does not see the mystery over yonder, beyond words, but is that which intuitively feels the mystery of the words that manifest themselves in the present, in the here and now. The inconceivable lies not over there but right here; this is truly the inconceivable nature of words. They are not signs or concepts, but light that embraces us.

Outer World: Yuichi Kajiyama and Oka Ryōji

In response to a question at a 1992 symposium entitled "The Cosmology of Pure Land" sponsored by the Hongwanji Doctrinal Research Institute, Yuichi Kajiyama expressed a view based on science that was rather unexpected coming from a noted Buddhist scholar of the Indian philosophical tradition. He was asked what would be the contemporary equivalent of *shihō-rissō* (giving direction and establishing form), a concept attributed to Shandao (613–681), which served as an appropriate teaching in keeping with the needs of the worldview of that period. Kajiyama answered:

> Simply put, it (an appropriate teaching for the contemporary world) would be space (*shinkū*) [as] talked about in physics. We ordinarily think of space as void or being totally empty, but it certainly is not like that. In fact space is filled with moving particles in their motion mode, and they are all wavering. And that wavering was the source that produced the universe.
>
> The Buddhist *śūnyatā* also does not mean void. It's my view that the nonsubstantiality of *śūnyatā* becomes a form of energy that produced Amida Buddha as well as the Pure Land. This means that there are the wavering particles within emptiness.
>
> This *śūnyatā* is the wisdom of [*pāramitā*]. It is also the wisdom of Amida Buddha and wisdom of dharma-body. That wisdom of dharma-body is not simply an empty space. There are the wavering particles, which constitute Amida's compassion. Thus, I believe that *śūnyatā* is always accompanied by compassion, and that is the very energy that makes up the world as well as the Buddhist teachings.[36]

Kajiyama saw space as the most appropriate framework through which contemporary people could understand the Buddhist teachings. By drawing on current findings in physics, he found a parallel between space and the Buddhist teaching of *śūnyatā,* which produced the universe, and Amida and the Pure Land, respectively. Kajiyama does not go so far as to say that *śūnyatā* produced the physical universe (his clarification of the relationship between space and *śūnyatā* would have been even more provocative) but does feel that compassion produced by *śūnyatā* makes the *world and the Buddhist teachings possible.*

Oka Ryōji, a Shin Buddhist scholar and priest, similarly turns to the outer world. In his case, he finds that the outer world serves as an active participant in his Shin spirituality. Oka explains that when one listens and awakens to the deeper meaning of the sacred story and Amida's vow, one feels a profound sense of gratitude for the reasons he explains:

> The entire universe has been working solely on my behalf. . . . In order to liberate me, the entire universe has been working to become [*Namu Amida Butsu*] itself. And as I hear this truth, I am made to realize the truth that I am supported and embraced within the great compassion itself of [*Namu Amida Butsu*].[37]

So for Oka, the workings of the entire universe become *Namu Amida Butsu.* He does not elaborate much further on what he means by "the entire universe," but I understand it to be referring to the totality of the nurturing causes and conditions that ultimately involves the entire universe. While I realize that Oka is not necessarily thinking about the "universe" in the sense of physics, I find it significant that a noted Shin scholar and former professor at Ryūkoku University, a Shin-based institution affiliated with the Nishi Honganji branch, would identify Amida with a nontraditional referent such as "the totality of universe" in such an unambiguous manner.

Unseen Life Force: Hase Shōtō

This identification of Amida with the universe is also found in the writings of Hase Shōtō, formerly a professor at Kyoto University and now teaching at Ōtani University, a Shin-based institution associated with the Higashi Honganji branch.

Hase Shōtō delves deeper into this issue as he makes a distinction between "creative nature" (*nōsanteki shizen*) and "created nature" (*shosanteki shizen*), a distinction derived from classical Western thought. He explains creative nature as follows:

> Creative nature is said to be [God's] nature. This creative nature takes place at a much deeper level than the creation of creatures and the natural world. Creative nature refers to the "life force" (*inochi*) of the Buddha of Immeasurable Life. Amida Buddha is called "Immeasurable Life" or "Amitāyus," and refers to life force that transcends the life force of ordinary life or of biological life. In other words, it is none other than the boundless life force that dwells as the foundation of ordinary life.[38]

Hase also clarifies the role of the "sacred story" of Bodhisattva Dharmākara and Amida in relationship to his understanding. For Hase, the sacred story is treated as "image" through which a seeker awakens to the boundless life force that transcends the self but also courses deep within oneself. Hase stresses the importance of relating to the story-image on an "emotive-intentional" (*jō'i*) level, not on a rational (*risei*) level. Amida is not something that exists objectively somewhere out there, but must be realized as the boundless life force found deep within. And this life force is none other than "creative nature," as different from "created nature" that can be perceived and felt.

And this life force is realized as "inner manifestation" (*eigen*) as opposed to "outer manifestation" (*ōgen*). Inner manifestation transcends history, while outer manifestation is within history, which is why Hase sees the former as Amida and the latter as Gautama Buddha. His distinction has basis in Shinran's poem:

> Tathāgata [Śākyamuni] appeared ("outer manifestation") in Kapilavastu Castle, while Tathāgata Amida appeared ("inner manifestation") in the Realm of Ease and Nurturance (i.e., the Pure Land).[39]

A Practical Engagement with the Narrative as Figurative Symbol

As seen above, the circumstances of contemporary society call for non-traditional approaches to understanding and engaging the teachings of Amida and Pure Land. This became more urgent with the fundamental discrepancy between Shinran's literal symbolic orientation and the figurative symbolic perspective of most contemporary people. I would now like to propose some practical guidelines for engaging the teachings.

As indicated by the "affirmation of form" approach of Corless, we should not reject outright the narrative, for it helps us to be moved spiritually. To reject it and even eliminate it, as Nonomura did in his rationalistic approach, would effectively make it no longer a Shin teaching. Nonomura rejected it, unnecessarily in my view, because he understood the narrative in the substantialist manner. It would also be problematic to regard the Pure Land (and Amida) as "this dirty world" or the "purified mind" as advocated by Suzuki, for that would deviate too far from the core Shin position.

Instead, in taking the cues from Ōhara's "religious existence" and Ōmine's "poetic language" approaches, we should understand the narrative to be pointing to the reality of a different order from the ordinary. The narrative does not call for us to reject the ordinary but calls for us to approach and see the ordinary differently. The narrative should serve to provide us with the "image" for cultivating our spiritual life, as encouraged by Hase.

In his "unseen life force" proposal, Hase encourages us to relate to the narrative on an "emotive-intentional" level, not on a rational level, thus enabling us to perceive and feel this unseen life force that dwells as the foundation of ordinary life. So, this life force needs to be realized as "inner manifestation." Hence, while the narrative seems to be "out there," it needs to be approached primarily to transform the emotive-intentional aspect of our inner selves. In other words, the concern is with our spiritual dimension.

This spiritual dimension is often best expressed and nurtured by narratives or myth. As Joseph Campbell so aptly explained, myth does not mean false or untrue, but helps explain a deeper meaning that cannot effectively be explained by rational or other modes of expression.

This manner of approaching the narratives or myths has been supported by the writings in the "Mahayana philosophy" approach (Ueda, et al.) mentioned above. Many of them refer to the Mahayana concept of the two levels of truths, conventional (*saṃvṛtti-satya*) and ultimate truth (*paramārtha-satya*), which serve as a generalized framework for supporting the figurative symbolic understanding of Amida and the Pure Land. The conventional or the forms are to be cherished, and the seekers are, thus, encouraged to find the spiritual meaning symbolized by the particulars of the forms in the narrative.

For example, from my personal perspective, Bodhisattva Dharmākara's forty-eight vows symbolize for me the *fundamental compassionate nature* of my existence. Despite all the unfortunate events in this world from wars, natural disasters, and interpersonal conflicts, compassion and love suffuse our existence. There courses a caring force that lies at the basis of our very existence, which I see symbolized in Bodhisattva Dharmākara's subsequent self-cultivation for innumerable *kalpa*s in order to make our enlightenment and existence possible. Findings in physics have revealed that enormous amounts of energy are consumed to sustain life and its activities, which becomes apparent as we note how much water, energy, food, and plastic wrappings we consume to sustain our daily lives. This is the basis for the "outer world" approach we saw above by Kajiyama and Oka, who call for us to awaken to the sense of indebtedness we should have toward the supportive world and universe.

The narrative also tells us that Bodhisattva Dharmākara became Amida Buddha and since then has resided in the Pure Land billions of buddha lands to the west. What is the meaning that we are to derive from this? The fact that Bodhisattva Dharmākara has attained buddhahood as Amida symbolizes the potential liberation of all living beings as noted in his vows, in which his becoming a buddha was contingent on all beings having the conditions in place for their birth in the Pure Land. Thus, since he *has become* Amida, all beings will be assured of birth if they fulfill the conditions as stipulated in the vows. This, in my view, offers a reason for us to face life now and in the future with a greater sense of optimism and gratitude, since the basic conditions for our spiritual emancipation have already been met.

As a third example, the narrative states that those who vow to help others will upon birth in the Pure Land return to this *sahā* realm and to other worlds to lead others to attain buddhahood. This returning, referred to doctrinally as "the phase of returning" (*gensō*), need not be taken literally but can be seen to symbolize the seeker's participating in the workings of a deeper spiritual reality. When a person realizes *shinjin* in this life, one "joins" in the dynamic compassionate workings called "Amida." In that capacity, a person participates in the life force, which can be "accessed" by those who have yet to realize *shinjin* by reciting the name, *"Namu Amida Butsu."* And as they recite and attain *shinjin* in their lives, they also join this immeasurable light and life called "Amida" in an ongoing, cyclic working to lead as many beings to buddhahood as possible.

Because this working of Amida ultimately transcends the dichotomy of this life and life after death, as well as that of post-*shinjin* and pre-*shinjin,* everyone who seeks earnestly by uttering the name is already embraced by this life force. The specific element in the narrative helps to open us up to an existence that is magnanimous, inviting, and assuring.

Importance of Concerted Effort with the Name and the Light

As stated above, in this process of engaging the narrative, the name is the principal tangible representation of Amida (and indirectly of the Pure Land). In this life, the name *"Namu Amida Butsu"* is the manifestation of Amida. For that reason as well, to effectively engage the narrative we must cultivate the practice of reciting the name (nenbutsu) in our daily life. Shinran talks about the importance of the name:

> Truly we know that without the virtuous name, our compassionate father, we would lack the direct cause of birth. Without the light, our compassionate mother, we would stand apart from the indirect cause of birth.[40]

Here, I cannot emphasize enough the importance of making the effort, particularly in voicing and saying, *"Namu Amida Butsu."* I am not alone among the growing number of people who feel that Shin Buddhists have become too cerebral and rationalistic with an overemphasis on *shinjin.* While *shinjin* certainly deserves our attention, it has come at the expense of effort, which should involve our personal engagement with the name *"Namu Amida Butsu."* Its importance is the reason for Shinran regarding the name as "father" in the passage given above.

In that passage, Shinran also makes mention of the importance of light. Hence, I wish to focus on light as a process of spiritual maturation, since light has played a central role in the soteriological experiences of Pure Land Buddhists, and Shinran was no exception.

In our ordinary daily context, light can be tangibly understood as insight or understanding that was planted in us and nurtured by our families, and by countless teachers, friends, and even strangers. This insight enabled me, for example, to feel uplifted by the exquisite beauty of fluttering maple leaves in the autumn breeze or to appreciate the reassuring aroma of my favorite French roast coffee.

It is also this insight that allows me to acknowledge the shortcomings in my character and conduct without a great deal of resistance (at least, with less resistance than if I had I not received this endowed insight) and turmoil on my part. And more importantly, the insight helps me realize that the shortcomings of which I am aware are actually only the tip of the iceberg.

Others who do not experience this "light of nurturance" (*chōjuku no kōmyō*) may not be able to feel the same level of appreciation and acceptance even when experiencing the same tree, coffee, or personal shortcomings. A famous Buddhist parable of "one water, four perceptions" demonstrates that the same water is seen as jewels by heavenly beings, as drinking water by humans, as an abode by fish, and as mucus or phlegm by hungry ghosts. Hence, the quality of insight or understanding determines one's reality.

I believe the light as endowed wisdom as described above will help to serve as the means *within our ordinary daily lives* by which Shin seekers can come to feel more closely connected to Amida in its figurative symbolic sense. This departs from the more substantialist portrayal of Amida as a divine being residing in a distant buddha land. It also fosters more concrete ways of understanding the meaning of "wisdom and compassion," the most common epithet by which Amida is expressed.

In reality, wisdom and compassion are not attributes of Amida but are Amida itself, just as the name *"Namu Amida Butsu,"* as experienced in a profoundly spiritual manner, is none other than Amida. In its purest experience, a person is embraced completely by this light and name and not forsaken (*sesshu fusha*).

Some Concluding Remarks

We have covered quite a great deal of territory in responding to Gordon Kaufman's questions, which are the same questions that many contemporary Shin Buddhists themselves have been asking. If I were to summarize my arguments made in this paper, they are as follows.

First, the two dharma bodies concept first advocated by Tanluan (and affirmed by Shinran) actually represents two distinct developments within Mahayana, with roots in earlier Indian Buddhism. This constitutes more than a process of "demythologizing" by Tanluan, but rather a "synthesis of two discrete traditions," *a point that previously has not been, at best, strongly emphasized.*

Second, Shinran held a much more literal understanding of Amida and Pure Land than heretofore thought, particularly in the so-called pre-*shinjin* mode. I refer to his position as that of "literal symbolism," and as different from that of "figurative symbolism," which he embraced in the post-*shinjin* mode. And it is this latter mode to which many contemporary Shin Buddhists subscribe.

Third, a discrepancy—that between Shinran's literal symbolic understanding and the contemporary figurative symbolic understanding—forces us to deviate from Shinran on this point, encouraging us to reevaluate our relationship to the "founder."

Fourth, some of the representative kinds of approaches proposed by contemporary scholars on Amida and Pure Land were summarized, most of which, in my view, were carried out from the figurative symbolic perspective.

Fifth, based on these approaches, I proposed some practical approaches to understanding and engaging the teachings concerning Amida and Pure Land.

Having made these points, my hope is that I have addressed at least some of the questions posed by Kaufman. However, the nature of spiritual reality forces us to acknowledge that ultimately his questions cannot be answered conceptually but must be experienced personally, which prompted me to close this paper with sections devoted to effort and practical engagement.

Notes

1 "Where is the Pure Land? Controversy in Chinese Pure Land Buddhism on the Nature of Pure Land," *Pacific World*, n.s., 3 (Fall 1987): pp. 36–87 (reprinted in *Shin Buddhism: Historical, Textual, and Interpretive Studies*, ed. Richard K. Payne [Berkeley, CA: Institute of Buddhist Studies and Numata Center for Buddhist Translation and Research, 2007], pp. 99–113); "Symbolism of Amida and Pure Land in the American Context," *The Pure Land*, n.s., 8 & 9 (December 1992): pp. 64–88.

2 Gordon Kaufman, "Religious Diversity and Religious Truth," in *Shinran and the Contemporary World: Internationalization and the Encounter with World Religions* (Kyoto: Ryūkoku University, 1989).

3 Tanaka, "Symbolism of Amida and Pure Land in the American Context," pp. 68–72. An informal survey was designed to ascertain the nature of some beliefs and values held by selected members of the Buddhist Churches of America concerning Amida and the Pure Land. The respondents filled out the questionnaire in June 1990. The questionnaires were sent to twenty lay members associated with the Institute of Buddhist Studies (Berkeley, California) and to twenty randomly selected ministers who were asked to find any four to five lay members from their temples. A total of thirty-eight responded (eighteen females, eighteen males, two unknown gender), including thirteen "converts" (those who were not raised a Buddhist). Their ages were as follows:

Age (in years)	No. of Respondents
0–19	7
20–29	4
30–39	6
40–49	6
50–59	10
60–69	9
70+	1

4 Dennis Hirota, et al., trans., *The Collected Works of Shinran* (hereafter CWS), vol. 1 (Jōdo Shinshū Hongwanji-ha, 1997), pp. 460–462. Emphases added.

5 See Kenneth K. Tanaka, *The Dawn of Chinese Pure Land Buddhist Doctrine: Ching-ying Hui-yüan's Commentary on the Visualization Sutra.* (Albany, NY: State University of New York Press, 1990), pp. 3–9.

6 T. 1819: 40.830a.

7 T. 1819: 40.839b.

8 T. 1819: 40.841b.

9 CWS I, p. 428.

10 I realize that "symbol" is a complex issue that deserves much fuller discussion, but due to space limitations of this essay I wish to proceed to the next section, where my usage of the term "symbol" will be made clearer, particularly in relation to Shinran's understanding.

[11] Paul Tillich, "The Religious Symbol," in *Symbolism in Religion and Literature*, ed. Rollo May (New York: George Braziller, 1960), pp. 76–77.

[12] Ibid., p. 76.

[13] Ibid., p. 75.

[14] Mircea Eliade, ed., *The Enclyclopedia of Religion* (New York: Macmillan, 1987), p. 206.

[15] T. 47: 11c27.

[16] CWS I, p. 477.

[17] Tillich, "The Religious Symbol," p. 75.

[18] John S. Yokota, "Understanding Amida Buddha and the Pure Land: A Process Approach," in *Toward a Contemporary Understanding of Pure Land Buddhism*, ed. Dennis Hirota (Albany, NY: State University of New York Press, 2000), p. 82.

[19] CWS I, p. 662.

[20] CWS I, p. 539.

[21] Yokota, "Understanding Amida Buddha and the Pure Land," pp. 82–83. Shinran's passage is found in CWS I, pp. 110–111.

[22] Furusawa Katsuhiro, "Kedo-kan no kenkyū" (A Study on the "Chapter on Transformed Land"), *Shūgakuin ronshū* 65 (March, 1996): p. 55. This journal is published by one of the institutes for traditional learning in Kyoto.

[23] Dennis Hirota, "Images of Reality," in *Toward a Contemporary Understanding of Pure Land Buddhism*, pp. 42–53. Hirota delves into greater detail regarding the features of these stages or modes, which cannot be discussed here due to space limitations; it is highly recommended for readers interested in this area.

[24] Nonomura Naotarō, *Jōdokyo hihan* (*Critique of Pure Land Buddhism*) (Kyoto: Chugai Shuppansha, 1923), referenced throughout the book.

[25] D. T. Suzuki, "Shin Buddhism: Part I," *Eastern Buddhist*, n.s., 17, no. 1 (Spring 1985): p. 2.

[26] T. 85: 1236–1242.

[27] Ryūkoku University, trans., *Kyō gyō shin shō: Teaching, Practice, Faith, and Enlightenment* (Kyoto: Ryūkoku University Translation Center, 1966), p. 84.

[28] John Cobb, *Beyond Dialogue: Toward a Mutual Transformation of Christianity and Buddhism* (Philadelphia, PA: Fortress Press, 1982), p. 128.

[29] Abe Masao, "The State of Buddhist-Christian Dialogue," lecture given at the Third International Buddhist-Christian Conference (Berkeley, CA: August 10–15, 1987).

[30] Ishida Mitsuyuki, *Shinran kyōgaku no kisoteki kenkyū* (*A Fundamental Study of Shinran's Thought*) (Kyoto: Nagata Bunshōdō, 1970); John Ishihara (Yokota), "Shakyamuni Within the Shin Tradition," *Pacific World*, n.s., 2 (Fall 1986): pp. 31–35; Ueda Yoshifumi and Dennis Hirota, eds., *Shinran: An Introduction to His Thought* (Kyoto: Hongwanji International Center, 1989); Hoshino Genpō, *Jōdo* (*Pure Land*) (Kyoto: Hōzōkan, 1957); Taitetsu Unno, *River of Fire, River of Water: An Introduction to the Pure Land Tradition of Shin Buddhism* (New York:

Doubleday, 1998); Alfred Bloom, *The Promise of Boundless Compassion* (Honolulu: Buddhist Study Center Press, 2002); David Eckel, "Defining a Usable Past: Indian Sources for Shin Buddhist Theology," *Pacific World*, 3rd series, 5 (2003): pp. 55–84.

31 Alfred Bloom, ed., *Living in Amida's Universal Vow: Essays in Shin Buddhism* (Bloomington, IN: World Wisdom, 2004).

32 Roger Corless, "The Brilliance of Emptiness: T'an-luan as a Mystic of Light," *Pacific World*, n.s., 5 (1989): pp. 13–16 (reprinted under the title "The Brilliance of Emptiness: Tanluan as a Mystic of Light," in *Shin Buddhism: Historical, Textual, and Interpretive Studies*, ed. Payne, pp. 275–284).

33 Ōhara Shōjitsu, *Shinshu kyōgaku no dentō to koshō* (*Tradition and Realization of Shinshū Doctrinal Studies*), Shinshū-kyōgaku-shi kenkyū 5 (Kyoto: Nagata Bunshōdō, 1965), pp. 202–206.

34 Ōmine Akira, "Language and Transcendence," *The Pure Land*, n.s., 3 (December 1986): pp. 144–147.

35 Ibid., pp. 150–151.

36 Kajiyama Yuichi, *Jōdo no kosumoroji* (Kyoto: Jōdo-Shinshū Kyōgaku Kenkyūjo, 1993), p. 67.

37 Oka Ryōji, "Shinran no jūnen shisō," *Shinshūgaku* 107 (January 2003): p. 71.

38 Hase Shōtō, "Jōi no sekai to shiteno shūkyō—eigen suru hōzōbosatsu," *Shinshūgaku* 107 (January 2003): p. 104.

39 CWS I, p. 349. This passage actually appears over two poems (nos. 87 and 88) in *Hymns to Amida Based on Various Sutras.*

40 CWS I, p. 54.

Contributors

Harvey B. Aronson is founding Co-Director of Dawn Mountain Tibetan Temple, Community Center, and Research Institute, and a psychotherapist in private practice in Houston, Texas.

Gordon Bermant is a Lecturer in the Department of Psychology, University of Pennsylvania, and a past president of the Buddhist Churches of America.

Alfred Bloom is Professor Emeritus of the University of Hawai'i, and a former dean of the Institute of Buddhist Studies, Berkeley, California.

Ruben L. F. Habito is founder of the Maria Kannon Zen Center in Dallas, Texas, and Professor of World Religions and Spirituality at the Perkins School of Theology, Southern Methodist University.

Arthur Holder, John Dillenberger Professor of Christian Spirituality, is Dean and Vice President for Academic Affairs at the Graduate Theological Union, Berkeley, California.

Charles B. Jones is an Associate Professor in the School of Theology and Religious Studies, The Catholic University of America, Washington, D.C.

Charles D. Orzech is a Professor in the Department of Religious Studies, University of North Carolina, Greensboro.

Richard K. Payne, Yehan Numata Professor of Buddhist Studies, is Dean of the Institute of Buddhist Studies, Berkeley, California.

Charles S. Prebish is the Charles Redd Professor of Religious Studies, Religious Studies Program, Utah State University.

James H. Sanford is Professor (ret.) of Religious Studies, University of North Carolina, Chapel Hill.

Kenneth K. Tanaka is Professor at Musashino University, Tokyo, and a former professor at the Institute of Buddhist Studies, Berkeley, California.

Bibliography

Abe, Masao. "The State of Buddhist-Christian Dialogue," lecture given at the Third International Buddhist-Christian Conference, Berkeley, CA: August 10–15, 1987.

Abé, Ryūichi. *The Weaving of Mantra: Kūkai and the Construction of Esoteric Buddhist Discourse.* New York: Columbia University Press, 1999.

American Heritage Dictionary. Boston: American Heritage Publishing Co., Inc., 1969.

Amstutz, Galen. *Interpreting Amida: History and Orientalism in the Study of Pure Land Buddhism.* Albany, NY: State University of New York Press, 1997.

Aponte, Harry J. "Clinical Applications of Spirituality: Questions and Answers," Texas Association for Marriage and Family Therapists 2000 Annual Conference. Houston, TX: Sounds on Tape, 2000.

Araki, Kengo. *Myōmatsu shukyō shisō kenkyū (Studies in Religious Thought at the End of the Ming*). Tokyo: Sōbunsha, 1979.

Aronson, Harvey B. *Buddhist Practice on Western Ground.* Boston: Shambhala, 2004.

Baker, Sharon. "The Three Minds and Faith, Hope and Love in Pure Land Buddhism," *Buddhist-Christian Studies* 25 (2005): pp. 49–65.

Benn, Charles David. "Taoism as Ideology in the Reign of the Emperor Hsüan-tsung (712–755)." Ph.D. dissertation. University of Michigan, 1977.

Berlin, Isaiah. "The Hedgehog and the Fox: An Essay on Tolstoy's View of History," in *The Proper Study of Mankind: An Anthology of Essays,* ed. Henry Hardy and Roger Hausheer. New York: Farrar, Straus and Giroux, 1997.

Bermant, Gordon. "Growing American Jōdo Shinshū: Are There Lessons in the Christian Missionary Model?" in *Sharing the Dharma with Others: Eleven Perspectives on Shin Buddhist Outreach,* ed. Gordon Bermant and Anna Tecson. San Francisco: Membership and Outreach Committee, Buddhist Churches of America, 2005.

Berra, Yogi. *When You Come to a Fork in the Road, Take It.* New York: Hyperion, 2001.

Bloom, Alfred. *Essentials of Shinran.* Bloomington, IN: World Wisdom Press, 2006.

—. Ed. *Living in Amida's Universal Vow: Essays in Shin Buddhism.* Bloomington, IN: World Wisdom, Inc., 2004.

—. *Shinran and the Gospel of Pure Grace.* Tucson, AZ: University of Arizona Press, 1965.

—. *The Promise of Boundless Compassion.* Honolulu: Buddhist Study Center Press, 2002.

Blum, Mark, and Yasutomi Shin'ya, eds. *Rennyo.* New York: Oxford University Press, 2005.

Bodiford, William M. "Dharma Transmission in Sōtō Zen: Manzan Dōhaku's Reform Movement," *Monumenta Nipponica* 46, no. 4 (Winter 1991).

Brook, Timothy. *The Confusions of Pleasure: Commerce and Culture in Ming China.* Berkeley, CA: University of California Press, 1998.

Burnham, Frederic B., ed. *Postmodern Theology: Christian Faith in a Pluralist World.* New York: Harper and Row, 1989.

Buswell, Robert, ed.-in-chief. *The Encyclopedia of Buddhism,* 2 vols. New York: Macmillan Reference USA, 2004.

—. *The Zen Monastic Experience.* Princeton, NJ: Princeton University Press, 1992.

Carpenter, J. Estlin, ed. *The Dīgha Nikāya* (1911). London: Luzac & Company, Ltd., 1960, reprint.

Carrithers, Michael B. "'They Will Be Lords Upon the Island': Buddhism in Sri Lanka," in *The World of Buddhism: Buddhist Monks and Nuns in Society and Culture,* ed. Heinz Bechert and Richard Gombrich. New York: Facts on File, 1984.

Chadwick, David. *Crooked Cucumber: The Life and Zen Teaching of Shunryu Suzuki.* New York: Broadway Books, 1999.

Chappell, David W. "The Formation of the Pure Land Movement in China: Tao-ch'o and Shan-tao," in *The Pure Land Tradition: History and Development,* ed. James Foard, Michael Solomon, and Richard K. Payne. Berkeley, CA: University of California Press, 1996.

Chaves, Jonathan. *Pilgrim of the Clouds: Poems and Essays from Ming China by Yüan Hung-tao and His Brothers.* New York: Weatherhill, 1978.

Chiba, Jōryū. "Orthodoxy and Heterodoxy in Early Modern Shinshū: Kakushi Nenbutsu and Kakure Nenbutsu," in *The Pure Land Tradition: History and Development,* ed. James Foard, Michael Soloman, and Richard K. Payne. Berkeley, CA: University of California Press, 1996.

Chih-ping Chou. *Yüan Hung-tao and the Kung-an School.* Cambridge: Cambridge University Press, 1988.

Chou, I-liang. "Tantrism in China," *Harvard Journal of Asiatic Studies* 8 (1945): pp. 241–332.

Chün-fang Yü. "Ta-hui Tsung-kao and Kung-an Ch'an," *Journal of Chinese Philosophy,* v. 6 (1979).

Cobb, Jr., John B. *Beyond Dialogue: Toward a Mutual Transformation of Christianity and Buddhism.* Philadelphia: Fortress Press, 1982.

Corless, Roger. "Pure Land and Pure Perspective: A Tantric Hermeneutic of Sukhāvatī," *The Pure Land,* n.s., 6 (1989): pp. 205–217.

—. "Self-Power Practice with Other-Power Attitude: An Interpretation of Mind in Shin Buddhism," *The Pure Land,* n.s., 8–9 (December 1992): pp. 166–205.

—. "T'an-Luan: The First Systematizer of Pure Land Buddhism," in *The Pure Land Tradition: History and Development,* ed. James Foard, Michael Solomon, and Richard K. Payne. Berkeley, CA: University of California Press, 1996.

—. "The Brilliance of Emptiness: T'an-luan as a Mystic of Light," *Pacific World* (n.s.) 5 (1989): pp. 13–16. Reprinted under the title "The Brilliance of Emptiness: Tanluan as a Mystic of Light," in *Shin Buddhism: Historical, Textual, and Interpretive Studies,* ed. Richard K. Payne. Berkeley, CA: Institute of Buddhist Studies and Numata Center for Buddhist Translation and Research, 2007.

—. "The Pathless Path for North America," *The Pure Land,* n.s., 13–14 (December 1997): pp. 6–18

—. "The Playfulness of *Tariki,*" *The Pure Land,* n.s., 4 (December 1987): pp. 34–52.

—. *The Vision of Buddhism: The Space Under the Tree.* New York: Paragon House, 1989.

Davidson, Ronald M. *Indian Esoteric Buddhism: A Social History of the Tantric Movement.* New York: Columbia University Press, 2002.

Davis, Winston. *Japanese Religion and Society: Paradigms of Structure and Change.* Albany, NY: State University of New York Press, 1992.

Delumeau, Jean. *Sin and Fear: The Emergence of a Western Guilt Culture 13th–18th Centuries,* trans. Eric Nicholson. New York: St. Martin's Press, 1990.

Dharmapala, Anagarika. "Opening Address," in *The World's Parliament of Religions. An Illustrated and Popular Story of the World's First Parliament of Religions, Held in Chicago in Connection with the Columbian Exposition of 1893,* ed. Rev. John Henry Barrows, 2 vols. Chicago: The Parliament Publishing Company, 1893.

Diagnostic and Statistical Manual of Mental Disorders, 4th ed. Washington, DC: American Psychiatric Association, 1994.

Dobbins, James. *Jodo Shinshu: Shin Buddhism in Medieval Japan* (1989). Honolulu: University of Hawai'i Press, 2002, reprint.

Duquenne, Robert. "Daitoku myōō," in *Hôbôgirin: dictionnaire encyclopédique du Bouddhisme d'après les sources chinoises et japonaises,* vol. VI, pp. 652–70, ed. Paul Demiéville and Jacques May. Tokyo and Paris: Maison franco-japonais and A. Maisonneuve, 1929–1967.

Eckel, David. "Defining a Usable Past: Indian Sources for Shin Buddhist Theology," *Pacific World,* 3rd series, 5 (2003): pp. 55–84.

Eichmann, Jennifer Lynn. "Spiritual Seekers in a Fluid Landscape: A Chinese Buddhist Network in the Wanli Period (1573–1620)." Ph.D. dissertation. Princeton University, 2005.

Eliade, Mircea, ed. *The Enclyclopedia of Religion.* New York: Macmillan, 1987.

Elman, Benjanim A. *A Cultural History of Civil Examinations in Late Imperial China.* Berkeley, CA: University of California Press, 2000.

Falk, Nancy E. Auer. "Pûjâ," in *The Encyclopedia of Religion,* ed. Mircea Eliade. New York: Macmillan, 1987, vol. 12, pp. 83a–85a.

Fan Jialing. *Zibo dashi shengping ji sixiang yanjiu* (*A Study of the Life and Thought of Master Zibo*). *Fojiao lun cong,* no. 28. Taibei: Chung-hwa Institute of Buddhist Studies, 2001.

Feer, M. Leon, ed. *Saṃyutta Nikaya* (1884–1894). London: Luzac & Company, Ltd., 1960, reprint.

Foard, James H. "In Search of a Lost Reformation: A Reconsideration of Kamakura Buddhism," *Japanese Journal of Religious Studies* 7, no. 4 (December 1980): pp. 274–281.

Foulk, T. Griffith. "The Ch'an Tsung in Medieval China: School, Lineage, or What?" *Pacific World,* n.s., 8 (1992): pp. 18–31. Reprinted under the title "The Chan *Zong* in Medieval China: School, Lineage, or What?" in *Shin Buddhism: Historical, Textual, and Interpretive Studies,* ed. Richard K. Payne. Berkeley, CA: Institute of Buddhist Studies and Numata Center for Buddhist Translation and Research, 2007.

Fredericks, James. "Interreligious Friendship: A New Theological Virtue," *Journal of Ecumenical Studies* 35, no. 2 (Spring 1998): pp. 159–174.

—. "Masao Abe: A Spiritual Friendship," *Spiritus* 3, no. 2 (2003): pp. 219–230.

Fujita, Kōtatsu. "The Textual Origins of the *Kuan Wu-liang-shou ching:* A Canonical Scripture of Pure Land Buddhism," trans. Kenneth K. Tanaka. In *Chinese Buddhist Apocrypha,* ed. Robert E. Buswell. Honolulu: University of Hawai'i Press, 1990.

Furusawa, Katsuhiro. "Kedo-kan no kenkyū" (A Study on the "Chapter on Transformed Land"). *Shūgakuin ronshū* 65 (March 1996).

Geibel, Rolf W. *Two Esoteric Sutras.* Berkeley, CA: Numata Center for Buddhist Translation and Research, 2001.

Goldstein, Joseph. *One Dharma: The Emerging Western Buddhism.* New York: HarperCollins, 2002.

Griffin, David Ray, and Huston Smith. *Primordial Truth and Postmodern Theology.* Albany, NY: State University of New York Press, 1990.

Groner, Paul. "Shortening the Path: Early Tendai Interpretations of the Realization of Buddhahood with This Very Body," in *Paths to Liberation: The Mārga and Its Transformation in Buddhist Thought,* ed. Robert Buswell and Robert Gimello. Honolulu: University of Hawai'i Press, 1992.

Guo Peng. *Ming-Qing fojiao* (*Buddhism in the Ming and Qing*). Fuzhou: Fujian Renmin chubanshe, 1982.

Habito, Rubin L. F. "Nichiren's Way of Being Religious: A Case Study in East Asian Buddhism," in *Kimura Kiyotaka Hakase Kinen Ronshu* (*Commemoration Volume in Honor of Dr. Kiyotaka Kimura*), ed. Sueki Fumihiko, et al. Tokyo: Shunjūsha, 2001.

—. *Originary Enlightenment: Tendai Hongaku Doctrine and Japanese Buddhism.* Tokyo: International Institute for Advanced Buddhist Studies, 1996.

—. *Shinran to Seisho no Yomikata* (*Reading Shinran and the Bible*). Tokyo: Akashi Shoten, 1989.

—. "Uehara Senroku's Hermeneutic of Shinran: Prospects for Shin Studies," *The Pure Land,* n.s., 8–9 (December 1992): pp. 47–63.

Hanshan Deqing. "Shi xiu jingtu famen" ("Expounding the Practice of the Pure Land Dharma Gate"), in *Hanshan Deqing, Hanshan Laoren meng you ji,* 4 vols. (1879). Taibei: Xinwenfeng, 1993, reprint.

Hase, Shōtō. "Jōi no sekai to shiteno shūkyō—eigen suru hōzōbosatsu," *Shinshūgaku* 107 (January 2003).

Hatta, Yukio. *Shingon jiten*. Tokyo: Hirakawa shuppansha, 1985.

Hawking, Stephen W. *A Brief History of Time*. New York: Bantam Books, 1988.

Hirakawa, Akira. *A History of Indian Buddhism: From Śākyamuni to Early Mahayana*, trans. and ed. Paul Groner. Honolulu: University of Hawai'i Press, 1990.

Hirota, Dennis. *Toward a Contemporary Understanding of Pure Land Buddhism: Creating Shin Buddhist Theology in a Religiously Plural World*. Albany, NY: State University of New York Press, 2000.

Hirota, Dennis, et al., trans. *The Collected Works of Shinran*. Jōdo Shinshū Hongwanji-ha, 1997.

Hodge, Stephen. *The Mahāvairocana-abhisaṃbodhi Tantra with Buddhaguhya's Commentary*. London: Routledge Curzon, 2003.

Horner, I. B., trans. *The Book of the Discipline* (1952). London: Luzac & Company, Ltd., 1962, reprint.

Hoshino, Genpō. *Jōdo* (*Pure Land*). Kyoto: Hōzōkan, 1957.

Howard, Angela Falco. *Summit of Treasures: Buddhist Cave Art of Dazu, China*. Trumbull, CT: Weatherhill, 2001.

Hsing-li Tsai. Ch'en Hung-shou's 'Elegant Gathering': A Late Ming Pictorial Manifesto of Pure Land Buddhism. Ph.D. dissertation. University of Kansas, 1997.

Hunter, Harriet. "Late Tang Chinese Handbooks for the *Garbhakośa* Rite," in *Embodying Wisdom: Art, Text and Interpretation in the History of Esoteric Buddhism*, ed. Rob Linrothe and Henrik H. Sørensen. Copenhagen: Seminar for Buddhist Studies, 2001.

Hurvitz, Leon. *Chih-I (538–597): An Introduction to the Life and Ideas of a Chinese Buddhist Monk*. Mélanges chinois et bouddhiques, vol. 12. Bruges, Belgium: Inprimerie Sainte-Catherine, 1960–1962.

Inaba, Masamaru, ed. *Rennyo Shōnin Ibun*. Kyoto: Hōzōkan, 1972.

Inagaki, Hisao. *The Three Pure Land Sutras*. Kyoto: Nagata Bunshōdō, 1994.

Ingram, Paul. "Faith as Knowledge in the Teaching of Shinran Shonin and Martin Luther," *Buddhist-Christian Studies* 8 (1988): pp. 23–36.

Ishida, Mitsuyuki. *Shinran kyōgaku no kisoteki kenkyū* (*A Fundamental Study of Shinran's Thought*). Kyoto: Nagata Bunshōdō, 1970.

Itsuki, Hiroyuki. *Tariki: Embracing Despair, Discovering Peace*. New York: Kodansha America, 2003.

Jackson, Roger, and John Makransky, eds. *Buddhist Theology: Critical Reflections by Contemporary Scholars*. Surrey, UK: Curzon Press, 2000.

Jiang Canteng. "Li Zhuowu yu wan Ming fojiao sixiang yi ji dui 'kuang chan' de piping" ("Li Zhuowu and Late-Ming Buddhist Thought and a Critique of 'Crazy Chan'"), in *Zhongguo jindai fojiao sixiang de zhengbian yu fazhan*. Taibei: Nantian Shuju, 1998.

Kajiyama, Yuichi. *Jōdo no kosumoroji*. Kyoto: Jōdo-Shinshū Kyōgaku Kenkyūjo, 1993.

Kanamatsu, Kenryo. *Naturalness: A Classic of Shin Buddhism.* Bloomington, IN: World Wisdom, 2002.

Kato, Bunno, et al., trans. *The Threefold Lotus Sutra.* New York and Tokyo: Weatherhill/Kosei, 1973.

Katz, Nathan. *Buddhist Images of Human Perfection: The Arahant of the Sutta Piṭaka Compared with the Bodhisattva and the Mahāsiddha.* Delhi: Motilal Banarsidass, 1982.

Kaufman, Gordon. "Religious Diversity and Religious Truth," in *Shinran and the Contemporary World: Internationalization and the Encounter with World Religions.* Kyoto: Ryūkoku University, 1989.

Khetsun Sangpo Rinbochay. *Tantric Practice in Nying-ma,* trans. and ed. Jeffrey Hopkins, co-ed. Anne Klein. Ithaca, NY: Gabriel/Snow Lion, 1982.

Korten, David. *The Great Turning: From Empire to Earth Community.* San Francisco: Berrett Koehler Publishers, 2006.

Ko Sa Myun. *Idakite: Tannishō to no Deai* (*Embracing One Teardrop: My Encounters with the Tannishō*). Tokyo: Mainichi Shinbunsha, 1977.

Kripal, Jeffrey J. "Psychoanalysis and Hinduism: Thinking Through Each Other," in *Vishnu on Freud's Desk: A Reader in Psychoanalysis and Hinduism,* ed. T. G. Vaidyanathan and Jeffrey J. Kripal. Delhi: Oxford University Press, 1999.

Lamotte, Étienne. *History of Indian Buddhism: From the Origins to the Śaka Era,* trans. Sara Webb-Boin. Louvain: Institute Orientaliste de l'Universit, Catholique de Louvain, 1988.

Lee, Kenneth. "Comparative Analysis of Shinran's Shinjin and Calvin's Faith," *Buddhist-Christian Studies* 24 (2004): pp. 171–190.

LeVine, Sarah, and David N. Gellner. *Rebuilding Buddhism: The Theravada Movement in Twentieth-Century Nepal.* Cambridge, MA and London: Harvard University Press, 2005.

Linrothe, Rob. *Ruthless Compassion: Wrathful Deities in Early Indo-Tibetan Esoteric Buddhist Art.* Boston: Shambhala, 1999.

Löwy, Michael, and Robert Sayre. *Romanticism Against the Tide of Modernity.* Durham, NC and London: Duke University Press, 2001.

Markus, Rose, and Shinobu Kitayama. "Cultural Construction of Self and Emotion," in *Emotion and Culture,* ed. Shinobu Kitayama and Hazel Rose Markus. Washington, DC: American Psychological Association, 1994.

Matsunaga, Daigan, and Alicia Matsunaga. *Foundation of Japanese Buddhism.* Los Angeles and Tokyo: Buddhist Books International, 1976.

May, Gerald G. *Will and Spirit: A Contemplative Psychology.* New York: Harper SanFrancisco, 1982.

McDonald, Joren. "The Importance of Self Effort," *The Wheel of Dharma,* vol. 24, no. 7 (July 1997).

Ming-shui Hung, "Yüan Hung-tao and the Late Ming Literary and Intellectual Movement." Ph.D. dissertation. University of Wisconsin, 1974.

Mochizuki, Shinkō. *Bukkyō daijiten*. Tokyo: Sekai Seiten Kangyō Kyōkai, 1974–1977.

—. *Chūgoku jōdō kyōri shi (A History of Chinese Pure Land Thought)*. Kyōtō: Hōzōkan, 1978.

Nattier, Jan. *Once Upon a Future Time: Studies in a Buddhist Prophecy of Decline.* Berkeley, CA: Asian Humanities Press, 1991.

Nonomura, Naotarō. *Jōdokyo hihan (Critique of Pure Land Buddhism)*. Kyoto: Chugai Shuppansha, 1923.

Numrich, Paul. *Old Wisdom in the New World: Americanization in Two Immigrant Theravada Temples.* Knoxville, TN: University of Tennessee Press, 1996.

—. "Vinaya in Theravāda Temples in the United States," *Journal of Buddhist Ethics* 1 (1994): pp. 23–32.

Ōhara, Shōjitsu. *Shinshu kyōgaku no dentō to koshō (Tradition and Realization of Shinshū Doctrinal Studies)*. Shinshū-kyōgaku-shi kenkyū 5. Kyoto: Nagata Bunshōdō, 1965.

Oka, Ryōji. "Shinran no jūnen shisō," *Shinshūgaku* 107 (January 2003).

Olcott, Henry Steel. *A Buddhist Catechism* (1881). London: Theosophical Publishing Society, 1904.

Oldenberg, Hermann, ed. *The Vinaya Piṭakaṃ*, vol. 1. London: Luzac & Company, Ltd., 1964, reprint.

Ōmine Akira. "Language and Transcendence," *The Pure Land*, n.s., 3 (December 1986): pp. 144–147.

Ōmura, Chōkaku, et al. *Mikkyō daijiten.* Kyoto: Hōzōkan, 1970.

Orzech, Charles D. *Politics and Transcendent Wisdom: The Scripture for Humane Kings in the Creation of National Protection Buddhism.* University Park, PA: Pennsylvania State University Press, 1998.

Osabe, Kazuo. *Tōdai mikkyō shi zakkō.* Kobe: Kōbe shōka daigaku gakujutsu kenkyūkai, 1971.

—. *Tō Sō mikkyō shi ronko.* Kyoto: Eiden bunshōdō, 1982.

Ouyi Zhixu. "Xifang helun xu" ("Preface to Comprehensive Treatise on the West"), in *Ouyi Dashi Quanji (The Collected Works of Great Master Ouyi)*, 21 vols. Taibei: Fojiao chubanshe, 1989, reprint.

Pagels, Elaine. *The Gnostic Gospels.* New York: Vintage Books, 1979.

Pan Guiming. *Zhongguo jushi fojiao shi (A History of Chinese Lay Buddhism)*, 2 vols. Beijing: China Social Studies Press, 2000.

Pas, Julian F. "The *Kuan-wu-liang-shou-Fo-ching*: Its Origin and Literary Criticism," in *Buddhist Thought and Asian Civilization: Essays in Honor of Herbert V. Guenther on His Sixtieth Birthday*, ed. Leslie S. Kawamura and Keith Scott. Emeryville, CA: Dharma Publishing, 1977.

—. *Visions of the Sukhāvatī: Shan-Tao's Commentary on the Kuan Wu-Liang-Shou-Fo Ching.* Albany, NY: State University of New York Press, 1995.

Patrul Rinpoche. *The Words of My Perfect Teacher: A Complete Translation of a Classic Introduction to Tibetan Buddhism*, trans. Padmakara Translation Group. New Delhi: Vistaar Publications, 1994, rev. ed.

Payne, Richard K. "Hiding in Plain Sight: The Invisibility of the Shingon Mission to the United States," in *Buddhist Missionaries in the Era of Globalization,* ed. Linda Learman. Honolulu: University of Hawai'i Press, 2005.

—. "Introduction," in *Tantric Buddhism in East Asia,* ed. Richard K. Payne. Boston: Wisdom Publications, 2005.

—. "Review of *Why Religion Matters: The Fate of the Human Spirit in the Age of Disbelief* by Huston Smith," *Theology and Science,* vol. 5, no. 1 (March 2007): pp. 109–117.

—. Ed. *Re-Visioning "Kamakura" Buddhism.* Honolulu: University of Hawai'i Press, 1998.

—. Ed. *Tantric Buddhism in East Asia.* Boston: Wisdom Publications, 2005.

—. "The Five Contemplative Gates of Vasubandhu's Rebirth Treatise as Ritualized Visualization Practice," in *The Pure Land Tradition: History and Development,* ed. James Foard, Michael Solomon, and Richard K. Payne. Berkeley, CA: University of California Press, 1996.

—. *The Tantric Ritual of Japan. Feeding the Gods: The Shingon Fire Ritual.* Delhi: Aditya Prakashan, 1991.

Peng Jiqing. *Jushi zhuan* (*Biographies of Buddhist Laymen*), in *Wanzi xu zang jing,* vol. 149. Taibei: Xinwenfeng, 1978.

Piyadassi Thera. *The Buddha's Ancient Path.* Kandy, Sri Lanka: Buddhist Publication Society, 1974.

Powers, John. *Introduction to Tibetan Buddhism.* Ithaca, NY: Snow Lion Publications, 1995.

Prebish, Charles. *American Buddhism.* North Scituate, MA: Duxbury Press, 1979.

Prothero, Stephen. *Religious Literacy: What Every American Needs to Know—and Doesn't.* San Francisco: HarperSanFrancisco, 2007.

Przyluski, Jean. "Les Vidyaraja, Contribution à l'Histoire de la Magie dans les Sectes Mahāyānistes," *Bulletin de l'École Française d'Extrème Orient* 23 (1923): pp. 301–318.

Qian Bocheng, ed. *Yuan Hongdao ji jianjiao* (*The Collected Works of Yuan Hongdao with Annotations*), 3 vols. Shanghai: Guji chubanshe, 1981.

Qiu Minjie. *Can chan yu nianfo: Wan Ming Yuan Hongdao de fojiao sixiang* (*Chan Practice and Buddha-Recitation: The Buddhist Thought of Yuan Hongdao in the Late Ming*). Zongjiao wenhua cong shu, vol. 3. Taibei: Shang Ding, 1993.

—. "Yuan Hongdao de 'Xifang helun' de jingtu sixiang" ("The Pure Land Thought of Yuan Hongdao's 'Xifang helun'"), *Diguan* 73 (1993): pp. 73–98.

Rahula, Walpola. *What the Buddha Taught.* Bedford, England: Gordon Fraser, 1959.

Rambelli, Fabio. "'Just Behave as You Like: Prohibitions and Impurities Are Not a Problem': Radical Amida Cults and Popular Religiosity in Premodern Japan," in *Approaching the Land of Bliss: Religious Praxis in the Cult of Amitabha,* ed. Richard K. Payne and Kenneth K. Tanaka. Honolulu: University of Hawai'i Press, 2004.

Ray, Reginald. *Buddhist Saints in India: A Study in Buddhist Values and Orientations.* New York: Oxford University Press, 1994).

Rogers, Minor L., and Ann T. Rogers. *Rennyo: The Second Founder of Shin Buddhism.* Berkeley, CA: Asian Humanities Press, 1991.

Roof, Wade Clark. *Spiritual Marketplace: Baby Boomers and the Remaking of American Religion.* Princeton, NJ: Princeton University Press, 1999.

Rubin, Jeffrey B. *Psychotherapy and Buddhism: Toward an Integration.* New York: Plenum, 1996.

Ryūkoku University, trans. *Kyō gyō shin shō: Teaching, Practice, Faith, and Enlightenment.* Kyoto: Ryūkoku University Translation Center, 1966.

Sanford, James H. "Amida's Secret Life: Kakuban's Amida Hishaku," in *Approaching the Land of Bliss: Religious Praxis in the Cult of Amitābha,* ed. Richard K. Payne and Kenneth S. Tanaka. Honolulu: University of Hawai'i Press, 2004.

—. "Breath of Life: The Esoteric Nenbutsu," in *Esoteric Buddhism in Japan,* ed. Ian Astley. Copenhagen and Aarhus: Seminar for Buddhist Studies, 1994.

—. "Shakuhachi Zen: The Fukeshū and Komusō," *Monumenta Nipponica* 32, no. 4 (1975): pp. 411–440.

Scharf, Robert H. "The Zen of Japanese Nationalism," in *Curators of the Buddha,* ed. Donald S. Lopez, Jr. Chicago: University of Chicago Press, 1995.

Schepers, Gerhard. "Shinran's View of the Human Predicament and the Christian Concept of Sin," *Japanese Religions* 15, no. 2 (July 1988): pp. 1–17.

Schuon, Frithjof. *The Transcendent Unity of Religions.* Wheaton, IL: Quest Books, 1993, rev. ed.

Schwartz, Jeffrey M., with Beverly Beyette. *Brain Lock: Free Yourself from Obsessive-Compulsive Behavior.* New York: Regan Books, 1996.

Seager, Richard H. *Buddhism in America.* New York: Columbia University Press, 1999.

—. *The World's Parliament of Religions: The East-West Encounter, Chicago, 1893.* Bloomington, IN: Indiana University Press, 1995.

Shengyan, Ven. Dr. *Mingmo fojiao yanjiu* (*Studies in Late Ming Buddhism*), Zhihui hai 9. Taibei: Dongchu Publications, 1992.

Shigaraki, Takamaro. *A Life of Awakening: The Heart of the Shin Buddhist Path,* trans. David Matsumoto. Kyoto: Hōzōkan, 2005.

Shi Guangding, ed. *Yinguang Dashi quanji* (*The Collected Works of the Great Master Yinguang*), 7 vols. Taibei: Fojiao Chubanshe, 1991, rev. and exp. ed.

Shinshū Shōgyō Zensho. Kyoto: Kōkyō Shoin, 1957.

Shweder, Richard, with Joan G. Miller. "The Social Construction of the Person: How is it Possible," in *Thinking Through Cultures: Expedition in Cultural Psychology,* ed. Richard Shweder. Cambridge, MA: Harvard University Press, 1991.

—. Ed. *Thinking Through Cultures: Expedition in Cultural Psychology.* Cambridge, MA: Harvard University Press, 1991.

—. "You're Not Sick, You're Just in Love," in *The Nature of Emotions: Fundamental Questions,* ed. Paul Ekman and Richard J. Davidson. New York: Oxford University Press, 1994.

Silk, Jonathan A. "The Composition of the *Guan Wuliangshuofo-jing:* Some Buddhist and Jaina Parallels to Its Narrative Frame," *Journal of Indian Philosophy* 25 (1997): pp. 181–265.

Smith, Huston. *The Religions of Man.* New York: Harper and Bros., 1958.

—. "The Universal Grammar of Religion," *Religion East and West* 5 (2005): pp. 1–5.

—. *The World's Religions: Our Great Wisdom Traditions.* San Francisco: HarperSan Francisco, 1991.

—. *Why Religion Matters: The Fate of the Human Spirit in an Age of Disbelief.* New York: HarperCollins, 2001.

Smith, Huston, and Philip Novak. *Buddhism: A Concise Introduction.* San Francisco: HarperSanFrancisco, 2004.

Smith, Jonathan Z. *Drudgery Divine: On the Comparison of Early Christianities and the Religions of Late Antiquity.* Chicago: University of Chicago Press, 1994.

Snodgrass, Adrian. *The Matrix and Diamond World Mandalas in Shingon Buddhism,* 2 vols. New Delhi: Aditya Prakshan, 1988.

Staal, Fritz. "Ritual Syntax," in *Sanskrit and Indian Studies,* ed. M. Nagatomi, et al. Dordrecht, Holland: D. Reidel Publishing Co., 1980.

Steinfels, Peter. "Beliefs," *New York Times,* March 10, 2001.

Stone, Jacqueline I. *Original Enlightenment and the Transformation of Medieval Japanese Buddhism.* Honolulu: University of Hawai'i Press, 2003.

Streng, Frederick J. *Understanding Religious Life.* Belmont, CA: Wadsworth, 1985.

Suzuki, D. T. "Shin Buddhism: Part I," *Eastern Buddhist,* n.s., 17, no. 1 (Spring 1985).

Suzuki, Shunryu. *Zen Mind, Beginner's Mind,* ed. Trudy Dixon. New York: Weatherhill, 1970.

Takeuchi, Yoshinori. *The Heart of Buddhism: In Search of the Timeless Spirit of Primitive Buddhism,* ed. and trans. James W. Heisig. New York: Crossroad, 1991.

Tamura, Yoshiro. *Kamakura Shin-bukkyō Kenkyū.* Kyoto: Hōzōkan, 1969.

Tanabe, Hajime. *Philosophy as Metanoetics,* trans. Takeuchi Yoshinori. Berkeley, CA: University of California Press, 1986.

Tanaka, Kenneth K. "Ethics in American Jodo Shinshu: Trans-ethical Responsibility," in *Living in Amida's Universal Vow: Essays in Shin Buddhism,* ed. Alfred Bloom. Bloomington, IN: World Wisdom, Inc., 2004.

—. *Ocean: An Introduction to Jodo-Shinshu Buddhism in America.* Berkeley, CA: WisdomOcean Publications, 1997.

—. "Symbolism of Amida and Pure Land in the American Context," *The Pure Land,* n.s., 8 & 9 (December 1992): pp. 64–88.

—. *The Dawn of Chinese Pure Land Buddhist Doctrine: Ching-ying Hui-yüan's Commentary on the Visualization Sutra.* Albany, NY: State University of New York Press, 1990.

—. "Where is the Pure Land? Controversy in Chinese Pure Land Buddhism on the Nature of Pure Land," *Pacific World,* n.s., 3 (Fall 1987): pp. 36–87. Reprinted in *Shin Buddhism: Historical, Textual, and Interpretive Studies,* ed. Richard K. Payne. Berkeley, CA: Institute of Buddhist Studies and Numata Center for Buddhist Translation and Research, 2007.

ten Grotenhuis, Elizabeth. *Japanese Mandalas: Representations of Sacred Geography.* Honolulu: University of Hawai'i Press, 1999.

Tharchin, Lama. *A Commentary on the Dudjom Tersar Ngrondro: The Preliminary Practice of the New Treasure of Dudjom.* El Cerrito, CA: Pema Osel Ling, n.d.

The Random House Unabridged Dictionary of the English Language, 2nd ed. New York: Random House, 1987.

Thondup, Tulku. *Boundless Healing: Meditation Exercises to Enlighten the Mind and Heal the Body.* Boston and London: Shambhala, 2000.

—. *The Healing Power of Mind: Simple Meditation Exercises for Health, Well-Being, and Enlightenment.* Boston and London: Shambhala, 1996.

Thornton, S. A. *Charisma and Community Formation in Medieval Japan: The Case of the Yugyo-ha (1300–1700).* Ithaca, NY: Cornell University Press, 1999.

Tillich, Paul. "The Religious Symbol," in *Symbolism in Religion and Literature,* ed. Rollo May. New York: George Braziller, 1960.

Toshimaro, Ama. "Toward a Shin Buddhist Social Ethics," in *Living in Amida's Universal Vow: Essays in Shin Buddhism,* ed. Alfred Bloom. Bloomington, IN: World Wisdom, Inc., 2004.

Trungpa, Chögyam. *Cutting Through Spiritual Materialism.* Boston: Shambhala, 1987.

—. *The Myth of Freedom and the Way of Meditation.* Boulder, CO and London: Shambhala, 1976.

Tsuji, Kenryu T. *The Heart of the Buddha-Dharma.* Berkeley, CA: Ekoji Buddhist Temple and Numata Center for Buddhist Translation and Research, 2003.

Ueda, Yoshifumi, and Dennis Hirota, eds. *Shinran: An Introduction to His Thought.* Kyoto: Hongwanji International Center, 1989.

Unno, Taitetsu. "Constructive Buddhist Theology: A Response," in *Buddhist Theology: Critical Reflections by Contemporary Scholars,* ed. Roger Jackson and John Makransky. Surrey, UK: Curzon Press, 2000.

—. Introduction, in Kenryo Kanamatsu, *Naturalness: A Classic of Shin Buddhism.* Bloomington, IN: World Wisdom, 2002.

—. *River of Fire, River of Water: An Introduction to the Pure Land Tradition of Shin Buddhism.* New York: Doubleday, 1998.

Unno, Taitetsu, and James Heisig, eds. *The Religious Philosophy of Tanabe Hajime.* Berkeley, CA: Asian Humanities Press, 1990.

Urban, Hugh B. *Tantra: Sex, Secrecy, Politics, and Power in the Study of Religion.* Berkeley, CA: University of California Press, 2003.

van Bragt, Jan. "Does Jodo Shinshu form a Bridge between Jodo Shinshu and Christianity?" *Japanese Religions* 18, no. 1 (1993): pp. 47–75.

Varela, Francisco J., Evan Thomson, and Eleanor Rosch. *The Embodied Mind: Cognitive Science and Human Experience.* Cambridge, MA: MIT Press, 1991.

von Brücke, Michael. *Einführung in den Buddhismus.* Frankfurt am Main and Leipzig: Verlag der Weltreligionen, Insel Verlag, 2007.

Welch, Holmes. *The Practice of Chinese Buddhism 1900–1950.* Cambridge, MA: Harvard University Press, 1967.

Wheelock, Wade T. "The Mantra in Vedic and Tantric Ritual," in *Mantra,* ed. Harvey P. Alper. Albany, NY: State University of New York Press, 1989.

Woodward, F. L., trans. *The Book of the Kindred Sayings* (*Saṃyutta Nikāya*) (1884–1904). London: Luzac & Company, Ltd., 1956, reprint.

Yamaoka, Seigen H. *Jodo Shinshu: An Introduction.* San Francisco: Buddhist Churches of America, 1990.

Yeats, William Butler. *The Collected Poems of W. B Yeats.* New York: Macmillan, 1959.

Yokota, John. "Shakyamuni Within the Shin Tradition," *Pacific World,* n.s., 2 (Fall 1986): pp. 31–35.

—. "Understanding Amida Buddha and the Pure Land: A Process Approach," in *Toward a Contemporary Understanding of Pure Land Buddhism,* ed. Dennis Hirota. Albany, NY: State University of New York Press, 2000.

Yuan Zhongdao. *Kexue zhai qianji* (*Earlier Anthology from Kexue Studio*), 5 vols. (1618). Taibei: Weiwen, 1976, reprint.

Zhang Ruzhao. "Yuan Zhonglang de Foxue Sixiang" ("Yuan Zhonglang's Buddhist Thought"), *Renjian shi* 20 (January 1935).

Zhou Qun. "Lun Yuan Hongdao de foxue sixiang" ("A Discussion of Yuan Hongdao's Buddhist Thought"), *Chung-Hwa Buddhist Studies Studies* 6 (2002): pp. 383–417.

—. *Ru-Shi-Dao yu wan Ming wenxue sixiang* (*Confucianism, Buddhism, Daoism, and Late-Ming Literary Thought*). Shanghai: Shanghai Bookstore Publishing, 2000.

—. *Yuan Hongdao ping zhuan* (*A Critical Biography of Yuan Hongdao*). Nanjing: Nanjing University Press, 1999.

Index

A

"A" 62, 63, 64–65
Abe, Masao 233
Abé, Ryūchi 54
abbot(s) 15, 138, 139, 175, 176, 177
  eighth, of the Hongwanji (*see also* Rennyo) 175, 201
  third, of the Hongwanji (*see also* Kakunyo) 176, 177, 182
abhidharma(s) xiv, 163
  masters 131
abhiṣeka (*see also* consecration) 32, 38, 42, 44, 45, 50, 140
absolute 61, 62, 83, 94, 116, 163, 166, 167, 185, 227
  other-power xiv, xv, 177, 180
  time 225, 226
ācārya (*see also* preceptor) 38, 42, 130
acharyas 141
Achu rulai nian song gongyang fa 49
Adam and Eve 181
Adamantine Lotus Dharma 39
Adamantine Pinnacle Sutra (*see also* *Vajraśekhara-sūtra*) 52
adhiṣṭhāna (*see also* empowerment) 35, 55, 70
Afro-Brazilian Candomblé 153
age(s) 69, 72, 73, 176, 177, 178, 183, 192, 201
  declining 229
  five, of decay, of the five deteriorations 45, 95–96
  last, of the last period of the teaching (*see also mappō*) 32, 44, 183, 191
  of right dharma 191
  of semblance dharma 191
  of true dharma 190
AIDS 136, 141
Aitken, Robert 134
Ākāśagarbha 33
alaṃkāra 231
alchemy vii, x
Allah 203
altar(s) xii, 33, 35, 68
  five-buddha 39
Amaterasu 74
America, American(s) (*see also* Anglo-Americans; Euro-American; Latin America; North America; United States) 6, 14, 77, 78, 79, 80, 81, 85, 133, 134, 135, 137, 138, 139, 147, 148, 158, 161, 172
  Jōdo Shinshū practice 77, 78, 79
  Protestant 153, 161
  Shin 80, 205, 216
American Buddhist Congress 142, 145
American Heritage Dictionary 79
Amida (*see also* Amitābha; Amitāyus) xiii, 5, 59, 60, 61, 62, 63, 64, 65, 66, 67, 68, 69, 70, 71, 159, 164, 166, 167, 171, 179, 180, 182, 183, 184, 185, 186, 192–93, 194, 195, 196, 197, 199, 204, 215, 216, 217, 218, 220, 221, 222, 223, 224, 225, 226, 227, 228, 229, 230, 231, 232, 233, 234, 235, 236, 237, 238, 239, 240
  compassion 81, 167, 177, 178, 183, 185, 187, 192, 193, 194, 195, 196, 197, 198, 199, 203, 204, 208, 209, 212, 233
  hongaku 61, 68, 71
  image 59, 70
  myth, narrative, story 221, 223, 225, 226, 236
  name 62, 64, 179, 194, 195, 197, 198, 199, 203, 204, 209, 220, 221, 239

Amida (*continued*)
other-power xv, 178, 179
primal vow, Primal Vow 182, 184, 191, 192, 224
Pure Land (*see also* Pure Land [as place]) 66, 74, 79, 184, 203
salvation, salvific grace of 19, 59, 64, 182, 185
vow(s), Vow xv, 4, 159, 175, 177, 178, 180, 181, 183, 184, 192, 195, 216, 234, 237
welcome 184, 196
Amidism, Amidist(s) 61, 63, 70, 73
Amitābha (*see also* Amida; Immeasurable Light) 40, 44, 46, 47, 62, 71, 97, 105, 106, 107, 111, 112, 115, 116, 117, 192, 194, 218, 219
body 111
cult 34, 39
name 46, 105, 109
paradise, Pure Land, Western Pure Land (*see also* Pure Land [as place]) 31, 104–105, 106, 109, 112, 114, 115, 116, 117, 181
Amitāyus (*see also* Amida; Immeasurable Life) 14, 33, 34, 35, 36, 39, 43, 47, 54, 71, 192
dhāraṇī 32, 34, 35, 40, 46, 47
mantra 33, 51
marks 33, 47
mudrā 33, 35
samādhi 35, 36, 47
Amituo guyin sheng wang tuoluoni jing (*see also Sheng wang jing*) 125
Amituo jing tong zanshu 102
amoebic dysentery 15
Amoghavajra 31, 37–38, 39, 40, 41, 42, 43, 44, 45, 49, 52, 53
Anagarika Dharmapala 133
Ānanda 129
Anglo-Americans 159
anjin (*see also* faith) 178, 179, 180
Anle ji 112
An Lushan 94
An Lushan rebellion 38
Anselm 157
anti-modernism 155, 156, 165
apocryphal 38, 32
apoha, apohic 230, 231
Araki, Kengo 90
arhat(s), arhatship 8, 128
Arjuna 162
Armstrong, Lance 81
Aronson, Harvey B. xix, 3–29, 83, 243
Asia, Asian (*see also* Central Asia; East Asia; South Asia) xiii, xiv, 13, 15, 16, 22, 24, 127, 135, 137, 138, 140, 141, 142, 150, 206, 210
aspiration(s) 84, 178, 194, 214, 232
for enlightenment (*see also bodhicitta*) 82, 187
assimilation 16, 17, 38, 39, 43, 59
Atigupta 50
Augustine 162
Austrian 164
Avalokiteśvara (*see also* Guanyin) 33, 34, 35, 39, 44
samādhi 36, 47
Avataṃsaka-sūtra 231
Awakened One (*see also* Buddha) 191
awakening(s) xix, 5, 7, 61, 63, 66, 68, 70, 75, 83, 94, 95, 109, 153, 159, 160, 162, 177, 181, 231
acquired 61
Awakening of Mahayana Faith 97, 102

B

Baker, Richard 138, 139, 145
Bamboo Grove 92
Bankei xvi
Baoding shan 51
BCA (*see also* Buddhist Churches of America) xvii, 79, 81
Ministers' Assistants Program 77
Bedi, Freda (*see also* Kechog Palmo, Sister) 136
Beijing 97, 99

being (*see also* non-being) xiii, xviii, 25, 61, 69, 154–55, 158, 194, 195, 203, 209
great chain of 154, 171
being(s) (*see also* human being; living being; sentient being) x, xvii, 5, 9, 10, 11, 12, 32, 33, 35, 44, 53, 63, 64, 105, 112, 115, 116, 129, 157, 169, 177, 178, 179, 183, 192, 193, 196, 197, 198, 216, 218, 237, 238
foolish. *See bonbu;* foolish being(s)
great, marks of 181
heavenly. *See* heavenly beings, realms
nine grades of 182
ordinary 115, 219
unenlightened 105, 107, 113, 117
Benedictine ix
Benicia, California xii
Berkeley, California vii, xix, xx, 3, 136, 147, 175, 240, 243
Bermant, Gordon xi–xviii, xix, xx, 77– 86, 147, 179, 184, 243
Bertolucci, Bernardo 140
Bhaiṣajyaguru. *See* Medicine Buddha
*bhāṇaka*s. *See* text reciters
bhikṣu(s) (*see also* monk) 128, 129
bhikṣuṇī(s) (*see also* nun) 128, 129
Bhubaneswar 17
bhūmi (*see also* stage) 32, 75
Bible 160, 181, 206, 207
biblical 207, 208, 212
Biographies of Buddhist Laymen 120
bio-psychological 10, 13, 16
birth (*see also* no-birth, non-birth; rebirth) 32, 66, 67, 100, 129, 134, 177, 178, 182, 183, 184, 186, 194, 195, 196, 206, 228, 237
birthless 66, 67
cause(s) for, of 193, 194, 237
four modes of 198
highest, upper, uppermost 31, 32, 40, 47
in the Pure Land, Sukhāvatī xv, 32, 47, 95, 159, 160, 164, 184, 196, 199, 222, 224, 237
birth and death, birth-and-destruction (*see also* samsara) 68, 75, 191
blessing(s) 19, 69, 70
bloodline 60, 71, 72
Bloom, Alfred xix, 79, 175–87, 210, 213, 230, 243
Board of Rites 98, 99
bodhi (*see also* enlightenment) 34
bodhicitta 64, 109, 161
Bodhidharma 57, 132
Bodhiruci 50, 55
bodhisattva(s) 8, 10, 20, 33, 34, 46, 47, 51, 62, 75, 105, 109, 131, 152, 159, 177, 182, 216, 219, 230
celestial 117
four *pāramitā* 41
lay 131
monastic 133
path, way 51, 82
state (*see also* bodhisattvahood) 34, 47
tenth-stage 75
vows 8, 81
bodhisattvahood (*see also* bodhisattva, state) 32, 49
bodhisattvayāna. *See* bodhisattva, path, way
Bodiford, William 132
body(ies), of buddha 63, 111, 218
dharma (*see also dharmakāya*) 193, 217, 218, 219, 220, 223, 224, 232, 233, 239
enjoyment (*see also sambhogakāya*) 8
form 218
four 67, 69
fulfilled 193, 217
reward (*see also sambhogakāya*) 108
subtle 61
three, triple 61, 62, 74, 230
tranquility 65
true 193
two 217, 218, 219

body, speech, and mind 33, 41, 49
bonbu (*see also* foolish being) 183, 224, 226
Bope Vinita Thera 135
Boston University 3
Boxiu (*see also* Yuan Zongdao) 95–96
Brahma 181
brahma-conduct 110
Buber, Martin 164
Buddha viii, x, xiv, 4, 5, 14, 19, 21, 32, 45, 49, 51, 65, 83, 95, 96, 102, 107, 108, 112, 121, 127, 128, 129, 130, 131, 132, 133, 137, 138, 151, 152, 162, 183, 186, 191, 193, 217, 220, 229, 232
  compassion 177, 178, 184
  disciples, followers, spiritual family, sangha 127, 128, 131, 137, 138, 142, 143
  historical (*see also* Gautama; Śākyamuni) 81, 221
  land(s) (*see also* buddha land) 95, 104, 224, 229
  name 4, 46, 95, 96, 110, 112
  teaching(s) 152, 224
  thirty-two major and eighty minor marks of 55
  of unhindered light (*see also* Amida) 193, 195
  vow(s) 45, 191
buddha(s) 4, 8, 10, 11, 12, 20, 33, 50, 51, 61, 62, 63, 64, 67, 68, 73, 104, 105, 108, 109, 112, 113, 114, 115, 116, 118, 129, 131, 152, 154, 159, 161, 178, 179, 181, 183, 184, 192, 197, 218, 220, 221, 237
  bodies, manifestations (*see also* body[ies], of buddha) 5, 61, 73, 218
  dhyāni- 47
  effulgent-, light-, 40, 53
  five 39, 41, 42
  name(s) 46, 53, 108
buddhadharma 57, 70, 127, 179, 185
Buddha, Dharma, and Sangha 140
Buddha Gong (*see also* Gong Daqi) 91
buddhahood 5, 8, 10, 12, 15, 21, 24, 59, 64, 67, 71, 102, 106, 109, 110, 115, 140, 181, 184, 187, 197, 198, 199, 236, 237
buddha land(s) 33, 65, 66, 105, 109, 112, 113, 187, 216, 218, 231, 236, 238
buddha-nature 64, 106, 112, 113, 193, 217
Buddha of Endless Life (*see also* Amida) 66
Buddha of Immeasurable Life (*see also* Amitāyus) 234
Buddha of Infinite Light (*see also* Amida) 226
buddhānusmṛti. *See* nenbutsu; *nianfo*
Buddhism vii, viii, ix, x, xiv, xv, xvi, 3, 17, 37, 57, 69, 70, 73, 81, 83, 84, 85, 90, 93, 100, 101, 107, 109, 111, 115, 117, 118, 119, 120, 121, 127, 128, 130, 131, 133, 135, 137, 139, 142, 148, 149, 150, 151, 152, 153, 154, 155, 156, 157, 158, 159, 160, 164, 165, 166, 168, 169, 179, 181, 202, 214, 228
  in America (United States), American, Americanization of 133, 135, 137, 141
  Chinese 54, 107, 117
  early 65, 131, 142, 153, 169
  East Asian 38, 54
  esoteric 32, 36–39, 41, 42, 43, 48, 50, 51, 53, 54, 60
  exoteric 59
  gentry 91, 120
  global, globalization of 140, 142, 143
  Heian 54
  Indian 128, 153, 169, 217–18, 239
  Indo-Sinitic 164
  Japanese 152, 159, 161, 214
  Kamakura 73, 207
  lay 111
  Mahayana xix, 21, 84, 130, 161, 218
  Ming 111
  modernist reinterpretation, representation of (*see also* Buddhist, modernism) 150, 151, 152

monastic 111, 169
Nara 54
Nichiren 58, 147
"original" 151, 152
"Protestant" 150
Pure Land (*see also* Pure Land [as sect, school, tradition]) ix, x, xix, 31, 101, 147, 148, 149, 152, 158, 159, 160, 161, 162, 164, 165, 189, 196, 203, 205, 207, 210, 228, 230
Shin xvii, 5, 83, 148, 159, 160, 165, 175, 176, 177, 180, 181, 183, 184, 185, 200, 203, 205, 207, 209, 216
"state-protection" 38
Tang 32, 42
Tantrayana, tantric 8, 130
Tendai 176
Theravāda 130, 141, 142
Tibetan 3, 14, 133, 140, 149
Vajrayana 141
Zen 201, 228

Buddhism: A Concise Introduction 148, 149, 151
Buddhism in America 137
Buddhist xii, xiv, xvii, 13, 15, 19, 22, 23, 26, 32, 37, 51, 65, 90, 101, 102, 103, 108, 110, 111, 120, 128, 131, 133, 141, 142, 150, 151, 154, 155, 159, 160, 163, 164, 165, 170, 182, 189, 204, 230, 231, 232, 233
belief, concepts, ideas, notions, philosophy 93, 111, 113, 154, 193, 201, 204
canon, catalogues, scripture(s), text(s) 40, 100, 101, 106, 120, 218
clergy, monk, priest(s) ix, 104, 127, 205, 210, 233
community(ies) xii, 101, 1128, 129, 130, 189, 190, 201, 202, 205, 207, 213
cosmogonies, cosmos 157, 170
doctrine, teaching(s) xiv, xv, 32, 67, 74, 171, 183, 190, 200, 207, 209, 211, 233
history 90, 130
intra- 140, 214
laity, layman, laymen xii, 90, 104, 124
literati 97
literature, parable, poems, writings 65, 93, 112, 114, 183, 238
modernism, modernist(s) 148, 150, 151, 152, 153, 165, 168
monasteries, temple 51, 135
practice(s), praxis 5, 13, 17, 19, 25, 46, 102, 103, 108, 111, 207
practitioner ix, 7, 16, 129
"revival," revivalists 93, 150
sangha 127, 130
scholar (*see also* Buddhologist) 6, 189, 233
sect(s), school(s) 115, 133, 176
societies 168
studies xix, 110, 137, 152
tantras 51
teacher(s) 17, 20, 138
theology 189, 190, 200, 209
thought xix, 90, 95, 107, 118, 163, 164, 202, 203, 218
tradition(s) 129, 130, 131, 132, 137, 140, 142, 145, 176, 184, 201, 205, 213, 214

Buddhist(s) ix, xi, 15, 109, 118, 129, 130, 131, 142, 159, 160, 161, 163, 166, 169, 214, 216, 217, 240
American, Caucasian, Euro-American, non-Asian, Western xv, xvi, 135, 137, 138, 143, 216
Asian 135, 138, 141
Chinese 97, 98, 100, 101, 112, 118, 119, 120, 132, 145
convert 137, 142
four groups of 128
immigrant 137
Indian 133, 215
Japanese 58, 74, 189
lay (*see also* laity) 128
Mahayana 131

Buddhist(s) (*continued*)
Pure Land (*see also* Pure Land [as sect, school, tradition]) 120, 189, 190, 199, 200, 202, 203, 205, 207, 209, 211, 214, 215, 218, 219, 229, 238
Shin xii, 147, 175, 180, 189, 190, 199, 201, 202, 203, 205, 206, 207, 208, 209, 210, 212, 213, 214, 215, 216, 226, 227, 233, 238, 239
Tendai 207
Theravāda 135, 141
Tibetan 5, 19, 20, 137, 140, 141, 145
Vajrayana 129
Zen 201
Buddhist Catechism, A 168
Buddhist-Christian dialogue, relations ix, 189, 229
Buddhist Churches of America (*see also* BCA) xvii, 77, 82, 200, 240
Buddhist Faith Fellowship of Connecticut 85
"Buddhist Thought and Practice" seminar vii
Buddhist Vihara Society 135
Buddhologist (*see also* scholar, of Buddhism, Buddhist) 58
Buddhoṣṇīṣa 42
Bureau of Ceremonies 97–98
Bureau of Honors 99
Burmese 135
Buswell, Robert 132

C

Caesar 179
cakravartin 38, 181
California vii, xii, xx, 3, 134, 136, 147, 164, 243
Calvin, John 152
Cambridge, Massachusetts 136
Campbell, Joseph 227, 236
cancer 13, 16
Carrithers, Michael 127
Catholic(s) (*see also* Christian, Christianity; Roman Catholic) ix, xx, 78, 83, 132, 147, 152, 154, 159
Catholic University of America 89, 243
cause(s) x, xv, xvi, 158, 192, 193, 195, 209, 217
of birth xv, 193, 194, 237
and conditions 77, 234
and effect(s) 62, 68, 107, 116
one great 68, 70, 71, 72
causality, causation 82, 171
Central America 206
Central Asia, Central Asian 37, 49, 51
Ceylon (*see also* Sri Lanka) 127
Chadwick, David 138
Chan (*see also* Zen) 37, 54, 91, 93, 94, 95, 96, 97, 98, 101–102, 104, 106, 112, 113, 115, 117, 118, 119, 120, 121, 126, 132, 229
"crazy" 98, 101, 110, 119, 123
Chang'an 37, 91
Chapel Hill, North Carolina 57, 243
Chappell, David W. 46
Chaves, Jonathan 95, 97
Chen Hongshou 101
Chiba, Jōryū 58, 59, 67
Chicago 133
Chicago Buddhist Temple 134
China 37, 38, 41, 42, 43, 49, 63, 74, 90, 100, 101, 102, 112, 119, 131, 149, 181, 196, 219, 229
Chinese 19, 24, 32, 37, 38, 43, 46, 48, 54, 63, 65, 74, 89, 100, 101, 131, 132
Buddhism, Buddhist(s) 54, 90, 98, 100, 101, 107, 112, 117, 118, 119, 120, 132, 145
Chan (*see also* Chan) 132
invasion, takeover of Tibet 6, 20
Pure Land (*see also* Pure Land [as sect, school, tradition]) 46, 90, 124, 125
Tiantai 207

Chinese language, literature viii, xiii, 31, 32, 49, 52, 53, 91, 93, 112
Chomsky, Noam 170
Christ (*see also* Jesus) 21, 154, 162, 229
Christian(s), Christianity (*see also* Catholic; Protestant) vii, viii, ix, x, xii, xiii, 21, 22, 148, 152, 153, 154, 155, 158, 159, 160, 163, 168, 169, 170, 171, 180, 189, 203, 204, 213, 215, 229
  missionaries 149, 150
  underground 74
Christmastime x
Chūinryū tradition, of Shingon 36
Chün-fang Yü 93
Cimarron Zen Center 135
cittaprasāda 161
City South Literary Society 122
clergy (*see also* monk; priest) 104, 183
Cloud Perch Temple (*see also* Yunqifa Temple, Yunqi Temple) 95
Cobb, John, Jr. 213, 229
Collected Works (of Yuan Hongdao) 90, 100
Colorado 139
Commentrary and Notes on the Shorter Sukhāvatī-sūtra (*see also Xu zang jing*) 97
Commentary on the New Huayan Sutra 103
Commentary on the Pure Land Treatise (*see also Commentary on the Upadeśa on the Sūtras of Amitāyus with Stanzas on the Resolution to Be Born by the Bodhisattva Vasubandhu*) 217, 218
Commentary on the Upadeśa on the Sūtras of Amitāyus with Stanzas on the Resolution to Be Born by the Bodhisattva Vasubandhu (*see also Commentary on the Pure Land Treatise*) xix, 47, 49
Communist 90
community(ies) xvi, 8, 29, 128, 129, 130, 134, 135, 136, 139, 140, 141, 142, 143, 158, 180, 190, 199, 200, 201, 202, 205, 206, 207, 208, 209, 213, 214, 221
  academic, scholarly xii, 101
  American, convert 137, 138
  Jōdo Shinshū 200, 201
  lay 128
  monastic (*see also* sangha) 128, 130, 131, 142
  Shin 80, 180, 189, 190, 201, 202, 205, 207, 213
  Theravāda 135, 141, 142
  Tibetan, diaspora 133, 136
  twofold (*see also* sangha, *ubhayato-*) 128
  wanderers' 128
  Zen 134, 139
compassion 25, 72, 82, 84, 97, 106, 109, 178, 184, 197, 198, 199, 204, 209, 233, 236
  of Amida 68, 167, 177, 178, 183, 185, 187, 192, 193, 194, 195, 196, 197, 198, 199, 204, 208, 209, 212, 233
  great 9, 78, 187, 194, 197, 198, 199, 234
  wisdom and 81, 84, 238
compassionate means (*see also* expedient, expedient means; skillful means) 179, 183
  dharma body as 193, 217, 218, 220, 223, 224, 232
Comprehensive Treatise on the West. *See Xifang helun*
confession 8, 9, 19
Confucian, Confucianism (*see also* Neo-Confucian) 22, 91, 93, 120, 185, 189, 202
consciousness vii, viii, xi, xv, 25, 193
  clouded, impure xv, 84
consciousness-only (*see also* Faxiang school; mind-only; Weishi) 117

consecration (*see also abhiṣeka*) 38, 50, 51
consort 8, 9
contemplation(s) 32, 44
  of emptiness 108
  of the middle 109
  of the phrase 93
  of the provisional 108
  three 108–109
Coral Grove (*see also Shanhu lin*) 91
Corless, Roger J. vii, x, xi, xix, xviii, 3, 29, 46, 47, 62, 80, 82, 85, 147, 166, 189, 209, 215, 230–31, 235
cosmogony(ies), cosmos 117, 157, 170
cosmology 160, 216
Crews, Frederick 169–70
Crooked Cucumber: The Life and Teaching of Shunryu Suzuki 138
crosscultural 3, 6, 7, 10, 20, 26
Csikszentmihály, Mihály xiii
cult 34, 39, 47, 227

D

Dahui pujue chansi yulu. See Recorded Sayings of Dahui Zonggao
Dahui Zonggao 93, 94–95, 123
Dainichi (*see also* Mahāvairocana) 59, 61, 63, 64
Daizong, Emperor 38, 39
Daizong chao zeng si kong da bian zheng guang zhi sanzang heshang biaozhi ji 52
Dake, Mitsuya 3, 4
Dalai Lama 140
Dallas, Texas 243
Dānapāla 52
Dante xiii
Dao, Daoism, Daoist 22, 46, 52, 100, 157
Daochuo 112, 124, 222
Daśabhūmika-śāstra 103
Daśabhūmika-sūtra 75
Da Tang zhenyuan xu kaiyuan shijiao lu 53
Davidson, Ronald M. 51
Dawn Mountain Tibetan Temple, Community Center, and Research Institute 3, 243
defilement(s) 9, 3, 34, 116, 176, 183
  five 65, 115, 191, 197
deity(ies) 4, 5, 33, 34, 35, 36, 37, 38, 39, 41, 44, 55, 64, 70
delusion(s) 108, 199
demonic, demons 9, 11, 12, 15, 181
Deng 95
Denison, Ruth 135
depression 11, 23
Deshung Rinpoche 135, 136
deva(s) (*see also* god) 182
Devānampiya Tissa, King 127
devotee(s) 105, 107, 114, 203, 205, 206, 207, 208, 209
devotion, devotional xii, 65, 69, 96, 98, 183, 196, 201, 214
dhāraṇī(s) 34, 35, 36, 38, 43, 46, 55
  of Amitāyus 32, 34, 35, 40, 46, 47, 51
dharma(s) (*see also* buddhadharma) xiv, xvi, xvii, 57, 58, 61, 65, 66, 68, 74, 75, 77, 79, 105, 107, 116, 130, 131, 132, 137, 143, 178, 179, 185, 193, 217, 219, 222, 229, 230
  family(ies) 138, 139, 140
  heir(s), successors 134, 138, 139, 145
  last age of, latter days of (*see also mappō*) 183, 190, 191
  lineage 132, 139
  master(s), teacher xii, 130, 131, 133
  name 138
  semblance, age of 191
  transmission (*see also shihō, shihō risso*) 138, 139
  true, age of 190
dharma-bhāṇakas 131
dharma body(ies) (*see also dharma-kāya*) 217, 218, 233
  as compassion, compassionate means 193, 217, 218, 220, 223, 224, 232

as suchness 217, 218, 220, 224
two 217–18, 219–20, 239
dharma-dharas. *See* dharma, master(s)
dharmadhātu 116
dharma gate(s) 97, 120
Dharmākara 67, 68, 69, 193, 219, 223, 224, 230, 232, 236
forty-eight vows of 236
vow(s) of xvi, 67, 218, 225
dharmakāya (*see also* dharma body) 61, 62, 64, 66, 68, 72, 73, 224
buddhahood, Buddha's, *tathāgata* 61, 64, 68, 107
dharmatā 61, 62
double xv, 62
expedient, of expedient means 61, 62
dharmalessness xvii
Dharma-lineage of Chan Master Zonggao of Jing Mountain. *See Jingshan Gao chansi fasi*
dharma-nature 217
dharmatā 61, 62, 72
Diagnostic and Statistical Manual of Mental Disorders 13
Diamond Sangha 134
Dickwela Piyananda 135
Dīgha-nikāya 131
dilettante, dilettantism xx, 110, 119
disc 9
lunar, moon 8, 9, 34, 35
of the sun 70
disciple(s) 37, 38, 41, 42, 43, 49, 51, 67, 128, 130, 131, 132, 134, 138, 139, 145, 191, 198, 200, 225
Discussion of the New Huayan Sutra. *See Xin Huayan junglun*
divine, divinity 19, 33, 36, 59, 68, 109, 160, 163, 169, 238
doctrinal, doctrine xv, xvi, xvii, 60, 106, 117, 130, 131, 134, 154, 160, 163, 166, 184, 203, 205, 215, 217, 218, 220, 221, 230
Buddhist xv, 130, 207
Mahayana 219, 230
orthodox, of Christianity 21
Pure Land, Shin 58, 62, 63, 164, 171, 203, 229
Doctrine of the Mean, The 103
Dōgen xvi, 207
dogma viii, 163
Dragon Lake 95
Dresser, Marianne xx
dualism, dualist, dualistic xix, 5, 70, 75, 103, 108, 112, 117, 118, 156, 165, 172, 226, 228
duḥkha (*see also* suffering) 129
Duke Chapel Choir x
Duke University vii, xii, 147
Dusum Khyenpa (*see also* Karmapa, first) 133

E

Earth Community 209
East, the 180
East Asia, East Asian 31, 37, 38, 44, 51, 54, 61, 89, 192, 196, 215
Eastern Citadel 69
Eckel, David 3, 230
"eclectic left" 169
Eichman, Jennifer 90
eighteenfold sequence (*see also* Eighteenfold Way) 41–42, 49, 51, 53
Eighteenfold Way (*see also juhachi dō; Shiba dao*) 31, 33, 34, 35, 36, 41
eightfold path 153
Ein Sof 154, 155
Ekoji Buddhist Temple xii, 79, 82
Elegant Gathering 101
Eliade, Mircea 222
Elman, Benjamin 92
emanationist metaphysics, thought 154, 155, 157, 164, 165
Embracing One Teardrop: My Encounters with the Tannishō. *See Hitotsubu no Namida wo Idakite: Tannishō to no Deai*

empowerment(s) (*see also adhiṣṭhāna*) 70, 136, 137, 140, 141
emptiness(es) (*see also śūnyatā*) 68, 84, 101, 102, 106, 108, 109, 110, 182, 204, 219, 233
emotional, emotions 7, 11, 18, 24, 60, 75, 219
English (language) xiv, 6, 16, 74, 75, 77, 79, 83, 103, 104, 135, 136, 153, 195, 210, 212, 213
enlightenment (*see also* awakening; *bodhi*) vii, xv, 11, 32, 65, 66, 70, 81, 94, 97, 98, 101, 119, 162, 177, 187, 190, 191, 198, 199, 236
  aspiration for (*see also bodhicitta*) 82, 187
  full 109, 221
  original 207
  path to xv, 183
  sudden 106, 110
Enlightenment, post- 189
entrust, entrusting, entrustment (*see also* trust) 64, 82, 180, 195, 198, 208, 211, 217, 222, 224, 225
  mind (*see also shinjin*) 194, 195, 196, 197, 203, 204, 225
  true (*see also shinjin*) 177, 179, 184, 225
Episcopal vii
epistemological, epistemology 161, 163, 165, 172
Eshin-ni 181
esoteric, esotericism, esotericized (*see also mikkyō;* tantra) 31, 32, 34, 36, 37–48, 49, 50, 51, 52, 53, 54, 55, 57, 58, 59, 60, 61, 63, 64
  gates, three (*see also* body, speech, and mind) 32, 49
  manual(s) 31, 36, 38, 39, 41, 42, 44, 49
Essentials of Shinran 210
ethic(s), ethical 7, 10, 24, 106, 131, 203, 205, 209, 232
eunuchs 98
Euro-American 135, 150
Europe 139, 163
evil(s) 34, 154, 158, 170, 177, 178, 183, 184, 204, 208
  karma, karmic 32, 183, 231
  ten 183
  world, of five defilements 65, 197
Ewam Choden Tibetan Buddhist Center 136
examination system, in China 91, 92–93, 95, 96, 98, 99, 100
  jinshi degree 89, 91, 92, 93, 95, 96, 99
  juren degree 92, 99
expedient(s), expedient means (*see also* compassionate means; skillful means) 62, 68, 73, 108, 114, 116
  dharmakāya as 62
Exposing the Heart. See Kaishinshō

F

Fairfax Station, Virginia 82
faith ix, xiii, xv, 4–5, 20, 45, 65, 67, 71, 74, 102, 111, 160, 161, 176, 178, 179, 180, 181, 183, 187, 203, 225
  bad 152, 158, 165
  religious 5, 163, 177
  settled 179, 180, 184
Fang 95
Fanwang jing 102
Faquan 42, 43 44, 53
Faust legend xiii
Faxiang school 106, 117
Fazang 106
feeling(s) (*see also* emotional, emotions) 20, 24, 25, 114
fire(s) 16, 63, 66, 102, 222
  sacrifice 51
  vajra- 34, 41
fire and ice, metaphor of 222
Five Cloud Mountain 97
five grave offenses, five heinous acts (*see also* sins, five major) 8, 196
five obstacles. *See* women, five obstacles of

foolish being(s) (*see also bonbu*) 71, 178, 183, 193, 224, 226
Fo shuo guan wuliangshoufo jing. See Guan jing
four assemblies, groups of Buddhists (*see also* sangha, fourfold) 128, 129
Fredericks, James 212
Freud, Sigmund 23
friend(s), good, spiritual (*see also kalyāṇamitra; zenchishiki*) 71, 129, 130, 133
Furusawa, Katsuhiko 225

G

Gampopa 133
Garbhakoṣa Maṇḍala *(see also Garbha maṇḍala;* Womb Maṇḍala) 63
Garbhakośa manuals 43
garbhakoṣa realm 62
Garbha maṇḍala, techniques (*see also* Garbhakoṣa Maṇḍala) 41, 42
gate(s), gateway (*see also* dharma gate) 101, 107, 115, 159, 175
  five contemplative 55
  ten, of Huayan thought 115
  three esoteric (*see also* body, speech, and mind) 32, 49
gāthā(s) 40, 41
Gautama (*see also* Buddha; Śākyamuni) 81, 235
Geertz, Clifford 18
Gellner, David N. 150, 168
Gelug, Gelukba 27, 133, 135
Genku (*see also* Hōnen) 67
gensō. See returning, phase of, to the world
George, Christopher 135
German Idealists 162
geshe 133
giardiasis 16
Giebel, Rolf W. 52
Glassman, Bernard 139, 140
Gnostic, Gnosticism 21, 158, 172
Gnostic Gospels, The 21
Gobō 57, 73
Gobunshō (*see also Ofumi*) 186, 187
God x, 19, 154, 160, 163, 169, 170, 179, 229, 234
god(s) 50, 179, 183, 184, 216
goddess(es) 10, 14
gohonzon (*see also* altar; *honzon*) 69, 72
Gold Shavings (*see also Jinxie bian*) 90, 91
Goldstein, Joseph 135, 143
Gongan County 91, 93, 98
Gongan school 89, 99
Gong Daqi 91
good, goodness 14, 22, 24, 105, 110, 114, 129, 154, 158, 169, 179, 183, 204
  act(s), deeds, practices xiii, 32, 191, 194, 198
good family, daughters, sons of 131
good friend. *See* friend(s), good, spiritual
grace 19, 55, 62, 80, 151, 153–54, 159, 169
  Christian 153, 154, 155, 159, 169
Graduate Theological Union vii, 3, 243
Grape Society 97, 98, 99
gratitude x, xiv, 3, 62, 71, 177, 178, 179, 180, 197, 209, 210, 214, 234, 237
"great chain of being" 154, 171
Great *Samaya* True *Lakṣana* Mantra 40, 47
Great Sun. *See* Dainichi
Greek viii, 21, 74, 157
Green Gulch Farm 139
Greensboro, North Carolina 31, 243
Groner, Paul 163
Guan jing 31, 33, 35, 36, 40, 43, 45, 46–47, 48, 49, 53
Guan wuliangshou fo jing shu miao zong chao 103
Guanyin (*see also* Avalokiteśvara) 41
Guanzizai pusa ru'ilun niansong yigui (*see also Ru'ilun*) 41, 49

Guénon, René 156
Guide to the Eighty Thousand Dharma Principles (*see also Hōri hachiman chō*) 60–72
Guo Peng 101
guru 60, 67, 130, 140
Gutoku (*see also* Shinran) 72
Gyalwa Karmapa (*see also* Karmapa, sixteenth) 137, 141

H

Habito, Ruben L. F. xix, 189–214, 243
haengja(s) (*see also* postulant) 132
Haidong shu 112
Hakamaya, Noriaki 214
Handel x
Hangzhou 96
Hanlin Academy 93
Hanshan, Deqing 120
Harvard University 135, 215
Hase, Shōtō 234–35, 236
Hawai'i xii, xvi, 134
Hawking, Stephen W. xviii
Hayagrīva (*see also vidyārāja*, horse-headed) 34, 41
healing 3, 5, 6, 7, 10, 11, 12, 13, 15, 16, 26, 205, 209
heart-mantra. *See* mantra, heart-
Heart of Buddhism: In Search of the Timeless Spirit of Primitive Buddhism, The 213
Heart Sutra 73
heaven(s) 68, 70, 71, 97, 109, 116, 154
  of equal enlightenment 70
  of the formless realm 109
heavenly beings, realms 12, 159, 238
Hebrew x, 157, 160
Heian period 31, 49, 54, 58
hell 116, 224
Henepola Gunaratana 135
heresy, heretical 21, 58, 74
hermeneutical, hermeneutics 54, 208
"Hermeneutic of Shinran, A." *See* "Shinran-ninshiki no hōhō"
hierarchical, hierarchy(ies) xvi, 12, 129, 155, 158, 169–70, 171, 206
higher power 23, 159
hiji bōmon 58, 74
Hinayana 106
Hindu, Hinduism 51, 157, 181
Hippolytus 21
Hirota, Dennis 210, 213, 225, 230, 241
Hitotsubu no Namida wo Idakite: Tannishō to no Deai 212
hōben (*see also* compassionate means; expedient, expedient means; skillful means) 179
hōben-hosshin. See dharmakāya, expedient, of expedient means
homa 38, 42
home, leaving (*see also* renunciation) 131
Hōnen xiii, 67, 152, 162, 163, 164, 176, 182, 192, 195, 207, 224
hongaku 61, 74
  Amida 61, 65, 68, 71
  shisō (*see also* enlightenment, original) 207, 214
Honganji (*see also* Hongwanji) 200, 201
  Higashi (Eastern) branch 200, 234
  Nishi (Western) branch 200, 234
Hongwanji (*see also* Honganji) 175, 176, 177, 182
Hongwanji Doctrinal Research Institute 233
honzon (*see also* altar; *gohonzan*) 59, 63, 69, 70, 71, 72
Hōonkō 180
Hopkins, Jeffrey 135
Hōri hachiman chō (*see also Guide to the Eighty Thousand Dharma Principles*) 57, 58–72
Hoshino, Genpō 230
hosshō-hosshin. See dharmakāya, dharmatā
householder (*see also* laity; lay; laypeople, layperson) 32, 44
Houston 3, 20, 27, 29, 243

Houston Ballet 13
hrīḥ 33, 34, 35
Huang Hui 93
Huayan 54, 93, 94, 97, 104, 105, 112, 113, 115, 116, 117, 118, 119, 126
Huayan jing helun 104
Huayan Sutra 103, 104, 106, 115, 116, 126
Hubei province 91
Huguang province 91
Huiguo 38, 41, 42, 43, 49, 53, 54
Huiyuan (*see also* Zhingying Huiyuan) 55
Huizinga, Johan xiii
hūṃ 8, 62, 63, 64
human, humanity, humankind xx, 21, 58, 60, 64, 89, 109, 116, 155, 156, 169, 171, 178, 182, 184, 190, 191, 200, 201, 202, 205, 208, 224, 229, 231
  act, capability, contrivance, effort, making xiii, 70, 159, 198, 199, 203, 204, 228
  condition, predicament, problematic 81, 105, 153, 154, 158, 190, 191, 192, 200, 203, 204
  existence 154, 190, 200, 216, 227
  failings, limitations, powerlessness 23, 82, 192, 203, 204
  history 152, 192
  nature 18, 204
  ultimate destiny 190, 192, 193, 194, 195, 196, 203, 204
human being(s), humans (*see also* being[s]; living being; sentient being) 157, 158, 169, 182, 190, 191, 192, 194, 195, 198, 202, 204, 231, 238
humanism, humanistic 11, 228
hungry ghosts 116, 238
Hunter, Harriet 42, 43
Huxley, Aldous 162
Hymn of True Faith. See Shōshinge
Hyms of the Pure Land 181, 182
"Hymns of the Pure Land Masters" 181, 182
Hymns to Amida Based on Various Sutras 242

I

"I Am" 162, 164, 166, 167
icchantikas 106
iemoto 58, 73
ignorance 9, 77, 108, 110, 153, 191
"I-It" 164
Ikeda-Nash, Mushim xx
illness(es) xi, xx, 11, 12, 15, 16, 17, 89, 147
illusions xi, 10
image(s), imagery 13, 20, 33, 51, 61, 64, 69, 70, 71, 84, 94, 116, 148, 150, 152, 164, 183, 234, 235
  of Amida, Amitāyus 33, 70
Immeasurable Life (*see also* Amitāyus) 70, 71, 192, 234
Immeasurable Light (*see also* Amitābha) 71, 192
Immigration and Nationality Act 141
imperial 37, 38, 45, 97
India, Indian, Indic 14, 17, 24, 32, 37, 50, 51, 53, 54, 63, 127, 128, 131, 132, 133, 136, 152, 153, 164, 169, 181, 192, 215, 217, 218, 228, 230, 233, 239
Indo-European 27
Indo-Sinitic 164
Indra 181
Infinite Life. *See* Amitāyus
inka, inka shōmei 132, 138, 139, 145
Inner Asia 140
Inner Asia program 136
Insight tradition (*see also vipassanā*) xvi
Institute for Canonical Translation 52
Institute of Buddhist Studies xix, 3, 147, 175, 240, 243
"Instructing Members of the Society" 123
intentionality 19, 20, 24, 25, 29
interdependence 12, 24
International Association of Shin Buddhist Studies xii, 213

interreligious vii, 140, 201, 202, 203, 212, 213, 229
Isaiah 162
Ise 74
Isetani, Isao, Rev. and Mrs. 210, 214
Isetani, Kuniko 210, 214
Ishida, Mitsuyuki 230
Islam 156, 203
"I-Thou" 162, 164, 166
Itsuki, Hiroyuki 167, 212

J

Jaffe, Richard M. 73
Jambu River 69
Japan xvi, 31, 38, 40, 54, 58, 63, 85, 100, 132, 134, 138, 139, 163, 164, 191, 192, 198, 200, 201, 202, 205, 206, 207, 208, 209, 210, 216, 228, 231
  postwar period 201, 208
Japanese xvi, 31, 38, 40, 41, 49, 54, 57, 58, 63, 64, 73, 81, 85, 134, 201, 206, 207, 208, 212
  Buddhism, Buddhist(s) 58, 74, 159, 161, 189, 214
  pilgrim(s) 38, 54
  Pure Land (*see also* Pure Land [as sect, school, tradition]) 45, 46, 74, 152, 184
  religion 58, 73, 75, 134
  Shingon 44
  Sino- 60, 64, 65
  society 192, 206, 207
  Tendai 54, 207
  Zen 73
Japanese American(s) 78, 79
Japanese language, text(s) viii, 53, 65, 71, 80, 138, 175, 202, 212, 214
Jesuit 139
Jesus (*see also* Christ) 152, 160, 179, 203, 229, 230
Jewish (*see also* Judaism) 164
Jiangbei 126
Jiangbei Scriptural Press 126
Jiang Canteng 123
Jiangsu province 96
Jiangxi 91
Jiangyou 91
Jiao Hong 93
Jiaxing da zang jing 101
Jigdal Dagchen Sakya 136
jinen 82, 220
Jin'gangding jing guanzizaiwang rulai xiu xing fa 39, 40, 44
Jin'gangding jing yuqie guanzizaiwang rulai xiu xing fa 39, 44
Jin'gangding texts 39–40
Jing River 91
Jingshan Gao chansi fasi 94
Jingtu jingguan yaomen 102
Jingtu jue 112, 125
Jingtu shengxian lu 124
Jingtu shi yao 101
jinshi degree 89, 91, 92, 93, 95, 96, 97
Jinxie bian (*see also Gold Shavings*) 90
jiriki (*see also* self-power) xiv, 82, 208
Jiujing yisheng baoxing lun 103
Jiu pin wang sheng Amituo sanmadi ji tuoluoni jing 39, 40, 55
Jōdo Shinshū ix, xiii, xiv, xvi, 3, 4, 5, 19, 58, 59, 77, 78, 79, 80, 81, 83, 134, 200, 201
  Higashi (Eastern) branch 200
  Nishi (Western) branch 200
Jōdo wasan. See Hymns of the Pure Land
John 162
Jones, Charles B. xix, 89–126, 243
Journal of Buddhist Ethics 127
Judaism (*see also* Jewish) 154, 207
juhachi dō (*see also* Eighteenfold Way; *Shiba dao*) 31, 41, 53, 55
jukai. See ordination, lay
Jungian theory 172
juren degree 92, 99
Jushi zhuan 124

K

Kabbalah, Kabbalistic 154–55, 160, 164, 172

Kagiya lineage 59, 60, 70
Kagyu lineage 133
Kaishinshō 57
Kaiyuan catalogue 53
Kaiyuan shijiao lu 52
kaji (*see also adhiṣṭhana*) 70
Kajiyama, Yuichi 233, 236
Kakuban 73
Kakunyo 176, 177, 182
kakure 74
kirishitan. See Christian(s), underground
nenbutsu 58, 59, 60, 74
kakushi nenbutsu 58, 59, 60, 67
Kālacakra 140
Kālayaśas 31
*kalpa*s 223, 224, 225, 236
kalyāṇamitra(s) (*see also* friend, good, spiritual; *zenchishiki*) 67, 129, 133, 143
Kamakura period 58, 207
Buddhism 73, 169, 207
Kamakura Shin-bukkyō Kenkyū 214
kambun texts 175
Kanamatsu, Kenryo 167
Kaneko, Daiei 201
Kanshomon 125
Kantian 164
Kapilavastu 235
Kapleau, Philip 134
karma, karmic 7, 10, 11, 12, 13, 14, 15, 32, 140, 159, 179, 183, 193, 198, 211, 231
Karma Kagyu lineage 136, 137
Karmapa(s) 133
first (*see also* Dusum Khyenpa) 133
seventeenth (*see also* Trinley, Ngawang Ugyen; Wangyal, Ngawang) 133
sixteenth (*see also* Gyalwa Karmapa) 137
Karma Triyana Dharmacakra 137
Karmê-Chöling (*see also* "Tail of the Tiger") 136
Kaufman, Gordon 215, 216, 217, 239
Kawahashi, Noriko 210, 214
Kechog Palmo, Sister (*see also* Bedi, Freda) 136
kengyō (*see also* open teachings) 57, 58
Kennedy, Robert Jinsen 139
Kexue zhai jinji 122, 123
Khetsun Sangpo 5, 6, 18, 20, 29
kimyō 63, 64, 65
Kitayama, Shinobu 24
Kiyota, Min 3
Kiyozawa, Manshi 201, 212
Klein, Anne C. 27
*kōan*s 164
Kōbō Daishi (*see also* Kūkai) 57
Korea, Korean 132, 212
Kornfield, Jack 135
Ko Sa Myun 212
Kripal, Jeffrey 7
Krishna 203
kṣetra (*see also* buddha land; land) 32, 47
Kuiji 103
Kūkai (*see also* Kōbō Daishi) 38, 53, 58
kuladuhitṛ, kulaputra. See good family, daughters, sons of
Kunga, Thartse 135, 136
Kuroda, Hakujun 139
Kuroda Institute 139
Kyōgyōshinshō (*see also True Teaching, Practice, and Realization of the Pure Land Way, The*) 161, 175, 176, 181, 184, 186, 194, 210
Kyoto 59, 125, 200, 210, 241
Kyoto school 201
Kyoto University 234

L

Ladakh 14
laity (*see also* lay; layman, laymen; laypeople, layperson; laywomen) 104, 128, 131, 150, 151, 168
lakṣana (*see also* mark) 47, 49

lama(s) 15, 18, 19, 27, 48, 49, 135, 171
incarnate (*see also tulku*) 140
Lamotte, Étienne 129
land(s) 68, 69, 70, 104, 107, 111, 114, 116, 118, 140, 193, 195
of bliss, happiness, utmost bliss 178, 182, 217
buddha, Buddha's 33, 65, 66, 95, 104, 105, 109, 112, 113, 187, 216, 218, 231, 236, 238
fulfilled xv, 193
of peace, tranquil, of tranquility 65, 67, 72, 193, 216, 217
pure (*see also* Pure Land [as place]) 10, 53, 105, 109, 116
three 69, 70
Land of Peace (*see also* Pure Land [as place]; Sukhāvatī) 217
Land of Utmost Bliss (*see also* Sukhāvatī) 117
Larger Pure Land Sutra, Larger Sutra (*see also Larger Sukhāvatīvyūha-sūtra*) 181, 186, 210, 218
Larger Sukhāvatīvyūha-sūtra (*see also Larger Pure Land Sutra, Larger Sutra; Sukhāvatīvyūha-sūtra*) 218
last period of the teachings (*see also mappō*) 32, 44
Latin America 206
Latin, Latinate (language) viii, 153
Laws of Manu 181
lay (*see also* laity; layman, laymen; laypeople, layperson; laywomen) 44, 77, 79, 85, 90, 111, 118, 119, 128, 129, 131, 138, 205, 206, 240
layman, laymen xii, 90, 95, 120, 124, 128, 129, 229
Layman Stonehead (*see also* Yuan Hongdao) 91
laypeople, layperson(s) 77, 81, 111
laywomen 128, 129, 229
"lecture-mat sickness" 111
Levine, Sarah 150
Lianchi (*see also* Yunqi Zhuhong; Zhuhong) 97
liberation x, 8, 12, 13, 14, 15, 16, 17, 67, 128, 190, 191, 214, 236
liberation theology 206
life force 234, 235, 236, 237
Life of Awakening: The Heart of the Shin Buddhist Path, A 4
lineage(s) 4, 38, 57, 92, 127, 130, 131, 132, 133, 134, 139, 140, 145, 186, 221
Kagiya 59
Kagyu, Karma Kagyu 133, 136, 137
Pure Land (*see also* Pure Land [as sect, school, tradition]) 164, 221, 227
Rinzai 134
Sōtō 134, 138
Vajrayana 133
Zen 138, 139
literary xiv, 89, 90, 92, 95, 97, 98, 99, 100, 102, 120, 131, 201, 212
literati 93, 99
Li Tongxuan 102, 103–104, 115
Little Buddha 140
liturgy 8, 9, 11, 20, 25
Liu-Song dynasty 50
Liu zu tang jing jielu 90
living being(s) (*see also* being[s]; human being; sentient being) 109, 110, 115, 118, 236
Li Zhi 95, 98, 99, 110, 112, 120, 123, 125
Locho Rinpoche 27
Lokeśvararāja 224
Lokottaravādin school 218
Longqing era 91
Lord of Death 9
Los Angeles 135, 139
lotus 8, 33, 34, 41, 67, 69, 70, 72, 96, 116
maṇḍala 34, 41, 70
repository world 217
samādhi 72
Lotus family 33, 36, 40
Lotus Sutra 21, 102, 105, 106, 114, 181
Lovejoy, Arthur 156

lunar disc. *See* disc, lunar, moon
Lunzhu 47
Luther, Martin ix, 152, 159

M

Macheng 95
Mādhyamika(s) xiv, 113, 114, 230
Madihe Pannaseeha Thera 135
Maezumi, Taizan 134, 139
Mahabodhi Society of USA 145
Mahākāśyapa 132
Mahāsaṃghika 218
Mahāsi Sayadaw 135
Mahāvagga 130
Mahāvairocana (*see also* Dainichi) 39, 61, 63
Mahāvairocanabhisaṃbodhi-sūtra 37, 38, 41, 43, 44, 45, 53, 54
Mahāvairocana-sūtra (*see also Mahāvairocanabhisaṃbodhi-sūtra*) 42
Mahāvaṃsa 144
Mahāvyutpatti 50
Mahayana xv, 21, 42, 51, 106, 112, 130, 133, 141, 142, 154, 181, 218, 219, 221, 230, 236, 239
  Buddhism, Buddhist xix, 21, 84, 129, 161, 218
  literature, scripture(s), text(s) xv, 37, 47, 131, 218
Mahinda 127
Maitreya 109, 184
maṇḍala(s) 32, 33, 40, 44, 45, 47, 51, 53, 61, 70, 74, 75
  dual, twin 38, 41, 42, 44, 53, 63, 75
  eight-petaled, eight-section 33, 34
  Garbha, Garbhakośa 41, 63
  Womb 63, 70, 74
  Vajradhātu 53, 63
Mañjuśrī 38, 39
mantra(s) x, 4, 5, 9, 33, 34, 35, 36, 37, 40, 41, 42, 46, 51, 63, 73
  Great *Samaya* True *Lakṣana* (True Mark) 40, 47, 55
  heart- 51
  hundred-syllable 9
  seed 63
  siddham 49, 53
manual(s) 31, 32, 36, 38, 39, 41, 42, 43, 44, 45, 49, 52
  esoteric 31, 36–37, 38, 39, 41, 42, 44, 49
  ritual 36, 38, 39
mappō (*see also* age, last, of the last period of the teachings; dharma, last age, latter days of; last period of the teaching) 183, 190
māras 34
Maria Kannon Zen Center 243
mark(s) 31, 34, 35, 36, 47, 48, 55
  eighty minor 33, 50, 55, 85
  thirty-two major 33, 50, 55, 185
Markus, Rose 24
Marlowe, Christopher xiii
Marpa 133
martial arts 22
martyrs 21
Maruyama, Teruo 214
mātṛkā-dharas. *See* abhidarma, masters
Matsumoto, Shiro 214
Matsuoka, Soyu 134
Mauldin, Michael 29
May Fourth Movement 90
May, Gerald G. 18, 19, 20, 21
McDonald, Joren 81
medical, medicine xi, 10, 11, 13, 14, 15, 16, 78, 85
Medicine Buddha 15
meditation(s), meditative viii, xvii, 5, 11, 12, 13, 14, 15, 16, 25, 35, 43, 46, 47, 55, 65, 82, 84, 116, 118, 119, 120, 132, 135, 149, 150, 151, 214
  Vajrasattva 3, 5–6, 7, 8, 14, 15, 16
Meditation Sutra 111
Meiji Restoration 201
mendicants 128, 129
Mengxi village 91
mental 63, 81, 113, 161, 226, 228
mental health 11, 13, 16, 22, 23

merit(s) 10, 33, 128, 193, 194, 196, 198, 203
Messiah x
metaphysical, metaphysician(s), metaphysics 154, 155, 157, 162, 163, 164
Method of the Secret Dhāraṇī of the Three Types of Accomplishment That Obliterate the Hells and Convert and Expel the Karmic Obstructions in the Triple World 54
Miaoxi (*see also* Dahui Zonggao) 94
mikkyō (*see also* esoteric; secret) 57, 58, 59, 61, 65, 70, 71, 73
Milarepa xvi, 133
mind(s) xiii, 5, 6, 7, 24, 34, 35, 47, 60, 62, 63, 65, 66, 67, 69, 79, 81, 83, 85, 94, 95, 103, 107, 108, 112, 113, 114, 115, 132, 164, 166, 177, 180, 186, 194, 195, 197, 199, 201, 204, 211, 216, 217, 218, 222, 226, 228, 229, 231
  darkened, defiled, deluded xv, 46, 108
  enlightened 113, 116
  entrusting, of reliance (*see also shinjin*) 194, 195–96. 197, 203, 204, 225
  of great compassion 197, 198, 199
  one, single (*see also* One Mind) 96, 97, 106, 194
  pure, purified xv, 229, 235
  self-striving 177, 178
  settled 178, 179, 180
  true 178, 194
mind-only (*see also* consciousness-only) 65, 97, 105, 107, 108, 110, 112, 113, 118, 120, 121, 229
Ming dynasty 89, 90, 91, 93, 100, 101, 102, 111, 112, 115, 119, 120
Minghuang Xinshu (*see also* Xuanzong, Emperor) 94
minister(s) 79, 81, 114, 182, 240
Ministry of Personnel 99
Mipham Rinpoche (*see also* Ösel Rangdröl Mukpo) 137, 141
miscellaneous teachings 57
Mitsuya, Dake 3
Mochizuki, Shinkō 90
modern, modernity, modernization (*see also* anti-modernism; postmodern) xiii, xiv, 10, 12, 17, 18, 22, 23, 37, 90, 91, 101, 115, 128, 132, 133, 150, 153, 156, 157, 158, 161, 165, 168, 176, 201, 202, 216, 223, 228, 229, 230
  medicine, psychology 10, 11, 13
  science, scientific 150, 151, 216
modernism, Buddhist 148, 150, 151, 152, 153, 165, 168
Modon Dremo 9
Mohe zhiguan 103
monastery(ies) 38, 51, 192
monastic x, 45, 111, 118, 127, 128, 130, 131, 133, 136, 138, 139, 169, 181, 183
  community (*see also* sangha) 128, 130, 131, 142
monasticism, monasticization 128, 132, 150, 151, 168
Mongol 51, 207
monk(s) (*see also* clergy; priest) ix, 37, 67, 68, 69, 95, 97, 98, 100, 101, 111, 112, 117, 120, 127, 128, 129, 130, 131, 133, 135, 138, 141, 150, 151, 183, 229
monotheism 204
monshu. See abbot(s)
moon disc. *See* disc, lunar, moon
moral, moralistic, morality x, 14, 17, 20, 24, 80, 109, 110, 151, 154, 170
Mt. Baldy Zen Center 135
Mt. Hiei 80, 192
mudrā(s) 33, 34, 35, 36, 41
Musashino University 215, 243
mystical, mysticism 155, 161, 162, 164, 165, 172, 221, 230, 231, 232
mystics 156, 162
myth(s), mythic, mythological, mythology(ies) 24, 97, 120, 158, 181, 216, 220, 223, 225, 227, 228, 232, 236

mythopoetic 232

N

Nabeshima, Naoki 3
nāgā(s) 195
Nāgārjuna 102, 110, 166, 221
Nakamura, Hisashi 210
nalandabodhi.org 133
Nalanda Foundation 136, 141
namas (*see also namu, Namu*) 64
Name (*see also namu, Namu*) 4, 82, 193, 194, 232, 237
Namō Āmi-tuo-fo (*see also Namu Amida Butsu;* nenbutsu) 97
namu, Namu (*see also* Name) 59, 62, 63, 64, 65, 69, 178, 193
Namu Amida Butsu (*see also* nenbutsu) x, 59, 63, 64, 66, 162, 177, 178, 180, 221, 224, 232, 234, 237, 238
Nara 54
Nāropa 133
Native American 157–158
Naturalness: A Classic of Shin Buddhism 167
Near Eastern religion 160
nectar 9, 19
nenbutsu (*see also Namu Amida Butsu; nianfo*) ix, xiv, 3, 58, 63, 64, 68, 69, 71, 72, 77, 80, 83, 84, 85, 164, 178, 179, 180, 195, 196, 197, 198, 199, 237
  himitsu 58, 73
  kakure 58, 59, 60, 74
  kakushi 58, 59, 60, 67
Neo-Confucian, Neo-Confucianism (*see also* Confucian, Confucianism) 94, 100
Neoplatonic, Neoplatonism 154, 157, 158, 160, 163, 164
Nepal 6
neuroscience 85
New Jersey 135
New Mexico 139
New York 134, 137
New York Buddhist Academy 229
New York Times 22
nian (*see also* recollection) 46, 47, 49, 108
nianfo (*see also* nenbutsu) 46, 49, 97, 102, 106, 107, 109, 164
Nichiren 134, 207, 211
Nichiren school, Nichirenites 58, 74, 147, 214
nikāya tradition(s) 129, 131
nirmāṇakāya (*see also* body[ies], of buddha, three, triple) 61, 62, 68, 73, 218
nirvana xv, 63, 66, 67, 177, 184, 190, 193, 195, 217
  complete, final, supreme 67, 68, 196, 211, 220
  without retrogression 188
Nirvana Sutra 102
no-birth, non-birth 67, 72, 182, 219
non-Asian 135
non-being 69
non-Buddhist(s) 74, 128
nondual, nondualistic, nonduality xviii, 4, 5, 61, 63, 68, 74, 110, 113, 226, 228
Nonomura, Naotarō 228, 235
nonvirtue(s) (*see also* virtue) 8, 17, 18, 23, 24, 25
North America, North American 85, 135, 136, 137, 209, 210
North Carolina ix
Notes on "Essentials of Faith Alone" 217, 220
Notes on the Rebirth of Women. See Nyōnin ōjō kikigaki
Novak, Philip 149, 151
novice(s) (*see also śrāmaṇera*) 130, 132, 136
Numrich, Paul 127, 135, 141, 142
nun(s) 59, 70, 74, 128, 129, 229
Nyingma Institute 136
Nyingma tradition 3, 5, 6, 136
Nyōnin ōjō kikigaki 182

Nyoshin 57, 60, 61, 70, 72
nyūga ganyū 59

O

obsessive-compulsive disorder 13
obstruction(s) 7, 8, 9, 10, 12, 15, 51, 113, 126
Ocean: An Introduction to Jodo-Shinshu Buddhism in America 213
Odiyan Retreat Center 136
offering(s) 10, 33, 34
  four 39
  universal 35, 36, 41
Ofumi (*see also Gobunshō*) 186
Ōhara, Shōjitsu 231, 235
Ohtani, Koshin 210
ōjō (*see also* Pure Land [as place], birth, rebirth in) 66–67
Oka, Ryōji 233–34, 236
Olcott, Henry Steel 168
Ōmine, Akira 232, 235
omniscient 21
One, the 164, 167
One Dharma: The Emerging Western Buddhism 143
One Mind (*see also* mind, one, single) 106
oneness 4, 167, 177, 178, 186, 192, 217, 220, 222–23, 224
On Jinen Hōni 220
Ono, Gemmyo 125
"On Secret Teachings" 74
Open Court Publishing Company 134
open teachings (*see also kengyō*) 57
ordination(s) 130, 132, 138, 154
  full 130, 136
  lay 138
  monastic 138
  novitiate 130
Originary Enlightenment: Tendai Hongaku Doctrine and Japanese Buddhism 214
Oriyas 17
Orzech, Charles D. xix, 31–55, 243
Osabe, Kazuo 41, 50
Osaka, Koryu 139
Ösel Rangdröl Mukpo (*see also* Mipham Rinpoche) 141
Ösel Tendzin (*see also* Rich, Thomas F.) 136, 141
ōsō. *See* Pure Land [as place], going forth to
Ōtani University 202, 210, 234
other, Other, the 6, 7, 16, 148, 159
other-power (*see also tariki*) xiv, xv, xvi, 4, 19, 45, 55, 66, 80, 81, 153, 177, 178, 179, 180, 183, 204, 228
Outline of the Platform Sutra. See Liu zu tang jing jielu
Ouyi Zhixu (*see also* Zhixu) 100, 115

P

Pacific World: Journal of the Institute of Buddhist Studies 213
Pagels, Elaine 21
Pāli viii, xiv, 129, 130
Pan Guiming 90
paradox, paradoxical 162, 163, 166, 167, 178
parivrājaka. *See* community, wanderers'
passion(s) 21, 66, 68, 83, 191, 222, 224
path xii, xvii, xix, 19, 23, 79, 83, 84, 106, 161, 164, 195, 212, 225
  of awakening, enlightenment, realization xv, 160, 183, 192
  bodhisattva 82
  difficult 45, 195
  easy, quick 45
  eightfold 153
  of practice 77
  Pure Land (*see also* Pure Land [as sect, school, tradition]) 197, 227
  of sages 197
  self-power xvi, 80
  of transformation 84
patriarch(s) 140
  eighth, of the Pure Land tradition (*see also* Yunqi Zhuhong) 96

first Chinese Chan (*see also* Bodhidharma) 132
first Indian (*see also* Mahākāśyapa) 132
ninth, of the Pure Land tradition (*see also* Ouyi Zhixu) 100
Pure Land (*see also* Pure Land [as sect, school, tradition]) 120, 227
patriarchal 181, 185
Pavlova, Anna 80
Payne, Richard K. xix–xx, 3, 47, 51, 55, 74, 147–72, 243
Peng Jiqing 124
People magazine xvii
perennialism, perennialist 155, 156, 157, 158, 161, 162, 165
perfection 18, 20–21, 22, 23, 24
perfections, six 21, 109
Perkins School of Theology 189, 243
Philadelphia 22
Philippines 206
philological 193
philosopher(s), philosophical, philosophy 89, 96, 100, 103, 107, 113, 118, 119, 120, 152, 163, 164, 193, 201, 204, 230, 233
Mahayana 230, 236
Pilgrim of the Clouds 95
Platform Sutra 112
Platonic thought (*see also* Neoplatonic, Neoplatonism) 154
"Playfulness of *Tariki*, The" ix, xiii–xiv
Plotinus 154
Poden Gyalpo 9
poet(s), poetic, poetry (*see also* mythopoetic) 89, 92, 98, 99, 100, 111, 120, 163, 186, 201, 212, 232, 235
post-Enlightenment 189
postmodern, postmodernism, postmodernist xx, 7, 73, 189, 200, 201, 202, 213
postulant(s) (*see also haengja*) 132
power(s) xiv, 10, 25, 46, 68, 71, 81, 98, 105, 107, 109, 155, 162, 164, 166, 167, 177, 180, 182, 183, 192, 196, 199, 208, 209, 221, 225
of Amida, Amitabha (*see also* other-power) xv, 105, 192, 194, 198, 199, 204, 209
of the Buddha, buddhas 45, 107, 152
four, of confession 19
individual, personal (*see also* self-power) 82, 195, 198
innate 220, 221
transcendent 198, 199
powerlessness 159, 190, 192, 203, 204
PowerPoint viii
Powers, John 140
practice(s), praxis viii, ix, x, xvi, xvii, 4, 5, 6, 7, 10, 11, 12, 13, 14, 15, 16, 17, 19, 20, 24, 25, 35, 38, 45, 46, 47, 55, 59, 67, 77, 78–79, 80, 82, 83, 84, 85, 89, 93, 98, 101, 102, 103, 104, 105, 106, 107, 108, 109, 111, 113, 116, 117, 119, 120, 123, 133, 134, 138, 140, 150, 151, 161, 180, 190, 191, 194, 195, 196, 203, 204, 205, 207, 209, 214, 224
calming 135
Chan, Zen xvi, 118, 134
esoteric 45, 46, 47, 54, 55
great 194, 195, 196, 198
Insight xvi
Jōdo Shinshū 77, 79, 80
lay 77
mantra 42
meditative, meditation, meditational xvii, 12, 46, 55, 149, 151, 214
mikkyō 58
mixed, sundry 180, 184
nenbutsu, *nianfo* ix, 3, 102, 106, 109, 164
Pure Land (*see also* Pure Land [as sect, school, tradition]) 47, 66, 75, 95, 96, 97, 100, 102, 106, 107, 108, 110, 112, 114, 115, 116, 117, 118, 218
of releasing life 97

practice(s) (*continued*)
  recitation 5, 35, 203, 204, 237
  self-power 83
  Shingon 51
  of the six perfections 21
  tantric 3, 4, 47, 60
  Tibetan 4, 5, 22
  Vajrasattva 4, 5, 6, 7, 12, 13, 15, 19, 20, 21–22, 27
  visualization 9, 15
Practice of Chinese Buddhism 1900–1950, The 131
praṇidhāna. See vows, of Amida
pratyekabuddhas 106
Pratyutpannasamādhi-sūtra 102
Prebish, Charles S. xix, 127–45, 243
precept(s) 102, 110, 111, 138
  five lay 119
  ten grave 138
  three pure 138
preceptor(s) 38, 130
priest(s) (*see also* clergy; monk) 52, 139, 168, 206, 229, 233
  Episcopal vii
  Jesuit 139
  Nichiren 214
  Shin 171, 205, 210
primal vow, Primal Vow. *See* vow, primal
propagation 147, 175, 176, 178, 200
Protestant, Protestantism (*see also* Christian, Christianity) 150, 151, 152, 153, 158, 161, 165, 168, 220
psychological, psychology (*see also* bio-psychological) 6, 10, 11, 12, 13, 14, 16, 24, 25, 26, 151, 163
psychosomatic 11, 25
psychotherapeutic, psychotherapist(s), psychotherapy (*see also* therapeutic, therapist) 3, 11, 22, 243
puṇya. See merit
Pure Land (as place) xv, 31, 33, 34, 36, 39, 44, 45, 48, 54, 64, 65, 66, 67, 68, 70, 102, 105, 106, 107, 108, 109, 111, 112, 113, 114, 115, 116, 118, 167, 181, 182, 184, 194, 195, 196, 197, 198, 199, 203, 208, 211, 215, 216, 217, 218, 219, 220, 222, 223, 224, 225, 226, 227, 228, 229, 230, 231, 233, 235, 236, 237, 239, 240
  birth, rebirth in 31, 32, 34, 44, 45, 47, 59, 67, 74, 79, 95, 107, 109, 110, 112, 114, 117, 180, 181, 184, 196, 222, 237
  going forth to 194, 196
  of nine classes 53
  seven decorated forms of, seven-jeweled 114, 216, 219, 228
  of Vairocana 115, 116
  vision, visualization of 31, 33, 35, 36, 45, 46, 47
  Western 31, 61, 105, 109, 116, 229
Pure Land (as sect, school, tradition) 36, 39, 46, 47, 55, 58, 59, 62, 63, 64, 65, 73, 89, 96, 97, 98, 101, 102, 103, 104, 105, 106, 107, 108, 112, 113, 115, 116, 133, 148, 149, 153, 155, 158, 159, 164, 165, 176, 192, 215, 218, 219, 221, 222, 231
  belief, faith, piety 102, 196, 198, 201
  Buddhism, Buddhist(s) ix, x, xix, 31, 101, 147, 148, 149, 152, 158, 159, 160, 161, 162, 164, 165, 189, 190, 196, 199, 200, 201, 202, 203, 205, 207, 209, 210, 213, 214, 215, 217, 218, 219, 228, 229, 230, 238
  in China, Chinese 46, 90, 101, 112, 124, 125
  devotee(s), practitioner(s) 108, 113, 114, 124, 203, 208, 209
  doctrine 58, 62, 63, 171
  esotericized 58, 67
  concept(s), ideas, notion 45, 46, 105, 115, 160
  Japanese 45, 46, 75, 152, 184
  lineage, lineage-holders, patriarchs 120, 164, 221, 227
  mind-only 105, 112, 120, 121, 229

normative 58, 65, 75
other-direction 112
path, way 197, 204, 218, 227
practice(s) 47, 66, 75, 95, 96, 97, 100, 102, 106, 107, 110, 112, 114, 115, 116, 117, 118, 218
sutras 181, 191, 215, 218, 221, 231
teaching(s) 107, 117, 164, 181, 182, 184, 190, 195, 200, 203, 209, 213, 218, 224, 235
thinker(s) 45, 46, 100, 115, 215
thought 58, 67, 70, 90, 91, 96, 97, 98, 100, 102, 108, 112, 115, 120, 159, 161, 171, 202, 203, 232
western-direction 112, 113, 117, 118, 120, 121, 226
writings, work, text 111, 112, 115, 118, 120
Pure Land: Journal of the International Association of Shin Buddhist Studies, The xii, 213
purification, purificatory, purified, purify(ing) 6, 8, 9, 10, 11, 12, 13, 15, 19, 33, 34, 35, 36, 41, 46, 112, 115, 140, 150, 152, 231, 232, 235

Q

Qian Bocheng 90
Qing dynasty 89, 101, 120
Qiu Minjie 90, 115, 125
Qixin lun shu bi xiao ji 125
Questions about the Pure Land 102
Quli, Natalie xx
Qu Ruji 93

R

Ragnaröok 157
raigō, raikō 184, 185
Rambelli, Fabio 73
Ray, Reginald 128
reality 11, 12, 26, 69, 71, 80, 83, 102, 108, 110, 115, 117, 132, 148, 154, 160, 171, 178, 195, 216, 221, 222, 223, 227, 230, 231, 232, 235, 237, 238, 239
conditioned 11
ordinary, physical 19, 113
true 194, 195, 226, 232
ultimate viii, 107, 113, 117, 190, 192, 193, 194, 196, 200, 204, 222, 232
realization(s) x, 4, 5, 24, 31, 110, 117, 166, 179, 185, 190, 191, 192, 194, 195, 204, 211, 231
ultimate 194, 203, 204, 205
realm(s) 11, 31, 44, 48, 63, 109, 178, 193, 205, 218, 229, 231
ethereal, formless 109, 159
garbhakoṣa 62, 63
inconceivable 46
lower, unfortunate 44, 68
of nirvana, transcendent 162, 217
of non-birth 219
pure heavenly 12
sahā (*see also sahā* realm, world) 231, 237
six 10, 198
vajrakoṣa 62, 63
of wisdom 107
Realm of Ease and Nurturance (*see also* Pure Land [as place]) 235
Realm of Immeasurable Light (*see also* Pure Land [as place]) 226
rebirth 7, 11, 13, 17, 32, 70, 102, 109, 114, 115, 116, 117, 129, 178, 184
highest, upper 34, 40, 47
nine classes, levels of 31, 40, 74
in the Pure Land, Sukhāvatī 31, 32, 34, 45, 59, 67, 107, 109, 112, 114, 117, 180, 181, 184, 193
six realms of 10
in Tuṣita Heaven 109
in the universal self 162, 167
of women 181, 182, 183
receptivity (*see also* willingness) 20, 22
recitation 3, 4, 5, 8, 20, 35, 36, 45, 48, 63, 80, 105, 108, 109, 164, 179, 180, 195, 196, 197, 199, 203
recollection(s) 32, 35, 46, 47

Recorded Sayings of Chan Master Tianmu Mingben 93
Recorded Sayings of Dahui Zonggao 93
Record of Lament of Divergences, A (*see also Tannishō*) 198
Reformation, the 161
refuge xiv, 8, 9, 19, 25, 64, 140, 182, 184
  formula 130
refugees 91, 136
religion(s) vii, viii, ix, x, 39, 54, 58, 78, 83, 90, 120, 127, 148, 150, 151, 152, 153, 155, 156, 157, 158, 160, 162, 163, 165, 166, 167, 168, 170, 171, 172, 176, 177, 180, 205, 230
  civil 20
  five characteristics of 159, 160
  Christian, Protestant 154, 161
  of East Asia, Eastern 54, 160
  Greek 157
  of India 152
  Japanese 58, 73, 75, 134
  Western 58
Religions of Man, The (*see also World's Religions: Our Great Wisdom Traditions*) 147, 149, 152, 158
religious ix, xii, xiii, xv, 15, 19, 21, 22, 38, 58, 77, 85, 89, 98, 104, 120, 129, 131, 139, 147, 148, 150, 156, 160, 161, 163, 164, 171, 172, 176, 177, 182, 189, 190, 200, 202, 203, 205, 206, 207, 209, 214, 216, 228, 229, 231, 232, 235
  centers, circles, community(ies), group(s), institution(s), organization, sanghas 74, 128, 136, 176, 190, 199, 200, 201, 202, 204, 209, 213
  concepts, ideas, notions, teaching, thought 73, 90, 91, 100, 148, 150, 155, 156, 165, 189, 204, 207, 212
  cultivation 98, 109, 110
  culture, environment, landscape, milieu 12, 32, 37, 39, 100, 133, 161, 201
  devotion, faith xii, 5, 163, 177
  experience 5, 7, 192, 201
  history 151, 161, 201
  life 21, 89, 90, 123, 137, 177, 179, 196
  message 190, 192, 200, 201, 203, 204, 205
  practice(s), praxis xvi, 13, 89, 116, 123, 204, 205, 209
  studies 27, 147, 153, 158
  symbol(s), symbolism 163, 205, 220
  tradition(s) viii, 155, 156, 163, 184, 189, 190, 202, 203, 204
  value(s) 150, 151, 161
  view(s), worldview 163, 165, 180, 192, 196, 199, 202
Rennyo 58, 74, 79, 167, 175–85, 186, 201, 210
renunciation 130, 181
Renwang jing. See Scripture for Humane Kings
returning, phase of, to the world 196, 208, 235
Revelation 163
revival, revivalism, revivalists 93, 150–51, 159
Rhodes, Robert 210
Rice University 27
Rich, Thomas F. (*see also* Ösel Tendzin) 136, 141
Rigpa Fellowship 136
Rinzai 58, 134
rite(s), ritual(s) 32, 33, 35, 36, 37, 39, 40, 41, 43, 44, 45, 47, 50, 52, 54, 59, 132, 140, 151, 168, 176, 196
  area, arena 33, 34, 35, 36, 38, 41
  commentaries 45, 53
  esoteric, *mikkyō* 36, 38, 41, 42, 44, 45, 46, 50, 52, 54, 70
  Kagiya 60
  manual(s), text(s) 36, 38, 39, 43, 44, 176
  Pure Land (*see also* Pure Land [as sect, school, tradition]) 59
  sequence 34, 36, 40, 41, 42, 50

Shingon 64
Vajradhatu 42
yankou 54
Rites for Contemplation and Offerings to Amitāyus Tathāgata. See Wuliangshou yigui
River of Fire, River of Water: An Introduction to the Pure Land Tradition of Shin Buddhism 213
Robinson, Richard H. 3
Rochester, New York 134
Roman Catholic (*see also* Catholic) 201
Romantic, Romanticism 156, 161, 162, 165
Rome 21
rōshi 138, 139
Rubin, Jeffrey 14
Ru'ilun 41, 42, 53
rūpakāya. See body(ies), of buddha, form
Russell, Bertrand xviii
Ryūkoku University 3, 210, 215, 228, 234

S

Saddharmapuṇḍarīka-sūtra. See Lotus Sutra
Sages and Worthies of the Pure Land 120
sahā realm, world 112, 114, 223, 231, 237
Saichō 58
Śākya, sons of 129
Sakya Center for Buddhist Studies and Meditation 136
Sakya Monastery of Tibetan Buddhism 136
Śākyamuni xiv, 57, 62, 68, 70, 73, 114, 116, 118, 131, 132, 191, 192, 197, 221, 223, 224, 227, 230, 235
Sakya Phuntsok Ling Center for Tibetan Buddhist Studies and Meditation 136
*Śākyaputrīyas-śrāmaṇa*s 128
Sakya Sheidrup Ling. *See* Sakya Center for Buddhist Studies and Meditation
Sakyong 143
salvation, salvific xiii, 18, 19, 45, 59, 64, 65, 105, 153, 154, 169, 184, 185, 198, 208
of women 175, 180, 181, 182, 185
Salzberg, Sharon 135
samādhi(s) 5
Amitāyus 35, 36, 47
Avalokiteśvara 34, 35, 36, 47
lotus blossom 72
of recollecting the Buddha 32, 49
Samantabhadra 38, 117
sāmanta feudalism 37, 51
Samantapāsādikā 144
samatha. See practice, calming
saṃbhogakāya (*see also* body[ies], of buddha, enjoyment, reward) 61, 62, 68, 69, 108, 218
samsara (*see also* birth and death) xv, 63, 65, 66, 69, 109
samurai 179
Saṃyutta-nikāya 129, 144
Sanford, James H. xix, 57–75, 243
San Francisco ix, xx, 134
San Francisco Zen Center (*see also* SFZC) 133, 138
sangha(s) (*see also* community) xiv, 127–28, 129, 130, 209
bhikṣu- 128
bhikṣunī- 128
cāturdisa- 128
fourfold, of the four quarters (*see also* four assemblies) 128, 129, 142
ubhayato- 128
Sanlun (*see also* Three Teachings) 117, 118
Sanskrit viii, 50, 52, 64, 71, 127, 133, 140, 161, 194, 230, 231
Santa Cruz, California 136, 148

Sanzhong xidipo diyu zhuan yezhang chu sanjie bimi tuoloni fa. See Method of the Secret Dhāraṇī of the Three Types of Accomplishment That Obliterate the Hells and Convert and Expel the Karmic Obstructions in the Triple World
Sarnath, India 14
Sartre, Jean-Paul 169
sarvajña. See omniscient
Sasaki, Joshu 135
scholar(s), scholarly, scholarship viii, ix, xii, xiii, xv, xix, 4, 37, 51, 85, 90, 93, 98, 101, 132, 147, 149, 166, 171, 175, 176, 213, 229, 230
  of Buddhism, Buddhist (*see also* Buddhologist) x, 6, 152, 207, 214, 233
  in China, Chinese 89, 90, 93, 101
  Christian, of Christianity ix, x, 229
  contemporary, modern, twentieth-century 37, 41, 89, 101, 115, 128, 227, 239
  Japanese 40
  Pure Land (*see also* Pure Land [as sect, school, tradition]) 189, 207
  Shin 160, 207, 215, 234
  Western viii, 58, 89, 90, 93
Schuon, Frithjof 156, 163, 170, 172
science, scientific (*see also* neuroscience) xiv, 60, 150, 151, 158, 160, 216, 232, 233
scripture(s) (*see also* sutra; treatise) 42, 48, 51, 55, 70, 104, 105, 106, 109, 110, 111, 117
Scripture for Humane Kings 38, 45, 53
Scripture on the Contemplation of the Buddha of Limitless Life (*see also Guan jing*) 31, 54
Seager, Richard 137, 140
"seal of approval." *See inka, inka shōmei*
Seattle, Washington 136
Second Founder. *See* Rennyo
Second Great Awakening 161
secret (*see also* esoteric; *mikkyō*) 51, 58, 59, 60, 72, 74, 80
  teaching(s) 57, 67, 74
  transmission 57, 60, 72
sect(s) 54, 58, 142, 159, 176, 180, 183
sectarian, sectarianism xix, 32, 42, 58, 169, 206
secular, secularism xiii, 5, 23, 132, 136, 157, 179, 185
Sedgwick, Mark 156, 170
seed mantras, syllables 9, 10, 63
self xiv–xv, 3, 24, 30, 51, 59, 67, 69, 70, 84, 116, 167, 229, 234
  universal 165, 166, 169
self-attachment, self-oriented, self-profit 20, 83, 62, 183
self-cultivation, self-development, self-help, self-improvement 17, 45, 150, 151, 236
self-knowledge, self-realization, self-understanding 24, 25, 191, 203, 205
self-power (*see also jiriki*) xiv, xvi, 3, 4, 19, 80, 83, 196, 198, 199, 204, 214, 225
"Self-Power Practice with Other-Power Attitude: An Interpretation of Mind in Shin Buddhism" xii, xiv–xvi
self-reflection, self-reflective 83, 84, 176
self-reliance, self-responsibility 20, 25, 81, 82, 154, 179
self-righteous, self-righteousness x, 229
self-striving 177, 178
sensei 79
sense perception, senses 10, 48, 108
sentient beings (*see also* being[s]; human being; living being) 61, 63, 64, 67, 68, 70, 82, 105, 109, 113, 115, 116, 191, 192, 193, 197, 198, 199, 217
Senzaki, Nyōgen 134
seven jewels, seven-jeweled 33, 114
Seven Sages 92
SFZC (*see also* San Francisco Zen Center) 138, 139

Shaanxi 94, 99
shaman 67
Shambhala International (*see also* Vajradhatu) 137, 141
Shandao 67, 71, 124, 181, 224, 233
Shanghai Museum of Art 101
Shanhu lin (*see also Coral Grove*) 90, 104, 118, 119, 125
Sheng wang jing (*see also Amituo guyin sheng wang tuoluoni jing*) 111
Shengyan, Ven. Dr. 120
Shiba chi yin 41, 49, 53
Shiba dao (*see also* Eighteenfold Way) 31, 33, 41
Shigaraki, Takamaro 4–5, 81, 83, 86, 210
Shigong (*see also* Yuan Hongdao) 91
shihō, shihō-risso (*see also* dharma, transmission) 133, 138, 233
shikaku (*see also* awakening, acquired) 61, 65, 71
Shimano, Eidō 134
Shimazu 59
shin (*see also shinjin*) 5, 60
Shin Buddhism, Buddhist (*see also* Jōdo Shinshū; Pure Land [as sect, school, tradition]; Shinshū) xii, xiii, xvi, xvii, xix, 5, 80, 82, 83, 85, 147, 148, 155, 159, 160, 162, 164, 165, 166, 167, 175, 176, 177, 180, 181, 183, 184, 185, 189, 190, 199, 200, 201, 202, 203, 205, 206, 207, 208, 209, 211, 212, 213, 214, 215, 216, 225, 226, 227, 229, 230, 233, 234, 235, 238, 239
  Higashi Hongwanji branch 234
  Hongwanji branch 175
  Nishi Hongwanji branch 234
  orthodoxy 86, 229
  priest(s) 171, 210, 233
  theology 189, 190, 209
"Shin Buddhism as a Member in the Global Communities of Faith" xiii
Shingon 31, 40, 41, 44, 45, 51, 54, 55, 57, 58, 59, 61, 63, 64, 65, 66, 69, 70, 73, 134
  Chūinryū tradition 36
Shingon jiten 40
shingyō (*see also shinjin*) 195
shinjin xv, 5, 80, 83, 86, 160, 161, 177, 178, 179, 182, 184, 186, 193, 194–95, 196, 197, 198, 199, 203, 211, 217, 221, 222, 225, 226, 228, 237, 238
  post- 225, 226, 228, 237, 239
  pre- 225, 226, 228, 237, 239
Shinran ix, xiii, xiv, xv, xvi, 4, 5, 57, 58, 60, 72, 74, 77, 80, 152, 161, 162–63, 164, 165, 175, 176, 177, 178, 179, 180, 181, 182, 184, 185, 186, 187, 189–209, 210, 211, 212, 213, 214, 215, 216–217, 219, 220, 221, 222, 223–25, 226–27, 228, 229, 232, 235, 237, 238, 239, 240, 241
Shinran and the Gospel of Pure Grace 213
Shinran: An Introduction to His Thought 213
"Shinran-ninshiki no hōtō" 206
Shinshū (*see also* Jōdo Shinshū; Shin) xvi, 60, 62, 77, 82, 231, 232
Shintō 58, 74, 156
Shitou jushi (*see also* Yuan Hongdao) 91
Shōshinge xv, 175, 180
Shuntian province 99
Shweder, Richard 6, 10, 11, 16, 17
Sichuan 51
siddhi 35, 55, 68, 69
Sigālovada-sutta 131
Śikṣānanda 50
śikṣāpadas. *See* ten principles of training
śīla (*see also* precepts) 97
Silver Springs, Maryland 136
Singer, Rabbi Don Ani Shalom 140
Sino-Japanese 60, 64, 65
sin(s) 8, 9, 33, 153, 154, 169, 181
  five major (*see also* five grave offenses, five heinous acts) 182–83

six elements 63
six perfections 21, 109
six realms of rebirth 10, 198
skillful means (*see also* compassionate means; expedient, expedient means) 225
Smaller Sukhāvatīvyūha-sūtra, Smaller Sutra 219, 231
Smith, Huston 147–67, 169, 170, 171, 172
Smith, Jonathan Z. 172
Society for Buddhist-Christian Studies 140
Sōen, Shaku 134
Soga, Ryōjin 201, 212
Sogyal Rinpoche 136
Soka Gakkai International xx
Sōkatsu, Shaku 134
sokushin jōbutsu 59, 65, 69
Song dynasty 52, 98
Sŏn master 132
Sonoma County, California 136
sono mama xix, 80, 184
Sopa, Lhundrup 135
soteriological, soteriology 14, 40, 44, 45, 51, 153, 159, 160, 175, 177, 178, 180, 185, 221, 222, 238
Sōtō 58, 132, 134, 137, 138, 139
souls, *hun* and *po* 62, 65
South Asia, South Asian 37, 38, 41, 43, 44, 49, 50, 51
Southern Methodist University 189, 243
Spock 23
spiritual viii, 4, 8, 13, 15, 18, 19, 20, 22, 23, 25, 26, 63, 69, 70, 85, 129, 131, 132, 133, 138, 141, 167, 179, 183, 185, 203, 212, 236, 237, 238, 239
  accomplishment(s), attainments 10, 69, 181
  family(ies) 127, 129, 131, 137, 138, 140, 143
  friend, friendship (*see also* friend, good, spiritual) 129, 130, 133
  heirs 131, 138–39
  kinship 60, 127, 128, 129, 130, 131, 132, 133, 137, 138, 139, 140, 141, 142
  leadership 137, 181, 199
  life 14, 18, 216, 235
  lineage(s) 131, 132
  materialism 81, 82, 83, 86
  path 212, 225
  tradition(s) 4, 13, 18, 22
  transformation 180, 228
  yearnings 189, 201, 213
spirituality viii, 13, 22, 58, 83, 147, 166, 185, 233
śraddhā (*see also* faith) 161
*śrāmaṇa*s, *Śākyaputrīya-* 128
śrāmaṇera(s) (*see also* novice) 130
śrāvaka(s) 106, 182
Sri Lanka (*see also* Ceylon) 127, 135
Staal, Fritz 51
stage(s) 15, 161, 211, 225, 241
  of fruition 68
  post-*shinjin* 31, 226, 228
  pre-*shinjin* 31, 226, 228
  rain cloud of the dharma 75
  tenth 75
  of the truly settled 195, 196
  of the uncreated 67
Star Trek 23
Steinfels, Peter 22
St. Francis xiii, 162
St. Ignatius 162
Stone, Jacqueline I. 73
Streng, Frederick J. 190
Śubhakrasiṃha 37, 38, 39, 44, 49, 52, 53
suchness (*see also* thusness) 68, 69, 70, 97, 194, 195
  dharma body as 217, 218, 220, 224
Sudhana 116–117
suffering xvi, 7, 10, 17, 21, 46, 81, 105, 108, 177, 191, 198, 199, 209, 217
Sugiura, Myodo 210, 214
Sukhāvatī (*see also* Pure Land [as place]) 32, 33, 34, 35, 47, 49, 164, 191, 195, 218, 223

birth in 32, 34, 47, 159, 160, 164, 193, 194

Sukhāvatīvyūha-sūtra (*see also Larger Sukhāvatīvyūha-sūtra; Smaller Sukhāvatīvyūha-sūtra*) 31, 181

śūnyatā (*see also* emptiness) 230, 231, 233

superstition(s), superstitious 150, 151, 152, 177

Śūraṅgama-sūtra 106

Susiddhikara Sutra (*see also Susiddhi-mahākara-tantra*) 52

Susiddhimahākara-tantra 37, 41, 42, 43, 44, 45, 52, 53

Susiddhi tradition 41, 42, 44, 53

sutra(s) (*see also* scripture; treatise) 57, 104, 117, 224, 231

Pure Land (*see also* Pure Land [as sect, school, tradition]) 191, 215, 218, 221, 231

Suxidijielo gongyang fa 41, 45, 49, 53

Suzong, Emperor 38

Suzuki, Daisetsu (D.) Teitaro (T.) 134, 201, 228, 235

Suzuki, Ryowa 210, 214

Suzuki, Shunryu 134, 137–38, 145

Swan Lake 13, 14

syncretic, syncretism xii, 58, 73

T

Tabrah, Ruth xiii

"Tail of the Tiger" (*see also* Karmê-Chöling) 136

Taimadera Temple 74

Taima Mandara (Mandala) 61, 74

Taimitsu 54

Taishō canon, edition 32, 39, 40, 53, 55, 125

Taiwan 90, 120

Taiyuan 38

Takeda, Ryusei 212

Takeuchi, Yoshinori 212

Tamamitsu, Junsho, Rev. 210, 214

Tamamitsu, Katsuko 210, 214

Tamura, Yoshirō 207, 214

Tanabe, Hajime 201

Tanaka, Kenneth K. xix, 55, 210, 215–42, 243

Tanaka, Kimie 210

Tang dynasty, period 31, 32, 36, 37, 38, 39, 41, 42, 43, 44, 45, 49, 52, 53, 94, 103

pre- 34

Tanluan xv, xix, 45, 46, 47, 49, 54, 55, 62, 74, 124, 217, 218, 219, 231, 239

Tannishō (*see also Record of Lament of Divergences, A*) 186, 198, 234

tantra(s), tantric, tantrism (*see also* esoteric) 3, 4, 8, 37, 47, 51, 60, 61, 63, 69

Tantrayana (*see also* esoteric; Vajrayana) 130

Tao Wangling 93, 97

Tara 14

tariki (*see also* other-power) xiv, 82, 83, 86, 153, 204

Tariki: Embracing Despair, Discovering Peace 167, 212

Tarthang Tulku Rinpoche 136

Tassajara Hot Springs 139

tathāgata(s), Tathāgata 68, 159, 193, 217

of the fulfilled body 193, 217

of unhindered light 193, 194, 217

tathāgatagarbha xix

Teigen 59–60, 70

Tendai school 40, 54, 57, 58, 61, 73, 134, 176, 207

Ten Essential Texts of the Pure Land. See Jingtu shi yao

ten principles of training 130

Texas 27, 29, 243

text reciters 131

Thai monks 135

theist, theistic 165, 204

theologian(s) 164, 213, 215, 220

theological, theology 58, 73, 85, 139, 148, 151, 155, 156, 157, 158, 170, 201, 203

theological, theology (*continued*)
Buddhist 189, 200, 202
Christian, of Christianity 169, 170
liberation 206
Protestant 151
Pure Land (*see also* Pure Land [as sect, school, tradition]) 89
Shin 189, 190, 209
therapeutic, therapist(s) (*see also* psychotherapeutic, psychotherapist, psychotherapy) 13, 22, 23, 151
Theravāda, Theravādin(s) 3, 19, 127, 128, 130, 131, 135, 141–42, 149, 154
Third International Buddhist-Christian Conference 241
three bodies. *See* body(ies), of buddha, three, triple; three-bodies theory
three-bodies theory 62, 69, 218
three classes of disease 9
three demonic influences 9, 15
Three Jewels (*see also* Buddha, Dharma, and Sangha) 138
three poisons 9, 15, 191
three subordinations. *See* women, three subordinations of
Three Teachings (*see also* Sanlun) 91, 94, 100
Thurman, Robert 135
thusness (*see also* suchness) 61, 65
Tiantai school, thought 101, 106, 108, 115, 117, 118, 119, 126, 207
Tiantai Zhiyi (*see also* Zhiyi) 102
Tibet, Tibetan(s) 6, 15, 17, 18, 19, 20, 23, 24, 133, 135, 136, 171
Chinese takeover of, holocaust 20, 133
refugees 136
Tibetan Aid Project 136
Tibetan Buddhism, Buddhist, tradition 3, 4, 5, 12, 14, 18, 19, 20, 22, 133, 136, 140, 141, 145, 149, 171
Tibetan language viii, xiii, 133, 135, 140
Tibetan Nyingma Meditation Center 136
Tibetan Relief Foundation 136
Tillich, Paul 220, 221, 222, 223, 227
Tilopa 133
Tōji Temple 73
tokudō (*see also* ordination, monastic) 77, 138
Tokugawa era 59, 74
Tokyo 134, 215, 243
Tokyo University 210
Tönnies, Ferdinand 158
Tour de France 81
Tracy, David 189
Traditionalism, Traditionalist 148, 149, 155–57, 158, 162, 163, 165
transcendence, transcendent 5, 7, 22, 23, 73, 162, 163, 198, 199, 215, 218, 222, 225, 231
Transcendent Unity of Religions, The 156, 163, 170
transformation vii, 7, 84, 105, 128, 177, 180, 181, 197, 209, 213, 228
of gender 79, 183, 184, 185, 187
transgression(s) 19, 196
transmigration(s) (*see also* rebirth) 72, 225
transmission 12, 38, 54 60, 61, 70, 72, 132, 133, 138, 139, 200
one-to-one 60, 61, 73
secret 57, 60, 72
Treasure House of Merits 161
treatise(s) (*see also* scripture; sutra) xv, 104, 117, 210
Treatise on Ten Doubts about the Pure Land 103
Treatise on the Mass of Doubts about the Pure Land 103
Treatise on the Pure Land 211, 217, 219
Tricycle magazine xvi
trikāya. *See* body(ies), of buddha, three, triple; three-bodies theory
Trinley, Ngawang Ugyen (*see also* Karmapa, seventeenth; Wangyal, Ngawang) 135
triśaraṇa. *See* refuge, formula

True Teaching, Practice, and Realization of the Pure Land Way, The (*see also* *Kyōgyōshinshō*) 194, 210
Trungpa, Chögyam 83, 86, 136–37, 140–41
trust (*see also* entrust, entrusting, entrustment) 5, 64, 65, 177, 178, 179, 180, 184
truth(s) 4, 5, 69, 72, 73, 81, 106, 107, 108, 113, 114, 115, 116, 121, 148, 156, 163, 176, 178, 179, 180, 219, 234
  conventional 113, 114, 118, 219, 236
  two 108, 219, 230, 236
  ultimate 113, 114, 117, 118, 156, 219, 236
Ts'ai Hsing-li 124
Tsuji, Kenryu (K.) T. xii, 79, 82, 179
tulku (*see also* lama, incarnate) 140
Tulku Thondup 6, 12, 15, 16, 19, 20, 27, 29
Tuṣita Heaven 68, 70, 109
two truths. *See* truth(s), two

U

Ueda, Yoshifumi 213, 220, 236
Uehara, Senroku 206, 207, 208
Ueyama, Daishun 210
Understanding Religious Life 190
United States (*see also* America) xvi, 16, 18, 134, 135, 136, 139, 141, 200, 216
universal monarch (*see also* *cakravartin*) 181
University of California Extension, Santa Cruz 148
University of Hawai'i 175, 243
University of North Carolina 31, 57, 243
University of Oregon 3
University of Pennsylvania xi, 77, 243
University of Washington 135
University of Wisconsin 3
Unno, Mark 3
Unno, Taitetsu 80, 166, 167, 189, 200, 202, 210, 212, 213, 230
ŭnsa 132
Upadeśa on the Sūtras of Amitāus with Stanzas on the Resolution to Be Born 47
upadhyāya (*see also* preceptor) 130
upāsaka(s) (*see also* layman, laymen) 128, 129
upasampadā. *See* ordination, full
upāsikā(s) (*see also* laywomen) 128, 129
upāya. *See* compassionate means; expedient(s), expedient means; skillful means
Urban, Hugh B. 51
Utah State University 127, 243

V

Vaidehī 184
Vairocana (*see also* Mahāvairocana) 32, 39, 104, 105, 107, 115, 116, 118
Vajirarama Temple 135
vajra 9, 33, 34, 41, 63, 65, 72
Vajrabodhi 37, 38, 39, 40, 42, 43
Vajradhatu (*see also* Shambhala International) 136, 141
Vajradhātu 42, 53, 63
  maṇḍala 53, 63
Vajra family 33
Vajragarbha 33
Vajrakoṣa Maṇḍala, *vajrakoṣa* realm 62, 63
Vajrapāṇi 32, 44
Vajra Regent (*see also* Ösel Tendzin) 136, 141
Vajrasattva 4–5, 6, 7, 8, 9–10, 12, 13, 15, 19, 20, 21, 27
  meditation 3, 5–6, 7–10, 14, 15, 16
Vajraśekhara-sarvatathāgatasatyasaṅgraha-mahāyāna-pratyutpannābhisambuddhamahātantrarājā-sūtra. *See* *Vajraśekhara-sūtra*
Vajraśekhara-sūtra 37, 38, 39, 40, 41, 42, 43, 44, 52, 54

Vajrayana (*see also* Tantrayana) 129, 133, 141, 142
vak-karma 46
Vasubandhu xv, 55, 193, 211, 217, 219
Vedānta 156
vegetarian, vegetarianism 98, 99
vidyārāja(s) 51
horse-headed (*see also* Hayagrīva) 34, 41
Vietnam 132
Vietnam War vii
Vimalakīrtinirdeśa-sūtra, Vimalakīrti Sutra 102, 105, 112
vinaya 97, 130
masters 131
*vinaya-dhara*s. *See* vinaya, masters
Vinaya-nidāna 144
vipassanā (*see also* Insight tradition) 135, 149
virtue(s) 62, 129, 151, 155, 177, 194, 195, 196, 206, 221, 222
Vision of Buddhism: The Space Under the Tree, The viii, ix
visualization(s) 4, 9, 10, 15, 20, 31, 34, 35, 36, 45, 46, 47, 164
vow(s) xv, 19, 24, 35, 66, 67, 82, 99, 109, 111, 136, 159, 180, 181, 87, 192, 194, 217, 220, 223, 224, 225, 229, 237
Amida's, of Amida xv, 4, 159, 175, 177, 178, 180, 181, 183, 184, 192, 195, 216, 234, 236
bodhisattva 8, 81
Buddha's, of Buddha 45, 177
of Dharmākara 67, 69, 218, 225, 236
eighteenth xvi
forty-eight 217, 236
of individual liberation 8
nineteenth xvi
primal 66, 67, 69, 82, 167, 182, 184, 191, 192, 193, 196, 217, 222, 224
thirty-fifth 181, 182, 183, 185, 186
twentieth xvi
vow-kings, ten great 116
vulnerability 18, 20, 21, 23, 24, 83

W

Wangyal, Ngawang (*see also* Trinley, Ngawang Ugyen) 135–36
Wanli era, period 98, 100, 120, 124
Wanshan tonggui ji 103
War Crimes Trials (1946) 134
wasan 65
Washington Buddhist Vihara 135
Washington, D.C. 89, 135, 243
Wat Thai 135
way 194, 204
of being religious 189, 190, 200, 203
bodhisattva 51
of easy practice 45
Pure Land (*see also* Pure Land [as sect, school, tradition]) 204, 218
of secret dharmas (*see also hiji bōmon*) 58
of secret mantras 51
triple-worlds' 31, 48
to ultimate destiny, reality, realization 190, 194, 196, 204, 205
Way, the 97, 110, 111
Weishi (*see also* consciousness-only) 117
Welch, Holmes 131
West Coast 135
West, Western, Westerner(s) viii, xiii, xiv, xv, 4, 5, 10, 12, 13, 14, 16, 17, 18, 19, 20, 21, 22, 23, 24, 25, 30, 58, 85, 93, 128, 136, 138, 140, 141, 142, 149, 161, 163, 165, 171, 180, 181, 201, 202, 206, 228, 229, 234
academics, scholars, scholarship viii, 58, 89, 90, 101
dharma heir(s), families 139, 140, 145
students 17, 23, 24, 27, 138, 140, 141
Western Citadel 69
Western Paradise, Pure Land (*see also* Pure Land [as place]) 31, 61, 67, 105, 109, 116, 229
Whitefield, George 159
White Plum Sangha 139

Why Religion Matters 155, 156, 160, 166
Will and Spirit 18
willfulness (*see also* intentionality) 18, 19, 20, 21, 25, 83
willingness (*see also* receptivity) 18, 19, 20, 21, 22, 83
Willow Wave hermitage 98, 99, 118
Winters, Harry 16
wisdom(s) vii, xiv, 22, 32, 46, 62, 69, 70, 85, 107, 110, 133, 140, 155, 165, 182, 193, 197, 207, 222, 233, 238
  of Amida, Amitabha's 40, 233
  buddha- 184, 187
  and compassion 81, 84, 177, 178, 238
  "crazy" 110
Womb Maṇḍala (*see also* Garbhakoṣa Maṇḍala) 63, 70, 74
women 89, 111, 114, 131, 175, 180–85, 187, 209, 210
  birth, rebirth in the Pure Land 79, 182, 183, 184, 187
  five obstacles of 181, 182, 185
  salvation of 175, 180, 181, 185
  sexuality and femininity of 181, 184, 185
  three subordinations of 181, 182, 185
Woodstock, New York 139
world(s) xii, 7, 11, 18, 22, 23, 37, 51, 64, 70, 72, 81, 84, 95, 96, 105, 107, 109, 117, 141, 153, 154, 156, 157, 158, 162, 166, 167, 170, 177, 178, 181, 182, 183, 191, 192, 193, 197, 200, 202, 204, 205, 207, 208, 209, 215, 216, 221, 226, 231, 233, 234, 236, 237
  contemporary, modern, twenty-first–century 133, 150, 189, 200, 208, 209, 213, 223, 233
  culture(s) 18, 204
  defiled, of the five defilements, dirty, lower, sordid 32, 64, 65, 167, 197, 235
  history 206, 207
  impermanent 199
  lotus repository 217
  outer 233, 236
  phenomenal 154
  present 95, 112, 113, 118
  -realms 218
  returning to 196, 197, 208
  sahā, samsaric 17, 112, 114, 223
  triple 31, 48
World-honored One (*see also* Buddha) 32
worldling(s) 102, 112, 113, 115, 118, 121
worldly 96, 183, 184, 228
World Parliament of Religions 133, 145
world-ruling king (*see also* *cakravartin*) 38
World's Religions: Our Great Wisdom Traditions, The (*see also* *Religions of Man*) 147, 149
worldview(s) xiv, 6, 7, 154, 196, 199, 202, 221, 226, 233
World War II 134, 206
Wu County 96, 99
Wuliangshou jing yupotishe yuansheng ji 55
Wuliangshou jing yupotishe yuansheng ji Posoupantou pusa zao, zhu 54, 55
Wuliangshou rulai genben tuoloni 34
Wuliangshou rulai guanxing gongyang yigui. *See* *Wuliangshouyigui*
Wuliangshou rulai niansong yigui 39
Wuliangshou rulai zantan 34
Wuliangshou yigui 31–32, 34–47, 51, 53
Wuyon shan. *See* Five Cloud Mountain

X

Xifang helun 89, 90, 91, 97, 98, 100–101, 102, 103–104, 111, 112–121, 123, 124, 125, 126
Xingzhuang 42

Xin Huayan jinglun 125
Xuanzong, Emperor 37, 52, 94
Xu zang jing 93, 97

Y

Yahweh 160
Yaji tu. *See Elegant Gathering*
Yangjuemoluo jing 102
yankou rituals 54
Yasutani, Hakuun 134, 135, 139
Yeats, William Butler xviii
yin and *yang* 62, 63
Yinguang 117, 126
Yixing 37, 38
Yogācāra xiv, 47, 55, 218, 225, 230
Yoga-sūtra 38
Yoga teaching 43
Yokota, John 223, 225
Yongming Yanshou 91, 102, 103, 110
Yuan brothers, family 90, 91, 92, 93, 94, 98, 124, 125
Yuan Hongdao 89–121, 122, 123, 124, 125, 126
Yuan Shiyu 91
Yuanzhao 53
Yuan Zhongdao (*see also* Zhongdao) 92, 94, 99, 122
Yuan Zongdao (*see also* Zongdao) 92, 93, 95
Yuichi, Kajiyama 233
Yui-en 198
Yungifa Temple, Yunqi Temple (*see also* Cloud Perch Temple) 95, 97
Yunqi Zhuhong (*see also* Lianchi; Zhuhong) 96, 101, 115

Z

ZCLA. *See* Zen Center of Los Angeles
Zen (*see also* Chan) xvi, 16, 57, 58, 70, 73, 85, 132, 133, 134, 138, 139, 140, 158, 159, 201, 228, 229
  in America, American 134, 138, 139
  in Japan, Japanese 73, 132, 139
  Korean 132
  master, teacher(s) 132, 137, 138
  Rinzai 58, 134
  Sōtō 58, 132, 134, 138, 139
Zen Center of Los Angeles 134, 139
zenchishiki (*see also kalyāṇamitra*) 67
Zendō. *See* Shandao
Zen Mind, Beginner's Mind 137
Zenran 60, 70
Zenshuji Temple 139
Zhang Ruzhou 90
Zhang Zishao 94
Zhao Qian 42
Zhenyuan catalogue 39, 53
Zhen yuan xin ding shijiao mulu 53
Zhili 103
Zhingying Huiyuan (*see also* Huiyuan) 218
Zhiyi (*see also* Tiantai Zhiyi) 103, 107
Zhixu (*see also* Ouyi Zhixu) 101, 126
Zhongdao (*see also* Yuan Zhongdao) 89, 91, 92, 95, 98, 101, 123, 124
Zhonglang (*see also* Yuan Hongdao) 91
Zhou Qun 90, 94, 115, 118
Zhuangzi 98
Zhuhong (*see also* Lianchi; Yunqi Zhuhong) 97, 117, 120
Zibo Zhenke 101
zogyō. *See* miscellaneous teachings
Zongdao (*see also* Yuan Zongdao) 89, 92, 93, 98
Zongjing lu 91, 103, 110
Zongjing shelu 91
Zonkaku 182, 183
Zuzōshō 53